Val Wilmer was born in Yorkshire in wartime and headed for London as the Armistice was signed, baby's green ration-book in hand. She sold her first photograph – a Scout troop – to the local newspaper when she was sixteen, her first written commentary on jazz appearing soon after. She has photographed weddings and worked for African newspapers, written and broadcast on music throughout the world. The Victoria and Albert Museum, London, held an exhibition of her music photographs in 1973, and she is a founding member of Format, Britain's first all-women photographic agency. She lives in North London, where is she is owned by an elderly cat named Animal, and does not have a cottage in the country or a wife. She is working on two books about the Black presence in British jazz.

She is the author of: *Jazz People; As Serious As Your Life; The Face of Black Music;* and has illustrated: *The Jazz Scene; Jazz at Ronnie Scott's; The Illustrated Encyclopaedia of Jazz; Black Talk.*

val wilmer

mama said there'd be days like this

my life in the jazz world

The Women's Press

First published by The Women's Press Limited 1989
A member of the Namara Group
34 Great Sutton Street, London EC1V 0DX
This edition, 1991

British Library Cataloguing in Publication Data

Wilmer, Val.
  Mama Said There'd be Days Like This.
  1. Jazz. Criticism. Wilmer, Val
  I. Title
  781.65092

  ISBN 0-7043-4120-4

Printed and bound in Great Britain by
BPCC Hazell Books Ltd
Member of BPCC Ltd
Aylesbury, Bucks, England

Mama said there'd be days like this
            There'd be days like this
My mama said.

The Shirelles

Contents

Acknowledgments

At times it may seem the book is overburdened with names, but it is important to me to acknowledge who did what, when and where, especially as history is so often written by people who were not actually there at the time. George Padmore, one of the important Pan-Africanists, said he could not 'write history like the Stalinist — leave out the names of people because I disapprove of their policies'. Me neither.

I've tried to thank all my teachers, friends and inspirational figures, but inevitably, have had to leave some out of the narrative. I hope I'll be forgiven for that. But there are many to thank individually.

It was Carole Spedding who got me started on this book in the first place and encouraged me at times when I queried the usefulness of such an endeavour. Kitty Grime helped me enormously in my early days on the jazz scene and read Chapter 4, making constructive and informative suggestions. I'm grateful to her and to Maggie Nicols, another old friend, for her comments on this and further chapters, and to Terri Quaye, without whom I would never have learnt so much about music, about life, and myself.

No creative endeavour is possible without the input of others and while I was writing I spoke to many individuals who reminded me of 'the way it useta be' or otherwise provided encouragement. My thanks to Chris Albertson, Juliet Ash, David A. Bailey, John and Priscilla Batcheldor, Sally Bradbery, Bea Campbell, Dianne Ceresa, Joy Chamberlain, Elaine Cohen, Maggie Colbeck, Janet Coleman, Lindsay Cooper, Jayne Cortez, Terry Cryer, Laka Daisycal, B. J. Denba, Johnny Edgecombe, Georgie Fame, Mike Flood Page, Verna Gillis, Bob Glass, Jewelle Gomez, Ken Gordon, Peter Guralnick, Pam Holland, John Hopkins, Terry Hunt, Max Jones, Pam Jury, Nick Kimberley, Reva Klein, Patsy Maguire, Wendy Marshall, Maggie Murray, Humphrey Okoh, Jan Parker, Polly Pattullo, Angela Phillips, Simon Prager, Pat Preston, Brenda Prince, Alison Rayner, Chris Render, Sonia Sanchez, Victor Schonfield, Alyn Shipton, Louis Stephenson, Sue Steward, Mike Thelwell, Roberta Uno Thelwell, Sheila Thompson, Olu Timehin, Jackie Tracey, Floyd Webb, Vicki Wickham, Dave Wilkins, Rhonda Wilson, Rae Wittrick, Dot Worrell and my brother, Clive, who survived the rigours of our childhood together to stay a good friend.

Nothing can adequately convey my gratitude to those friends who read the first draft and took valuable time out of their busy lives to tell me what they honestly thought of what I had written. They are Paul Gilroy who also provided the Padmore quotation, Susan Hemmings, Pratibha Parmar, Penny Valentine, Vron Ware and Sue O'Sullivan who also, through her cookbook *Turning the Tables*, allowed me to try out the beginning of Chapter 23. I love you all.

I am indebted to those who helped me with translations,

spelling and 'sociological' explanations concerning their respective societies: Akwe Amosu, Mije Barnor, Buchi Emecheta, Mr Hassan of the BBC Hausa Service, Latifa Lazghoui, Bayo Martins and Abdul Razaq Yunusa.

For special kindnesses to me on the music scene, I would like to acknowledge Fontella Bass, Leroy Cooper, Andrew Cyrille, Richard Davis, Art Farmer, Red Holloway, Benny Golson, Ronald Shannon Jackson, Elvin Jones, Yusef Lateef, Marian McPartland, Esther Marrow, Allen Murphy and Chris White, and the late Henry 'Red' Allen, Roy Brown, Call Cobbs Jr., Eddie 'Lockjaw' Davis, Eddie Durham, Joe Gordon, Benny Green, Howard McGhee, Wes Montgomery, Jerane 'Doc' Pomus, Willie Guy Rainey, Stuff Smith, Eddie 'Cleanhead' Vinson, Josh White and Trummy Young.

A North Londoner now, I miss my Transpontine neighbours. For their friendship over the years and their understanding, my love to Janet Coleman, Olive Gallimore, James Lampley, Sandra Stimpson, Peter and Jenny Tudor Miles, Melba Wilson and Liz Spiro who also provided me with a space to write away from turmoil, making useful comments on parts of the manuscript and jogging my memory about our teenage years. To her, to Jane Harper and David Pallister for their resources, to Liz Woodcraft who reminded me of Peetie Wheatstraw and incidentally, gave me the title for Chapter 12, to Jan Diakow for finding the *Jazz News* with my Sonny Criss interview, and to D. Genders of Enco Products for information on the company history, more thanks.

For the use of their photographs I extend my appreciation to Terry Cryer, Chris Hardin, John Hopkins, Graham Keen, Joanne O'Brien and Mark Rusher, to Helen Warby at Report, and to Barbara Pendleton for access to the old *Jazz News* files.

Above all, I thank Lindsey Paget-Cooke, who is far more than a neighbour, for support and caring in a period of great personal crisis, and Tim Caton who always 'keeps eye'.

And finally, my gratitude to Margaret Busby, who not only published my first two books but, keeping patience with me, edited this one with thoroughness and feeling and a minimum of prodding. With love and in friendship, I salute you.

If anybody ask you who I am, here, at least, are some of the answers.

Val Wilmer
March 1989

Preface
If Anybody Ask You Who I Am

If anybody ask you who I am,
     Who I am, who I am,
If anybody ask you who I am,
     Tell 'em I'm a child of God.

Afro-American gospel song

Preface
If Anybody Ask You
Who I Am

People often write autobiographies as if they had no mother, no children, as if sexual love had passed them by. This is not one of those. At various times in history, such personal revelations may be neither possible nor productive; yet for the most revolutionary, as for the most reclusive, the total picture is incomplete without them. From Frederick Douglas to Alexandra Kollontai, Mary Wollstonecraft to Samora Machel, everyone has known the warmth of love and the pain of loss. Mao and his wife lost their children on the Long March; what effect must that have had on them? And yet we seldom read about these things. Men, for the most part, pretend that experiences of a personal nature are unimportant, ignoring them altogether or relegating them to the periphery of their story. Women cannot do this so easily. It is how we are treated as *women*, rather than as individuals, what happens to us *because* we are women, that dictates the direction of our lives. To us the personal is political, whether we like it or not.

In 1961 I was 19 years old. Nineteen was young in those days and I was pretty naïve despite my interest in jazz and blues. I'd started to write about Black music three years earlier and was already finding it remarkably easy, as well as rewarding, to track down those Americans who were beginning to play in Britain after a long period of musical starvation. Their appearance here was highly significant in the days predating the rise of British Beat and the period of affluence to come.

One of the blues artists so lionised during this period was Little Brother Montgomery, a versatile pianist from Louisiana via Chicago. I saw him play at the 100 Club in London and approached him for an interview. 'Just come by the hotel,' he said, and I did. He was in bed at the time but, excusing himself, struggled into a shirt and trousers and proceeded, with a characteristically sardonic air, to answer my tentative teenage questions.

A friend took a photograph of us: Brother sitting on the bed, his shirt hanging open to reveal a rather daunting paunch, me sitting on a chair beside him, pen and notebook in hand, legs crossed demurely. I'm wearing a Paisley dress made by my mother and an expression of truly painful seriousness. I rather liked the picture, though, so I submitted it for publication along with the article.

'Very nice, dear,' said The Editor, 'But we can't really use that, can we? I mean, what would our readers say if we printed a picture of a white girl sitting next to a darky with his shirt undone?'

I've never forgotten those words and they have taken on increasing significance for me as the years have gone by. They say a lot about the patriarchal divide-and-rule system under which women and Black people are forced to live. Writing about the music was something that men did. There was a penalty to pay for being a woman in a man's world, and there were many who made sure to exact it. Often it took the form of sexual pressure, and surviving that required strength of a particular kind. But for a white woman to be concerned with something that Black people did meant to experience additional pressure. Ostracism was the penalty there and to survive that it was necessary to recognise why it occurred.

Why people cannot measure their worth in terms other than power over others is one of the questions posed by personal politics which has always disturbed me, though I doubt whether it would have been so immediately obvious to me without getting to know people from worlds outside my own. Through becoming immersed in Afro-American music I was made aware of certain realities that would surely have remained hidden had I stayed within the secure boundaries of my own culture. The experience was so startling, went so deep, that there is little I write that does not reflect this contact.

It was music itself that first opened the path to discovery, that helped me in knowing myself. A powerful force that carried within it the seeds and the story, a learning-tree from which I could grow. It was through meeting musicians and others from their various worlds that I began to realise the potential for personal change that exists in us all, and it is because of this recognition that this book has been written in a particular way.

If I'd wanted, I could have glamorised my encounters with the famous in a way that aggrandised both them and myself and ignored what had actually taken place on the way. But to do that would have been a relatively pointless exercise, just something to add to the library of anecdote with which the literature of jazz music abounds. When I sat beside Little Brother Montgomery, when I was rebuffed by The Editor, life was doing me a favour. I was tripped up and taunted, made hideous gaffes of my own, but went on to reflect, to my lasting benefit. I haven't attempted to hide my mistakes or modify descriptions of my behaviour at various points, for to do so would be to gloss over and disguise the very real hardship of the process of motion. Often it was one step forward and two steps back, for change, like life itself, is never even. But for better or worse, the young woman who asked Little Brother why the blues was a twelve-bar, and worried others to death for the date of a long-lost recording, had embarked on a lifelong journey of discovery and personal growth from which there would be no return.

Always in the background for me there's been music. Musicians, like writers, are weavers of dreams, singing our songs for us when we can't find the tune. The music came to play an almost organic role in my life, identifying situations and events, reviving emotions and discovery. From the very beginning *Jazz on a Summer's Day* was *my* film – for the singers as much as the horn players. Chuck Berry singing about his 'Sweet Little Sixteen' who 'got the grownup blues': that was me, making my way into a world that seemed almost totally male and white. Dinah Washington playing the vibes like a *demon* when you thought all she could do was sing. All? And Mahalia Jackson, 'the world's greatest gospel singer', to close the show. The wonderful, words-are-not-enough Mahalia, with the no-nonsense stomping piano of Mildred Falls behind her. Memorable moments that have carried me through.

Really, I stayed a fan for ages. To this day I can't pass the Odeon in Hammersmith, West London, without remembering the dozens of times musicians smuggled me through the backstage labyrinth to a seat in the stalls. Or the Royal Festival Hall without seeing drummer Shelly Manne emerge from the lift to rescue my brother and me when the doorman wouldn't actually believe that one of the two kids at the stage door actually wrote for 'the press'. Long before the days of fanzines, college magazines and the like, journalists were invariably male, and they carried themselves with an air of importance that left me standing on the sidelines.

I survived, though, and went on to make some kind of name for myself as a writer on music, as a photographer, too. But it annoyed me that I always had to explain myself. The question was repeated *ad nauseam*: 'How come a white girl like you got into this music as much as you did?'

The reason this white girl 'got into' the music was that she liked what Johnny Dodds, Billie Holiday and John Lee Hooker had to say. She preferred their version of events, just as the questioner might lean towards Mendelssohn, Callas or Presley. Growing up, she found the music out there to learn from, alongside the paintings of Rembrandt and Degas, the poetry of Lorca and Donne, the movies of Huston, Truffaut and Hitchcock, the language of Shakespeare. It was mind-altering, life-enhancing. The question says more about the questioner than it does about this white girl.

It would be easy to explain it away if such thinking were not part of a pattern. When Liverpool 8 erupted in an angry uprising in 1981, an apoplectic Conservative councillor described the inhabitants of the area as 'the descendants of African seamen and local prostitutes'. For over a century, historians have used this thoughtless terminology to describe those white women who, in the mid-nineteenth century journeyed with their Black partners to settle Sierra Leone in West Africa. It caused someone I know to repeat hearsay linking Black servicemen with Soho prostitution in an otherwise instructive book about music in Britain. It's in the look I still occasionally catch on the face of an older white male if I walk down the street with a Black man. It denies the possibility of relationships existing between Black and White on anything other than mercenary terms, and tried to deny my right to take seriously the music and the people who made it.

It is hard to decide at what point something that has been a hobby becomes a part of life. Like many Whites caught up in the diversity of the African Diaspora, I've been challenged for attempting to document something outside my own experience. But I've been out here learning for thirty years or more and proximity has taught respect. I have always felt that those white people admitted as guests in the culture had a responsibility to support Black endeavour and make the information we gathered as well as the history as widely available as possible. There has been a pressing need for this, given the paucity of information available until lately. It has been my privilege to live with the constant realisation that the people I was meeting were part of history, or might very soon be.

Part One
Such a Sight to See

Oh, Mommy, Mommy,
      Please may I go
It's such a sight to see
      Somebody steal the show

Chuck Berry

1
Good Morning, Little Schoolgirl

I was about 12 years old when I walked into the Swing Shop in Streatham, south London, and asked if they had any jazz records. I remember what I was wearing: a navy-blue windcheater and pleated grey flannel shorts, the tomboy outfit I put on to play football and cycle around the common, smoking cigarettes stolen from unlocked parked cars.

The Swing Shop, as it happened, sold *only* jazz records. But Bert Bradfield, massive behind the counter in his loud checked shirt and thick hornrimmed glasses, was probably relieved that I didn't want the Beverley Sisters. I'm sure he was hiding a smile as he indicated the three modest secondhand racks: 'There's one or two over there.'

I sifted through the 78s in their cardboard sleeves until I came to a familiar name. 'Fidgety Feet' by the Humphrey Lyttleton Band seemed a lively enough title, and it cost only half a crown. Bert said I could have it for two shillings and I rushed home right away with my prize. The gramophone was an ancient portable covered in green imitation crocodile-skin, bought for seven shillings and sixpence in a junkshop. I cranked up the clockwork mechanism and dropped the steel needle on to the shellac. My mother rushed into the room. 'What's *that*?' she demanded in total amazement. 'That's *jazz*,' I said, looking her dead in the eye.

It's a tribute to my mother's tolerance that this wasn't Lyttleton's swansong in Streatham. Jazz didn't exist in the cultural world she inhabited, underpinned by 'the classics', Strauss waltzes and singers such as Richard Tauber, with Ivor Novello floating frothily on the surface. To her, as to many of her generation, 'jazz' was a catch-all word that stood for Vera Lynn, 'the Forces' sweetheart', and the sedate brand of dance music we heard Henry Hall playing on the radio each week. She could hardly have known she would actually grow to like Afro-American music and meet some of its greatest exponents.

For me, the idea of a life in the music business was just as remote. Although Mum had once been a music teacher, ours was not a musical home. If I wanted to be anything at that time it was a surgeon, miraculously saving lives (I already had a collection of *British Medical Journals* donated by the Egyptian doctor next door), or a forensic scientist, solving gruesome mysteries. This odd choice was brought on by growing up near a police station, where obsolete case reports and witness statements could be filched from the dustbins and surreptitiously stuck into a scrapbook, alongside reports of the trial of mass-murderer John George Haigh. I'd also considered being a detective, which had something to do with early exposure to Sherlock Holmes.

Where writing was concerned, I suppose there was a presage. I'd taught myself to type two-fingered at the age of 10, and when, soon after, I wrote a detective story I thought nothing of submitting it to the *Evening News*. My first rejection-slip didn't bother me over much. It was early preparation for the wonderful ways of the world of journalism.

Little girls, we are often told, want to grow up to be ballet dancers, but I certainly never knew any who did. Nurses, yes, teachers maybe, and often during puberty – at least among the middle classes – champion show-jumpers. I don't think it ever crossed my mind to consider the usual female options, resolutely opposed as I was to anything that smacked of feminine pursuits and did not involve going places, being and doing.

I always wanted to know how everything worked. On Saturdays I'd visit the Science Museum with its beautifully constructed working models of machinery, all shiny brass and precision engineering; and, whenever the opportunity arose, I'd dismantle any clocks that had ground to a halt, though the task of remedying their condition proved too much for inexperienced fingers. Yet I persevered in my quest for knowledge, the library being an invaluable source of how-to-do-it books, and chemists' shops of the raw materials.

I read boys' story-magazines, *Hotspur* and *Rover*, as well as the more acceptable *Girls' Crystal* and *School Friend*, and when I wasn't painting cavaliers or cowboys was constantly involved in 'scientific' pursuits. Taxidermy, fortunately, didn't last long, getting no further than curing rabbit skins brought from the butcher, but at different times in my early life I wanted to be a chemist, an astronomer and, because of pressure from my mother, a physiotherapist. (She had a thing about 'nice girls in white coats'.)

None of it worked out that way. If I regret anything about what did happen, it's that no one encouraged me to play music; when I did eventually try the guitar I was already too involved in writing and photography to make the commitment. If there had been another choice open, it would probably have been carpentry. I've often wished that Auntie Gladys, a 'maiden lady' friend of my father's who gave me a tool set for my tenth birthday, could have known how grateful I've been over the years for such far-sighted encouragement.

My early interest in science and manual skills was a result of the household in which I grew up. My father, the son of a Victorian army officer and a mother of whom I know little, was born in 1882. He was in his sixties when I was born, on the day Pearl Harbor was bombed, and America came into World War II. He died the day before my seventh birthday and I can remember my mother's face as she gave me the news. I came home from school to find her resolutely reddening with Ronuk, the brick-and-tile doorstep of our south London semi, trying to maintain a 'business as usual' façade for the sake of the children. My father remains a shadowy figure, a stooped old man in dressing-gown and pyjamas, coughing and panting with emphysema.

It has never really bothered me that I grew up without a father because Sybil, my mother, was a loving provider who never stopped treating my brother and me with the tenderness reserved for children. There were rebellious years when I refused to go to church and joined the Young Communist League to shock her as much as anything, but I could generally identify with her whatever our differences. The absence of a father does, I think, worry my brother Clive, who misses the mutual learning process he shares with his own children. And then, because he was three years younger than me, he did not get nearly as much from the substitute world we created.

Mum decided that, rather than go out to work, she would take in lodgers. For years our house was filled with 'paying guests', the polite term in suburbia. It was hard for Mum to break the habit of hospitality; even when well into her seventies she could be persuaded to help out with somebody's holiday visitors. By the time my childhood friend Janet got married, Mum had given up having lodgers on a regular basis, but she agreed to accommodate the prospective in-laws, who were coming over from Canada for the occasion. The family were Sikhs who had settled in Toronto, and I was rather taken aback the day before the ceremony to find the house full of superior-looking men in turbans, with a general air of something important going on. But Mum, in her quiet way, had everything under control. Though it was hard work running the house single-handed, she actively enjoyed having people to stay. In doing so, she made it into a home from home rather than a boarding-house. 'Your kitchen table is one of the friendliest places I know,' was one of many tributes paid her by contented visitors.

It's significant given England's colonial history that our first two lodgers came from Ireland and India respectively. David, I think, down-played his Indian-ness – it was only later that I realised his mother was Indian – but it aroused familiar echoes. My father had been born under the Raj in India, and although I don't think Mum ever really grasped the significance of his having been raised by an *ayah*, she was intrigued when names he'd mentioned – places such as Multan, Murree and Lahore – came up in conversation.

As children, we always played on a thick *dhurrie*, hand-woven in dark blue, white and pink, and polishing the large brass trays in the hall to a mirror-like shine was a regular ritual. These and some classical blue Multan pottery were the legacies of our father's colonial childhood, sepia photographs of a Punjabi battalion surrounding white officers the only visual evidence we had of what the British Raj was all about.

Most of our paying-guests were men and, with a couple of nasty exceptions, they befriended us like surrogate uncles. One or two were uncomfortable with children, but in the main we profited considerably from these men who were in the unusual position of being able to share their knowledge and experience without also having to exert authority.

Years before the Cuban Revolution, we often used the nickname 'Che' around the house. That was how I was addressed by Malcolm McGregor Robertson who had lived in Guevara's homeland, Argentina, where the word means 'buddy' or 'pal'. Mac was a generous Scotsman who liked my mother almost as much as he liked his dram. He gave many childhood ventures his financial support and bought me a rabbit for my tenth birthday.

We had brash German importers and girls from their office, a Hungarian refugee and even, at one stage, Richard Attenborough's personal secretary. Later there were East African Hindus, a Malayan Chinese and a couple of Sikhs. From several I learned different skills, something generally denied my brother because of his relative youth and lack of aggression. I was always pushy as a child and in retrospect I realise this was because Mum was often too busy housekeeping to pay us attention. But I learned how to put those tools to use building what was more a rabbit palace than a hutch, roofed with linoleum. Under the tuition of a countryman from Devon, I could clinch nails (bend over the ends) like an expert by the time I was eleven, straighten old ones for re-use with a hammer and steady the panelsaw with my forefinger. He taught me how to identify wild flowers and plants, too, especially those of interest to rabbits!

The nature trail had begun long before with David, who was to remain a champion of my mother's sweet nature throughout her life. On the common together we'd search for the first signs of spring, then he'd read to my brother and me in front of the coal fire, taking pressure off Mum as she cooked their evening meal. David was the only person I ever knew who resharpened his old razor-blades. Britain was yet to recover from the war, and wages were a pittance; economies had to be made. He was also the first man I saw sewing. His Robin Hood outfit for a fancy-dress dance — Sherwood green topped with a tail-feathered hat — was the talk of the town for ages.

Every weekend, at lunch and at teatimes, we'd sit and listen to the grownups talking. There was always a roast on Sundays (Mum was an excellent traditional cook), with homemade cakes for tea, but Sunday breakfast was best of all. Then we had sausages, and if one of the 'PGs' didn't want breakfast you might even manage an extra one before getting ready for church.

Sausages made with meat were a real treat after the deprivations of the war. They were the most important item on the shopping-list for Saturday mornings and came either from Sainsbury's, where they curled on the counter in fat pink anticipation, or from Kennedy's, a rather superior shop specialising in a spiced variety, greyish in colour, which hung in long strings from hooks behind the counter. (To my surprise the shop still exists, its marble counter and tiles intact, a bastion against the plastic future in forever upwardly-mobile Streatham.)

In those days shopkeepers knew all their customers by name. During the war those older men who stayed at home often managed to 'save a little something' for 'their' ladies, and during the rationing that followed, the personal under-the-counter touch continued. At Shillingford's, the butcher, huge sides of meat hung perilously from steel racks while the blood dripped on the sawdust-covered floor. The massive horns of an Angus bull sprouting from curly black wool were mounted above the desk where sat a grey-haired lady known only as 'Miss'. She wore fingerless cashier's gloves against the chill of the coldstore and never lacked a kind word for the children. Like Norman the butcher, she had worked there for years. Shillingford's was a mainstay in my mother's life; it was a source of real distress to her when the shutters came down for the final time.

Another institution that was gradually to disappear after the war was the wet-fish shop with its decorative tiling and men in shiny white aprons and with huge red, raw hands. Streatham boasted three such grand emporia, where bloodstained rabbits and woodpigeon hung alongside the haddock and herrings and where the dreaded boiled cod was purchased each Friday. There was Cordeaux, too, run by a French

6

family, which called itself 'the charcutiers', although few locals knew what the word meant; there we bought corned beef and rissoles for special occasions. Then there was Cooper's the grocer, where a shortish man named Mr Big dispensed good humour and dry goods from between tins of tea piled up in a counter display, and, believe it or not, a tall man named Mr Small was in charge of greengrocery. I loved going to these shops with my mother, being greeted by name and allowed to weigh out ounces of dried fruit and the like. Occasionally we'd drop into the ABC cafeteria for a cup of tea, a bun and an orange squash or a special treat: icecream served in a tall glass with ginger-beer.

Ever intrigued by unusual mechanical devices, I was fascinated by the centralised system of paying for goods at Sharman's the drapers and haberdashers. Handwritten bills and money were placed in a metal container, which was inserted into a highly polished brass tube and conveyed to the cashier via a pneumatic system of pipes. The receipted bill and change came back the same way, falling with a plop into a wire basket. At Tyrell's, another draper, and at the Co-op grocery, money was sent overhead by a system of wires and pulleys. The cash containers whistled across the store and I occasionally wondered what would happen if they collided. Of course they never did. Favourite of all the shops was Benbrook's, the ironmonger and oilshop, where linseed oil, turps and paraffin were dispensed straight from barrels. You'd go down two steps into the dim-lit shop where everything smelt of oil and was made from dark, ancient wood. There, nothing was too much trouble, even if the customer was only a little girl in search of a handful of staples to fix the rabbit-hutch wire.

A science teacher brought home test-tubes and chemicals for the aspiring young chemist and I acquired a book of instructions for simple experiments. What fun to put different salts in the tumblers and indicator in the water jug on Sundays and appear to turn water to wine! But it was even more fun to experiment unsupervised. I found out how to make chlorine, of all things, and when I grew bored with doing this in a test-tube, substituted a two-pound jam jar. Recklessly I hurled hydrochloric acid on to purple permanganate and the chemical reaction was overwhelming. The kitchen filled with lethal green fumes; I choked and spluttered and rushed outside. It was days before I could breathe without some discomfort.

And then there was old Mr Channon who lived with us for sixteen years and owned the first television set I ever watched. It never ceased to amaze me that someone with such an obvious inferiority complex could have won the Military Medal, saving cannon and comrade under fire in the First World War. We'd make fun of him for his endless recollections of fighting at 'Wipers' (Ypres) and on the Somme, where 20,000 died before breakfast, though in later years we came to realise he was actually part of history. We prompted the frequent retelling of his gruesome tale of the dead Uhlan. Mr Channon had come across this Prussian cavalry officer apparently asleep under a tree, his horse grazing beside him. We knew what was coming, but always managed to look aghast when he described how the man's head had come apart when he took off his ornamental helmet: 'A bit of shrapnel had got him right between the eyes, old boy.' We were in fact more shocked when he told how his battalion had shot a tyrannical sergeant in the back during a battle, though later I could well understand it. More sobering were his tales of gratuitous beating and kicking meted out to the enslaved Chinese who dug the trenches. Their presence in the Great War is seldom acknowledged, but his casual retelling of this brutality disgusted me at age 13, already becoming aware of racism in what seemed, in suburbia at least, a white-skinned Britain.

It was a funny world for a child to grow up in. My father, Eustace, was 22 years older than my mother and had been a friend of her parents. They had raised her in a rather genteel way in Purley, Surrey: Ernest, a gentle, unassuming man, and Cissie, a dynamic, no-nonsense woman who dressed with great style and managed to retain the centre of attention — and her high-heeled shoes — right up to her death at the age of 92. They were wonderful grandparents and excellent role-models for me. Our home life was fairly spartan, despite the large Edwardian house in which we lived, so it was always a treat to go to stay in their comfortable, dark-smelling semi. There you could have as many sausages as you could eat and stay up as late as you liked.

Bathnights with Grandma were among my earliest delights. She'd soap me with Wright's Coal Tar, her hands, protected with glycerine and olive oil, soft in contrast to my mother's, which always seemed rough and careworn. Long after I'd learnt to do it myself, I'd get her to bath me, a sensuous pleasure that stays with me still.

The long garden which ran down to the railway embankment was filled with beans and brassicas and fragrant sweetpeas, all of which won prizes for my grandmother wherever they were shown. In spring, lily-of-the-valley emerged from beneath a fallen tree covered with ivy, and later in the year there were raspberries to eat when no one was looking. Grandma was an inveterate gambler. Luck was something that stuck to her fingers, and whatever she won she would share. She would enter the crossword competitions, take part in whist-drives and raffles, carrying home prizes with a regularity completely over the odds. When it came to horse-racing, time and again she'd pick a winner. Only the football pools stumped her. Her generosity to family, friends and tradespeople alike was legendary, but it was partly as a result of her success at the wheel of fortune that she was able to help my mother to clothe Clive and me.

In their hall and front room, which smelled of lavender-water and tobacco, hung three massive portraits in oils, distinguished ancestors from my grandfather's family. Bewigged and frockcoated, they looked out at us across two centuries. One, a judge, stern in brilliant scarlet, followed you everywhere with his intimidating stare. In the bookcase were heavy tomes on aspects of jurisprudence, the work of my grandfather's brother Arundel, another relation 'at law'. But any intellectual activity in my immediate family lay more on my father's side, Grandma's reading being confined to popular weeklies and the *News of the World*, which she took 'for the crossword', Grandpa's to the *Daily Telegraph*, read at the library. There he and I would trek together, hand in hand, he in cloth cap, muffler and herringbone overcoat, occasionally allowing me to walk with his stick. A group of retired men congregated there daily and I'd be patted approvingly, the occasional penny or toffee thrust into my hand. Then it was home via Markwick the butcher for the sausages, like Shillingford's in Streatham a seemingly incorruptible institution.

During the day I'd be let loose to explore the railway embankment. There were orchids to find and chalk-loving snails; their contrasting stripes were a thrilling discovery for a child raised on London clay, where snails came in uniform drabness. In the evening we'd sit by the fireside and listen to the radio and I'd roll my grandfather's cigarettes. He'd smoke the results, misshapen and leaking strands of tobacco, without complaint. We'd play games like Corinthians, a forerunner of pinball, and cards, sometimes for pennies as I got older. They'd usually let me win.

But if I enjoyed a free rein in the uncritical atmosphere of my grandparents' home, they were nevertheless Victorians. It was according to the strict moral standard and class-ridden views of that era that my mother was raised, values that were doubtless reflected in my father's philosophy, for he was after all her parents' contemporary. Certainly Victorian mores and attitudes were alive in my mother, and it was a long time before she shook them off. That she did so and radically altered her perspective on race and religion, on food, music and fashion, was due in part to the influx of lodgers and the influence of her children, but mainly to her willingness to learn. She had an open nature anyway, but she developed a genuine curiosity at a stage of life when most people are becoming set in their ways. This curiosity was her most outstanding quality and I like to think that I've inherited it from her.

It could not have been easy being left a widow in 1948 with two small children and no money. No doubt about it, Mum had her work cut out to keep things running smoothly at home. Every morning there were jugs of water to be heated for shaving, and fry-ups to bring to the table on time. She preferred male lodgers because they were less trouble. Unlike women, she reasoned, they washed their hair in the bath and sent their wash to the laundry. Still, it was hard to get into the bathroom some mornings if you missed your turn, and I'd often find her grabbing a cat-lick at the old Butler sink in the kitchen, struggling with cami-knickers and shoulder-straps in case one of the men should catch her undressed. In those days even people with bathrooms only took a bath weekly, but with three lodgers and the rest of us, the boiler had to be stoked and kept in each night. There was coal to be fetched and grates to be blacked, and there could be hell to pay if the hot water ran out on somebody's 'night'.

Whenever she could, Mum would take us to places of interest, museums and so on. In summertime we took the Green Line bus into the countryside, where the cornfields were dotted with blue flax and poppies, and we'd walk for miles across the fields to picturesque country churchyards. Most exciting of all was going to Piccadilly Circus to see the West End lights after the war. Being allowed to stay out well past nine o'clock was unusual, and for many years the words 'Coca-Cola', lit up in red neon, were synonymous for me with growing up. Mum always encouraged us to bring our friends home, whoever they were. She did draw the line when I brought home a drape-suited Teddy-boy, though later events showed that, in this case, her intuition had been right.

Despite Mum's central position in our lives, it was actually a very male world, filled with the ideology of both middle- and working-class men of the period. I am often surprised to discover how much more I know of the way men rather than women lived at that time. Certainly I've never met any other woman of my age who grew up on Westerns such as *Texas Mesa* or American pulp-magazines such as *Weird Tales*, *Black Mask* and *Texas Ranger*. Not that my mother actively discouraged me from feminine ways – I wore bows in my hair and floral frocks with white collars – but I was a forthright kind of child, set on a collision course with life, and it was probably far simpler for her to pass me into the care of whichever lodger was willing, faced as she was with the strict regime of running the household. It was thus I absorbed so many male-centred values. From racing-form, boxing and football to the intimate details of collarstuds, shaving and razor-stropping, it was a world of total fascination. With such unrelenting maleness as a model, I'd write off for brochures on courses in Mechanical Engineering – even, at one point, to bodybuilder Charles Atlas for details of his secrets of 'dynamic tension'.

My father, despite his infirmity, had started me reading before I went to school and I still can't pass a secondhand bookshop without slowing down. Mum's relative poverty meant that pocket money was limited; when other children got sixpence we were getting a penny. So when I discovered secondhand books and realised that selling as well as buying was possible, I never looked back. I'd read all the classics, the Victorian novels and Edwardian school stories lying around the house and I wanted to move on. On Saturdays I'd drag Clive from door to door while we were out doing the shopping. We would ask for old books and magazines, then take them to Jennings Secondhand Book Shop after school. Even magazines such as *Woman's Own*, with a cover-price of twopence ha'penny, were recycled; Jennings resold them for a penny, which meant you got a halfpenny for each. With the proceeds I built up a collection of paperback Westerns, sci-fi and thrillers, Dennis Wheatley and 'The Saint' in particular. Occasionally I'd venture into other fields. Once I picked up a medical journal filled with vivid colour photographs. 'You don't really want this, do you?' said a dubious Mr Jennings, but I insisted. Later, I realised the lurid illustrations showed the chancre sore of syphilis.

To supplement our pocket money, we did odd jobs: cleaning windows, polishing furniture and shopping for anyone who would have us. Newspapers, too, could be converted to cash. The fish-and-chip shop paid a penny for 7 lb of old newsprint, and our door-to-door forays would always produce a few bundles. And then shoplifting became all the rage in our street. At the time I was collecting an expensive glossy series of comics, based on famous books, called *Classics Illustrated*. I worked out that by sidling up to the counter at W.H. Smith I could slip one of these under my coat. I built up a reasonable collection in this way until the day I met Mum coming out of the grocer's next door 'What are you doing here?' she demanded, just as, to my horror, I felt the magazine slipping from its position of safety. I wriggled in desperation, but, with a guilty plop, it landed at my feet. 'You stole that!' she exclaimed. 'Now just you take it back.' Having to repeat the process in reverse was the most salutary of lessons. Just as well; shortly after, two older girls down the road, orphaned by the war, were sent to an approved school for their efforts in this direction –

albeit linked to a little amateur prostitution.

One of these girls, June, I remember particularly, because she was the first person I ever knew who made it into 'show business', even though at a humble level. I can still see her, standing resolutely in front of the screen at the Saturday morning pictures, dressed in a long green hand-me-down coat, giving a sturdy rendition of 'Now is the Hour' to an audience of rowdy ABC minors.

It was the rowdiness of our Saturday morning excursions to the Regal that set my mother against this particular social activity. June, like others in our road, was a 'requisitioned' girl, and that meant she didn't speak 'properly'. During the war, unoccupied property was requisitioned to house homeless families, many of whom came from the blitzed East End of London – much to the dismay of middle-class Streatham, which had always had a very high opinion of itself. At the Saturday morning pictures – 'We love to laugh and have a singsong/ Such a happy crowd are we-e/We're all pals together/We're Minors of the A-B-C-e-e' – the classes mingled recklessly. According to Mum, my accent and my behaviour suffered. To my lasting dismay, she stepped in and prevented me going.

Clive and I were both great collectors, and in a further effort to raise money, we put on a Grand Exhibition in our dining-room. Everything on display was carefully documented: birds' eggs, skulls and seashells laid out on cotton wool, cigarette cards, coins, cheese labels and matchboxes identified. There were photographs of revolutionary jet aircraft, butterflies and moths caught by my father in India and a sliver of fossilised treetrunk carefully chipped from an exhibit in the grounds of the Natural History Museum. The *pièce de résistance* was a sparrow's skeleton which I'd mounted in a standing position, bones glued with Seccotine and fixed together with fusewire. It was a great success; the visitors were duly impressed and generous with their contributions. With Barbara and Zane, the Egyptian doctor's children, we held a funfair in the back garden. Zane and I, inveterate builders of balsa wood aircraft and manufacturers of genuine gunpowder, attempted in vain to build a small roundabout, settling for corks in a bucket instead. At Christmas time Clive and I made a few attempts at door-to-door carol singing, and I played cards with the lodgers for money: whist, crib and Beg o' my Neighbour. The only time Mum was obstructive was when we attempted to take a Guy into the street to raise money for fireworks on November 5th. 'I'm *not* having my children begging,' she said. All in all, our efforts earned a fair bit of revenue during those lean times. My brother said to me recently, 'You know, for someone who's so socialist-minded, you were a pretty good capitalist at an early age!' Whatever – it's helped me survive the freelance life with all its uncertainty and pitfalls. I'm glad for that early experience.

We were, of course, lucky to have such freedom. It was not that Mum didn't care where we went or what we got up to. On the contrary: she actively encouraged every creative activity. She was not to know what the saltpetre and sulphur, deliberately purchased from separate chemists, were used for, and not overkeen when she caught me shinning up our huge chestnut tree to raid the woodpigeon's nest, but otherwise she was pleased to see us occupied, especially if she thought we were learning.

As my fascination with science developed, I was allowed to turn the boxroom into a laboratory. There, surrounded by my collection of animal skulls and abandoned photographs of Victorian ancestors, I set about putting into practice knowledge gleaned from the 'how-to-do-it' books I picked up at the library. I plastered the walls with dissection-plans for various creatures and imagined myself making discoveries like Faraday working with frogs' legs. Through a second-hand microscope I discovered the secrets of pond-water, and learnt how to sandwich sections of everyday substances in glycerine to examine their structure. Dissection tools could be improvised from razor-blades and needles bent into hooks with the aid of a gas-flame, and Janet recoiled in horror one day when she came upon me at work on a mouse professionally pinned-out on a board. It wasn't only the smell to which I was oblivious, I was unaware of what was expected of girls of my age – or at least ignored it.

Somehow I located a supplier of laboratory requisites, and began ordering chemicals and anything else in my price range that took my fancy. Crayfish drenched in stinking formaldehyde came through the post, sea-urchins, too, and one half-term holiday I dragged my hapless mother to their premises in Pentonville Road to load up with test-tubes, beakers and coverslides, much to the astonishment of the technician in charge.

Along with science and reading, I had another love in my life. In the Girl Guides I became a part of a world where my 'unfeminine' skills were appreciated and a sense of responsibility encouraged. It is fashionable now to belittle the Scouting movement as out-of-date and jingoistic, but for many children like myself it provided a place to develop potential of a kind that was not always encouraged at school. It was classless, too, and to my lasting benefit, I was thrown together with the fireman's daughter and later, when I became a Cub Instructor, the postman's son. And, because the Guides was seen as a 'good thing', there was nothing my mother could do about that.

I loved the outdoors and the sense of adventure that camping made possible. We'd pile into the back of a pantechnicon-type furniture lorry and ride off into the great unknown, doing something all our own in which grown-ups, discreetly, played a peripheral role. I bought Baden-Powell's *Scouting for Boys* and *The Scout's How-to-do-it Book of Gadgets and Dodges*, and became a dab hand at fire-lighting and woodcraft. Above all I learned the secrets of making gadgets that wouldn't collapse. Other little girls had difficulty in lashing two twigs together; I found a felled ash-tree, trimmed and bundled some of its branches and took them with me, cross-lashing them firmly on site. My racks kept our gear out of the mud, and no greater compliment could be paid to a 14-year-old than to catch the officers admiring my work, cameras in hand.

But there were other things apart from the smell of sausages and woodsmoke and singing 'Land of the Silver Birch' at nightfall. I'd shrugged off my mother's attempts to domesticate me, but here I had to learn to cook and to sew, so I did. The 1957 World Camp and Jamboree were held in Britain, and it was there that I met African people for the first time. I met Scouts from what is now Pakistan, too. They came from Multan, my father's birthplace, and gave me badges for my collection. For many girls the Guides was a period of marking time until the first boy came along, but for more than seven years the movement was an important part of my life, developing self-respect and encouraging internationalism and the idea of working with others. It was a lot more fun than school.

My aptitude for wheeling and dealing stood me in good stead when the spring on the old gramophone finally broke. A schoolfriend had an old wind-up model for sale. Thirty bob was all she wanted, and, as luck would have it, my doe rabbit had just given birth to a litter of six. I pinned a notice to the front tree — 'Baby Rabbits For Sale, 5/- each' — and sold the lot. I told Sandra I'd have her portable gram with its nursery-rhyme pictures on the lid, but could only manage 29 shillings (I needed a shilling for a box of needles). It worked and I had to put up with Little Miss Muffett and Co. until I finally acquired a Dansette.

But music was still a complete mystery to me when I started at grammar school at the age of 11. As a small child I remember Mum playing 'The Blue Danube' on the piano and singing us songs from old musicals such as 'If You Should Care for Me', but she never suggested that I should try to play. Eventually the piano disappeared and I tuned out. Like most families in the days before television became common, we'd sit and listen to the radio together. But, she said, I cared only for 'talking', with programmes such as *Jennings at School* at the top of my list.

Then Diana and Michael moved, separately, into our house. They were young, lively and flirtatious, and had quite an impact on me. I suppose I was a little in love with them both; certainly I hung on their every word. They were both obsessed with music, and so, as a result, was I.

On the eve before rock 'n' roll shook up the music business, the first number I learned to sing along with was Jo Stafford's 'My Resistance is Low' ('You touch my fingertips and my heart is aglow'). Doubtless reflecting the aftermath of war and continuing National Service in Britain, songs about home and traditional values were popular: Guy Mitchell's rousing 'There's Always Room at Our House', Rosemary Clooney's 'Come On-a My House', and later Pat Boone's 'I'll Be Home', a cover of Black group the Flamingos. I listened to radio programmes such as *Family Favourites*, which linked service personnel abroad with relatives, featuring requests for Frank Sinatra, Nat 'King' Cole and Ella Fitzgerald alongside the well-scrubbed Ruby Murray. With my burgeoning passion for music, I even wanted to be like some of the singers. It was a desire that afflicted Clive in an equally trans-sexual way. He'd rush around dressed in Western gear singing 'The Deadwood Stage', as featured by Doris Day in *Calamity Jane*, while I'd try to imitate the operatic marvel Mario Lanza's stirring 'Because You're Mine' in the bath. Eventually I had to accept that I wasn't a natural tenor.

Family Favourites came on just before lunch on Sundays. I began to resent being dragged away from the wireless – the classic Pye 'Q' model from the 1930s, its grille shaped like a sunset – especially when Johnny Ray, one of my earliest heroes, came on the air. An aura of mystery surrounded this frail singer with the conspicuous hearing-aid, not least because his 'suggestive' recording of 'Such a Night' had been banned in America and by the BBC. A friend of mine had a copy, however, and as Michael brought home all the music papers I was beginning to know what was going on.

The BBC often banned records with dubious sexual connotations; Nat 'King' Cole's 'Teach Me Tonight' was another victim. But Johnny Ray was clearly a rebel, castigated by *Melody Maker* writers for the histrionics of 'Cry', which had millions of bobbysoxers doing just that. More to the point, he was influenced by blues and gospel music, and sang in a more 'open' manner than other white singers of the day. His overwhelming popularity, though partially based on the 'desire to mother him' syndrome, was an indication of the shattering of comfortable values that lay just ahead. I thought he was exciting; he obviously had the edge on Perry Como and the virtuous Vic Damone.

When it came to instrumental music, dance bands predominated, with interludes from close-harmony vocal groups such as the Stargazers: 'The Stargazers are on-the-AIR!' they sang, and I was fascinated to learn that one of them lived in Streatham. There was jazz on the radio, too, from solo artists such as Louis Armstrong as well as the American and British big bands. Michael was inclined towards the 'progressive'; he raved about Stan Kenton's Orchestra and the internationally respected dance band led by England's own Ted Heath. Somewhere along the way I got into swapping football programmes and autographs with a penfriend who was also a Heath fan, thereby picking up even more information.

And then I met my first boyfriend, at a church fête. His name was Laurence and he played the trumpet. His main interests in life were jazz and sex, and I didn't take much persuading to be converted to both.

It was inevitable, I suppose, given the history of the way white society has dealt with Black music, that the first jazz record I bought should have been by an imitator rather than an original. However, the imbalance didn't last long. Laurie thought Humphrey Lyttelton was terrific, but he told me that Louis Armstrong was even better. In the library I found a history of jazz called *Shining Trumpets*, and on one of my more legitimate trips to W.H. Smith came across the Pelican *Jazz*. This, like most similar literature of the period, insisted that the 'real' jazz ended with the advent of bebop in the 1940s. Years later when I met the author, Rex Harris, he told me he wished he'd never written the thing; but it was from these two books that I learned how the music had been created by former slaves in America's Deep South following Emancipation, and noted the names of the early innovators. I also became familiar with the legends of jazz, many repeated without question up to this day.

New Orleans was renowned as a trumpet player's city and *Shining Trumpets* painted romantic word portraits of all the 'kings'. There was Kid Buddy Bolden, credited with 'inventing' the music, Freddie Keppard, who played with a handkerchief over his right hand to stop rivals copying his fingering. And King Joe Oliver, in whose band Louis Armstrong first came to prominence and whose 78 record 'Dippermouth Blues' I'd seen displayed at the Swing Shop. These were tough guys with tremendous reputations in the community, who one day played for parades perched on the back of a lorry and the next for a funeral, accompanying hearse and mourners to the cemetery. With their iron lips and their formal way of dressing, they stood four-square on the pages of history, offering an alternative view of what might have been culturally significant in bygone days.

Much was made of Storyville, the city's 'sporting district', where prostitution, booze and gambling flourished unchecked before Prohibition, and where pianists such as Jelly Roll Morton played for the patrons of brothels. This lurid connection was to capture the imagination of the prurient and for years be stressed out of proportion to other elements in the music's evolution.

I began going to the Swing Shop regularly and, with Bert Bradfield's help, found out how the music sounded. I came home with 'Dippermouth Blues', where Armstrong and Oliver's cornets dovetailed in classic virtuosity – albeit a little hard to hear over the decades – and played it and other records to death. I discovered Keppard, Morton and other New Orleans key figures, such as Sidney Bechet and my particular hero, clarinettist Johnny Dodds. And, of course, the blues.

I'd always been miserable at school, a consequence of being moved up a year at the age of 7 and seldom managing to make any real friends. The one or two girls I got close to were usually 'outcasts' too. The problem was that I was too bright and too boisterous, generally at the top of the class and detention lists alike. It was a dangerous combination, given the conservatism of children. But my new-found knowledge gave me a chance to shine in Music Appreciation. We were allowed to pursue a project of our own choice and I wanted to do a history of jazz. There was only one other girl who knew anything about the music – indeed she gave me a Count Basie 78 I have to this day – but I managed to persuade the hopelessly innocent Miss Ivermee that jazz was a 'classic music' that had nothing to do with this new rock 'n' roll, which had already caused cinema riots when the film *Blackboard Jungle* was shown.

Some girls were upset about this; they felt they should be allowed to write theses on Elvis or Gene Vincent but their efforts were quashed. I rehashed part of the Harris book, illustrating the text with pen-and-ink drawings copied from *Melody Maker* and photographs cut – disgracefully – from my library copy of *Shining Trumpets*. I decorated the cover with brass instruments, coloured in with gold ink (we were all heavily into coloured inks in those days, always in trouble for doing homework in green). But school in general, apart from drama class led by the lovely Miss Lee with the beautiful violet eyes, was a drag.

Laurie and I met after school a few times but there was an enormous amount of letter-writing in our relationship. I must have been pretty bold for those days. 'Are you the kind of boy who kisses girls?' I remember writing, adding: 'I hope you are.' No sooner was this out in the open than we put it into practice down by the running-track. The way we went about it seems amusing now, looking over our shoulders and hastily grabbing each other until somehow our lips met, but 1955 was light years away from today where sex is concerned.

Growing up in an area where kerb-crawling flourished ensured that I knew plenty about sex from an early age; one nastier early pastime was wandering over Tooting Bec Common counting the abandoned condoms. Erect pink flesh could often be glimpsed through the hawthorns as the flashers prowled in search of children to shock, while at the cinema and on the buses, seeking refuge from groping paedophiles was a constant. There were few among my acquaintances who did not suffer from this aggravating and, for some, distressing abuse, as men pressed up against you, destroying screen concentration, feverishly unbuttoning themselves beneath raincoats strategically placed. Yet the thought of 'doing it' with Laurie was unimaginable to both of us. Despite our obsession with sex, we never got further than a bit of fondling. Nevertheless, our letters blazed with passion. He exhorted me to look out for historical romances by an author called, I think, Phillip Lindsay, who wrote quite explicitly about sex. I looked in the library and, sure enough, there they were, all falling open at well-thumbed pages.

We were well into Hank Jansen by now, the tough-guy American crimewriter whose women were always having their dresses ripped by panting men. What a disappointment to find out years later that he was a south London schoolteacher, or something equally unexotic. We reeled back in excitement at the passage in *The Cruel Sea* where the adulterous wife is caught with 'come' all over her nightdress, fumbled in the back row at the Regal while Humphrey Bogart acted out his role as the paranoid Queeg in *The Caine Mutiny*. Laurie wrote to me about his 'new invention for lovers: bras that open down the front'. I wrote from the Cloisters at Westminster Abbey during a school visit that I was having my plaits cut off – at last. Laurie wrote back that he knew I'd look terrific, and promised more passion when next we met.

Too late. My mother found the 'front-opening bra' letter and that was that.

2
About a Half a Million . . .
Famed Autographs

In 1966 my mother was 62. On the morning of her birthday I received a phone call from a Nigerian diplomat who wanted me to take photographs at a party that night. I did a lot of this type of work at the time and did not want to lose the job, but I'd promised my mother a night out. 'Bring her with you,' he said.

As soon as we walked in, Mum was whisked away and a drink put in her hand. Whenever I looked around, there she was talking earnestly or working her way rather delicately through a well-piled plate of red jollof rice. I was constantly on call, trying to organise straggling group photos to order, but Mum experienced no social inhibitions as she danced with students and chatted. Later she said it was one of her best birthdays ever.

Her enthusiasm to go anywhere and talk openly won her a lifetime of friends from different cultural groups as well as her own. A Nigerian boyfriend of mine, long after we'd stopped seeing each other, would call by to visit her with a bottle of wine; and there was an Australian car salesman, a real 'rough diamond', who stayed at the house as a lodger for a while and became quite attached to her. He'd take her out for sophisticated dinners when she was a sprightly 70-year-old, then call her from Australia on his return. Once, when I was away and the Duke Ellington Orchestra came to town, saxophonist Harry Carney invited her to a telerecording and offered to send a taxi.

People liked her because she took them as she found them, but it had not always been that way. Her open response to the people she met through her children has been a lifelong lesson for me in showing how racism, when based on ignorance, can turn into something quite different when myths are debunked and exploded.

The first Black people I recall seeing were leaning on the railings, passing the time, outside the Prince of Wales pub in Brixton. Ever since I can remember, Westindians have stood on that corner where Coldharbour Lane meets the High Street, and as I passed there often as a child they became a familiar sight, particularly at weekends when the men were out to relax. (The first wave of postwar migration being predominantly male, it was too early for there to be many Black women about.)

The male style of the day was flamboyant: wide-brimmed hats worn at a jaunty angle, knitted waistcoats sometimes with suede panels, hand-painted ties and double-breasted jackets with padded shoulders – the kind of people filmed by Pathé News arriving on the *Empire Windrush* from the Caribbean to work in Britain after the war. I was fascinated by their 'different-ness' and wanted to know more about them, especially as I had begun to realise that jazz was a Black people's music. Information was sketchy, however, and I detected that the subject was taboo.

From time to time there were Black faces in our church congregation, sober-suited Africans and people from other parts of the Diaspora. Then a Canon from the Sudan came to preach. We became friendly and took photographs together and I invited him home for tea. He visited us several times during a long stay in Britain and wrote to me regularly about his adventures as he travelled around the country visiting various churches. Together with our vicar and Canon Ngama I went to see the film *The Ten Commandments*. Halfway through, the vicar turned to me. 'Well, Valerie,' he said with a smile, 'you ought to go straight from now on – watching *The Ten Commandments* sitting between two parsons!'

But whatever relationships might be established between pew and pulpit at Immanuel Church, Streatham Common, everyday realities were different. The 'sordid anthropological heresy' of African inferiority, created to justify the slave trade and colonial rule, still infected Britain. Tolerant views might be expressed by more liberal members of society, yet the traditional prejudices surfaced as Afro-Caribbean settlers came to stay in increasing numbers. Among the books I devoured as a child were plenty by Victorians such as Kipling, Conrad, Henty and Haggard, racists all, whose stories of European supremacy in the face of savagery operated, a century on, as the backdrop to public opinion. Indeed, in the Mau Mau struggle of the 1950s against British colonial rule in Kenya the 'savage' deeds of the freedom fighters were emphasised. Britain, of course, was incapable of savage behaviour. The country wallowed in a ludicrous self-image of decency, as dishonest then as it is today. It was not an auspicious climate in which to enquire about the men in the wide-brimmed hats.

Whenever we now advertised a room to let, African students were among those who came to the door. My mother, who had welcomed light-skinned Indians into the house, turned them away politely and expected me to do likewise. When I asked for an explanation, I was told that 'they' were 'different', that the people at church who were 'trying to lead good lives' were all right but the wide-brimmed hats were a sign of immorality. and she wasn't going to risk having *that* sort of thing in the house – despite the fact that the African students didn't dress like that anyway.

I was upset and angry. Something was clearly wrong. Canon Ngama had been made welcome, after all, and wasn't he a good friend of the vicar? I'd been brought up to believe in a worldwide brotherhood and sisterhood, all walking hand-in-hand to Heaven; and we attended a church with a long history of involvement in missionary work. Regardless of the paternalistic attitude of British missionaries and preachers toward their 'coloured brethren', as far as I was concerned a tacit belief in equality existed. It was a point I made over and over; but it was useless to argue. My mother had made up her mind. I refused to collude by lying, and whenever an African came to the door left it to her to tell him that the room 'was let'.

From time to time I'd bring up the subject and saw that my mother wavered. It was not that she was an evil racist; far from it. She was unworldly, alone and, frankly, frightened. For her, as for most

Whites brought up on Victorian ideas, Africans represented the unknown. Not that contact with Black society had been totally absent on her side of the family. At the turn of the century my grandfather played tennis with Samuel Coleridge-Taylor, the eminent composer of African descent. They lived near one another in Croydon and the man who wrote *Hiawatha's Wedding Feast* was sufficiently respected for my grandfather to recall this personal contact with pride. Yet, as I later learned, the newspapers of the day ran a continuing – and libellous – correspondence about the Black man's 'propensity' for rape.

The attribution of base qualities to all Black people, as happened during slavery in order to justify 'this cruel and unnatural institution', persisted into my childhood and beyond. At school the lily-white First Year learned to recite, unquestioning, a poem about a 'Darky Sunday School' where the worshippers had 'a place to check [their] chewing-gum and razors at the door'. At the same time, we would often hear pianist-entertainer 'Hutch' on the radio, singing songs such as 'These Foolish Things' and 'Begin the Beguine' with effortless charm and the merest 'hint' of his colour. Hutch (Leslie Hutchinson) was a longtime British resident, a Black man beloved by the public; he'd win nods of approval whenever his familiar light baritone boomed over the airwaves. Paul Robeson, too, was deeply revered, epitomising what good, serious singing was all about.

One of our lodgers was a great fan of the popular Black vocal group, the Deep River Boys, frequent visitors to Britain, and when I revealed my interest in jazz he proudly produced a postcard photograph of them signed: 'To Derek'. Such reverence for Black entertainers was a far cry from the myth of the African's 'bestiality' which, I would learn later from reading Malcolm X, was to some degree created by the white man to manipulate the white woman and justify his own access to Black women. White rape, too, was used as a form of control. But the myths continued, and where Black people were concerned, 'immorality' was something that 'everyone knew'.

But at the same time as I was being made to believe in the 'inferiority' of people of African descent, I was beginning to learn how much they had contributed to the world. The double standard was confusing. Here I was, reading that people like Duke Ellington were among the most respected of modern composers – their names were in *books*, after all – so why should these 'other' people be so different?

Like any child told to leave something alone, I was curious about this forbidden society. I went up the road to post a letter one night and walked into a situation that was to confirm my mother's worst fears. I met a man from Sierra Leone. His name was Moses, he was studying law, and he asked me to go out with him. I was really excited. Here was a grown man taking an interest in me. I felt sure that my mother would not allow me to see him, so we met at the cinema and parted a distance from home. On our third meeting he gave me a ring and invited me back to his house. He cooked me a meal of rice and tinned meat and we listened to the radiogram, Nat 'King' Cole singing 'Walking my Baby Back Home'. We drank VP wine and he asked me to go to bed with him. I told him I couldn't and he settled for a kiss and more wine.

I got into the habit of going to see Moses regularly. He called me 'Bo', the name for 'friend' in several Sierra Leonean languages (and one of the African words that survive in America), and indeed our relationship felt more like a friendship than an affair. Some Saturdays we'd go to the pictures, but generally the pattern was: food, music, wine or sherry, and the 'heavy petting' that some other girls had already begun to report. Although he wanted the 'real thing', he was gentle and never tried to force me. I told someone at school whose friendship with an Indian had incensed her father, and we confided in each other in our plight. I'd hidden the ring from my mother but I showed it off to people at school.

Then disaster struck. Mum and I were summoned to the school and interviewed separately about what was going on. My mother was distraught when I confessed all. The police were involved because I was under-age and intercourse was presumed to have occurred, despite my denials. It was decided that it would be better for all concerned if I didn't return when the new term started. I spent the most miserable time of my life so far, chastised for my sins all summer, racked with guilt and even, at one stage – although I knew it was impossible – with fear of pregnancy.

Eventually another school was found where I had to play catch-up for a year, but before this my form teacher wrote to me telling me to repent and sent me a copy of *The Imitation of Christ* by St Thomas à Kempis. Only Miss Lee, of the beautiful violet eyes and casual, offbeat humour, showed any understanding. 'Don't worry about what people say,' she wrote. 'I always think it is best to help the individual forget in these circumstances. Let me know how you get on in your new school.'

The aftermath of my harmless affair was weeks of misery and more early education in racism. I'm sure that any 14-year-old girl suspected of having sex with a man would have been similarly treated then, but doubt whether the story would have come to light so readily had the man not been Black. A girl in my class had spent some time in the USA and been infected by the kind of white American thinking that sought to ban rock 'n' roll records because of the music's 'savage' origin; she, I'm sure, stirred things up. As it happens, she did me a favour, simultaneously raising my consciousness and my academic standards. My next school was clearly superior and there for the first time I made good friends who really counted.

Moses continued to send me birthday and Christmas cards, and from time to time I'd run across him in the street and we'd stop and exchange greetings. I noticed that increasingly he wore a raggedy coat several sizes too big for him and a greasy brown hat perched on the back of his head. I'd see that his eyes were bloodshot and he walked with his arms swinging sideways in a distinctly unbalanced way. I never found out how his studies were going. Perhaps he was not cut out for the academic life or had become drink dependent. All I knew was that whenever we met I felt badly for him and sensed that his shabby state was connected with what had happened.

Years later my grandfather told me how the police had threatened Moses to make him confess. That they believed in his innocence only shows how much he was forced to grovel. What he had done, in forming a sexual friendship with a 14-year-old, was a perfectly normal practice in Africa, though what subsequently happened was a confirmation of something Diasporean Blacks would have been taught to avoid. For me, it was a rude awakening from childhood, a lesson in how this society operates that I have never forgotten.

Through my visits to the Swing Shop I got to know the literature of jazz as well as the music. Some critics felt that the only authentic jazz was limited to the prewar period, but their views were subverted by Bert Bradfield, who would give me any 78s that had been chipped or cracked in transit. On my old portable gramophone such defects were a mere inconvenience and it was in this unorthodox way that I became familiar with 'modernists' such as Charlie Parker, Bud Powell and Stan Getz, while simultaneously hearing them referred to as heretics.

I decided to catalogue my growing collection with details of who played what, where and when. I had become aware of the little research publications and my aptitude for letterwriting, practised on the muscular Charles Atlas and honed to perfection with penfriends from Brunei to Boulogne, stood me in good stead when I began looking for data.

Max Jones who worked for the *Melody Maker* was a veteran commentator on Afro-American music, having actually seen Armstrong and Ellington at the Palladium in the 1930s. He was understandably surprised to receive a letter from a 15-year-old schoolgirl. This, he said later, he just had to see. He invited me to his office off Long Acre and gave me a stack of old magazines. In his trademark black beret, Max swanned around the scene in a rather proprietorial manner. As co-editor of the periodical *Jazz Music* he had published work by people such as George Padmore, pioneer of Pan-Africanism, and the Black American writer Langston Hughes, as well as the 'Negrophile' Nancy Cunard. Max had known Billie Holiday and many other jazz names, and his 'Collectors Corner' and 'World of Jazz' columns were packed with information on many of the lesser known musicians.

The music's early white chroniclers notable for such perspicacity wrote in isolation in Britain. It has been said that, not having to confront the Black reality in their presence to any extent, they could afford to be liberal; and it became increasingly apparent that the role Whites played in defining the music irked many people from inside the culture. Nevertheless tribute is due to those pioneering white spirits who went beyond the love affair with the 'Negro' that existed from the days of Blackface minstrelsy, to realise there was more to the music than fashion or instant thrills. Max Jones was certainly one of these. I read his every word avidly and he encouraged me to write, eventually for *Melody Maker* itself.

I must have been about 15 when I conceived the idea of writing a book about Johnny Dodds. His clarinet playing on early records by Louis Armstrong, Jelly Roll Morton and others really touched me, particularly on 'Perdido Street Blues' by the New Orleans Wanderers. His solo was sparsely constructed but it went deep. Years before I walked along Perdido Street itself, and even longer before I discovered that a *woman* was responsible for this particular arrangement (and marvelled that this should have gone unremarked for so long), Johnny Dodds was my hero. An unpopular choice, as it turned out.

He had died in 1940, the year before I was born, so I wrote to his brother for help. Historically, Warren 'Baby' Dodds is one of the elders of modern percussion, the cornerstone of New Orleans drumming. In the 1920s he played with King Oliver in the company of brother Johnny, the young Louis Armstrong and Louis's pianist wife Lil, the 'Perdido Street' arranger. Baby Dodds had been incapacitated for some time, but to my surprise he wrote back right away:

> In regard to my brother I can't tell you anything about him unless I see you face to face. I am on the road to recovery. I would like for you to see if you can get me booked over there. Maybe so if I can come to Europe we can get together. Then I can help you and you can help me.

It seemed like a reasonable deal, but he lived in Chicago and distance was against us.

To this day I find it remarkable that someone who was part of Armstrong's epochal Hot Seven should have actually written to me, especially when I was only 15. But Baby Dodds was the first of many musicians who responded to my need to know more of the people behind the sounds. I still have most of their letters to me. For a while I maintained a correspondence with several veterans of New Orleans music. People such as Lawrence Marrerro, who had played banjo with the legendary Bunk Johnson band, appeared genuinely pleased in the interest I showed, and, for me, it seemed perfectly normal that such heroes should enter my life. Other people corresponded with tennis players and footballers, after all, or wrote to film stars for photographs. I received a signed picture from singer Alberta Hunter and a Christmas card from Omer Simeon, who had once played clarinet with Jelly Roll. But it was about much more than mere acquisitiveness. Getting a letter with a New Orleans postmark established it as a *real place*, not just a name on the map or in history books – a place where people lived and made music, far more believable than cowboys or film stars. Exchanging such letters was the perfect antidote to any tendency I might have developed to rate records above the people who made the music.

'Junk-shopping' has always been a collectors' pursuit. In the days before albums took over, jazz rarities originally issued as 'Dance Music/Foxtrot' were constantly found in the piles of dross that accumulated in secondhand shops. Among my contacts was the eccentric collector Brian Rust, who worked at the BBC. Like Max Jones, he was intrigued to know the identity of the teenage girl behind the many queries for discographical information, and he invited me to lunch at Broadcasting House. Brian looked like someone out of Greyfriars School with a 'Gee whizz' kind of hairstyle and way of speaking, but he pointed me in the right direction and introduced me to sounds that might have otherwise escaped me, such as Troy Floyd's 'Shadowland Blues'. Then, for my sixteenth birthday, he presented me with my very own rarity, a copy of the original Victor 78 of Duke Ellington's 'Mood Indigo'/'The Mooche'. I was bowled over by such incredible kindness. He also made me aware of the relative values of 78s other than jazz and, armed with a list of desirable items, I'd rummage through stacks of old records on my way home from school. With my beady eye primed for the telltale labels sought by collectors – I hoped to find early Bessie

Smiths bearing the legend 'Vocal Novelty' — I came across Valaida Snow, 'The Queen of the Hot Trumpet', who played with the power and verve of Louis Armstrong and spent several years in Europe before being interned by the Nazis. I turned up a few saleable items and traded them with Brian for sides that I really wanted.

This was the kind of music I was listening to in my teens while my schoolmates were immersed in rock 'n' roll. I was not entirely immune to 'popular' music — one of the paying-guests gave me a copy of Bill Haley's 'Rock Around the Clock', and I was absolutely crazy about the Crew Cuts singing 'Earth Angel' — but my main interest lay in sounds recorded a couple of decades earlier. I still have the 78s: the ebullient Fats Waller, recorded in London, Bessie Smith doing her 'Empty Bed Blues' and Peetie Wheatstraw, a.k.a. The Devil's Son-in-Law, singing 'Santa Claus Blues'. Across the decades, the brave souls who ventured into the early recording studios can be heard, barely audible in some cases. Among the earliest was Papa Charlie Jackson, recorded with Freddie Keppard's Jazz Cardinals in 1926 when the entire band would play into a massive horn. He sang: 'God made a woman/He made her mighty funny/You kiss her 'round the mouth/Sweeter'n honey/You salty dog/Sweet Mama, you salty dog.' I was immersed in sounds recorded thousands of miles away, when my mother was young. And if I didn't really know what a 'salty dog' was, I knew the records backwards, the solos note for note.

Just to look through the old 78s I collected so lovingly in those days, I can hear how they sounded without even having to play them. From the powerful surge and urgency of the early Ellington and Fletcher Henderson big bands going full tilt, to the rough-and-tumble of the Basie orchestra translating the blues for city-slickers, the sound comes rushing into my mind's ear. There's Billie Holiday singing 'Crazy he calls me', the strings claustrophobic behind her, Buck and Bubbles creating an aural experience out of tap-dance, Albert Ammons and Meade Lux Lewis delivering the ultimate boogie-woogie. Most moving of all was a Vocalion by an allegedly incarcerated pianist named Jesse James, about whom nothing is known. His one-off 'Lonesome Day Blues' made me shake when I heard it. His was a desperate shout which worked on me subliminally, telling me something of 400 years of struggle that just couldn't be learned from books.

As time went by I discovered that a number of early 78s by women singers were sought after for the rare trumpet accompaniments by people such as Louis Armstrong rather than for the name on the label. When it came to the women themselves, only the redoubtable Bessie Smith and a handful of other so-called 'classic' blues singers — that is, women who sang in theatres, drawing on the traditions of vaudeville, and earned their living as professional entertainers — were considered worth collecting in their own right.

So deep did this collectors' prejudice against women artists go that it took almost half a century for such 'obscure' singers as Ida Cox, a massive record-seller in the 1930s, or just about any of the early female instrumentalists, to achieve recognition on anything approaching their own terms. Men were seen as the architects of Afro-American music, the upholders of its rites and rituals. Sad to say, I, too, was influenced by the prevailing standards of white male 'authorities'. With the notable exception of Derrick Stewart-Baxter, another of my early supporters and a source of encouragement, who wrote lovingly about the women singers of the 'classic' period, women were very much regarded as also-rans. I liked Billie Holiday, of course, Bessie Smith and her teacher Ma Rainey, and a handful of others, but for quite a long time few representatives of womankind were allowed on my shelves.

As for the blues itself, the idea that it could be cathartic, a renewing and strengthening force or a source of resistance, was yet to be advanced in collectors' circles. When I first met the blues, I learned it was a music of sorrow, born out of slavery, and that was all. It certainly seemed sad to me.

Although I was eager to gather more information about the music, I managed to avoid the 'collector mentality' which can sometimes make catalogue numbers seem more important than people. I've been grateful to collectors for sharing their knowledge and have enormous respect for the science of discography, but the music itself was always the important thing, a living entity rather than a piece of plastic stuck in a sleeve. Getting to know the older musicians later made holding this view more plausible. The rarest of records often held little significance for the artists themselves I discovered — at least in the early days. At a period when musicians were frequently forced to sell their skills (and their compositions) outright, records had neither the potential for future earnings nor the status of works of art that became possible later. Nevertheless, collecting records the way people did in the 1950s meant becoming enmeshed in the idea of discography. It is arguable that a knowledge of who played what, when and with whom was a substitute for contact with the real thing, but thumbing through record sleeves that made a point of listing each participant taught me something which went beyond the music itself. For a start, there was the collective nature of the process to consider, despite the fact that the music was sold as the creation of 'stars'.

Being involved with discography meant that you automatically knew the identity of the most obscure player. Someone listed as 'imitation string-bass' turned out on closer examination to be the voice going 'doom-doom-doom' on some of the early blues recordings. His name was Alfred Elkins and I knew about him just as I knew about the virtuoso Coleman Hawkins, who strode across the pages of history, rewriting the saxophone handbook as he went. These were the history-makers, the humble as well as the mighty, not 'only sidemen', as some would have you believe. And knowing their names set the music apart. It had to be different from what someone like Elvis was up to, for he worked with anonymous bands. Thus through discography, it became possible to see the music as a cultural repository, an idea seldom voiced in those days, but something I now know that I realised unconsciously. And it meant that years later, at a jam-session in New York, I'd experience a thrill of recognition when an older trumpeter climbed on the bandstand and turned out to be Herman Autrey, who'd cut dozens of sides with Fats Waller before I was born. He could still play, as well — a name from the card-index file made flesh.

Through the weekly papers I kept in touch with what was going on outside the world of Okehs, Brunswicks and blue-label Deccas.

I remember the headlines when respected British jazzmen formed rock 'n' roll bands, and when saxophonist Charlie Parker died. 'Bird', one of the key innovators in the history of Afro-American music, breathed his last in March 1955 in the apartment of the music's legendary benefactor and patron, Baroness Nica de Koenigswarter. There was scandal aplenty; Nica was a Rothschild and Parker was Black, and it was assumed they were having an affair. (Years later I would meet Nica's niece, an early member of the team which started the British women's liberation magazine *Spare Rib*, and find we had a most unlikely something-in-common.)

There was another surge of excitement the year that Parker died. For almost two decades a mutual union ban had prevented American and British musicians from playing in each other's countries unless they did so for charity (Ella Fitzgerald and Lester Young were among those who gave their services after the devastating floods of 1952–3), or could qualify as 'variety artists'. In 1953 Stan Kenton's Orchestra played the Theatre Royal, Dublin, and an airlift and coach-parties were organised for jazz lovers starved of American originality, but it was not until 1955 that news filtered through that the impasse was about to be breached. In March 1956 the ban was finally lifted when Kenton played the first British date of a nationwide series of concerts arranged in exchange for a comparable tour of the United States by Ted Heath. Less than two months later, the mainstream element in the jazz world was rewarded. Louis Armstrong brought his All-Stars to play a week-long series of concerts held at Earls Court Arena.

I insisted we went to see Louis and bought tickets for my brother Clive and my mother. The odd thing is that I remember little about the concert, a kind of quasi-variety show which took place in a particularly unpleasant arena, with the musicians revolving on a stage like circus performers. But the press coverage of the visit was incredible. I compiled a scrapbook of cuttings; each of the dailies and the three evening papers carried reports of varying lengths, with the *Daily Express* serialising Louis' diary in four-column chunks as he toured the country.

At the end of the tour, I read in Max Jones' column that a group of musicians would be gathered at London Airport to give the All-Stars a send-off. It was half-term holiday from school, so off on the bus went the family. We had no idea where the momentous event would take place, but the sight of Humphrey Lyttelton, the towering ex-Etonian trumpeter, solved the dilemma. He was dressed in box-back coat, cap and matching plus-fours in grey tweed, a faithful replica of Armstrong's own 1920s style, and decidedly eccentric for the 1950s.

Suddenly there was Louis, small, polite and friendly in a speckled tweed jacket and green on white tartan shirt. He signed autographs for us and posed for a couple of pictures. I was still using my mother's box Brownie, but I felt like Karsh of Ottawa. The meeting was brief, but it didn't matter. It was as if we'd met God, and that was enough.

3
Sweet Little Sixteen

I was 13 going on 14 in 1955 when rock 'n' roll entered the British Hit Parade. I knew all about it, but for the next couple of years I stayed immersed in the prewar sound. None of my schoolfriends could understand my peculiar tastes and I didn't try to convert them. In order to survive, however, I had to keep in touch with the world that revolved around coffee bars, the cinema and the ice-skating rink. At the Coffee Cabin in Streatham the Gaggia machine dispensed espresso and capuccino into Pyrex cups, and I watched the older girls from school dallying with their boyfriends in front of the jukebox. Ponytails, adolescent crushes and Dansette record-players were the thing as the cult of 'teenage' and a room of one's own was growing. I went through a wimpish phase when I bought records by Pat Boone and Tab Hunter and sighed along, like everyone else, as Paul Anka pleaded, 'Oh, please stay by me, Diana'. But, other than as objects that male singers crooned about, women hardly got a look in. There was no way then I could identify with Brenda Lee, the gutsy Mississippi Miss, or the young Helen Shapiro singing 'Please Don't Treat Me Like a Child' as having anything to do with the idea of women being strong. With the exception of the outrageous Marie Adams, who sang the triumphant 'Ma (He's Making Eyes at Me)' with the Johnny Otis band, pop music was another domain of the male.

I was so involved with my New Orleans heroes at the time rock 'n' roll was being born as a marketable commodity that it almost escaped me that Black people were visible in it too, albeit playing second fiddle to the Fabians and Frankie Avalons. I did like the New Orleans pianist Fats Domino, but who wouldn't? Like Louis, he was Mr Goodtimes. And Little Richard was undeniably exciting, but his wildness was a bit decadent for someone reared on the idea that honking saxophones were somewhat out of order. I must confess that for a long time I preferred the Everly Brothers' comfortable version of 'Lucille' with its dove-tailing country harmonies, to Richard's devastating original.

As schoolgirls growing up in south London, we didn't know exactly why the words 'rock 'n' roll' were shunned by some older people, though there was a hint that they were not particularly 'nice'. Later, some of us would discover the ambiguity of the term which, like 'jazz' and 'balling', can be used interchangeably for 'having a good time' or, more specifically, sexual activity. At the time we had no cause to consider how it was used to disguise *what* we were hearing. 'Rock 'n' roll' was an expression coined to obscure the fact that Whites were dancing to Black music – that is, the blues. It was also used to relegate the music to the realm of 'natural' sensuality rather than 'intellectual' creativity, as has happened to every African-derived form, from ragtime and the cakewalk up to the rapping and styling of today.

In the 1950s there was little writing that analysed Black music in this way or discussed its political implications. Most histories were a combination of sentimentalism and sociology. There were plenty of references to slavery and suffering, but the slave revolts went unmentioned in any story of jazz. Although many of the early writers were quite radical, they preferred to write about the evils of segregation at a distance. Magazines such as the erudite *Jazz Monthly* featured Frederick Ramsey's documentary pictures of the Deep South, conveying a romantic image of Rabbit Foot Minstrels and the like while the civil rights movement was gaining ground in the USA. Only Max Jones wrote about world events, instituting a forum for discussion on ways of combating the colour prejudice that increased with the 1958 'race riots' in Nottingham and Notting Hill.

Among British jazz enthusiasts there was a general interest in Afro-American culture: when revues such as *The Jazz Train* or plays such as Lorraine Hansberry's *A Raisin in the Sun*, Langston Hughes' *Simply Heavenly* and, later, James Baldwin's *Blues for Mr Charlie* came to London, we all went to see them. By and large, though, the music press offered no indication of the movements of change taking place internationally and the idea that Afro-American music could in itself function as a kind of resistance was unknown. Yet the music would lead me to discover the literature of protest and struggle and to go beyond, eventually to recognise how the Afro-American oral tradition has, as one writer put it, offered a radical alternative to Western literary values.

These ideas were far away as I immersed myself in dusty old records and my dreams of becoming a writer. To my dismay, my correspondents poured scorn on the Johnny Dodds idea. They said he was technically limited, unimaginative even, that if I wanted to hear really good jazz clarinet I should look out for players with a lighter, more virtuoso touch.

One of those who spurned my hero and his bluesy ways was a researcher who had helped me considerably from the start. Sadly, he had become infected by the racist fantasies of Nick La Rocca, leader of the white Original Dixieland Jazz Band – generally referred to as the first jazz band to record but now identified by some researchers as in fact a non-improvising 'novelty' band (thereby allowing credit for the honour to pass to a Black band, Kid Ory's). La Rocca appeared to be more than a little deranged. To him, only white men played the 'true jazz'; Blacks, he claimed, weren't up to scratch. When my old friend told me he didn't care if he never heard Louis again, I was horrified. Later I came to see this as part of a process, as common in the jazz world as elsewhere, whereby praise is reserved for those Blacks who have internalised the values and attitudes of white teachers. Such 'acceptance' occurs at the expense of acknowledging Africanisms in Diasporean expression – an odd stance if you consider that the music's supposed exoticism was what attracted Whites in the first place – with integration being used to defeat Black self-determination.

Like other English people of my generation, I grew up with the civilising mission of Empire a reality still. I absorbed many of the peculiar ideas that formed the backbone of most writing about the music. Years had to pass for me to unlearn these and, as with other prejudices created in a society based on class, race and gender discrimination, I'm sure I haven't totally succeeded. But change I did.

While working for GCE O-levels I had a musical experience that challenged some of my purist assumptions. French radio was always in the vanguard in airing Black music, and in the evenings I would flick across the dial from Radio Luxembourg via the AFN broadcasts from Germany, searching for a French accent and a helping of soul. I was sitting in the kitchen, boning up on biology, when an unforgettable sound came *scorching* through the crackling atmospherics. The voice was hoarse, taut with emotion, the piano stabbing out whirlpools of notes. I didn't need to wait for the announcement. The name of Ray Charles was already being spoken with reverence in the jazz world, and it could be nobody else. The song was called 'Sinner's Prayer', and nothing I had heard before went as deep. It made me go cold, and it still does. It challenged the validity of everything I'd believed about music up until then. Ray Charles was supposed to be a 'pop' artist and thus beyond the pale for us 'jazzers'. Clearly this division counted for little. His revolutionary use of church elements and his unchained delivery created a musical shock wave. For me, it was an early taste of gospel, the profoundest music of all.

School itself was pretty hard going, with friendships consolidated long before my abrupt arrival, and the serious business of O-levels at hand. In the course of a Latin lesson, however, I encountered a lifelong friend. Her name was Liz Spiro and she intrigued me by spending the best part of the period perched by the window, straining for a glimpse of some boy she fancied. Such rebellious behaviour set her apart from the nicely spoken daughters of clerics and the like intent on Caesar's *Gallic Wars (Part IV)*, and it was to her crowd that I gravitated as the fifth year came to a close. With them I found the sense of belonging that had eluded me throughout my schooldays.

In the middle of all this, however, I was laid low with a bad chest infection. My mother, constantly mindful of bronchial matters following my father's long illness, kept me at home for a long time, and my writing pretensions prospered as a result. Most prolific among my musical correspondents was the Georgia-born folk 'songster' Jesse Fuller. Fuller had generously given me his life story in a series of lengthy pencil-written letters and, confined to bed, I assembled these into an article. I sent the results to *Jazz Journal* and to my delight it was published. In May 1959, I was some kind of a writer at last.

Somehow school drifted on. Some of the gang went off to Italy on holiday, acquiring Italian boyfriends called Sergio and the clout of maturity that goes with such inconsequential liaisons. New, fanciful names were temporarily adopted, one girl becoming, unaccountably, 'Kim', suggesting a pertness at odds with her rather blowsy persona. To counter the drabness of uniform, we put fashionable dents in our hats, wore our ties at half-mast and carried our satchels rakishly under one arm. Whenever we could get away with it, we wore shoes with low heels and a smear of eye make-up. We were women, after all, not girls any more, and I was no longer a tomboy.

We did the Russian Revolution in History, and Liz revealed to a startled class and teacher that her parents had been in the Communist Party. Together we joined the Young Communist League, one day that

28

shook the world.

I don't remember learning much about Marxist theory in the YCL, but because of my interest in 'jazz' I was soon co-opted into writing for the League paper, *Challenge*. With considerable aplomb and a certain amount of nerve, I previewed visits by Count Basie and Jazz at the Philharmonic, using the prevalent critical standards of the day. Then Liz and I got involved in the Campaign for Nuclear Disarmament and went on the Aldermaston marches, where New Orleans-style brass bands led each demonstration. I didn't stay long in the YCL, and it was years before I actually got around to reading the *Communist Manifesto*. But socialist ideas and contacts were to crop up continually in my life from then on, even during years when my main preoccupation was with having a good time.

At the YCL I met a student named Donald. He came from Guyana and my mother, with recent events still fresh in her mind, was not keen. This time I put my foot down. I was 17 years old and I made my own choices. Gradually she relented, won over by Don's gentle nature and his willingness to come round for tea at weekends. We were really in love with each other and I can still see his anxious face, peering through the glass in the front door on a Sunday. But our affair was confined to cuddles and kissing, and by mutual consent unconsummated.

How I managed to juggle the various elements in my life is a considerable mystery. I talked Communism every Thursday, still going to church parade once a month because of my lingering commitment to the Wolf Cubs. At the same time I had started going to concerts, sometimes with Clive, but often accompanied by my mother who, after her early naïvety, had developed a healthy suspicion of men. What she must have made of musicians who played without reference to written scores is a matter for some speculation. The big bands, Basie, Ellington and so on, had their music stands set up, of course, the instrumentalists reading off intricate arrangements that formed the backdrop to improvised solos, but practically all the other musicians we saw relied on 'heads', memorised routines based on improvised patterns. I think the music's informality was one of its attractions for me as for others. Certainly without sheet music coming between players and audience there was a feeling of being included in the proceedings.

Surprisingly, after her initial hesitation, Mum took in her stride the business of actually meeting the musicians. She soon realised that getting close to the artists was part of the routine for the avid enthusiast. I wanted to greet the visitors as well as the locals, even to take some snapshots should the opportunity arise. When the legendary Count Basie singer Jimmie Rushing came to tour with Humphrey Lyttelton's band, Mum was astonished at his girth — he was known, unflatteringly, as 'Mr Five by Five' — but more remarkable to her was the fact that the band used written arrangements for the first half of the concert. These they laid on the floor at their feet, straining their eyes to read the notes. 'Look,' she whispered loudly as we craned forward in the cheap seats in the gallery at Croydon Civic Hall, 'they've got *music*!'

The first spiritual music I heard in person came from an American group called the Eureka Jubilee Singers. They gave a concert at a church in Wandsworth, signing my autograph book with biblical references alongside their names. Their musical style was relatively 'Europeanised' in the tradition of the Fisk Jubilee Singers, who crossed the Atlantic in the latter quarter of the nineteenth century and sang for Queen Victoria and the Kaiser, thereby beginning the European craze for Black music. Despite numerous visits by various Black troupes in the decades that followed, such spiritual singing, 'well-regulated', with melisma and vibrato at a minimum, was the only kind of Black religious music most Europeans knew. Then the Clara Ward Singers, the Queens of 'hot' gospel, paid a visit and stood the jazz world on its ear. They wore frothy, sequinned robes and their hairstyles were twisted upwards and outwards. They appeared with the Humphrey Lyttelton band at his club in Oxford Street, singing with such drive and sheer joy it was hard to associate them with what I knew of religion.

Paul Robeson came to England around this time, too. His name was a byword in progressive and musical circles alike, both on account of his extraordinary talent and for his commitment to humanity through the Black liberation struggle, and we rushed to hear him. After his concert at Hammersmith Mum joined Clive and me outside the stage door until he emerged. He was a giant of a man, as moving and impressive as his music had promised. This visit marked the beginning of his second lengthy self-exile from the United States, the country which had denied him a passport for years.

Big Bill Broonzy brought his guitar and the Mississippi blues to the Royal Festival Hall and we missed the last bus home waiting for him to sign our programme. The 'live' music I went to hear was not limited to jazz, although there was plenty of that.

Schooldays were grinding to a close, with consternation expressed when I proclaimed my desire to become a journalist. The culmination of the sixth year was the School Dance, to which boys from a nearby school were invited. Mum had made me take dance classes — 'All girls *have* to be able to dance. How else can you meet people?' she reasoned — and during a succession of dreary Saturday lessons I made a half-hearted stab at the waltz and the quickstep. For the Great Day I wore a new dress, sewn by my mother from flame-red satin. I felt ridiculous waiting to be asked to dance by the spotty boys who lurked nervously at the end of the hall. The evening drew to a close, for me, as for many, without a single invitation. What humiliation.

What a waste of time, too, I can now say with hindsight; but in truth the feeling that not being chosen meant you were somehow a failure would linger for years. The event certainly marked my disillusionment with boys of my own age from my own social background. Nevertheless, there were to be a series of hapless suitors who would escort me faithfully to the pictures. There I would clutch the inevitable box of Black Magic chocolates, while they clutched at straws and any bit of flesh that happened to be accessible.

Jeff was the longest-lasting, a Senior Scout well into manhood. He wore a maroon waistcoat under blue serge suiting, his short-back-and-sides slicked back with Brylcream. Out of uniform he chainsmoked untipped cigarettes with macho bravado, fingers stained yellow and a wheezing, chesty cough on its way. I'd let him walk me home after a dance, although my heart wasn't in it; but he was polite and grown-up, and when he asked for a date, I agreed. Unlike other young men I met at this supposed peak of virility and sexual awareness, Jeff was not out for only one thing. He was a *suitor*, and that put an entirely different complexion on matters. His reticence when we held hands at the pictures was a measure of inexperience rather than anything nobler, but he made up for this through his family. Jeff had *parents*, and in his plan for seduction they worked as a team. They'd call on my mother with bottles of sherry, a ploy that bemused her, unaccustomed to anyone seeking my hand, then his mother would prepare incredible spreads – cold chicken and salad, trifle and cake – and 'just happen' to be out when we got back from our date. I'd gorge myself, then look at Jeff and wonder what on earth I was doing there. We had little to say to each other and, since he was reluctant to attempt more than tight-lipped kisses and an excruciating kind of arm-lock that was meant to be passionate, nothing to do.

It was his parents who were most upset by our break-up. 'Where did we go wrong?' his father demanded, wringing his hands on our doorstep while Mum looked oblivious. Poor Jeff, I thought, although secretly I had to admit that I was to going to miss his mother's teas.

At the end of the summer of 1959, I moved listlessly towards a course in photography, having received no helpful suggestions about following a writing career. I'd been doing my own developing and printing for a while – had even contrived to sell a snap of the Scout Troop to the local paper – so it seemed like a reasonable alternative. I still had my sights on Fleet Street, though; the vision of myself in green eyeshade, cigarette in mouth while I banged out the news on the typewriter, persisted for years. But I didn't know where to start and no one was there to advise. Women just did not have a role in that world then. It was with little enthusiasm for the camera that I signed up at the Regent Street Polytechnic.

For the generation preceding mine, jazz had been very much a part of the educational background, and at different stages popular jazz and blues musicians such as guitarists Josh White and Django Reinhardt were absorbed by the general public as a matter of course through their frequent broadcasts on the BBC. The establishment of a Jazz Book Club in the 1950s made it clear that appreciation of the music was no passing phenomenon. By the time I started to listen to the music, however, the jazz world was divided into two distinct, and often warring, factions.

Sharp young working-class boys constituted the bulk of the 'modernists', who listened seriously, without dancing, to the music known as bebop. The advocates of 'Trad' (Dixieland), on the other hand, tended to be middle-class tearaways, often from an art-school, 'beatnik' background. The clubs they frequented catered for dancing – or jiving, as it was known (in an odd misappropriation of an Afro-American word that means something completely different). But what-ever the differences between the two worlds, they had one thing in common: jazz was something that men did; women's function was strictly decorative. Few, indeed, would be the women who would seek out this music without a male escort, but my childhood friend Janet, like

31

me, was not about to be held back by such cultural considerations.

Janet, who lived two doors away, thought of herself as a bit of a beatnik. She attended the Art College, where Humphrey Lyttleton himself had once studied, and dressed in the Bohemian style of the day, dyed woolly stockings, baggy sweater and duffel-coat. To my mother, pubs were taboo for women alone, but it was with Janet that I escaped from such traditional strictures and made one of my first visits to a local hostelry to listen to jazz – a group led by Dave Carey who owned the Swing Shop. There was some desultory dancing but we didn't join in. We just sipped our cider and contrived to look bored. Already we both knew jazz was a serious business.

At college I met other art students who were devotees of such local heroes as Chris Barber and Acker Bilk, and wore bowler hats emblazoned with CND symbols. There were people like this around the Communist Party, too, which seemed odd to me then given the reactionary views of some 'mouldy fygges', as the traditionalists were sometimes known. The belief in New Orleans jazz as a people's music still persisted, even as Bilk, Barber and others were taking their popularised version of it into the charts.

'Trad' was now mainly a commercial proposition, only tenuously related to the idealism of the original revivalists. A few purist strongholds such as the Ken Colyer Club still existed, but the working-class musicians, earning their living with their instruments, were unaffected. They were interested in getting to grips with something living, not fossilised replicas. With a little ingenuity, some of them got dance band gigs on ocean liners, enabling them to get to New York, where they ate massive steaks for the first time in their lives and could purchase butter by the pound. And, of course, they went to hear Charlie Parker play.

But not all the 'revivalists' were interested in trying to sound like old-timers whose lip-muscles were past it. For Chris Barber, the leading Trad trombonist, blues and gospel music were important sources of learning. In New York he found his way to Harlem and the legendary Rainbow Records on 125th Street and brought back recordings by Afro-American church singers. Then he began to bring over blues and gospel artists to play with his band.

One afternoon Clive and I waited outside the stage door at the Royal Festival Hall for two bluesmen from the south-eastern United States who were appearing in concert with Barber. Guitarist Brownie McGhee, from Knoxville, Tennessee, and Sonny Terry, a Georgia-born virtuoso who gave a new definition to the word 'harmonica', were to have quite an impact on the course of local music. On this occasion they stopped, considerately, to talk. It was nothing like the rushed autograph-collecting of the past, where people such as Big Bill or Sidney Bechet had brushed us aside with a smile and a scribble; and they allowed us to take a series of photos together with them. The duo became perennial favourites with the British public, playing endless parties for blues fanciers and taking part in the Dixieland-style River-boat Shuffles held on the Thames each summer. Years later, they would still enquire about us from mutual friends.

Barber's most redoubtable coup was persuading guitarist Muddy Waters to leave his homebase at Smitty's Corner on the Chicago

South Side. Muddy, probably the greatest single influence on a generation of rock musicians, brought his half brother with him to play piano. He also brought the deep Mississippi blues. Backstage at St Pancras Town Hall I met him and pianist Otis Spann. Carrying themselves with tough dignity, hair and faces glistening with Vaseline and sweat after a concert of intense music, they dealt expertly with the fans who plied them with whisky and questions. The guitarist was handsome in a way all his own. He had a wide face and sensual eyes, his high cheekbones proclaiming a degree of Native American ancestry, and he stuttered slightly as he spoke — surprisingly, in view of his confidence on stage. Otis, a smallish man with a reserved manner and a slow, easy smile, squeezed my hand and expressed the hope that we might meet again.

As far back as the early 1950s, guitarists Lonnie Johnson and Josh White had played the blues for Londoners. Both were skilful musicians, Johnson in particular having been responsible for innovations thirty years earlier. Yet, in Europe they, like Big Bill Broonzy, were forced to adopt a 'country boy' persona in order to deliver the fantasy version of the Deep South that listeners apparently craved. It didn't matter that Broonzy had been a sophisticated guitarist, much in demand for studio work in the years between the wars, or that White was a progressive, closely aligned with the civil rights movement: in Europe they had to play 'minstrel', despite the professed liberalism of their audience.

With Chris Barber the blues artists got a chance to be *musicians*, even if it must have seemed a trifle odd to them — if not actually reflective of a certain stereotype — to have to perform with the band's regular banjo accompaniment when electric music had been around for some time. The Trad boom marked the beginning of a move away from the purism of the New Orleans revivalists, but pedantry still existed. Muddy himself created controversy by playing the electric guitar in Britain in 1958, in fact. Eventually droves of authentic blues artists would tour Europe as a purely commercial proposition, but Barber just brought over those people whose music he liked, with no concern for whether the tour would break even. The musicians were taken aback at their reception, treated like kings and queens in a foreign land, and their delight in their new audience was obvious. As for Chris, his dedication was tangible, and when I went autograph-hunting at one of his concerts we started talking.

He was a lanky, awkward man who seemed all legs and trombone. An unfortunate stammer added to the feeling of schoolboy enthusiasm he projected. I confided my desire to write about music and he recognised a sincere fellow-traveller. He suggested trying to get something into *Jazz News*, a newspaper published fortnightly by the National Jazz Federation, which also ran the Marquee. Chris, involved with both enterprises, was married at the time to Ottilie Patterson, a diminutive Irish woman who wore lace dresses and floral prints with disarming simplicity, then proceeded to stun everyone when she opened her mouth in a fair imitation of Bessie Smith. Ottilie and Chris took me under their wing for a while. Among their American guests were such people as blues-harpist (harmonica player) Jimmy Cotton and saxophonist Louis Jordan, the first Black artist to cross from the 'race' market into the mainstream, whose music was a forerunner of rock 'n' roll. Chris and Ottilie made it easy for me to get to know such musicians and never made fun of my naïvety and earnestness.

In the autumn of 1959, a group of former Count Basie musicians led by trumpeter Buck Clayton toured Britain as part of a package. Somehow or other, Clive and I found our way backstage at the Royal Festival Hall, where the musicians responded to us with exceptional friendliness. Some were veterans of foreign travel, the war having given many Americans a taste of overseas life. Trombonist Dicky Wells had worked in Europe in the 1930s, trumpeter Emmett Berry in Paris twenty years later; Buck Clayton had even travelled to China. For the others, war service apart, this was their first time out of America which was still, in the main, a segregated society. The warm reception they received came, they said, as a pleasant surprise. The urbane Wells, a highly inventive trombonist, was a particular hero of ours. He was one of the first to translate the pleas and moans of the blues singer to an instrument that had seldom been exploited for more than its obvious characteristics. He used a 'pepperpot' mute pierced with holes, his own invention, and showed off his rootedness by opening a solo with a handful of phrases straight out of one of the first blues 78s I ever owned. Dicky was an introvert compared to most of the others but he and Clive hit it off right away. For years we exchanged cards at Christmas, his being addressed to both of us: 'Sis' and 'Bro'.

The Clayton-ites, like other Americans I'd met, seemed almost like people from another planet, with their fine clothes and jewellery and the smell of cologne that wafted around them. Their uniforms were creased just so, cuff-links displayed, tie-clips precisely positioned. Backstage I gazed with fascination at their lacquered horns which nested on luxurious velvet cushions inside custom-made cases, and watched with interest while reeds were selected, adjusted and trimmed.

Herbie Lovelle, the sharp young drummer, stood apart from the others as they discussed obscure recording dates with veteran collectors. Herbie was the drummer on some of the early King Pleasure recordings that first introduced the art of 'vocalese', but in this company he was an unknown; it seemed inevitable that we'd gravitate to each other. Like outsiders seeking some kind of homebase, we lingered while he assembled his drumset. He showed us how the snare drum worked, the metal snare stretched across the bottom head to vibrate against it when the upper skin was struck, and gave me a pair of his sticks, splintered from playing rim-shots. I was wary of imposing on him but he was, he said, glad to find someone to talk to. As it turned out, the show was playing our local cinema a few days later, and we wondered whether he'd consider coming to our house for tea. Sure, said Herbie, he'd look forward to that.

Backstage at the Astoria he was already waiting for us. Earle Warren, the alto saxophonist, came with us too. Herbie suggested that it might be safer to travel the three blocks by taxi and we were astonished. Not only was street crime as remote as the moon-walk then, but cruising taxis just didn't exist in places like Streatham.

Mum had made tea and laid out all the best pink china. Herbie and Earle were on best behaviour and so was she. Mum had never met people like them before and was easily bowled over by their manners and practised charm. She had already come across Louis, Big Bill and Jimmie Rushing at close quarters and could not help but notice the enormous respect with which they were regarded by people such as Humphrey Lyttelton, the kind of Englishman whom she, in her turn, admired. Her prejudice was beginning to falter.

It helped initially, I suppose, that Earle was light-skinned, being a man of European, African and Native American ancestry. It was the latter that was most apparent physically. Playing the segregated South with Count Basie, he'd been able to 'pass' (for white) in order to eat, a ruse that had understandably angered some of the other musicians. But he came from a Black family and insisted in talking of 'my people' whenever racial questions arose.

Herbie was the kind of person who was always out on the town. An entrepreneur as well as a musician, he would end up producing various artists and recording with Aretha Franklin, Procul Harum and Bob Dylan as well as the you-name-it of jazz. He was strongly enjoying his introduction to Europe and whenever we spoke in later years he'd always ask after Mum.

Although he didn't know it at the time, Herbie was taking part in an important movement in American musical history. As a member of the Atlantic Records 'family', he was one of the musicians who played a transitional role in the changeover from 'race' records to rock 'n' roll, his steady backbeat shoring up countless historic recording sessions. In those days, however, jazz élitism meant that this side of his career went undiscussed. The fact that he'd played backbeat on LaVern Baker's 'Tweedle-Dee' was not a matter to raise with jazz musicians or writers, aspiring or otherwise.

The band spent two weeks in Britain and I interviewed my two new buddies during their stay. At that time my method was to follow the musicians around, taking down comments in longhand as they got ready to leave for work, or in quiet moments between sets backstage. I would work the results into an article later, portable tape-recorders being virtually unknown among reporters then. But Earle was one of the easiest subjects I've ever interviewed. He talked of his Basie days with fondness. Billie Holiday (who had recently died) sang with the band for a while. Earle said: 'She could sing "I Cried for You" like nobody I ever heard. I don't expect to ever hear anyone else doing with those tunes what Billie did.' Living communally on the road, Billie often cooked for the band. 'She was always jovial and entertaining, very seldom moody or obstinate.' It was good to hear that, after the bad press she'd received following her appalling treatment by the New York police during her final illness.

I wrote up an abridged version of the conversation with Herbie in which he spoke about the employment problems faced by outspoken musicians. Following Chris Barber's advice, I sent it to *Jazz News*. There it appeared under the shock-horror heading: 'Herbie hits out at US music racket.' When they left Britain, Herbie had taken time out to write me a postcard, *en route* to Algiers. Bassist Gene Ramey wrote, flirtatiously, from Paris. But all was innocent still, and when some of the band came back to London to spend a weekend shopping and renewing acquaintances, Clive and I went to their hotel. Shyly, I showed Herbie the article I'd written. 'Oh, God,' he exclaimed in mock horror, 'I'll never work in the States again!'

Tentatively at first, I began to interview other visiting Americans. Starting right at the top I talked first to the 'Divine' Sarah Vaughan, one of the most accomplished singers of this or any age. It never occurred to me that what I was doing was unusual, talking to the 'greats', whom the public at large held in awe. *Jazz News* ran the story over most of a page, illustrating it with two of my portraits, very classy, but when my byline began appearing in print, I was approached by another photographer who saw my ingénue's interviews as a potential outlet for work of his own. His name was Ken Palmer. He worked as staff photographer for EMI Records, and from our first meeting I developed a serious crush. Having been fortunate enough to find an editor who liked my pictures as well as my writing, I had no intention of letting someone else in on the act and told him so, but I followed him around all the same, hoping my devotion might lead to more. He was amused by my interest and helpful, showing me what kinds of shots would make the papers, and took me along on a couple of jobs, one being an historic event in local rock 'n' roll annals.

Gene Vincent, the legendary teen hero of 'Be-Bop-A-Lula' fame, was appearing at the Tooting Granada just down the road. He was headlining a package of young boy singers assembled by promoter Larry Parnes who, it was alleged, named his discoveries according to their extra-musical prowess. Lodged in the wings I watched the leather-clad Vincent drag himself across the stage to a chorus of screams – injuries sustained in a motorcycle accident had left him with a disability that added to the mystique, in the same way as did Johnny Ray's hearing-aid – absorbed and astonished at my first taste of live rock 'n' roll. Backstage I met the notorious 'Mr Parnes, shillings and pence' and rubbed shoulders with Billy Fury, Marty Wilde and Dickie Pride. It was completely at odds with my jazz purist's ideology but I enjoyed the glamour of it all in spite of myself. Such proximity worked on me subliminally, too, making me aware of what the business might have to offer if I played my cards right.

Much more in keeping with my idea of authenticity was the appearance in London of Sister Rosetta Tharpe, a dynamic singer and guitarist whose 'Up Above My Head' is one of the all-time great gospel recordings. I took time off from the Poly to spend a day with her and her husband, eating lamb chops for lunch in her hotel room – 'not seasoned like I make them, darling' – and sitting in on a BBC radio interview.

Sister Rosetta, making her second tour with the Barber band, was an ebullient woman who went on stage in tight-fitting green satin and carrying a white guitar, a modified Gibson SG. She wore golden or auburn-coloured wigs, combed into cherubic ringlets around her face. She told me about the foot-stomping 'Holy Rollers' of the Sanctified Church, who had inspired Ray Charles, and she shed some light on the deep connection between gospel and blues that many religious Blacks were anxious to deny at this point. Blues, she said blithely, 'is just the theatrical name for gospel'. Ottilie Patterson had told me how easy it was to duet with Rosetta, a good teacher; and when I disgraced myself by asking whether she felt Black people were better at music because of their 'natural sense of rhythm', she did not bat an eyelid, leaving husband Russell to explain gently that Whites could not expect to do anything more than approximate a feeling Black people had grown up with since birth. Like all of us swept into another culture on the wings of enthusiasm and little else, I was totally ignorant of the offensive nature of my assumptions. A generous woman, Sister Rosetta showered me — literally — with Lanvin's Arpège and gave me two pairs of her earrings. I wore them for years, still reeling in admiration long after she'd left town with her red-hot guitar.

It was around this time that Jesse Fuller made his first visit to London. Jesse was the musician about whom I'd written my first published article and I was excited at the prospect of meeting him. He was not strictly a bluesman, although his composition 'San Francisco Bay Blues' became a theme of the flower-power generation. He was, in his own words, a 'folk songster'. He played twelve-string guitar with one string removed to prevent unwanted vibrations, and blew a mouth-harp and a kazoo, which he wore around his neck on a harness. He kept time with one foot on a sock-cymbal and the other on a large bass-like instrument of his own creation, the fotdella.

At Streatham he was welcomed with open arms and after tea he played for us at length. His repertoire of stories was enormous, for he'd worked in Hollywood in the 1920s, appearing in walk-on roles with Mary Pickford and Douglas Fairbanks Sr, among others. He told us about riding the freight trains and had horrific recollections of cruelty in rural Georgia: being smoked over a fire in a gunny-sack was one punishment meted out by a white family with whom he lived as a child.

By the end of the tour, however, he felt pretty homesick and distinctly uncomfortable with British ways; but he had more dates to fulfil on the Continent. So he came to stay at our house for a few days — the first of several American artists to do so — where he could at least have what he wanted to eat, and he began to feel a bit brighter.

We went for a walk around town one day. Sister Rosetta was rehearsing at the Marquee and we dropped by to say hello. Jesse had his instrument with him and I suggested that the two guitarists jam together in order that I could take some pictures. I saw nothing wrong with the suggestion, but it was with some reluctance that Sister Rosetta agreed. She played a sophisticated, electric style, while Jesse was an older-style musician from the South, some of whose forms actually pre-dated the blues. It was the first time I became aware of the antipathy that sometimes existed between musicians of different styles. Enthusiasm had led me to believe that all was sweet harmony where music was concerned, that a note didn't care who played it. In time I would understand how divide-and-rule has operated historically to help hide the value of the Afro-American cultural experience in all its diversity, thereby promoting an alienation from the past. Just a few years later it was a totally different story. Younger Black musicians would consciously seek out the older players in order to learn, blues exponents among them. Over the years, though, I was saddened whenever I observed antipathy expressed towards the 'downhomey-ness' of old-timers.

It was Billie Holiday who said of Buck Clayton that he was 'the prettiest man' she ever saw, the word 'pretty', like 'baby', used between men, implying no diminution of masculinity for the Afro-American male. Certainly the man with whom I had my first 'real' sexual experience had the prettiest eyes that I'd seen, mobile, full-lashed and strictly 'bedroom'. John Graham (not his real name) was a trumpeter whom Charlie Parker said he always liked to play with. As the single Black member of a white band that toured here in 1960, he had to be super-careful to come up to the requisite All-American ideals of the day. He was supercool and superclean, sharp in Ivy League suit and Tyrolean hat, his hair cropped almost to baldness. He spoke in the way I imagined a jazzman should, his conversation peppered with jive-talk. When Clive and I went to see him, he was still lying in bed in the afternoon. He chainsmoked English cigarettes while we talked, and expressed his 'colourless' views. 'All this jive about the Negro plays better than the white – shit! In my opinion, there's not such a thing as any one person's music. Everything is put here for everybody.' He was concerned, he said, that musicians be evaluated on ability, not on racial grounds. We asked John if he'd come over for dinner on his day off. But when I arrived at the hotel to collect him, he'd forgotten and gone out shopping. I waited until he got back, apologies followed and we went to his room for a drink.

We talked for a while, then sex was on the agenda. I was frightened. This would be the 'real thing', not teenage fumbling or procrastination. John took it all in his stride. He was considerate and careful, but when it was over I was left feeling shaky. I had no idea what I was going to say to my mother. To his credit he suggested he accompany me home, lengthy bus ride and all. There he was all charm and apology, cups of tea were drunk and the spoilt dinner forgotten.

We spent another day together and my sex education unfolded. The trumpet player was one of those individuals who had learned from the exceptional opportunities for sex (if not necessarily for sustaining relationships) that the music life provides. He was kind and sensitive and though I was later to give up on men altogether, I would always remember him with fondness.

But I learned other things from this brief encounter. John had used narcotics for some years. He had been clean for a while, but the problems of confronting life without drugs were always there. The pressure of being the only Black in an 'ofay' band were tremendous. He might be on good personal terms with the other musicians yet he always had to be on best behaviour, as he explained. And when it came to improvising, he often had to restrain the urge to 'get down' in favour of a more acceptable 'refined' approach that owed more to the conventions of straightahead bebop, a music of a technically complex nature, rather than the downhome blues, the staple of Afro-America. He stood in the bathroom, naked and beautiful, trimming his moustache to a line with a razor-blade. Then he started to snort enormous quantities of water up his nose. My body reacted in sympathy; what he was doing seemed impossible. He explained that he felt drugs were still in his system, and I was confused. Like most ignorant people in England, reared on sensationalist films like *The Man with the Golden Arm*, I had no idea that heroin was frequently snorted.

As we got to know each other, John related an anecdote that

rather conflicted with his more idealised view of the way that the music should be. The band were hanging-out in a Paris club when another Afro-American, pianist Hazel Scott, walked in and started singing the blues. John was in a 'jamming' mood after the stresses of keeping to the musical straight and narrow. He decided to sit in. He reported 'feeling a draught' (detecting racism) from the other musicians as he made his way to the stand, but this was forgotten as soon as he started to play. 'All that jive I told you about everybody owning the music didn't figure any more. I mean, like it was the blues with all that *soul* and all I could think of was this is *mine*. It's our music, and I'm playing the shit out of it. I think that was the greatest ball I ever had.'

The story he told illustrated the complexity of the situation in which people like him found themselves: the necessity, indeed the desire, to be an American, and the deep-seated need to be *rooted*, to acknowledge something as one's own, unshared with the people who had raped and stolen your grandparents. The dominant white sociological view during those days was that the Afro-American was a white man with a black skin. It was an idea that might have been handy to espouse occasionally in the pursuit of constitutional rights but which rapidly fell into disfavour and ridicule as understanding developed of the importance of recognising and acknowledging racial difference across the spectrum, from definitions of culture to the identification of particular nutritional needs.

That John was willing to discuss all this with me showed something else, too. Men will often confide in a woman doubts they would never consider sharing with another man. With such confidences come another set of complexities: how woman's status is evaluated and what her role is considered to be – and whether *her* opinion actually matters, in fact.

When I wrote up our interview it contained few of these insights, of course, though John's confidences marked the beginning of my wider political education. (A rather bitter British musician once remarked sourly to a friend of mine: 'Oh, all *she* knows about music she learned in bed with musicians.' To that, I can only add, what better place to learn?) Versions of the interview were published in two places, a short extract even appearing in *Melody Maker* – a first, courtesy of Max Jones. I sent copies to John and, to my dismay, his wife wrote back. It was an exceptionally nice letter full of complimentary references to my family (Mum was 'a real cool chick', he had said), but I felt guilty, even though I'd known he was married and he'd assured me she was open-minded. Like many musicians out on the road, they probably had an 'arrangement', but when John died of burns sustained in a fire at his home, I could not bring myself to write to her. Now I wish that I had, because we did have something in common after all. And at 18 I could say I was now a grown woman.

4
Got the Grown-up Blues

The American musicians who played in Britain during the days predating the affluent 1960s and the rise of British Beat were treated reverentially, without exception, something I now realise was connected with the postwar feeling of optimism. Whether they were backwoods blues players or veterans of years on the road, racism was temporarily shelved in the face of genuine wonderment at the gods being here in our midst. Many British people have stressed the sheer physical impact of hearing Black music for the first time after years of listening to people who'd learned it from records. Local musicians did a creditable job but failed to assimilate the tension, power and excitement along with the technicalities. When Duke Ellington and Count Basie brought their polished big bands over it was, said one observer, 'like a dream'.

Reception committees were laid on when musicians arrived at the airport or left Victoria station for the Continent, and there were always parties and dinners. When he made his European debut in 1957 Count Basie was whisked away to appear on *Desert Island Discs*, the ultimate accolade from the starchy BBC, and Princess Margaret turned up at a concert. In fact, the Basie-ites were particular favourites, a combination of seasoned veterans and young Turks with a foot in the bebop camp. They were thrilled when strangers came up to them in the streets to say how nice it was to see them here. One or two rich admirers laid on parties at elegant private homes and places such as the Dorchester Hotel. For some, the most ancient of patriarchal practices prevailed: rumour hath it that one eager local musician even offered his wife.

Recovering from the war, Britain was still a pretty drab nation. It was not so long since coupons were needed to buy clothes, after all. So just the *way* these Americans looked, even wearing their band uniforms, had an enormous effect on someone used to economies, as I was. For a start, they were clearly well-fed. Well-dressed too, in mohair suiting and overcoats luxuriously lined with fur. Invariably these tours took place in the colder months, and the Black musicians' faces would be carefully creamed against the weather and ashy complexions, leaving them sleek and ageless. And there was an incredible neatness about their hair. Some of the older men wore it processed, flattened to a patent-leather lid overnight beneath a stocking-cap, others trimmed it short like the moustaches of manhood and the miniscule goatees grown under the bottom lip. All of them reeked of cologne.

After two decades of grappling with blue serge and utility underwear, those British women 'on the scene', as they were known, flocked around the visitors. There was the chance of a steak dinner, duty-free perfume, perhaps. Neither were to be shunned in the wake of rationing, and romances scented with the eminently forgettable 'Evening in Paris'. When the Basie band or Jazz at the Philharmonic travelled, there were always women aplenty on the bus and a general air of good times. The musicians were relaxed and convivial in the main, and in a holiday mood. There was little time or space for resentment.

At first I was just an observer of all that was going on, a little too young to participate in the partying. Most of the musicians adopted a protective attitude towards me, although there were exceptions. On their first trip to England the Basie band found rooms in an apartment block in Edgware Road, which became quite notorious during their stay. One of them wrote asking me to visit and offering cab-fare. My mother forbade it, which was probably just as well, for shortly afterwards the whole crowd were evicted as a consequence of their zealous entertaining.

The jazz world itself at this point was tolerant of Black men having a good time, indeed many male admirers got a vicarious buzz out of associating with the 'freer spirits', but this licence extended only so far. When the female contingent went to see off the Basie-ites at the airport there was much passionate kissing; they reported being treated as 'slags' by the airport staff. It would not be long before the same thing happened to me. Before this came about, however, my idealistic image of the musicians would take a tumble.

Back in 1960, Miles Davis was *the* jazz star. It is hard for people who grew up on Janis Joplin or the Sex Pistols to imagine just how revered the trumpeter was. John Coltrane had just left his group when Miles played here for the first time. Together they had cut the pivotal recording, *Kind of Blue*, and *everyone* played it all the time. In 1960, Miles was *hot*, so hot it almost hurt to listen to him. He came on stage at the Gaumont, Hammersmith, wearing a black tuxedo and a velvet bow tie, and glared at the predominantly white audience who had to come to pay homage. His behaviour provoked attitudes ranging from admiration to annoyance, and his habit of turning his back on the audience made the headlines. Only a few people realised he was making a statement condemning what had been expected from other Black artists who had preceded him. His generation no longer needed to be deferential. Their music spoke for itself; words were unnecessary. The man was admirable as much for his dignity as his music. He could switch from the white heat of a blues such as 'Walkin' ' to the 'walking on eggshells' delicacy of 'My Funny Valentine'. And I wanted to talk to him.

The sheer crudeness of his rebuff came as a shock. Later, after I talked to people who knew him personally, it became clear to me that Miles was not one to suffer fools gladly. He was a volatile individual whose responses were partially conditioned by racism. Nevertheless, for years I remained puzzled at how someone who played such beautiful music could act so mean. The contradictions have since been resolved, helped somewhat by an explanation offered by another trumpeter, Art Farmer: 'I guess Miles plays the way he would like to be.' At the time, though, I was hurt. This was the first time any musician had been unpleasant to me; I still thought the guys were as god-like as the music they played.

Wynton Kelly, the brilliant, bluesy pianist who played with Miles, had told me that people tended to take him too seriously when he spoke to them brusquely. He'd suggested Miles only laughed at those who took 'No' for an answer, so I persisted. But Miles made it clear that when he said 'Later', he meant: 'No way.' The wife of a British clarinet player on the tour looked on sympathetically. 'Oh, go on, Miles, be kind to the girl,' she cajoled. His reply came rasping, inches from my ear: 'If you lifted up your skirt I might give you an interview,' and he turned on his heel. Both Mrs Clarinettist and I were left somewhat shaken.

In those days 'unattached' women on the scene had to have a reason for being there, and it was generally imagined that sex was it. It was not enough to be there for the music alone. People would ask, 'Is she a scrubber?' meaning did you 'do it' with men. Strict moral codes had broken down during the war years but the 1950s and early 1960s were still a time of great sexual *angst*. The 'sexual revolution' had yet to come about and attitudes were confused and hypocritical even among people who fancied themselves as liberals. It was a time when men would grab you as you left a jazz club together and try for a 'knee-trembler' in the alleyway, a time of ignorance about contraception, and about women's sexual desire and needs. Men have written of their conquests during this period with jovial hindsight, but when I did succumb to one of the Trad scene's more notorious seducers, I found none of the tenderness and skills that had marked my more fortunate initiation. It was a brutal experience, albeit unintentionally so, all scratchy chin and ungainly bristly thighs. It had nothing to do with sensuousness or passion; any excitement came purely from shock.

It was an appalling climate in which to seek to learn more about this predominately man-made music, and were it not for the genuine friendship of some of the musicians and a couple of writers I doubt whether I would have survived.

One of the musicians was the Texas-born trombonist Henry Coker, whom I met when he came here for the second time with Basie in 1959. Henry, renowned for his romantic ballad playing, owned a horn given to him by Tommy Dorsey, the acknowledged master of the slow and sentimental. Henry was one of the first musicians to welcome my brother and me backstage, where we looked on with fascination as the Basie-ites wisecracked while warming up, preparing for another onslaught on the swing-starved British public. A heavy-set, muscular man who encouraged me to take photographs and even gave us a drink, he was to stay a good friend until his death. He had a substantial moustache and it was hard to believe him when he recalled how as a teenager he'd drawn on that moustache with eyebrow pencil to disguise his age and get into bars to hear music. it was hard to believe when he said he was nervous, too, but he certainly was. I sat in on an interview with a leading session trombonist who wanted to know about Henry's technique and style. The atmosphere was relaxed but Henry knocked back two tumblers of Scotch and still his hands were shaking.

Every band had its group of elders who took new recruits under their wing (something which, I later discovered, was part of a Black American tradition dating back to the days when musicians would leave home to go on the road, barely out of short pants). It was characteristic that Henry should have befriended Clive and me, for whenever a new musician joined Basie it was Henry who showed him the ropes. He was always my buddy, a real gentleman who treated me

42

with respect whatever the circumstances. Once, when I changed my strictly-for-the-music priorities as far as the Basie band was concerned and spent the night with one of his colleagues, he raised not an eyebrow when he saw us at breakfast next morning. From time to time we'd exchange letters.

In later years, he joined the Ray Charles Orchestra, a tight-fisted organisation whose operation contrasted widely with the *laissez-faire* Basie set-up. Henry invited me to a rehearsal in their London hotel and I, unwittingly, produced my camera. Immediately, two heavies appeared on either side of me and, when I began to protest, physically threw me out. Henry was disgusted. He put down his horn and came outside to join me. One of the road-crew came over to warn him: 'You'll be fined if you don't go back in.' 'Too bad,' said Henry. 'This lady is a writer and I'm buying her a drink.' Together we sat at the bar and after a while I began to feel better. The last time he was in London I was tied up the night of the concert, but I rushed to the hotel early so that we could have breakfast together before the band left. I'm glad that I did see him then, for it was not long afterwards that Henry's big heart gave out.

The music itself had a lot to do with my staying the course, naturally, as it did for the handful of other women I met who were not just there for whom they could 'pull'. Rae Wittrick was one of the first of these, a secretary from Essex who had founded the Bunk Johnson Appreciation Society in the wake of the New Orleans Revival and knew some of the oldtime musicians. She wrote me encouraging letters and sent me pictures of Johnson, the revivalists' trumpet-playing icon. Wisely, she stayed clear of the London Trad scene, appearing only when bands such as George Lewis or Kid Ory came to town.

I was vaguely aware of one or two others (such as Jackie Buckland, later to marry pianist Stan Tracey) who worked in the record business or were actively involved in promoting their 'old man's' career, and there were some musicians about, too – saxophonists Betty Smith, whom I heard on the popular radio show *Workers' Playtime*, and Kathy Stobart who played with Humphrey Lyttelton. Trumpeter Gracie Cole, formerly with the highly-regarded Squadronaires, had led her own band and got a good press, and there were the singers: Neva Raphaello, Yolande Bavan, Cleo Laine, Beryl Bryden and Marion Williams. Other women were equally dedicated to the music but by and large we were separated from each other, interacting only in terms of our relationships with individual men. And for those actually in sexual relationships, unless they stayed put with their husband or 'old man', no one was safe from ridicule. One woman in particular, a familiar face on the London scene, was treated like a 'non-person' after she split up with her saxophonist husband. Most women stay home when that happens but she liked music too much. She left for the States in disgust.

One of the few kindred spirits I met in the early 1960s was Kitty Grime, herself a writer (who, after years at the periphery of the business, was later to go on to sing). Kitty, starting out as a general factotum at a small record label, later handled jazz publicity at Decca. When we met she had graduated to the *Jazz News* staff, writing enthusiastically about the newer musicians in particular. She conducted a regular forum, too, 'How I feel about jazz', in which she managed to

43

extract profound observations from the most reluctant of interviewees. The daughter of a Derbyshire vicar, she had studied music the conventional way, but was not a good enough pianist to participate on the burgeoning bebop scene. She had excellent ears, though, and could pinpoint what was taking place musically in an instant. She was also pretty sophisticated about social relations, and it is to her that I owe many of the insights I've lived by.

Kitty was several years older than I was and had already made up her mind not to become involved in extra-musical activities. She was embarrassed at the backstage behaviour of the 'scrubbers'. So many men in this period (and later) spoke of their 'conquests' with disdain, and in order to keep a safe distance between herself and the chance of earning a questionable reputation she adopted the motto 'Come on your own, leave on your own.' When not singing tricky bebop lines for me, or the irreverent lyrics she'd written to Thelonious Monk compositions, she would do her best to help me out of the corners where I was pushed often by sexual pressure. Many was the time we huddled over a couple of cappuccinos at the San Remo in Charing Cross Road, with me trying desperately to unravel the contradictory mores that abounded and Kitty quietly guiding me towards an understanding and, often, away from one of the monsters of the scene.

The Miles Davis visit was an occasion of more than one rude awakening. Barely disguising their opportunism, the three-man rhythm section moved in on me, one after the other. Wynton, the pianist, was the least cynical of the three and he invited me to a restaurant with a record company executive, his publicist girlfriend, and a local pianist. I ended up passing one of the most awkward evenings of my life. After dinner we went to the record man's Mayfair flat, where row upon row of albums lined the walls. I had never seen so many records and said so. And that, apart from 'yes' and 'no', was all I managed to get out for the rest of the evening. It seems ridiculous now, but I just could not think of anything to say. I sat there, completely at a loss, while the 'grown-ups' made witty remarks, played Blue Note and Vee-Jay imports by the new heroes such as Wayne Shorter and Lee Morgan, and got high. I felt like a child, ignored and unloved. Wynton could not disguise his boredom and dropped me off before we even got back to the hotel. I don't blame him. That night I vowed never to get into such a situation again. From then on, however shy I may have been and in whatever company, I've always forced myself to find something to say.

By this time I was, apparently, known as a 'chick on the scene' and therefore available. Inevitably I did have sexual encounters with some of the visiting musicians, but with nothing like the degree of promiscuity that has been fantasised about by those who cannot imagine what a young white English woman and a middle-aged Afro-American man might have to say to one another. Quite simply, I got along well with a great number of musicians; having sex with all of them would have been impossible, not to say foolhardy. Yet I acquired an ignominious reputation that was to hound me for years and crops up even to this day. Only recently a woman I know was interviewing some dodo saxophonist and happened to mention my name. 'Oh, she just fucks all the Black musicians,' was his response.

Leaving aside what this says about him and his attitude towards women and towards Black people, it is extraordinary to think that a few years earlier he'd have been falling over himself to get to know the musicians and have something to talk about in years to come. When the music ceased to be such a mystery and local musicians began to develop voices of their own, attitudes changed towards the people who gave them something to play in the first place. At some point, the relaxed personal style and apparently effortless elegance of the visitors began to inspire resentment, just as the affluence of American GIs in Britain during the war had done. It is hard to pinpoint exactly when this happened. What was noticeable was that local musicians gradually stopped turning out for the Americans, whom once they had crowded round, eager for a blow on a special mouthpiece or a tip about playing, and taking delight in sharing a hip-flask or an 'African Woodbine' and the sexual gossip that is a staple of male dressing-room bonhomie.

The reaction of Whites to the postwar wave of Caribbean migration was not unconnected, of course. Once Black people became more vocal and challenging by their presence, the fantasy atmosphere created by the music's liberal chroniclers began to sour. It is, after all, a world in which macho values dominate. Alongside the good humour and exuberance the musicians are making a statement of intent that can be daunting to men from outside the culture. Indeed the music itself threatens notions of white supremacy and Black subservience. Increasingly in the Britain of the 1960s white men found Black settlers and their visiting heroes echoing each other in condemnation of the racist attitudes that existed on our own doorstep. Such resistance was intrusive on the faraway world of New Orleans and Chicago legend, and as British musicians developed a new self-confidence, so the idolatry began to vanish, the atmosphere becoming overtly racist at times.

In my own early days on the scene I experienced another form of resentment. There were some white men, 'enthusiasts', who did their best to make me feel uncomfortable. I traced this to a kind of jealousy, as if they felt personally slighted at not having their hero's undivided attention and at being unable to get as close as they imagined – usually erroneously – that I could. It would have been futile to point out that the music scene is structured around male activities that by their nature exclude women, making it difficult for women musicians ever to be really accepted as part of it. And equally pointless to suggest that when it came to 'important' matters a man was far more likely to get the serious attention of another male than I, a naïve young woman.

Ironically, it was sometimes only through giving in to sexual pressure that was, frankly, unwanted that I was able to establish any kind of dialogue with certain musicians. Thankfully, a compromise could generally be worked out, but the ludicrous hypocrisy of some of my countrymen plagued and exasperated me for ages.

Although photography was still seen as primarily a man's world, the set-up at the Regent Street Polytechnic provided enough encouragement to persuade a woman that it was possible to pursue a career with the camera. For a start, the department's head was the formidable Margaret Harker, one of the country's leading architectural photographers. 45

Women were outnumbered two to one by the male students, quite an enviable proportion given that this was essentially a technical course; arts degrees in photography came much later. Despite the usual prejudices, a couple of women were already working in Fleet Street; one of these, Ann Ward (later a Labour councillor), was the mother of a fellow student. Inevitably some of the older lecturers were at something of a loss as to how to treat 'twittering' females; but several of our tutors were women, strong and self-possessed characters, who made no such distinctions.

But in 1960 I was only really interested in the music and in working towards a career in journalism. At the end of my first year at the Poly, Margaret Harker called me in to see her. She said the lecturers had reported that I had no real interest in photography, 'And we don't advise you to come back.' I felt pretty hot under the collar but I knew my absenteeism had caught up with me. 'Don't worry,' I responded angrily, 'I'm not going to!' I swept out and took the first job I could find. For a while I worked in the bowels of the National Gallery, making black-and-white prints and slides of the paintings, in a cavernous darkroom with inch-thick steel doors where the nation's art treasures had been housed during the war.

It was an interesting job for the time that it lasted, and I managed to take ten days' holiday in Paris that October with Pam Bavin, who had been involved with the Canadian jazz magazine *Coda* while living in Toronto. Pam, a south Londoner like myself, was a couple of years older than me and she had travelled. I always thought of her as a 'woman of the world', in its positive sense. It was a relief to find another woman to share musical experiences with, and occasionally we'd go out on 'double-dates'.

In Paris where many Afro-Americans had moved to distance themselves from racism, or at least find enough peace of mind to fight the less obtrusive European version, we heard the great innovator Bud Powell, 'father' of modern jazz piano. Powell had suffered brain-damage as a teenage musician, the result of a beating at the hands of the police. Despite this condition which kept him in and out of institutions for years, he held down a residency at the Blue Note, a plush Right-Bank night club where drinks cost over £1/10/0 a time – astronomical then. We met Powell, plump and Buddha-like, and his wife Buttercup, and I attempted to arrange an interview. But when we sat down to talk, the words would not come out; what Bud had to say was said at the keyboard.

During our stay he also played a benefit concert for the children of bassist Oscar Pettiford, killed in a car crash. The concert was poorly attended (Miles Davis had played Paris earlier that week and few jazz fans could afford tickets for both events), but in the audience was Richard Wright, exiled author of the American classic *Native Son* and probably the first Black writer to make an impact on the American literary world. I had been stunned by his autobiographical novel *Black Boy*, although unaware at the time that he had been forced to present this as a work of fiction because of his declared communism. I discovered his work through the introduction he wrote to a book by blues authority Paul Oliver, one of the writers who befriended me. Oliver was another 'outsider' whose love for the music had a lot to do with its wider appreciation in the days ahead. The accuracy of his research, most done of necessity at a distance, led Wright to surmise that he wrote as if he had 'bummed around the Black Belt for years'. Seeing Wright at the Théâtre des Champs Élysées just a month before his untimely death was an experience not wasted on me. His presence was acknowledged in the manner reserved for royalty; he rose and took a bow. When I came across his 1941 book *Twelve Million Black Voices*, a powerful folk-history of Afro-American in words and pictures, which was to give me pause for thought over the years, I reflected on that brief glimpse of radical genius I'd been permitted across a half-empty concert hall.

Another long-term Paris expatriate was Bill Coleman, an easy-going veteran of the Swing era, who had first visited France in 1933. Since 1948 he had made his home there, speaking fractured French and still playing a tasty, lyrical trumpet. He and his wife Lily were always warmly welcoming whenever I visited Paris. Later they would become family friends, much loved by my mother, and when visiting Britain, would occasionally make the trip to Streatham for one of her famous afternoon teas.

Nearly every night we ended up at the Mars Club, a favourite afterhours spot with musicians. Françoise Sagan, who would visit the Mars nightly to hear Billie Holiday sing, named her first book, *Bonjour Tristesse*, after the Holiday classic 'Good Morning Heartache'. The Mars was located on the Right Bank, but I imagined it to epitomise *Rive Gauche* Existentialism. Pianist Art Simmons led the house trio, accompanying a woman who did evocative numbers such as 'I Wish You Love'. It didn't matter that the singer was unremarkable, the Mars had an authentic atmosphere of gin-soaked *ennui* and Gauloises that will remain with me always. I-felt *so* grown-up just being there and I loved it. One night I looked around and there was Miles Davis standing at the bar with actor Sidney Poitier, listening. I decided, warily, to keep my distance.

. We thought Paris was beautiful and couldn't get enough of it. Bill Coleman took us to a recording session, and we drank cognac with him and Lily and the other musicians in a café nearby. There was sightseeing to cram in, too, and we barely slept. At the Mars we met a suave American called Rick who took us to Les Halles for breakfast. We ended up in a cellar-bar along with two or three lesbian couples, most of whom seemed to be drunk and having a rather sordid time. Rick thought it was amusing but I didn't. I'd read *The Well of Loneliness* and the sight of all this misery only served to compound Radclyffe Hall's dreadful story of lesbian tragedy. I'd already had sexual feelings for women but this experience made me push them well into the background. I left Paris armed with some Olympia Press pornography, mandatory traveller's fare for the times. There were a couple of Henry Millers and a filthy Apollinaire, and I smuggled them nervously through Customs. But the images of women with their arms around each other kept on coming back with a kind of awful fascination. I didn't discuss it with Pam.

Back at the Gallery I answered a phone enquiry. The caller was Edward Scobie, the Dominican journalist and broadcaster who would later write *Black Britannia*, a book about the historical Black presence in Britain.   47

He was doing research and wanted prints of the Hogarth drawings that depict eighteenth-century London Blacks. We already knew each other. 'What are you doing there?' he asked. I explained my predicament and he suggested I went to see him at *Tropic*, the magazine he edited.

Earlier that year, when the singer Nat 'King' Cole appeared in London, I'd got to know his drummer Lee Young. Lee, the brother of the great saxophonist Lester Young, invited me to spend the day at a tele-recording Cole was doing for the new commercial channel. It was there that I had met the people who started *Tropic*. Black settlers had been publishing newspapers and periodicals in Britain since World War I but this was the first glossy magazine venture of its kind and the publishers wanted the singer's endorsement. Within a short time they had induced Cole to visit their office in an old corner shop in Bell Street, just off Edgware Road I'd been involved at the periphery of all this and was asked to contribute to the magazine. It was thus that I had met Ed Scobie, wrote a couple of pieces for the magazine while I was still at the Poly, and eventually ended up working there.

Charles Ross, who published the magazine, was a sometime bassist and drummer known as 'One-note Charlie'. He had little talent for music but obvious ambition and a personal style to match. He drove an Austin Metropolitan, an unusual car even then, in matching shades of cream and tan that toned well with his camelhair overcoat, and he smoked tipped cigarettes in a holder banded with gold. He really wanted a 'girl on reception who could do a bit of typing', but I saw it as an opportunity to continue writing about music and do some news photography. He agreed to put up with my hunt-and-pick typing and I put up with answering the phone. It turned out to be a venture of mutual benefit as long as it lasted, not without laughter and not without tears.

Tropic, which shared premises with a travel agent, was one of the unofficial cultural centres for Afro-Caribbean people who had come to work in Britain after the war. Just as other settlers would beat a path through Theo Campbell's Brixton record shop in order to talk to Claudia Jones at the *West Indian Gazette* offices upstairs, so they would drop into the *Tropic* office with their problems and news or just to pass the time. The Golden Gloves Hairdressing Salon next door was one of the few Black barbershops in London, a centre where opinions were aired, gossip and information exchanged, and customers would often check to see who else was around before moving on. More often than not it would be me alone; Charlie Ross and the others would be out chasing advertisers who had reneged on their bills. From insurance salesmen to writers, from boxers and tailors to night-club proprietors, a constant stream of ambitious individuals passed through that battered old shop-door. And along with them came ordinary women and men with a hundred and one problems. My help was enlisted to fill in forms and I would try to direct queries about housing and legal matters to the appropriate agency. If I'd harboured any illusions about the big times starting in Bell Street, the pressure of other people's needs soon changed that. I was frankly unequipped to deal with the situation in which I found myself, but I played catch-up fast. The lessons I learned have stayed with me always.

One of the people I got to know there was a trombonist and

composer who grew up in Jamaica. He invited me to tea one Sunday. He lived in a tiny room in a Westindian lodging-house off Harrow Road, where he had the most exhausted record-player I'd ever seen and a record collection worn grey with playing. He had worked in Paris with my friend Bill Coleman and there was plenty to talk about. He was very hospitable, too. For Christmas his mother had sent him a rich Caribbean fruitcake, packed with fruit and dripping with rum. He offered a slice and to my dismay, cut me the tiniest sliver. Coming from a home where cake came in slices that would not disgrace Royalty, I thought this a little on the ungenerous side. Only now do I realise how ungracious I was to harbour such thoughts. He had absolutely no need to share something so special, something that was, in fact, a lifeline to home.

Whenever I remember that incident and my shame at the way I reacted, I think of that room. Like many of the places where Black people lived in Britain then, it seemed claustrophobic to me. The sturdy old-fashioned bed groaned under the weight of the covers and took up most of the room, making freedom of movement difficult around it. A couple of wardrobes were piled high with suitcases and the inevitable brassbound trunk, effectively blocking out much of the light that came through the heavily-curtained window. In years to come I'd sit in dozens of such bedsits. I think it was in places like these that I began to understand, in an emotional rather than intellectual way, something of what it must mean to be separated from one's culture and homeland. To some so-called music-lovers the background to the music is of no import; they insist that to become involved in demands for justice and a fair deal for the constantly plundered creators has nothing to do with the way the notes affect you. Whenever I hear this view expressed, several images pass through my mind. The trombonist went on to become a composer of some repute, but his room of those days, its dimness enhanced by the sheer weight of dues-paying, is an image that stays with me yet.

The contents of *Tropic* were eye-opening, too. As Nigeria readied herself for 'nationhood', the magazine offered an editorial suggesting the eventual 'consummation of the dream of an "African personality", a proud and positive *négritude*' which would be the foundation of a 'United States of Africa' not unlike the recently formed Common Market. And there were articles about African and Diasporean history, mainly written by Edward Scobie and based on the work of pioneering Black journalist J.A. Rogers. He was concerned to put the Black view of history, a change from the prevailing perspective. It was here that I learned about the Black actor Ira Aldridge, who came to England from New York in 1825 to play Shakespeare; the Carthaginian general Hannibal – no one at school told us *he* was Black, although Rogers' claim is once more being disputed; the Haitian revolutionary Toussaint L'Ouverture and the Black Jacobins; and I became aware of others whose African ancestry was seldom acknowledged: Colette, Pushkin and Alexandre Dumas.

Scobie broadcast regularly for the BBC World Service, too. One programme on 'Eighteenth-Century Black Composers in England' discussed the work of Ignatius Sancho and others who wrote music in London in Georgian times. I began to realise that Black people played no role in any of the conventional history I had learned. Suddenly a new world was opening up all around me, peopled by individuals whose names were to remain unknown to most of the people with whom I grew up. Through *Tropic* I became familiar with the work of the brave South African photographer Peter Magubane, and there were writers by the dozen: Africans such as Wole Soyinka and Chinua Achebe, Westindians such as Jan Carew, Sylvia Wynter, Andrew Salkey and Donald Hinds, now a teacher, whose good-humoured 'Any more fares please?' described working on the buses as 'a job in which [he] had to be a cross between a psychiatrist and an adding-machine.'

There was little time to do much photography while I had to keep the office functioning, but I'd carry my camera each day, just in case. In this way I was able to photograph Jamaican premier Norman Manley, Aubrey Williams, the Guyanese painter, as well as a Nigerian baby born on Independence Day – the parents phoned into the office and I rushed out, recklessly, on my own initiative.

There were beauty contests to attend, diplomatic receptions and dances, and on one occasion a speech by Trinidad's Premier Dr Eric Williams observed by fellow Westindians Dr David Pitt, the politician and GP, now Lord Pitt, and singer/actor Edric Connor. On another occasion Charlie Ross took me to a meeting in a first-floor room off Edgware Road; it must have been one of the earliest autonomous gatherings of Afro-Caribbean transport workers.

Politics was in the air constantly with the African countries and Caribbean islands newly independent, and the picture I was piecing together of Black life in Britain bore little resemblance to the fantasies held in the jazz world.

A belief still existed that the music was born in New Orleans brothels and carried to Chicago on the riverboats, whence it moved to New York and lived happily ever after. It was a convenient theory; however much white enthusiasts thrived on direct contact with Black musicians, it kept the realities of the life beyond the music at a distance. Every musician had a mother, father, brother and sister and a cultural world of their own, but this was seldom allowed to impinge on the idea of 'good times' and 'high living' that is part and parcel of the legend of jazz. To be on first-name terms with a group of musicians and hustlers conveyed no contact with the realities of Brixton, the Grove or Bell Street.

Those Black musicians who lived in Britain tended to keep a low profile, relying as they frequently did on white bandleaders and fixers (contractors) for work. Any individual who resisted when called on to play 'minstrel' roles earned a 'troublemaker' reputation and suffered unemployment as a result. The status of Caribbean musicians was anyway relatively low in jazz circles, a common belief being that most of them were less than accomplished when it came to improvising, a damaging attitude that would prevail for many years.

There were quite a few hustlers among the non-musicians on the scene, patronised as they had always been for the 'atmosphere' they would lend to various gatherings. It was generally assumed, too, among whites on the scene, that any Black man would be a good source for cannabis. 'Charge', as it was still known, had yet to become freely available; socialising with those who 'smoked' was a source of excitement to people raised on pints of mild-and-bitter. There were, of course, several musicians who were sometimes forced to fall back on dealing, a traditional self-supporting last resort when they could not earn an adequate living from music. Then, as always, there were plenty of whites eager to hang out with Black people, yet when back on their own territory they could only talk badly about those white women they found when they got there. The realities of life for the Black settler were far removed from a cosy evening spent listening to Miles or Louis with a bottle of wine and a joint.

Shortly before I went to work for *Tropic*, the office fell victim to a racist attack. The British National Party, an organisation headed by Colin Jordan, was active in the area at the time, and a group of their thugs, armed with a rifle, had taken a shot at the window shortly after the office staff had left for the night. The window was never reglazed, just boarded up, business carrying on as usual. Spending the next three months huddled beside a paraffin stove in my overcoat while the cold seeped through the broken pane gave me plenty of opportunity to consider the political events then taking place. Mosley's Union Movement had been involved locally following their part in the so-called race riots of 1958 in Nottingham and London's Notting Hill, and the murder of Trinidadian carpenter Kelso Cochrane. The following year, in fact, they put up an election candidate who stood on an anti-immigration platform in nearby Kensington.

In 1958 the liberal conscience among the judiciary was still alive and white youths were imprisoned for their part in the racist attacks. Where the police were concerned, though, it was becoming clear that they were indifferent to the needs of Black people. Weeks after the shooting, which took place in 1961, Charles Ross had heard nothing. 'We, of the *Tropic* office, like the thousands of coloured people all over Britain are worried,' the magazine editorialised. 'We feel it's time the police did something so that coloured people in this country won't keep on saying: "The police are not on our side, man." ' The experience of police harassment was reported with increasing frequency, too. I would observe it first-hand as I started to move in Black company.

Among the creative people I met in Bell Street were a number of other photographers. One of these was called Maurice. He gave me a few useful tips about insurance and cameras and took me out for my first Indian meal — 'Try a biryani,' he suggested gently. One day he came into the office with a present for me. 'What's that in aid of?' I asked flippantly, without thinking. 'Nothing,' came the rejoinder. 'It not everyone must have a reason; sometime we just like to be giving.' I was suitably rebuffed and given a lesson in manners.

Another of the photographers I met was Julian, more generally known as 'Mooshie' on the music scene, where his speciality was a good 'draw'. Julian lived in a very smart if sparsely furnished flat near Marble Arch. He moved on the scene where rich white play boys came looking for kicks — drugs, 'fast' women and the vicarious pleasure of associating with jive-talking Westindian men, and handled dope as if it were water. We got high together sometimes and played *Kind of Blue* over and over. Whenever I think of those days, I see that record revolving on the Garrard deck, gradually turning grey with the playing. **51**

Miles had just left town and his influence still hung in the air.

In December 1960 Jazz at the Philharmonic, the unkindly dubbed 'travelling circus' of American star soloists, came to town. Julian had contrived to hang out with Miles the previous month, and so he suggested we go to the airport and meet the musicians, take some pictures and see what else we could get into. Charlie, a bewhiskered Welsh bass-player friend of his, drove us there. At the Arrivals desk the great names swanned about looking weary and blasé, secretly pleased at their reception committee, which included Max and Betty Jones and other local dignitaries. There were trumpeters Roy Eldridge and Dizzy Gillespie, saxophonists Coleman Hawkins, Don Byas and Benny Carter, and the legendary Cuban drummer Candido. In the middle of it all we came across Sam Jones, who played bass with Cannonball Adderley. His instrument had been smashed in transit and he had to play the Royal Festival Hall that night. He was in trouble.

Quick as a flash, Julian and Charlie swooped. Charlie had a bass to lend, if Sam would like to try it out. He agreed and off we all went to a club in Finchley Road. Sam tried the instrument and liked it. He borrowed it for the gig, then asked if he could buy it. It was only after Jazz at the Phil left town and Charlie had vanished that I learned the bass belonged to another. But that, like they say, is show business.

At the airport I met another bassist whom I'll call Albert Douglas. I'd met him before, when he was over on another tour. We'd had a peculiar, jousting exchange, and left it at that. This time our eyes met and it was a different ballgame. We got together after one of the concerts and I found myself feeling the way I hadn't felt since that innocent relationship back in the YCL days. Al was a brilliant bass player and arrogant about his talent. But he could be shy and awkward, too, and I found this rather appealing. He talked about politics and the position of Black musicians. It was the first time I'd heard the term 'Afro-American' and the first indication I had of a political consciousness existing among musicians. How important this was to me at the time I can't really say, but I liked Al's seriousness and saw him several times during the tour. Our lives were to be intertwined for a while.

5
Tight Dresses and Lipstick

In 1984 a major demonstration against a visit by South Africa's Premier Botha took place in London. It was the kind of occasion that brought white liberals of yesteryear out of the woodwork to march alongside Rastafarians and radicals. I saw people I hadn't seen since Martin Luther King's Memorial Tribute united in their opposition to apartheid. There, carrying a placard surmounted by a silver cup awarding opportunist South African athlete Zola Budd 'first prize for queue-jumping', was my old friend John Millington.

Johnny was a cook-turned-barber from Trinidad. We met backstage at a Miles concert in 1960 and hooked up to help each other get access to the musicians and to have a good time. He had a room full of those silver-plated trophies, and a fine line in survival hustles. It was Johnny who made me listen to saxophonist Ornette Coleman. His album *Change of the Century* was ridiculed by many of the established critics when it first came out, but Johnny didn't read the music press. 'Try this,' he said, as if offering a fine old liqueur, 'I think you might like it.' He also introduced me to Eric Dolphy, the multi-instrumentalist from California, who played his different reed instruments as though engaged in a private conversation with the listener. Johnny had the American issues of Dolphy's *Out There* and *Outward Bound* and he became 'our' discovery, to be played often and with the same combination of respect and familiarity accorded Brook Benton and Dinah Washington whose duets like 'Loving Good Way' were particular favourites then. We thought he was sublime.

I don't know when I first became aware that the music meant something different to Black people from what it did to Whites. What I do know is that it was nearly always people like Johnny who introduced me to the latest musical developments. When soul music was in its heyday in the 1960s, I had a friend named Abdul, a Nigerian diplomat, who seemed to get hold of every Atlantic album before it was released in Britain. Aretha, Sam and Dave, Otis and Carla, you name it, we danced the night away at his place to the latest sounds before most people in England had ever heard of them. Later it would be George Conley, a clarinettist from Chicago who introduced me to the music of the city's radical AACM (Association for the Advancement of Creative Musicians). There were notable exceptions, of course, but in general, the white critical establishment was always a half-step behind when it came to recognising the significance of ideas introduced on the Afro-American bandstand. Left to my own devices, I confess that I often tended to be pretty slow off the mark, too.

Al Douglas was one of those whose outlook affected me enormously. When he went back to New York, he started working with John

Coltrane, one of the most influential musicians of modern times. Together they explored the possibility of using two basses in the group, an idea that had originated when the saxophonist and another bassist listened together to Ravi Shanker. Ever since World War II, jazz musicians had been drawing inspiration from non-Western music. According to Al, this involvement with African rhythms and Eastern scales and tonalities came out of a growing desire to look beyond Europe for artistic and spiritual inspiration. It was a deliberate move to align themselves with others in the emerging Black and brown nations, and in music, Coltrane was one of the forerunners. Among the procedures they developed was that one bass should play the melody and improvise in the usual manner, the other being played mainly *arco*. Al wrote to me about what they were doing and told me how serious Coltrane was, devoted only to the music. This was the way he himself believed all musicians should be. He was opposed to alcohol almost as much as to narcotics, seeing both as destructive to Afro-American endeavour. He pointed to the example of a young man named McCoy Tyner, who had just joined Coltrane on piano: 'He doesn't drink or smoke, all he ever does is come to the gig and play music and then go home to his wife.' Al was a bit of a puritan, although he was not averse to a little sexual fun – provided it was sanctioned by monogamy.

The job at *Tropic* came to an abrupt end when the magazine's financiers stopped putting up money. Unable to find anything else that allowed me some degree of self-expression, I spent a miserable few weeks taking telephone orders for a commercial lab that prepared artwork for platemaking. When I begged to be allowed in the darkroom one lunchtime I was hauled out – literally – by the foreman for being too slow.

One day the phone rang and it was Jacko Smith (not his real name), a bass player turned photographer who had opened a studio in Soho. 'How would you like to come and work for me?' he asked. I needed no further bidding. Soon I was installed in the ancient darkroom, a deathtrap of dry rot, wet rot and ancient wiring. But it was mine, and I had it all to myself for over a year.

Jacko was a bearded man in his fifties who looked somewhat like Father Christmas and was occasionally hired as an avuncular model. Most of his work consisted of show-business portraiture (though every month he'd go to the local stripclub and take front-of-house stills for their latest production). The stars of yesterday, today and tomorrow came by to be photographed and sometimes he'd even send me out on a session. He was one of the few British musicians to listen with an unprejudiced ear to the new music being pioneered by Coltrane, Coleman and Dolphy and we were both pleased to have found someone to talk with about the latest record releases. Though Jacko himself was a fairly unadventurous player, he always appeared with bands that promised something out of the ordinary, in styles ranging from mainstream swing to rhythm 'n' blues or avant garde units led by people such as the freewheeling Indian saxophonist Ray De Milo.

I loved working in Soho and exploring the alleyways, shops and cafés, especially the nearby Nosh Bar, where the hot salt-beef sandwiches would fill you up on the coldest winter's day. The studio was near Archer Street, which for many years operated as an unofficial social club and hiring-place for musicians. On Monday afternoons from 2 until 5, traffic would be at a standstill there and in the adjacent streets; nothing could get through the hundreds of musicians who congregated on the pavement outside the Orchestral Association. The 'fixers' (contractors) would move from group to group looking for people to play their engagements. Dance-band and night-club work, weddings and barmitzvahs, all were there for the asking in the days before the electric guitar made countless skilled players redundant.

Every now and then I'd run into someone I knew. Sometimes Dave Wilkins, the Barbadian-born trumpeter who starred with Ted Heath and recorded with Fats Waller and Ambrose, would drop in to see me. One day I bumped into Rudy Jones, a tenor player from Jamaica who always dressed impeccably, and he invited me for a tea at George's, the café next door to the Rehearsal Club. There, where musicians passed the two afternoon hours when the pubs were closed, Rudy taught me the two golden rules of showbiz survival: always look slick, whatever's happening in your life, and carry enough money to buy a drink for yourself and someone else – even if it means walking home. He also asked me to take publicity shots for his band. I posed them holding their instruments on Tooting Bec Common, and it was my first really polished professional job. Rudy was pleased.

Then Al wrote to say he was returning to London. He had a two-month engagement accompanying Lena Horne at the Talk of the Town in Leicester Square, the most prestigious of nightspots. Lena had brought her own rhythm section and Al took me along to their initial rehearsal with the local musicians who made up the orchestra. As I sat in the stalls watching the elegant singer run through her repertoire, fur wrap slung casually across her shoulders, I felt really important. Al had given me special attention, made me feel like one of those long-legged, stylishly coiffeured creatures I'd seen on the arms of the Basie-ites when they first came to London. He'd made me into a woman of substance.

Lena, said to be the highest-paid cabaret artist of the day, was generous with her musicians but required faultless performances in return. She was notoriously tough. If a musician made the smallest mistake, said Al, she would make him pay for it for the rest of the night. She'd stop and start in different places, changing tempo and doing her best to throw him. She was nothing if not a perfectionist. I caught a couple of shows and can honestly say I have yet to see a performer who can measure up to Lena.   Everything she did was high-class, yet she was also mistress of the wittily risqué. She was another to suffer the BBC's puritanism: 'I Love to Love' ('Inflame me/Go on and maim me') was banned for being suggestive. Far stronger, though, was the contemptuous 'Don't Commit the Crime' ('If you can't afford the tickets/ Don't say we'll see the show'), still the ultimate dismissal of male sexual incompetence. Wicked and wonderful.

But if Lena had high standards, so did Al. Like other educated Black people of his generation, he was determined to have his share of the American pie. He had worked with the top Afro-American improvisers, symphony orchestras too, and felt justified in describing himself as 'the best' among contemporary bassists. He had surprisingly little time for other players of the instrument, reserving praise for the late

Oscar Pettiford alone. Much of Al's talk was about getting into the studios. A handful of Black musicians had begun to break through the barriers that had hitherto prevented them playing on the radio and commercial recordings. Such prized opportunities stayed lily-white for decades, but now one or two Black faces were beginning to be seen even on networked television shows. To hold down jobs like these required a not inconsiderable degree of personal discipline, he explained; one slip and the newcomer was out, with many willing to gloat. The financial rewards of such work were enormous, bearing little relation to what could be earned playing jazz. It was a rigorous obstacle course, however, which Al himself was just beginning to run. It was important to him to prove himself equally equipped to play European as well as Afro-American music. He felt he should be allowed to move from one to the other at will. However, discrimination kept Black players out of the top symphony orchestras and he had begun to work with other like-minded instrumentalists in co-ordinating a programme of challenges to the concert music establishment.

We got into the habit of seeing each other nearly every day. At the weekend we would walk in the countryside, visit theatres and concerts on his nights off. One evening before a concert, we dined with the Royal Philharmonic's French-horn soloist, Alan Civil. He joined us in an enormous meal of roast duck, unusual behaviour for any wind player so near to a concert. But Civil was a big man with stamina and an equally big sound, and he won me over with his effortless Mozart Horn Concerto.

Increasingly I had begun to listen to European concert music. At this period 'jazz' musicians and listeners were more likely to listen to the European composers than to pop music. I was aware of Cliff Richard singing about his 'Living Doll' and Helen Shapiro 'Walking Back to Happiness', but only peripherally. Symphonies and concertos were substantial in a way that Craig Douglas and Connie Francis could never be. On the darkroom radio one morning Janos Starker was featured playing Kodály's 'Sonata for Unaccompanied Cello'. At first hearing, I actually thought this virtuoso playing was the work of a string quartet! I worried the record shop to death till I got hold of a copy. The dramatic work impresses me enormously still.

I liked music that sounded substantial. Big Bill Broonzy, for example – his solos sounded more like two guitarists working in tandem as he accompanied his finger-breaking top string improvisation with a separate bass-line, fat and full. White pop music was trifling and one-dimensional to me and I just wasn't interested. Jazz, with its constant rhythmic invention, tension-and-release patterns and sheer breathtaking virtuosity, had to be best of all.

When it came to having the best, Al was obsessed with the idea. He went shopping for clothes at Simpson's and Aquascutum, bought handmade chocolates at Floris and gifts for my mother at Fortnum and Mason. He was earning plenty of money and liked to eat well, so we ate oysters at Bentley's (2 shillings a dozen), grilled sole at Wheeler's, unheard-of indulgences for someone who earned £10 a week. At the Victoria and Albert Museum we arranged to see a rare instrument, usually kept locked away, a nine-foot bass that required two players in performance. I photographed him gesticulating at its size and the story and picture appeared in New York's Black weekly newspaper, the *Amsterdam News*.

He and Jacko got along well superficially, exchanging tips on bass-playing and discussing valuable old instruments built by famous makers, but behind his back my employer made racist remarks about our friendship. It was still common for interracial couples to be stared at and abused in the streets, but I didn't expect this reaction from someone who played Black music himself. By this time, though, I had started to take photographs for a number of musicians who lived in London, many of whom were Black, and a couple of clients had dropped into the studio to see me. Jacko didn't like it and my relationship with Al merely served to fuel his prejudice.

Al was a frequent visitor to Streatham and enjoyed my mother's fine home-cooking. One day she did roast pork, scoring the skin and turning it into crackling in the traditional way. Al was surprised. 'Do you mean to say you eat *that*? That's what the old people eat in the South,' he explained, with some distaste. Back in 1961, such downhome ways were frowned upon by progressive Afro-Americans of diverse political views. The annals of cultural heritage had yet to be expanded to include respect for the African-influenced cuisine of the South; the Black Muslims were as down on sweet potato pie as they were on pork, in fact. It was pointless to explain that crispy roast pork fat was a delicacy in Europe. To civil rights advocates and Nation of Islam separatists alike it was 'slave-food' and Al was rather offended.

At the same time Clive and I were surprised to discover that he seemed uninterested in many of the older musicians whom we had taken for ganted as the people who had structured the music. To him, 'jazz' became significant in the 1940s when Dizzy Gillespie, Charlie Parker and the other architects of the new music began to clarify their position as Afro-American *artists*. Some people have blamed the pioneers themselves for their lack of foresight in keeping historical records, though this seems hardly fair given the educational priorities of earlier times. For years, though, many important facets of Afro-American history were obscured. With only the version of white historians on which to rely, information was often confused. The achievements of hundreds of self-sufficient organisations of the past only came to light more generally with the renewal of, and dramatic increase in, Black scholarship that grew out of the struggle of the decade ahead. In 1961, a musician like Louis Armstrong, an 'entertainer', was seen by many as representing the old ways. He had yet to regain his place in the pantheon of honour, and for Al his incandescent trumpet and generous, gritty vocals had the dubious, old-timey smell of chitt'lins.

Despite his seriousness, Al got along reasonably well with my mother, though I think she was rather daunted by him. Understandably, she preferred the easygoing charm of 'gentlemen' like Henry Coker and Harry Carney, another good friend whose baritone saxophone was a mainstay — the mainstay — of the Duke Ellington Orchestra. Such men were equally dignified and 'militant', but the fight for justice was not a constant topic for discussion with them. I think I was rather daunted by Al's seriousness, too, but by the end of his stay, I felt attached to him and he, I think, was quite fond of me.

We continued to write to each other and I made plans to visit 57 him in New York. At the same time he warned me against other musicians and sexual pressure. When one famous group came to London he suggested I stay away from them. 'Those guys are ruthless,' he said. 'They're not like the people you've been used to; they wouldn't take "no" for an answer.' Oddly enough, though I spent some time around this particular group, I experienced no problems. But it was always that way. People were constantly trying to warn me off this man or another, yet when we met we would generally end up getting along. It was the 'clean-living', 'respectable' names, in my experience, who gave me a hard time.

By this time I was interviewing musicians and, increasingly, taking photographs backstage at concerts. I got to know other music photographers – Terry Cryer who worked for *Jazz News*, Eric Jelly – and studied their techniques until I, too, could produce the crisp kind of work I saw weekly in *Melody Maker*. I acquired an electronic flashgun, a massive old Braun patched up with insulating tape, and learned how to hold the flashhead at arm's length to get the kind of sculptured modelling the others routinely produced in their portraits. When I saw those deep shadows separating the features on a subject's face appear on the negative for the first time, I knew I'd arrived. There was seldom much room for manoeuvre backstage, so my first 'serious' pictures were portraits taken in hotel rooms, cramped dressing-rooms and corridors. It never occurred to me then that I could actually instigate a photo-session and put the musicians where I wanted them. Indeed I was so tentative about what I was doing that I could hardly believe it when Basie saxophonist Frank Foster asked to buy some photographs to use for publicity.

I did take a few 'action' shots on stage but access was not always easy, despite the fact that I was by now a regular contributor to *Jazz News* and a couple of other magazines. In the days before backstage-passes, I'd been taken backstage either by the musicians themselves or by one tour manager in particular – who had actually suggested when we first met that I ask for him whenever I wanted to go backstage. It worked for a while and I'd call him at the office to find out when bands were arriving and where they'd be staying. But it was a situation which turned out to have mixed blessings. Always having to have this particular individual's clearance to go backstage meant that if one of the musicians took me into the theatre – a reasonable enough procedure if we'd just been doing an interview – he might well get difficult as soon as the musician's back was turned. It was all right as long as I was seen as a sweet young thing, but once that phase had passed, I ran the risk of being treated like a groupie or 'scrubber' – to use the terminology of the times – by such people. It still was not conceivable that I could be there as a journalist once I'd passed the obvious 'fan' stage and left my autograph book at home. From time to time, if something went wrong backstage, there'd be a purge on all visitors. This never extended to the 'bona fide' journalists who were, without exception, male, but was basically a round-up of drug-dealers, time-wasters and women, myself included. There was no point in protesting. There were one or two 'good-time girls' who did the rounds strictly for pleasure whenever the bands came to town, and on occasion management availed themselves

58

of their services, too. When things went wrong, however, out everyone went. It was the good old double standard in operation.

Another member of the road crew regularly fraternised with one of the bandleaders. Together they'd go to a Mayfair night club and 'take a couple of girls off the line' for a foursome back at the band-leader's hotel. That was neat and straightforward, but women who 'hung around', for whatever reason, were always considered a problem by managers who liked to run a tight ship.

Many feminists believe there to be an unspoken bond between males, the understanding that all women belong to all men. Where the white woman and the Black man are concerned, this understanding of the woman as shared possession, breaks down under the white man's gaze – unless the woman can be shown to be a 'prostitute'. If she wasn't, back in the 1960s, then in my experience the white men on the scene made sure she'd be treated like one. This was the penalty to pay for associating with Black men and breaking down the order of things white men had established. No woman was allowed to exist in her own right as an autonomous individual, if she was there, it had to be for the benefit of some man. As a result, hotel porters, bus drivers, stage doormen – real 'jobsworths' to a man – became a thorn in my side when it came to moving around with musicians. If the thought of sex had never crossed anyone's mind, these people certainly put it there.

For example, when I went to interview John Coltrane in his Mayfair hotel room, I had to run the gauntlet of sneering hall-porters and an under-manager who insisted I explain what I was doing going up to the room. Coltrane was polite and withdrawn, interested only in his music, but you'd think he was about to set up a pimping-ring from the way his female visitor was treated. On another occasion, a porter actually came upstairs and asked me to leave the room. As a result, interviews had often to be conducted in the relatively noisy lounge with constant interruptions and distractions.

The situation, peculiar to England at this time, contrasted with the experience of musicians elsewhere in Europe, where Black men tended to be treated with more respect, while hypocrisy about sexual matters seemed less pronounced. Not surprisingly, the censorship over women visitors was interpreted as racially motivated. There was a considerable element of racism in it, to be sure, although a few white guests did, in fact, report a similar denial of privacy unless an amount of money changed hands.

But it was not only hypocritical doormen and the like who would object to my presence. Occasionally I experienced the 'don't bring that girl with you' syndrome, the complainant being another white woman. There were a couple of women, one married to a writer, another to a musician, who had little time for me and my shyness. Having spent hours over a hot stove for the benefit of their husband's honoured dinner guest, they saw no reason why they should share the focus of male attention with me. Vying for prominence between women is a legacy of the way men separate us in order to keep control, but I now believe that racism was equally at the heart of this attitude. Even in the jazz community the stereotype of the Black man's 'animal' appetites flourished – indeed, for many it was part of his fascination. Black men were routinely called 'pimps' in the wider society, so any white woman

59

who associated with such people could be only a 'slag'. So, while he might be regarded as exciting, dangerous even, it was a bit too much, doncha-know, for Mr Blackman to bring his 'work' into the home. Whatever he might do on his own turf was fine, just as long as it didn't impinge on the family, nuclear and white.

Seeking out male protection is a strategy with which most women are familiar and in my early days on the music scene I was no exception. I don't know how deliberate it was, but whenever American bands came to town I would try to hook up with one particular individual as a safeguard against the sexual pressure I was beginning to encounter from young bloods — and some not so young — away from home. In some cases these relationships themselves turned into sexual friendships, but in most cases they did not.

Dave Brubeck's bassist Eugene Wright was one of my protectors for a while. He surrounded himself with a motley crew of adoring fans whom he dubbed his 'nieces and nephews' and Clive and I became part of this odd entourage. Unlike the other members of the quartet and the audience to whom their music mainly appealed, Gene was Black, on the surface of it an easy going character whose presence lent an acceptable degree of 'authenticity' to Brubeck's Ivy League image. But often he must have found himself beleaguered, and no doubt this had something to do with his insistence on inviting the 'nephews and nieces' backstage.

Harry Carney who played with Duke Ellington was my particular, and long-lasting, friend. He and Gene were solid, dependable middle-aged men and subconsciously, I think, I felt safe with them. Like Henry Coker, they got along well with my family, too, meeting Mum when she sometimes came to concerts with us. I noticed the respectful way they treated her, paying attention to what she said and showing a lively interest in the way we lived. It was so different from the way that people I grew up with related to their parents.

Harry carried himself with such dignity it would have taken a determined bigot to mess with him. He had played baritone saxophone with Ellington since 1926 and still liked to drive Duke himself whenever the band travelled by road. He was a big man, five feet eleven and well-built, who got a tremendous sound out of the solemn instrument he played. When he soloed, the notes seemed to hang from the walls. He had perfected the circular breathing technique that permits holding a note almost indefinitely, and people who had never heard the big saxophone before would gaze open-mouthed at his control and lung-power. He liked to wear a big overcoat and always went out well-muffled against the cold, a wise precaution after building up a sweat under the lights. And for extra protection, there'd be a bottle of Scotch in his pocket whenever he went out on the road.

We would invite our 'special' friends over to Streatham for a meal whenever we could. Harry loved my mother's cooking. He had got the business of flattering women down to a fine art, and Mum was enormously fond of him. Each year without fail he would send her a card at Christmas, making expectant noises about the next steak-and-kidney pie. She, in turn, was always welcome backstage.

Harry's close relationship with Duke was part of his *cachet*. He spent a good deal of time ensuring that the leader met some of his most loyal fans and always arranged for him to exchange a few words with my family. Once when they played a Sacred Concert in a Cambridge church, Clive was able to reciprocate. Musicians seldom got a chance to look around the cities they played and Clive, who was reading English at King's College, gave Harry a guided tour, when rehearsals were over, of parts of the university inaccessible to the public. Both of them felt grand, privileged in their respective ways.

In those days few places stayed open late enough for the musicians to get a meal after the show, but Harry always knew the whereabouts of a reasonable restaurant. Whenever the band played in London, we'd go for a steak in the West End, then back to the hotel for a drink. In the lounge the other Ellingtonians chatted and swapped stories with admirers, apparently oblivious of the pressing need for sleep. All the while the hotel staff kept watch, eagle-eyed and ready to pounce, should attempts be made to smuggle women up to the rooms. A fair number of successes occurred none the less. Room-keys were handed over surreptitiously in the bar, and the guest made her way to the lift via the 'Ladies'. But the need for such underhand action was demeaning and discouraged many women from pursuing invitations handed out backstage with cavalier charm and little thought for tomorrow.

Harry took it all in his stride, as equable with the 'jobsworths' as he was with the band's admirers. I never heard an angry or impatient word pass his lips, though some situations the musicians were forced to endure would have tried the patience of a saint. Neither was a word of scandal permitted where Ellington himself was concerned. Harry was not a great gossip, but on occasion, as the whisky flowed, he would share the odd story about the sexual pastimes in which some of the Swing-era greats indulged. In this way I found out the meaning, often erotic, behind the names of tunes collectors had bandied about innocently for years. But when it came to the legendary love-life of his oldest friend, his lips stayed firmly sealed. Duke expected loyalty from his sidemen, whatever else they might get up to on the road. He would bail people out of the most invidious situations, as loyal to the great artists he hired as he expected them to be in return. If anyone had the bad sense to cross him, that musician would be on his way. Rapidly.

One of Harry's hobbies was photography, an interest he shared with several other prominent musicians. He liked my own work, in particular a close-up portrait that accompanied an interview that we did. 'Maybe this could become your distinguishing style,' he suggested, and he commissioned me to shoot some pictures for the company whose instrument he played.

He also believed in keeping in touch with the many friends he had made worldwide. His Christmas card list was reputed to run into thousands, and from time to time he sent me postcards from exotic parts of the globe. Despite the band's hectic schedule, he found time to run down a couple of hard-to-find books that I wanted, mailing them to me with thoughtful dedications. On only one occasion did he forgo his usual diplomacy, showing me the Ellingtonian system for keeping in touch with friends — mainly women: a checklist in the back of a diary against which the despatch and receipt of correspondence was recorded. I think I must have done something to annoy him, prodding him for Ducal revelations or some such, for an admission like this was quite out of character. Whatever else happened when the band was in town, Harry was the person who could be counted on to smooth everything over.

I used to say, irreverently, that musicians on the road generally wanted three things only: to get high, to get laid, and to meet people who would not give them a hard time. It's a simplistic suggestion, of course, but there was definitely some truth in the idea of an easy life at all costs. Nothing upset a well turned out older musician more than to be badgered about some ancient recording when he had just embarked on a meaningful conversation with a likely young woman. As for me, I found that one of the reasons I got along so well with the musicians was that I was a good listener, genuinely interested in what I could learn from them and with no intention of giving them a 'time', hard or otherwise. The situation was not without confusion, though. On one occasion I invited a trombonist home who, I learned later, thought he was going to 'get laid'. To his surprise it turned out to be a family dinner, the only thing 'laid' (on) being a bottle of wine in honour of a special occasion. But, he later told my informant, the food was so good and the people so friendly that he quickly forgot about sex and went home feeling replete.

There were other men I used to hang out with who saved me from sexual pressure. John Millington, the Trinidadian cook/barber, was one of these. He'd come to Britain in 1948 as a stoker in the Merchant Navy. Back home he'd learned to cut hair and operated as a barber for a while in Cable Street, London's main Black centre before Brixton or 'The Grove' (Ladbroke Grove). At the turn of the 1950s there were only two Black hairdressers in London and Johnny was one of them. When I met him he was working as a cook at the first takeaway restaurant to offer barbecue chicken – quite an item in those days. Then, when the American musicians began to appear, he readied his razor and clippers again.

At that time Afro-American men either processed their hair straight, slicked it down with Vaseline or pomade or clipped it ultra-short for ease in combing. When I saw the Miles Davis band fingering their eighth-inch growth and muttering 'Damn, my hair getting *long*!' I was surprised. The African comb was one of the items that inexplicably disappeared during 400 years of exile. Cards used for combing wool were used in slavery days, but the days of the Afro-comb and the manageable 'natural' were a way away yet. To Johnny the short hair was 'GI-style'. He recognised the travelling musicians' need to stay neat but realised they did not have time to make their way to Bell Street or Brixton. So he came to them. He cut the hair of the Buck Clayton bandsmen and they were delighted. As he recalled later, 'They said, "Oh, it's just like home," and they really went out and played better.' He was a raging success.

In November 1961 we heard that Coltrane was coming to England and bringing Eric Dolphy with him. Together with what seemed like half the jazz fans in the country, Clive and I rushed to book tickets. Coltrane had been receiving a bad press because of his 'new directions', but nevertheless all the writers wanted to meet him. I managed to interview both saxophonists during their stay but I was too awed to do much more than ask the simplest of questions. Both men were quiet and seemed to be devoted to music, the atmosphere around Coltrane being definitely spiritual – although that was not a word I would have used at the time. Coltrane was polite but in a hurry to get the interview over so that he could phone his wife. He had recently adopted a vegetarian diet and wanted to eat some fruit before getting an early night. It was hardly the popular image of the wild, drug-crazed jazz musician. He needed a haircut, too, and I told him Johnny would be by at the weekend.

Clive and I went to the Gaumont State, Kilburn, where the Dizzy Gillespie group shared the bill. We were amazed at the length of Coltrane's set; an extended version of 'My Favourite Things' lasted over 35 minutes. Al had told me about the saxophonist's stamina, but his staying power was breathtaking. The music had an enormous impact, particularly on the local musicians. 'This . . . is living music,' wrote Kitty Grime in *Jazz News*, 'important enough to change quite a few jazz lives.'

Later that week Johnny and I caught up with them again at Walthamstow. Eric took us backstage, where we watched the concert from the wings, and we offered to show them around. The Fiesta on Westbourne Park Road was an Afro-Caribbean restaurant where musicians frequently hung out, and we suggested that they might like to cross town for a meal with us after the concert. Eric couldn't decide whether to come, but we did take McCoy and Aisha Tyner. Walking in the door at the Fiesta with them felt like a real coup. I was still a fan, after all, and McCoy, whom (thanks to Al's letters) I'd known about from the moment he joined Coltrane, was one of my heroes. I don't think we talked about anything in particular, everyone was tired. I just sat there, feeling 'cool' under the blue and green lights, sipping my ice-cold beer from a glass edged with salt, and grinning at our guests like a 12-year-old. Days like these made up for all the tedious hassles backstage.

6
Sportin' High-heeled Shoes

Central among the main music venues in the early 1960s was the Marquee, then situated beneath the Academy Cinema in Oxford Street. Harold and Barbara Pendleton who produced *Jazz News* also ran the club; as a journalist, I could go there whenever I liked. 'Modern' jazz was featured at weekends, with residencies from bands such as those led by 'our own' wizard of the tenor saxophone, Tubby Hayes, and Jamaican altoist Joe Harriott. I had already written a piece, a double-page spread, for *Tropic* about Harriott's revolutionary new music, and his first album featuring his 'free form' concept was released in the United States in 1961, a considerable accolade for a local player. The noted poet from St Vincent, Ellsworth 'Shake' Keane, played trumpet and fluegelhorn with Harriott, dividing his time between the group and literature studies at London University. Every Sunday, Johnny Dankworth's new orchestra held forth, featuring the unique voice of Cleo Laine, or expatriate American singer Joy Marshall. Interval piano came from Dudley Moore.

Later, the club opened nightly and the musical policy diversified. Trumpeter Dick Williams, who went on to find fame as an animator of cartoon films, led an impetuous, chaotic band much influenced by the American composer Charles Mingus. Like another bandleader, John Williams, whose saxophone section included a woman, his regular bassist was also female, Gill Lyons. As two of the few women musicians on the scene, they kept a low profile and upset no male egos, but I remember feeling a certain satisfaction at seeing women playing an equal role on the bandstand. Thursdays rhythm-and-blues sessions were presided over by guitarist Alexis Korner, and Cyril Davies the harmonica-player who was to die from heart failure before receiving the recognition he deserved. Several rock-stars-to-be would sit in with their Blues Incorporated, Mick Jagger among them. The atmosphere here and, to a lesser extent, at the Flamingo in Wardour Street, was very open. It was fertile soil for musical development. Mainly because of the influence of Chris Barber and Korner, another progressive thinker, a lot of crossover occurred between musicians with disparate styles. 'Jamming' or 'sitting in' was encouraged in those days, only becoming frowned on when musical arrangements grew less flexible. Harriott, a confirmed modernist, had a regular spot with Barber's band for a while, and the Stripes of Glory, a group of gospel-singing GIs from a base outside London, sometimes sat in with Korner. An aloof Nigerian who often joined the Barber band on trumpet was Fela Ransome-Kuti, then a music student at Trinity College. Later he dropped the colonial component of his name and became the notorious Fela Anikulapo-Kuti, King of Afrobeat and scourge of Nigerian neocolonialism. In those days, though, the advocate of polygamy and 'Black-ism' wore a houndstooth tweed jacket and grey flannels and a very proper, if angry, expression as he bent his playing to Barber's 'Traditional' style. Jagger was always around. He wore a Marks and Spencer's grey crewneck and a permanently worried expression and was never allowed on stage until the end of the evening.

Alan Vale, who managed the Marquee, had a little coterie of people he drank with, and through my friendship with Barber and Cyril Davies, I was one of the favoured few. I suppose I was seen as a 'likely bird', as was any woman not actually in a stable relationship, but Alan's good humour made up for a lot of the more cynical 'faces' around. One day he asked me to take some photographs for him. He was going to handle the bookings for Tubby Hayes' new group and needed some publicity shots.

Tubby was playing at the Flamingo, situated at the rougher end of Wardour Street opposite the sign that screamed 'DUREX' in red letters several feet high. It was the first time I'd ventured into that part of London but I mustered professionalism and introduced myself to the manager, a hard-headed Soho businessman with a reputation quite different from that of the music-lovers who ran the Marquee. When I'd taken the pictures, he asked me if I'd let him have one for the club wall – not a regular-sized print but a large blow-up. I said I'd be happy to do this and, being terribly new to the business, told him I'd send him a bill. 'A bill? Send me a *bill*?' he shouted. 'Whaddya mean, a bloody bill?' I was on my way up the stairs when this altercation began and he raised his hand as though to hit me. I began to apologise and he gave me a shove to help me on my way. I tripped up the stairs and fell forward on to my camera with his words ringing in my ears. 'Get the fuck out of my club, don't let me see you in here again!' I was startled at the whole affair but was beginning to learn how the business operated. People like him were always in control. Small wonder there was rejoicing among musicians when saxophonist Ronnie Scott opened up a club where the music was the most important thing and where they, at least, would be treated with respect.

At the Marquee I met several Africans who liked dancing as much as the music itself. One of these was Lucky Wadiri, a Nigerian sculptor. Whereas devotees of earlier forms of music commonly claimed that it was impossible to dance to bebop, Lucky showed me otherwise. He adored Miles, Thelonious Monk and the Modern Jazz Quartet, and played their records constantly. He demonstrated how Africans danced to the music, slow and easy without any feeling of pressure.

Lucky, a stocky man with the physique of a boxer, had worked as a seaman and put himself through college and a degree in architecture with six years of manual work. He combed his thick hair forward into a point, the sides closely cropped, a really rakish fashion in those days. At home he sometimes wore a *dansiki* and sturdy African sandals soled with recycled car tyres. Outside he dressed in chalk-stripe double-breasted jackets with wide lapels and padded shoulders, tapering trousers and crêpe-soled shoes. His attitude to life was basic; all he wanted was a bed, food and room to work. Several notable people owned pieces of Lucky's sculpture, a couple of them subsidising him regularly so that his work could continue. Lucky was friendly and quick to laugh, but after a while you realised the laugh was used to cover shyness. Yet as far as his own direction was concerned, he was strong and self-assured. He deliberated every move and always knew exactly where he was going and why.

I can remember watching him carve, deliberately and firmly, yet sensitively, thinking out every step as he decided to change the sweep of a line. His life revolved around whatever he was carving and he'd phone me and tell me what he had just altered. 'Ah, Val, you should see it now. It's just *fabulous*.' When Lucky modelled in clay, he would always build up the rough form around the central armature and carve away in the African tradition; he did not build up and add in the European manner. Ben Enwonwu, the Slade-trained sculptor from Nigeria who made an impact on the London art world in the 1950s, was commissioned by Hugh Cudlipp to create a family group for the new *Daily Mirror* building, and asked Lucky to do most of the carving. The group stood outside the building for some time, and when I passed through Holborn Circus in later years, I'd smile wryly in the knowledge of whose hand had actually worked all that wood.

Lucky lived in a house near The Brecknock in Camden Road, sharing cooking facilities with several other African tenants. It was there that I learned the 'right' way to cook rice, using the old parboiled 'brown' rice that some Africans favoured, with its rather rancid smell, and a basic West African stew, flavoured with palm oil and chillies. Lucky was the son of a fisherman, an Ijaw from the Delta Region, and would have followed in his father's footsteps had he not started wood-carving at an early age. He introduced me to African essentials such as sponges made from beaten bark-fibres and chewing-sticks, the bitter, mildly stimulating pieces of wood used for cleaning teeth. From him, too, I first heard the commonly held Black view of white people as spiritually and morally inferior; he was continually pointing out what was wrong and unnatural about the way Whites behaved.

On one occasion he left a social gathering abruptly when he judged that one of my friends was leading her boyfriend a bit of a dance. I'd told him all about Al and had thought that he respected my feelings. Jumping to conclusions I imagined that his hasty departure was somehow connected and wrote an apologetic letter. His reply was immediate and unexpectedly philosophical. 'I knew from when we met that you are new on the scene and that [you] had preconceived ideas of how you will want to swing,' he wrote. 'However, I will take this opportunity to stress my opinion that ideas of what constitutes "Love" differ in everybody . . . except the pretentious, and that you are still to find out the difference between WANT and NEED.'

It really made me think, not least to discover that such an apparently self-possessed man could be genuinely upset by what I felt was a minor breach of social etiquette. Over twenty years later I read Audré Lorde's biomythography *Zami*, in which she comments on the unsatisfactory nature of love that needs without wanting or wants but does not need. The memory of Lucky and his words came rushing back. But at this point in my life I was young, open and relatively innocent. Men were constantly making a play for me and, although I realised I should not be all *that* flattered by the degree of attention, the idea of fidelity seemed fairly unimportant.

One of Lucky's friends was Ida Kar, the photographer, born in Russia of Armenian parents in 1917. Her striking portraits of artists such as Epstein, Lowry and Chagall had just been shown at the Whitechapel Gallery. I was gradually overcoming my apathy about being a photographer and had studied Kar's work with admiration. There were still very few visible women photographers – or many women of recognised significance in most of the arts – and I was beginning to make a mental note of those who surfaced. Sandra Lousada and Zoë Dominic were two; a big revival was taking place in the British theatre and their publicity portraits and front-of-house stills for plays such as *A Taste of Honey* kept cropping up. Jacko often did publicity shots for *Spotlight*, the actors' shop-window, and I began to consider that I might work in this area, too. At the prompting of Ian, the gay retoucher, I wrote to several actors to ask if I could photograph them. Alec McCowan and a young Tom Courtenay agreed, but I did nothing with the shots that resulted.

No galleries existed for photography then; the only place to see quality work was in magazines such as *Vogue*, which featured outstanding single shots and picture-stories beside the fashion advertisements. Sandra Lousada's work appeared here, too, along with the Americans Richard Avedon and Irving Penn, masters of the technically superb. I looked at their pictures with awe and began to distinguish between the 'reportage' style and the classic Fleet Street procedure: holding up a flashgun and banging away. Among the people whose work I admired was Roger Mayne, probably known best for his 1950s street documentary, but whom I encountered originally through the pictures he took at the Trad clubs; he did the stills for Lindsay Anderson's innovative film *Mama Don't Allow*. There was Lord Snowdon, too, whose work for the *Sunday Times Colour Supplement* was far more sensitive than he has been given credit for by the envious with no photographic credentials of their own. However, I had yet to discover the great names of photo-documentary such as Walker Evans, Dorothea Lange and Eugene Smith. I liked Sanford Roth's 'insider's' shots of James Dean, and Wayne Miller, one of Smith's pupils, whose moving book about childhood, *The World is Young*, I'd picked up in Paris. In England, though, the working-class musketeers, Bailey, Donovan and Duffy were approaching their heyday. Their ideas would increasingly dominate the Swinging Sixties.

Partly through knowing Lucky, but also because I was intrigued with the idea of women handling anything so physically demanding, I became interested in sculpture too. A major festival of British sculpture was held in Battersea Park around this time and people were encouraged to touch the pieces. I liked the solid bronze figures of Elizabeth Frink and was particularly impressed by the serenity of the architecturally pure shapes Barbara Hepworth produced. Increasingly, though, it seemed to me that Ida Kar was the kind of woman I wanted to be if, indeed, I was to make a career with the camera. At the Whitechapel her huge prints, some up to nine feet high, quite unknown then, had captured the imagination of everyone who saw them. Indeed, it was because of her work that British art critics began to review photography seriously for the first time. I decided I wanted to meet her.

Lucky took me to Ida's Soho studio several times but we never found her at home. For years it remained a source of sadness that I never managed to meet such a powerful woman artist at a time when I could have drawn greatly from the experience. There were so few female role-models available then and I felt certain such a meeting would have been greatly encouraging. The only woman photographer I did meet was Dorothy Wilding, official portraitist for the Royal Family. I went to her for a job interview and she was so rude about my work and the way I presented myself that I flew out of her studio in dismay. Ida Kar went on to exhibit in Moscow but gradually disappeared from photography after her triumphs. She died in 1974, one of the many women whose fame came, in a sense, too early.

Pam Bavin, Lucky and I spent some enjoyable hours hanging out with pianist Roosevelt Sykes, a distinguished bluesman of the old school, from Arkansas. Roosevelt, who sold thousands of records in the 1930s and 40s under the name of 'The Honeydripper', came over on the wave of blues artists who had begun to play in Europe with increasing regularity. Roosevelt was a sophisticated man with a long experience of band-leading. He was quite a philosopher, too. And, he loved to sit back and puff on his fat King Edward cigar and analyse everyone around him. I'd never met anyone like him before. He told us he had converted to Islam and saw himself as 'a Moor, descended from Morocco'. He had adopted the Arabic name 'Bey' and explained that he only carried 'that slave-name of Sykes for the US government's sake'. He was the first Afro-American I had encountered to explain and describe this not uncommon procedure. He showed us a Mississippi driving licence in the name of Roosevelt Sykes Bey. There he was classified 'W' (for white) in deference to his adopted religion, a ploy which made him more mobile in segregated communities. Roosevelt always wore a stylish hat and kept his shoes highly polished. He carried himself with dignity and even when he related tales of riding the freight trains, you could imagine him flicking the smokestack smuts off an impeccable suit. He described how he'd sleep in the boxcars, rolling dollar bills up his arm inside his shirt-sleeves for safety, and you knew he'd always arrived in town looking just-so. His hoboing days were long gone, of course, but ironically we were to have our own train ride together.

His tour-manager was tired and asked if I'd like to take over one night. Roosevelt was booked for a gig in Brighton on the coast and had to get back for a midnight show at the Lyceum Ballroom. I never expected to be a roadie, but I agreed instantly. It was a chance to be alone with a fabulous musician, and we had a lot of fun. Ten years later I stayed with the pianist and his wife in New Orleans, but at this point I was only just beginning to find out something about life in the Black Belt South where the blues were born.

The blues musicians who played London in the early 1960s had to develop their own ways of dealing with white people who were in many ways very different to those they were used to at home. Some of the bluesmen, Sykes, for example, had been working the coffeehouse and college circuit of the folk boom that had developed alongside the civil rights campaign; they were accustomed to playing for young whites. Not all, however, had benefited from the attention of the folk revival which began in the 1930s and 1940s and helped push 'folk' songsters like Josh White and Leadbelly into the mainstream. Nearly all the blues players came from the South and had family there, still living under segregation, denied human justice and the right to vote. Some had been living in major urban ghettoes, where they catered for the needs of people like themselves, the urban proletariat, but they moved in a strictly Black world. Chicago's Southside, for example, was a strong, self-sufficient society where it was possible for people to live and work without coming into contact with Whites. In Europe, then, many of the blues musicians were, in effect, taking their first steps outside segregated society. It can hardly have been an easy journey, although it could be said that their 'outlaw' background went some way to prepare them. By choosing a way of life which many in their communities identified with immorality and evil, the bluesmen were accustomed to being outsiders.

Generally speaking, these pioneers took things in their stride. I think, for instance, of the fresh-faced Jimmy Cotton, whom Chris Barber met playing mouth-harp (harmonica) with Muddy Waters. For all his sharp white tuxedo and easygoing gold-toothed grin, it must have been unsettling to find himself onstage with the Barber band, trading choruses with Ottilie Patterson as if it were an everyday occurrence to be involved in such relatively intimate exchanges with a white woman. At the end of each triumphant set, the musicians would embrace Jimmy, Ottilie included. This must have been in some way disturbing, given a climate that still refused to sanction interracial relationships. Miscegenation was, in fact, illegal in many American states. And if anyone needed reminding, a mere half-dozen years had passed since 1955 when 14-year-old Emmett Till was kidnapped and murdered in Mississippi for allegedly speaking to a white woman in a familiar way. Yet Jimmy never batted an eyelid as he socialised with Ottilie or with me, treated with the utmost respect by Chris and the other musicians.

Jimmy kept his fingernails long and painted with clear varnish in a style still to be seen among a few older musicians, preachers and gamblers. (The single long nail exists in cultures outside Afro-America, proclaiming that the individual has no need to engage in manual work, that he is, in fact, 'clean to the bone'.) He 'konked' his hair, too, and wore it 'high' in a Black tradition of personal adornment not quite as extravagant as the pompadours of rock 'n' roll but splendid enough to impress English people who had never seen the effect outside publicity photos of Little Richard.With his fingers he moulded Marcel waves deep in his Vaselined 'process', keeping it in place at night with a head-wrap.

There was something distinctly 'feminine' about these bluesmen who preferred the soft-waved look and manicured hands. It puzzled white male writers, who got hung up on theories of sexual ambiguity and were rather embarrassed by this apparently less than macho streak in their idols. Yet I understood it when such men talked about 'keeping themselves pretty' for women; it was a reaction against the callouses of the field-hand and the grimy, broken nails of the assembly line.

I spent hours with Buddy Guy, Jimmy Cotton, John Lee Hooker and others, including Otis Spann, who would later occasionally drop me wishfully intimate notes from places such as Alabama, a location that suggested an act of defiance. I helped them find their way around London and the peculiar, unseasoned British food, at times taking one of them to Streatham for some home-cooking. Misunderstandings, sadly, abounded. When pianist Curtis Jones wanted to use the toilet in one of the new hamburger restaurants he was refused. He was upset and started to mutter about Jim Crow (segregation). The explanation was in fact that our cheaper cafés just didn't offer toilet facilities; but such awkward incidents, unintentional as they were, were regrettably common. My aid was enlisted to decipher recording contracts and fan-letters and to locate whisky or gin outside opening hours.

It would be wrong to suggest, as some have, that the bluesmen had cotton-balls clinging to their pants. The majority were professional musicians, literally and culturally a long way from home. Roosevelt Sykes had toured with his own band in his heyday, his name emblazoned on the side of the bus. Champion Jack Dupree had recorded frequently over two decades. A fast-talking ex-boxer from New Orleans and master of the *double entendre*, he embarrassed me and Liz Spiro, my erstwhile YCL comrade and schoolfriend, by announcing that we had requested the song about syphilis with the lines: 'You got bad blood, baby/I believe you need a shot/Let the doctor turn you over/And see what else you got.' Jack took a great liking to me and my family, writing to me constantly as he travelled around the Continent, and taking us out for steak dinners whenever we dropped by. Staying near Cecil Gee's, a clothing-store that was a favourite with musicians, he bought himself a new overcoat and jacket, giving Clive his discarded ones, which saw service for a number of years. He rapidly established himself on the jazz and folk circuit and moved permanently to Europe, marrying a woman from Halifax and settling into the role of Yorkshire gent for a while.

Like other visiting blues artists, Jack stayed at a small hotel off Haymarket called Airways Mansions. There no visiting restrictions operated and several rooms had cooking facilities as well. A dour Scotsman, permanently on Reception, would sometimes be involved in the partying, turning a blind eye to the constant stream of well-wishers who arrived bearing bottles of spirits, eager to learn more of the blues. Airways Mansions is long gone, but I can never pass the spot where it stood without recalling hilarious afternoons spent with bluesmen making their first trip outside America.

Another of these was Memphis Slim, the pianist and composer of 'Everyday I Have the Blues'. Unlike many others of his generation, he had shrewdly copyrighted his songs instead of selling them outright as others were persuaded to do. Pam Bavin came with me to meet him, and we found a musician considerably more aware of his rights and the injustices in the record business than other blues people we had encountered. In our interview he made a point of naming the corrupt director of Bluebird, one of the legendary companies that manufactured 'race' records. This man, he said, had cheated countless artists of thousands of pounds worth of royalties. Southern naïvety on arrival in Chicago was all he needed. 'How much do it cost to make a record?' a musician would ask, and into the studio he went.

Slim was amusing and became a good friend, although he did

have a rather unattractive tendency to tell tales on his peers. Some were instructive, of course, but you were left wondering what he might say about you as soon as your back was turned. His farsightedness on the matter of royalties paid off; he was able to move to France, where he drove a Rolls Royce and lived for a while alongside the embassies of Paris, in the exclusive 16th *arrondissement*.

He was still wearing a greasy yellow suede jacket, though, when Pam and I took him and fellow pianist Speckled Red on a tour of Soho nightspots. Red was an albino who immortalised a bowdlerised recorded version of the 'dozens', the ancient imprecatory ritual rooted in African tradition which can be improvised to suit any occasion. Afro-American songs were often cleaned up for Anglo consumption and Red stunned me one day by revealing the more usual 'Dirty motherfucker/ Old cocksucker' lyrics that were meat to his bar-room audience back home. At the Roundhouse in Wardour Street, a legendary blues room, the regulars shook their heads in disbelief as the two pianists took turns to beat the battered old upright into submission, stomping on down with 'Every Day' and a somewhat less ribald 'Dirty Dozens'. It was hard to believe that within the space of a few years such classic figures, the people who *are* the blues, would no longer raise a storm when they appeared in London. In those days, though, Black bluesmen and the white musicians they encountered in Europe held each other in mutual respect. Gradually this situation would change as whites such as Eric Clapton proclaimed that they, too, were 'Hoochie Coochie Men', capable of dealing the music with the same degree of 'authenticity' as the originators.

Slim recorded twice in London and I took photographs for his albums. Then he arranged for me to shoot the cover pictures for a Roosevelt Sykes session he had supervised in New York. Roosevelt was one of his earliest piano teachers, and the person who had advised him to copyright his material, long before this process had become common knowledge. Now Slim was returning the favour. He got me to write the liner-notes, too. My pictures were a long way from brilliant but, thanks to Slim, I felt I was going up in the world.

It was around this time that Charles Mingus came to London to take part in a film. *All Night Long*, based loosely on the *Othello* story, featured him and pianist Dave Brubeck in speaking roles and local musicians were involved as well. Mingus, who played bass, was one of the most important American composers, a major force in the 'roots' revival of the late 1950s and 1960s. He was one of the first to wrest the music from the Europeanised direction it was assuming in some quarters, and re-emphasise its source: the blues and the church. He was already a legendary character, a large, sensitive man, renowned for his outspokenness and racial pride. Everyone wanted to meet him.

Kitty had tried to interview him and he'd refused to let her make any notes. He reasoned that if what he had to say was important, she ought to be able to remember it. I decided against trying my luck but did ask whether I might go along to the hotel and photograph him. We took some amusing shots using an open umbrella as a prop and he was as friendly as anyone else had been. Bold as brass, I invited him home for a meal. On the day in question, though, he had to bow out

71

due to movie commitments. But he promised he would not disappoint us, 'Tell your mother I'm sorry,' he said. 'And *I'll* bring the food next time.'

When that day came, we drove to a barbecue chicken restaurant to pick up supplies. Pam and her boyfriend were with us and Mingus asked how many would be eating. A whole chicken was still something you saw only at Christmas, but to our utter astonishment, he purchased six of them, one for each of us.

Back at Streatham, Mum and Clive were waiting. Introductions were made, but Mingus headed straight for the kitchen. There and then he unwrapped his parcels, exhorting us to sit down and tuck in right away. He sat there surrounded by chicken bones and greasy newspaper, chomping away with a grin on his face, looking for all the world like a latter-day Henry VIII. I don't think he even took his coat off. We were awed at being in the presence of the Great Man, but Mum had no such illusions. She made her feelings clear and left us to it: 'I'm not sitting down with *that man*!'

Mingus didn't care. He was probably relieved to get away from all the movie-world bullshit and be with people who wanted nothing other than an ordinary evening with him. But no time spent with Mingus could be that simple. We talked for a while, then he asked if I would type a letter for him. For two hours he dictated, pacing up and down the lounge and leaning over me as I sat at my mother's desk. He was writing to the president of his local union branch to complain of injustices suffered at the hands of certain booking agents. It was an impassioned document, thousands of words long, and was not finished until the early hours. Everyone else had long disappeared and I called him a cab. As he left, he thrust £20 into my hand, an unbelievable sum in those days. That Mingus was a redoubtable character goes without saying. Being close to him that night, I absorbed something of the passion and love that made his music so special. I had begun to learn that even great people can be fallible. Certainly he wore his emotions on his sleeve for everyone to see. It made me feel warm and supportive towards him from then on, no matter what escapade he might be involved in.

Increasingly I began to learn about the 'other' London. I visited African and Westindian houses, many of which were severely dilapidated, with cramped cooking facilities and outside lavatories (a feature by no means confined to Black homes at that time). Not all the people I met lived in drab and dismal surroundings, but the reluctance of many landlords to let their better properties to anyone other than Europeans made it hard for Black people to find decent accommodation. African students, because of their relatively greater isolation, fared less well than Caribbean settlers in this respect. I got to know the areas of town where they battled with inadequate facilities – heating, lighting and plumbing – and to discover something of how the 'other half' lived and, despite such deprivation, managed to maintain a reasonable equilibrium.

Food was a problem – even rice, a major staple, when often the only kind available was that which we, the white English, used for puddings. It was better for those who lived near a market area such as Brixton or Shepherd's Bush. There yams, green banana, plantain and stockfish jostled cabbage, carrots and cod as north London's Enco Products, which had previously supplied the Jewish community, recognised a new market and began to import produce from Africa and the Caribbean. The red–blue Encona label identified gungo peas, gari and jars of bright orange palm oil, yet prices were high and distribution limited, forcing many to find substitutes for the basic carbohydrates of the African diet. Semolina and ground rice, which the British used for milk puddings, were employed to create an Anglicised version of *fufu* or *eba*; potato flour could be made to resemble pounded yam.

At the beginning of the 1960s, Indian restaurants were still few and far between, so anywhere that offered large helpings of rice took on special significance. Greek restaurants fell into this category, and there were several in Soho frequented by African students, who favoured the huge hunks of lamb on the bone. Among these was the legendary Jimmy's, still going strong at another location, but at that time a little underground hideaway in Frith Street. In the long, arched and tiled basement where service was hectic, there was an outcry among African patrons when the bread, previously gratis, was charged for: two slices for twopence.

Several nightspots in London were operated by Africans or Westindians, too. At Club Afrique, a basement in Wardour Street run by Nigerian Ola Dosonmu and his English wife, the Yoruba guitarist Ambrose Campbell, provided the regular entertainment, and in Greek Street the Afro-Caribbean Club had a fast-moving atmosphere. In such places interracial couples could socialise without fear of harassment, an important advantage in the days when male settlers still outnumbered females and those of them seeking companionship formed relationships with white women. Black men were still banned from some dancehalls in the early 1960s; indeed, in the previous decade, the Paramount in Tottenham Court Road had been the only place where dancing partners could be approached without fear of rejection. But gradually the colour-bar was breaking down. My own local, the notorious Streatham Locarno, had begun to admit controlled numbers of respectably dressed 'coloureds'. In contrast to the war years when many whites baulked at the segregated social behaviour required by the US Forces based here, inviting Afro-American service personnel into their social clubs and homes as a protest, white women who went out with Black men could now expect to be abused – attacked even – in the street. White people would stand and stare openly at 'mixed' couples; the general belief was that any white woman with a Black man could only be on the game, and even then, she should 'stick to her own'.

Inevitably, given my socialising and work routine, Lucky and I had a serious quarrel. He, too, assumed that the musicians I was constantly meeting were more than just friends. We stopped seeing each other and I missed him. Lucky knew his way around clubland and had introduced me to an underground of Black musicians who never made their way into the music papers. I enjoyed the intimacy of being in an insider's company, and whenever I went to the newly opened Ronnie Scott Club or the afterhours Downbeat, it wasn't the same without him. Lucky's mistrust was not surprising in view of the experience of most Black men in his situation, forced to rely on the night club or dance-hall as a meeting place. The fact that open-minded white

73

women existed, determined enough to shrug off the abuse and in many cases go on to marry their lovers, was not enough to change views reinforced time and again by the dull thud of rejection. The men in his immediate circle had their beliefs, and nothing could alter the idea that any woman prepared to leave a club in their company would almost inevitably be on the fringes of the game at the least.

But I refused to be daunted, just as I refused to be seen as a whore. I dropped by his house one day to find that another woman he knew had moved in. Lucky was embarrassed and wrote apologetically. Several months had elapsed since our fight and we started to meet again, going to the pictures and catching up on the latest musical sounds. Together we saw many of the key films of the era, from *A Bout de Souffle*, *Les Amants* and *Black Orpheus* to *Jazz on a Summer's Day* and the horrific *Warsaw Ghetto*, in which for the first time most people of my generation saw the Nazi atrocities on film — these were images that stayed with me for ages.

With Lucky I always felt comfortable, despite the cultural gap that separated us. He taught me much about life and about art. Most notably, he showed me the value of silence, of simplicity and, above all, of honesty. As with other men, we were better as friends than as lovers.

Lucky's sculpture prospered until he suffered a debilitating stroke that left him partially paralysed. He learned to sculpt again using his left hand, and, as I had done for him before, I continued to make a photographic record of his progress. Then, tragically, he suffered a second, fatal, stroke three days before he was due to marry. He was 32, the first friend I'd lost in this way. I missed him for ages.

Jacko was spending more and more time out of the studio, leaving things to be run by me and 'Sarah', who worked as his receptionist and secretary. I became pretty adept at forging his signature on cheques when materials were delivered, but business was not exactly booming. One weekend, there was a terrible storm and, turning up for work Monday morning, we discovered that rain had come through the roof of the studio. Water was beginning to damage the considerable stock of valuable negatives Jacko had inherited from his predecessor. As Sarah and I set about rescuing this material, we discovered a small shoebox hidden away on the top shelf behind rows of neg-bags. I opened it and to my surprise uncovered a series of pornographic pictures our employer had taken in his spare time of local strippers. We had just finished laughing at a shot of him measuring his dick alongside a ruler, when we heard his step in the corridor. Hastily I pushed the box aside and jumped down the ladder. He moved forward purposefully. '*I'll take care of that box.*' Fine, I said, and busied myself elsewhere. At the time the discovery seemed funny — pathetic, really — but it added to my diminishing respect for him. This, in turn, led to our final clash.

Backstage at a Jazz Messengers concert I met a Yoruba drummer named Bayo Martins, who was to be a good friend for years to come. Art Blakey, the Messengers' leader and drummer, had recently spent a couple of years in Nigeria and the atmosphere slipped warmly from the usual sycophancy of white fans to a relaxed, palm-slapping Pan-African exchange. I photographed Bayo and his wife with Blakey and one day he dropped in to see me at work. I was out of the studio so he showed Jacko the contact-sheet of my pictures. My employer was not best pleased. The business was in crisis and that, linked with his dislike of my friends, gave him the excuse he needed to harass me. He was always off with some woman or other, and I resented having to go and find him in whatever pub or café he was conducting his chat-up routine when clients turned up looking for him.

I told Jacko his business was going downhill because he didn't devote enough time to it. Take me, for example, I said, I've got lots of work. We had an almighty row and the following Monday he told me not to bother coming in any more.

As luck would have it, I didn't need the job. I'd thrown my bonnet over the windmill and decided to go to New York. I was going to stay with Al Douglas and thought we might end up getting married. It was a pleasure to give Jacko two fingers, and a pleasure to get on the plane.

Part Two
Three Times Seven

Well, I'm three, three times seven
        And that makes twenty-one,
Ain't nobody's business
        What I do.

Bessie Smith

7
First Bite at the Apple

When the plane landed at Idlewild, Al was there to meet me. He had put on weight and looked tired but I was excited to see him. We took the 'limo' into the city, driving past the massive cemeteries that line the highway, 'the biggest rock-garden in the world', as one waggish musician described it. The Manhattan skyscrapers had barely loomed up out of the haze when he turned to me and said, 'Don't expect me to be the way I was in London.' Sessions and students were keeping him busy, he explained. New York was nothing like London; he had to operate differently on his home turf. I don't know what I expected at 20, but I'm sure that even though the words made sense, I was left feeling disconcerted by what lay behind them.

Minutes after we arrived at his East-side apartment, a dozen red roses were delivered, and before long we were making love. Al's place bulged with music, scores stacked on chairs and blocking the doorway. With several double-basses leaning against the walls of the tiny apartment, freedom of movement was difficult. Such minor details were irrelevant, though; I was in New York! I'd planned to stay for a couple of weeks, to look up some of the people I'd met in London and hear some music. At the end of it all I imagined that Al and I would see if we had any grounds for making a more permanent arrangement. That was what everyone did in those days, so it seemed a reasonable idea. What's more, several American musicians had married women they had met in Europe, and the possibilities offered by such trans-national relationships were a matter for debate within the music community.

As the evening approached, Al started to get ready for work. I asked whom he was playing with and he reeled off a 'Who's who' of jazz. Great, I said, when do we leave? 'Oh, no,' he said, 'you're staying here.' I protested that I wanted to come and hear the music, and anyway had met some of the guys in England. He huffed and puffed and said he had no idea when the gig would be over and that I couldn't just hang around all night. I told him I was perfectly capable of getting a taxi home if need be, and off we went.

The gig turned out to be a special event presented by jazz dancers Leon James and Al Mimms at the famous Woodstock Hotel. Singer Jimmie Rushing was featured, with intermission piano provided by the 'stride' master, Willie 'The Lion' Smith. Trumpeter Clark Terry was the bandleader. Clark was one of the first American musicians I'd met when he played London with Duke Ellington in 1958. He had switched recently to the fluegelhorn, a more mellow instrument which suited his cheerful, bubbling style, and was pioneering the breakdown of barriers in the lucrative but racially-exclusive session-work world. Now he was in demand for radio, recording and television dates, where his combination of technical excellence and a lively style put him ahead of many of his more conservative counterparts. I thought what he was doing would make a good story for *Jazz News*, especially as Al had stressed the importance of what he was doing.

It was great to see Clark again. He'd kept in touch through Christmas cards and I was secretly a little in love with him. He dressed crisply, with a knitted silk tie and the kind of crease in his trousers you could cut yourself on and I thought he looked lovely. He had the Ellington charm in abundance, and I hung on his every word. New York was turning out to be just as I'd imagined.

A number of jazz writers with familar names were in the audience. Al pointed out Rudi Blesh, bearded and scholarly, the author of *Shining Trumpets*, my earliest primer, and introduced me to Bob Reisner who had just compiled a rather sensationalist collection of anecdotes about Charlie Parker, a book treated like gold-dust in hip London circles at the time. There were other musicians I'd met as well: Jimmie Rushing, the singer, and Gus Johnson, whom I'd interviewed for *Tropic* about playing drums with Ella Fitzgerald. All were friendly and welcoming.

On the way back, though, Al became bullish. 'I don't like you talking to all those guys,' he said as we squeezed in with his bass in the back of the Yellowcab. I was taken aback but managed to control my dismay, asking him how else he expected me to write about the music. 'Well, anyway, you were flirting with Clark Terry.' Nothing, I said, was further from my mind – no twinge of guilt was necessary, for Al was the man I'd come to see – and we left it at that.

The first person I called next day was Herbie Lovelle. He promised to drop by later but was noticeably sniffy when I announced where I was staying. Al was set to play an afternoon session. He left me with admonitions about 'running up the telephone bill' and 'calling up other men' ringing in my ears. There was a resolute look on his face as he struggled through the partially jammed door with his bass. I was beginning to feel a little perturbed.

Herbie was Mr Easy when he turned up, making me feel relaxed for the first time since my arrival. I explained that the relationship was serious and he nodded sagely. 'Look,' he said, 'I want to introduce you to some people.' We drove across town to Greenwich Village and the home of two newly-arrived fellow Britons. I recognised them from the previous night as acquaintances of Clark. Herbie had met Edgar and Barbara Blakeney during his earlier visit to England. They came from Blackpool, where Edgar taught at the College of Art and Barbara studied textiles, and they had an 11-year-old daughter. We all liked each other immediately.

Herbie was in the process of setting up a booking agency and his spare time was limited. But he wanted to make sure I would have somewhere to go if my living situation should get 'awkward'. Matters came to a crunch the following day when I wanted to phone Langston Hughes, the writer. Hughes was the poet laureate of Afro-America, a prolific essayist, dramatist and short-story writer, but it was through his poetry that I first came to know him. A verse of his had inspired the title of Lorraine Hansberry's *A Raisin in the Sun* the first drama by a Black woman writer to play Broadway; in company with other music enthusiasts, I had gone to see it when it was staged in London. And I wanted to know more of the poet's work. There is a recording of his, *The Weary Blues*, where he reads his poetry accompanied by musicians, one group from the Swing era, another led by bassist/composer Charles Mingus. I loved the way he sounded, like a blues singer – talking. The record was deleted but it was Al, ironically, who had found me a copy. He'd sent me Langston's *Selected Poems*, too. But now it was: 'You can't call up Langston Hughes just like that.' I explained that I'd written to ask if I might come and photograph him during my stay and he had agreed. Al muttered darkly about the cost of the telephone. 'Dammit,' I said, 'I'll pay for the bloody call!' With tears in my eyes – tears of anger, at being thwarted – I phoned Hughes' secretary to arrange an appointment.

'Egg' and Barbara had invited me for dinner that evening, after which it was planned to go and hear Herbie where he was working. At the Embers, one of the more pricey supper clubs which featured jazz for business people with expense accounts, trumpeter Louis Metcalfe was the bandleader, with Herbie and Leonard Gaskin on bass. Metcalfe was an oldtime musician who played with enough 'soul' to keep the clientele happy, without getting too funky and disturbing the status quo. He had once worked with King Oliver, too, and between sets we did a short, scribbled, interview.

When the gig was over, Herbie and Leonard took us for breakfast. It was the first time I'd heard of breakfast before bed. As we drove along neon-lit avenues thronging with nightpeople, I was awhirl with the strange new ideas of the city. It was four in the morning but I felt I'd only just started. We had 'sunnyside-up' eggs and bacon at a diner behind Birdland, the renowned night club named after Charlie 'Bird' Parker, then Leonard drove me downtown and home.

My head was spinning as I walked in the door. I'd met someone who had played with King Oliver, eaten breakfast as dawn was breaking, and socialised with musicians who treated me as though friendships between 'them' and 'us' were an everyday thing. New York was something else.

Al was something else, too. He sat up in bed with a face like thunder. 'Where have you been?' he demanded. I told him I'd been out with Herbie. 'You've been fucking!' he thundered. 'Of course I haven't,' I shouted, 'I've been out with the Blakeneys as well.' 'Freaks!' he shouted back. 'All those people are freaks. And she's a lesbian, too!' My heart started racing. I'd made the mistake of confiding in Al that I sometimes found women attractive and was trying to decide what this meant. 'Freaks' I knew was American slang for 'deviants' or 'swingers', but Al had gratuitously tagged on the word 'lesbian' as the ultimate attack against female morals. It was the first time I'd heard it used in this way and I felt as though the ground was slipping from under my feet. Barbara seemed like a lovely woman, blessed with earthy, dry Lancashire humour; I certainly hadn't had time to think of her as anything other than a jazz fan. I strenuously denied all the charges. They were just so unfair and it was with tears of disbelief that I crept into bed.

I slept little that night, and the next day my mind was in a turmoil. I realised I'd made a great mistake in thinking I could stay with Al and get on with my writing as well. I had no idea it would turn out this way, for we'd talked often about music and he had encouraged my interest. I had gone to New York on a package trip organised by Ronnie Scott's Club which included a hotel room; but I'd opted for staying at Al's and had taken little spending money along as a consequence. Our flight was a charter so there was no way I could think of going back before the appointed time. I was stuck in a tricky position, but I couldn't endure what was happening.

I told Al I was going for a walk. New York was experiencing one of its hottest May days on record and as I trudged miserably up Second Avenue the temperature hovered around the 100°F mark. I felt thirsty and went into a bar. At that time, bars outside the Village did not encourage women alone and the service was surly. I ordered a beer and a roast beef sandwich. Unaware of the Jewish dietary laws that influence food served in the city, I failed to stipulate 'mustard or mayo' and was left with an almost inedible slab of meat on dry bread. My hands shook as I attempted to eat it.

I felt sick as I walked back to East 19th Street but I'd made up my mind. I stepped into a phone-booth, the sweat mingling with tears as I sweltered inside its oven-like interior. This time, though, they were tears of sadness. I dialled Herbie's number and he told me to wait for him at the Blakeneys. I went back and started packing. Al was upset: 'Where are you going? You don't know anybody here!' I said very little. I cared for the man and respected him, but it was obvious that I could no longer stay there on his restrictive terms.

Barbara was all considerateness and Lancashire hospitality, throwing together a meal and offering chilled Miller Highlife. Herbie drove us Uptown, where his son had a small apartment near the edge of Harlem. I could stay there for the remainder of the visit. I couldn't believe my luck.

I began to explore New York City, making tentative forays along Broadway and seeing some of the sights. In a bookshop on Times Square I found a collection of Langston Hughes' 'Simple' stories from his column in the *Chicago Defender*. I also bought a copy of *Fight for Freedom*, his history of the NAACP (National Association for the Advancement of Colored People), and a book called *The Negro in American Culture*. Reading these, I began to know more of the society in which the music developed.

I arranged to see Clark Terry and met him in Jim and Andy's, the bar frequented by session musicians which was situated on 48th Street. We discussed his breakthrough into network television and he explained how Blacks had hitherto, as he put it, been *forced* to play jazz in America. Not that this was a disgrace, he hastened to add, it being a Black art form, but prejudice had made it hard to find employment outside that area. As many would explain·later, he felt that by working for NBC he was doing more than a job. 'I feel I am responsible for Negroes doing this kind of work in the future. I am determined to dispose of the "I told you so" fallacy.'

I contacted Moses Asch, too, the proprietor of Folkways Records, for whom I had annotated and photographed Roosevelt Sykes. Asch was an impressive, mustachioed man, the son of the renowned Jewish novelist Schlomo Asch. He had the superficially cynical New York manner but seemed to be warm inside. He had started Folkways with recordings by Big Bill Broonzy, Champion Jack Dupree and Leadbelly, and it had grown into an important record label offering everything from *Flamenco Music of Andalusia* to selections from the *Bhagavad Gita*; I decided to interview him, too. He told me to meet him at 8.30 for breakfast. Clearly breakfast was a big event in the city.

But Moses Asch introduced me to more than hashed browns and eggs-over-easy. He gave me a couple of albums of my choice, on one of which Langston Hughes read his 'Simple' stories. On the other side was poet Sterling Brown with some of his powerful work. Brown, veteran Professor of English for half a century at Howard University, America's most respected Black academic institution, shared with Hughes the title of Afro-America's poet laureate. In this way I became familiar with another of Afro-America's great literary figures. And a painter, as well: the stark black-and-white cover illustration, a sardonic comment on segregation, came from the pen of Jacob Lawrence, one of the major artists of the Harlem Renaissance. A new world was opening up for me, spearheaded by music but going far beyond the bandstand and bar-room.

Egg and Barbara were what we used to call 'ravers'. They had not been long in Manhattan but already knew people all over the Village. They lived on Horatio Street in an apartment I would come to regard as my New York home-from-home, and among their acquaintance were numbered most of the musicians who kept a high profile during that period. They had met pianist Dave Brubeck and his quartet at the same time as they got to know Herbie, and their scrapbook showed snapshots of Lesley, their little daughter, partying with Brubeck and his bassist the jovial Eugene Wright, one of my 'gentlemen guardians', from the early days. Clark Terry, Stan Getz, Gil Evans, Jerome Richardson and Brubeck's saxophonist Paul Desmond were among those who would sometimes drop by to see them. They introduced me to guitarist Jimmy Raney, too, who was playing at the Village Vanguard with Getz and we were able to do an interesting interview.

The Blakeneys' record-playing equipment included a huge speaker from a ship's Tannoy system which made the walls reverberate with the richness of its sound. Egg had nailed a 78 rpm copy of Charlie Parker's 'Lover Man' to the wall over the record shelves; under it was proudly displayed a saxophone reed that had belonged to Getz. The walls were lined with cork tiles, the smell of which I still find comforting for the memories it brings of touching base at their apartment whenever New York got too much for me.

There were plenty of fellow Britons with whom to share the experience of hearing saxophonist Charles Lloyd for the first time with the Chico Hamilton Quintet or catching the duets of Al Cohn and Zoot Sims at the Half Note. At the Jazz Gallery I went to hear Art Farmer and Benny Golson and spotted Ornette Coleman in the audience. I ran into several people who had come over on the Scott Club package, as well as two musicians trying their luck in 'The Apple', saxophonist Tubby Hayes and Welsh pianist Dill Jones. Dizzy Reece, the Jamaican trumpeter, kept cropping up, too. Reece played at the first 'modern jazz' concert I ever attended when he was living in London in the 1950s. Since then he had made his home in New York and was on hand to show tourists the ropes. Everyone was excited just to be able to walk into places like Birdland, and I went to one of the famous Monday night jam-sessions there. Enthusiasm was the keynote; 'Tubbs' had yet to experience the rejection by some American musicians wary of foreigners trying to take over their patch, and Dill the frustration of having to play cocktail music to pay the rent.

One of the Blakeneys' closest acquaintances was Tadd Dameron, whose clean-lined compositions are regarded as classics of modern jazz – beautiful pieces such as 'Our Delight' and 'The Scene is Clean', titles evocative of an era. Having spent some time in England (where he wrote for the bands of Ted Heath and Geraldo, among others, and lived in Mayfair), Tadd related well to English people and particularly liked Barbara and Edgar – he called him 'Eggy'. Tadd was at a precarious point in his life. After avoiding the addiction to heroin that caught up with so many of the bebop generation of musicians, he had himself succumbed to pressure and taken the narcotic route, ending up at the Federal Narcotics Institution at Lexington, Kentucky. He had been back in New York for just over a year and was trying to rebuild his career. His new works reflected his credo: 'There's enough ugliness in the world, I'm interested only in beauty,' and he already had plenty of writing commissions. He was working on an album of his own but was plagued by ill health, a weak heart making it hard for him to live a normal life.

Egg suggested we go by Tadd's new apartment on West End Avenue for a drink and see if he was up to an interview. We had an enjoyable evening, during which he played some of his new compositions on his little spinet, apologising for the fact that he only played 'arranger's piano'. He told us how, in his family group in Cleveland, Ohio, and at the age of 7 he had played for Bessie Smith, and of working as a singer himself. On one such date he was playing piano when Charlie Parker sat in. The saxophonist told him that they were developing similar harmonic ideas. Around that time, in 1939, Tadd composed 'Ladybird' and 'Good Bait', outstanding classics far ahead of their time. I went back the following day to take some photographs. He donned a smart black velvet shirt for the occasion, and I noticed his fingernails were finely manicured, too.

I was having a fine time wherever I turned, with music nearly every night. I tried not to think of Al, for whenever I did I felt upset. I began to hang out with Gene Ramey, the bass player who had played alongside Herbie in the Buck Clayton group. There had been a flirtatious atmosphere between us when the band had come back to London for a weekend stopover, but then I'd been moved by the whole experience, the closeness I'd reached with the guys and a certain look in the eye. I remember tears had appeared unbidden when the time came to say our goodbyes. Gene had chided me fondly and from then on addressed me as 'CB' ('Cry-Baby'). In New York I was drawn to him immediately, a comfortable older man with a white gunfighter moustache and an easy manner. Despite the flirtation that loomed in the air, he cast himself in the role of protector.

We drove around Manhattan together, Gene with his brown porkpie hat perched on the back of his head, me with what must have been an insufferable degree of enthusiasm. We went out to Jones Beach and called at a lot of bars. The American watering-holes with their abundant bottle displays, Tennessee sour-mash and all, were riveting in their magnificence for someone who had only just discovered Sauternes. On Broadway at Midtown, the musicians congregated outside the Turf, a famous showbusiness restaurant. Many were historical figures, a far cry from the mob that thronged Archer Street. At bars such as the Copper Rail and Beefsteak Charlie's I met people who'd only been names on a record to me. In the space of a few minutes I was introduced to the gymnastic vocalists of bebop, Joe Carroll and Babs Gonzales, the majestic saxophonist Ben Webster, and Zutty Singleton and Philly Joe Jones, two of the greatest drummers in the history of music. My head was whirling.

Gene introduced me to Harlem, too, the cultural capital of Afro-America. We ate delicious 'soul food' in a scrubbed-clean restaurant, and dropped in backstage at the Apollo Theater, where James Brown was just finishing his act. On 125th Street there was a church where the 'Saints' worshipped nightly, and from the street I could see the participants dancing and playing all kinds of music. At the corner of 125th Street and Lenox Avenue, another Harlem landmark was the National African Memorial Bookshop, outside which were displayed portraits of all the African leaders. Louis Michaux, a Black nationalist and respected community leader, ran this 'House of Common Sense: Home of Proper Propaganda', as hoardings proclaimed. He advertised it as 'Repatriation Headquarters of the Back-to-Africa Movement'. To stand outside such a place, rallying point in times of crisis and focus of race-awareness for Uptown people, was consciousness-raising for me, too, fresh out of England.

Intimations of the changing times had begun to surface in the music press. I'd begun to read the American music magazine *Downbeat* a year earlier and had noted in it some resentment at any expression of what I now know to be Black nationalism, although it was then misunderstood and derided by Whites as 'Black racism'. An article on the subject even appeared in *Jazz News*, written by a former *Downbeat* editor. Alarm was expressed in these pieces at a new trend taking place on the bandstand: some Black musicians – shock, horror! – had stopped hiring white players. Of course, colour bars had operated in music, as elsewhere, for years; yet only when racial exclusivity began to be practised by Blacks did it become newsworthy. The alarmists, however, maintained that 'reverse prejudice' was going to kill jazz.

Ira Gitler, a respected journalist, provoked a furore when he reviewed an 'outspoken' recording by singer Abbey Lincoln, saying among other things, 'We don't need the Elijah Muhammed [*sic*] type of thinking in jazz' (Muhammad was the leader of the separatist Nation of Islam). A forum entitled 'Racial Prejudice in Jazz' was organised in the magazine, the participants including Lincoln and her husband, the percussion innovator Max Roach. Only veteran radical journalist Nat Hentoff seemed to support the point of view they expressed.

All this took place against a background of growing political action in the South. The desegregation struggle which was concerned with civil rights had begun in the aftermath of World War Two. When Rosa Parks refused to give up her seat to a white man on an Alabama bus the pace of political action accelerated. British newspapers gave prominent coverage to the fight for voter registration and the rise of the Rev. Martin Luther King, Jr, catapulted to prominence by the Montgomery bus boycott which started in 1955.

The music press no longer remained silent once musicians became involved in the struggle for racial justice and democratic representation. The name of Little Rock echoed around the world when Daisy Bates and nine young students 'integrated' the Arkansas school system with the help of the National Guard, but even before that, *Melody Maker* put another redneck capital's name in the news. Nat 'King' Cole was attacked on stage in Birmingham, Alabama, as he sang with Britain's own all-white Ted Heath Orchestra, and the story made headlines back home. Many Black artists would not work in the segregated South, of course, but now white musicians joined in the protest. Pianist Dave Brubeck stipulated his concerts be open to everyone, and refused to leave bass player Eugene Wright at home when working the South with his otherwise white quartet.

As anyone connected with the music would be, I was aware of the events that were taking place but was hazy about the complicated politics behind it all. Al, when we'd discussed it prior to our split had done little to clarify matters. He had worked with Lincoln and Roach and shared some of their views. He commented favourably when Roach reproduced a lunch-counter sit-in picture on the cover of his *We Insist – Freedom Now!* album, something that had never been done before. But he was angry, and providing explanations for a young white woman was low on his list of priorities.

The civil rights movement grew bigger with each day, but I was too naïve, politically, to distinguish between the various courses of action that were being undertaken. I was still only 20 years old, and that was young in those days. I lacked the sense of enquiry that would develop later. All I knew was that the term 'Colored' was forbidden. It was segregational terminology, and any organisation that used it, like the essentially reformist NAACP, received the thumbs-down where Al was concerned. I still didn't understand why.

Langston Hughes had written admiringly about what the NAACP had accomplished, and, to me, he was what might be called then a 'militant Negro'. It would be a significant while before I would begin to grasp what differentiated and motivated the various routes in the struggle for justice. As for Michaux's Bookstore, I didn't go inside. The sight of it remained with me, though, an impressive, bold statement in the heart of Harlem. I doubt whether anyone else on our jazz-lovers' journey even passed by it.

Gene took me to Buck Clayton's house out on Long Island, where 'Cat Eye' – so-named for his light-coloured eyes, sometimes blue, sometimes green – cooked us a barbecue. We had a fine time with his family, filling up on 'mansize' steaks, sausage and sweetcorn. This, then, was America, all skyscrapers, candied yams, okra and barbecue, where whisky and music flowed freely and revolutionary political ideas were in the air. I was beginning to get over the emotional bruising I'd suffered. I found 'Rames' attractive but it was just a friendly thing as far as I was concerned, nothing like my feeling for Al. But I had a lot of love in me and didn't know where to put it. I was a ready catch for any man out for some fun, and as long as I didn't get hurt then I didn't mind doing a little swinging.

One morning I was lying in bed when there was a knock at the door. Herbie had told me never to open the door to anyone, and I was petrified. I lay there and the knocking continued. Eventually I asked who was there. It was Al. He'd followed me back from a club one night and wanted to try healing the breach.

He asked what I wanted to do and I said I hadn't yet been to Minton's. Minton's Playhouse, to give it its proper title, was a nightspot beneath the Hotel Cecil in Harlem where radical musical developments took place in the early 1940s. It was there that Charlie Parker and Dizzy Gillespie worked out the music that would become known as bebop, in the company of housedrummer Kenny Clarke and pianist Thelonious Monk. Visiting the club was a kind of pilgrimage for jazz fans, but Al wasn't happy about it. Minton's was situated on 118th Street in the heart of Harlem drug-country, and I suppose it grieved him to expose either me or himself to the dereliction and misery that surrounded the club. Nevertheless, we made our way there and I recall being disappointed. I suppose I'd imagined a re-creation of bebop's heyday was still possible, where sitting-in flourished and sweat and inspiration poured forth in equal amounts. Pianist Richard Wyands led the house-trio, playing adequate music, but there were no horn-players on hand and no fireworks. Al made his unhappiness obvious, acting nervously and setting up a critical commentary. We didn't stay long. He wanted me to go back to East 19th with him but I couldn't make it. Barbara had suggested I invite him for dinner next evening to smoothe things out. He agreed, the accusations of immorality conveniently set aside now that the scenario had changed.

Towards the end of my stay, I kept my appointment with Langston Hughes. School was just out for the day as I emerged from the subway, feeling a trifle apprehensive at being uptown alone for the first time. I had yet to work out the simple grid-system of streets and was unsure of the way to West 127th Street where the writer lived. I hesitated before asking directions, influenced by the racist attitudes about Harlem that abounded downtown. The reaction I received was so matter-of-fact that I realised I was being ridiculous. If you were white and asking the way, you obviously had someone to see.

Children played 'tag' and skipped rope all around me as I walked the two blocks to Hughes' brownstone. The poet was a night owl who did most of his writing in the early hours, his day beginning at four in the afternoon. His secretary, George Bass, kept me occupied until he emerged, dressed in a comfortable mauve striped shirt worn casually outside his trousers. He was a shortish, well-rounded man in his early sixties, with eyes that twinkled behind hornrimmed spectacles. His interest in strangers was genuine, something I was to observe again on another visit. He had a wonderful capacity to encourage others to open up.

He poured tumblers of Scotch-on-the-rocks and quickly got me talking about myself. I asked him about Sterling Brown and he showed me some more of Jacob Lawrence's striking pictures, full of what someone later described as his 'angular energy'. We took pictures

87

in his study, then went out into the street, where he was joined by some local youngsters. I shot more pictures on the steps of the elegant brownstone where he had an apartment, and some with the kids on the block. The overall mood of those photographs is of generosity and love, the qualities that enliven all his writing. I asked him to sign my copy of the 'Simple' stories and he did so, presenting me with a copy of his *Ask Your Mama: 12 Moods for Jazz*, 'enscribed especially for Valerie Wilmer with a hearty welcome to our USA'. When I got back to England, I sent him the photographs with extra copies for the 'young men' and he sent me his anthology, *The Poetry of the Negro*, 'with thanks for your sympathetic photographs'. From time to time he'd drop me a note, enclosing a poem or a write-up about one of his plays. I felt honoured that he knew of my existence.

I left New York early in June, after an unforgettable final day. For several hours I sat at the bar in Junior's, another musicians' watering hole. People kept buying me beers but I managed to stay fairly sober. It was, I felt, a sad reflection on the American brew. Al Grey was one of my drinking companions, a trombonist I had met on a visit with Basie, and he gave me a copy of his latest recording. There, in the band, on the front cover, wearing a tie that I'd sent him from London, was Al Douglas. I was getting ready to leave for the airport and I still hadn't called him. I had no idea what there could be left to say, so I left without saying a thing.

8
Move On Up

Back home again I started to look for a job. I had plenty of writing to occupy me, but I was still living at home and that meant contributing to the family finances. None of the jazz publications paid enough to cover the rent, indeed *Jazz Journal* somewhat derisively paid its contributors a couple of albums an article.

Peter Clayton was now editing *Jazz News* and he was more than happy with the interviews I had brought back from the States. Whenever possible he would find a way of using my photographs, too, even working a piece of copy around a picture he particularly liked. He actively encouraged my writing and was, I think, a little awed at my ability to get along so well with the American musicians. They rather floored him, a 'typical Englishman', with all their swagger and soul.

From time to time Egg and Barbara would write to me, filling me in on the latest happenings in 'The Apple' and offering their invariably accurate predictions about up-and-coming talent. Prestige, a New York jazz label, had rushed out a re-release of some of Tadd Dameron's early material to coincide with his comeback and Edgar persuaded them to use one of my pictures on the cover. Tadd had also recorded *The Magic Touch*, a beautiful album of his own compositions, but the Blakeneys were becoming increasingly worried about his health. He was hospitalised for a while, following a series of heart-attacks, but when he emerged he found time to write and thank me for the story I'd done and to ask for my help in collecting European royalty payments. Sadly, he was to die not long after, in 1965.

Al continued to write to me occasionally, too, his letters often the only indication I had of the social upheaval taking place in racially divided America. The music press kept more or less quiet on the subject but when the massive civil rights march on Washington was assembling in 1963, he expressed his ambivalence over whether to join what he saw as a non-autonomous form of expression or stay home and devote his energies to working in an Afro-American context. He sent me all Coltrane's recordings as they came out, and, at my request, a copy of *Blues People*, LeRoi Jones' iconoclastic look at how the music developed. Jones placed the music in a social context, explaining how it had changed as the people changed, and although a number of white critics rejected his theories and belittled the work, the way he wrote was beginning to make sense to me.

I began to contribute to two other periodicals, *Jazz Monthly* and a new musicians' magazine, *Crescendo*. Then one day Peter Clayton sent me to cover a music trade fair with a journalist named Danny Halperin, a Canadian who worked on one of the Fleet Street newspapers. There's a piece he wrote in a book about Duke Ellington which is still my favourite look at life 'on the road'. His recollections of the Ellington band in his native Toronto were loving, sensitive and funny, and brought the musicians alive as individuals in a way that most writing about the music seldom achieved. In person, though, Danny was fast-talking and abrasive, the kind of guy who'd give Mickey Spillane a hard time if he stepped in the door.

The instrument show was a pretty dull affair so we went to sit in Russell Square afterwards to thaw out over a cup of tea. Danny had spent time in Paris with Sidney Bechet, the master clarinettist and soprano saxophonist from New Orleans who had made his home in the south of France. When Bechet produced his wonderful autobiography, *Treat It Gentle*, Danny reviewed it in an unusual way. Rather than delivering a blow-by-blow commentary, he revealed the reedman's quest of many years to find someone who could help record his story so that he might hold an actual *book* in his hand, the words 'coming out at you'. I thought it a clever approach, even if his prose went over the top at times. But Danny really cared about music.

Now he talked casually about the legendary Ringside Club – modern jazz seven nights a week – where he used to hang out with other Americans in Paris, saxophonist James Moody, pianist Inez Cavanaugh, singers Annie Ross and Babs Gonzales and the painter Lobo Nocho, when France was the most 'jazz-minded' country in Europe. He talked knowledgeably about 'Bird' (Charlie Parker) and 'Pres' (Lester Young), and offered a view of these great artists unlike anything I had previously heard. His were the tales of an intimate, it seemed to me, not sensationalist as a lot of writing about Afro-American music tended to be, dwelling on alcohol, drugs and the low life. He made the sadly-departed Bird and Pres come alive as vital individuals, whatever their personal solution to racism and misunderstanding might have been, people who poured their hearts out through the music until there was nothing left to hang on for.

His ideas were romantic, it's true, but I felt that I learned something special that day about the depths that the music can reach and the toll that such honesty takes. Danny was very much a progressive, one of the few people in Britain to write enthusiastically about Ornette Coleman when his earliest records appeared, and to grasp the fact that Coleman's jettisoning of bar lines and key signatures was a reflection of the widening gap between the way politicised young Afro-Americans were thinking and the reformists who challenged discrimination through the legal process. Next time I met him he'd switched back to his hard-boiled persona, castigating some older musicians he'd heard for playing 'like tired, sad, old men who oughta stay home'. I never heard him talking that way again.

Afro-American music would stay my major preoccupation in the years ahead, but it was far from being the only music to which I responded. I listened to African music, Indian ragas and the sounds of the Caribbean, and there was European 'people's music' (folk), too, which I had begun to discover through a group of drinking companions I would know for many years. Most of these had connections with the Communist Party, if not actually members, and nearly all of us belonged to CND. We met regularly at The Falcon, a large Clapham Junction pub.

There were several painters in the group, and people who wrote poetry in their spare time. I went there for the first time with John Batcheldor, a boyfriend who worked as a printer and had actually been on Christmas Island with the Royal Navy during the first three H-bomb tests. He was the only person we knew in CND who could actually claim to have witnessed the havoc created by the dreadful weapon against which we campaigned, and had snapshots of the explosion in his album to prove it. With the exception of Paul, who held down an art-director's job, and around whom much discussion revolved, most of the group were working-class intellectuals for whom *The Ragged-Trousered Philanthropists* was a touchstone, and who were trying to make some sense of their existence. One of the regulars was Frank, a painter whose elderly adoptive parents had been on the 'halls' and were the artist's models for the original Bisto kids. At their golden wedding celebration, a down-to-earth Battersea knees-up, we all sat around the old kitchen stove while the older people carried on dancing and flirting with a spirit belying what seemed to me then their considerable age. Later on we started to meet at another pub, The Railway, where we got to know a group of semi-pro guitarists and banjo-players. Whenever we had parties in those days, someone would always produce an instrument and we'd join in the singing of 'The Wild Rover' or 'Will Ye Go, Lassie, Go'. I loved it and have always considered live music the essential to having a really great time.

John and I had an odd sort of relationship. We went out together off and on for years and he was a loyal friend, but I could never be as serious about him as he would have liked. He was a solemn man, an introvert, who smoked a pipe and puffed hard on it when at a loss for words, but he revelled in the chance of meeting musicians such as the Ellingtonians when they came to town. In their company he grew more expansive, encouraged by their friendliness. Because he had spent several years at sea, he seemed to have a wider view of the world than most other Englishmen I knew. It was he who suggested books for me to read that started me thinking along new lines. One of these was the magnificent Lewis Grassic Gibbon trilogy, *A Scots Quair*. Although a man was the writer, it was the first time I had come across a woman as *hero* – as opposed to *heroine* – of a story. In other books where a woman was the central figure, having 'adventures' was the best she could hope for. In *Scots Quair* Chris was deliberately carving out a life for herself against all the obstacles. I read it again and again. I'd already read Simone de Beauvoir's *The Second Sex* and was beginning to kick against the injustices I felt that we suffered. My brother called me a 'feminine-ist' when I declared an interest in the works of women writers and plunged into reading Colette. I didn't really know what the word meant.

John, oddly enough, was supportive. We discussed those historical figures who had struggled against their lot, whether shackled by race, gender or class. He was interested in Paul Robeson, a lifelong fighter for freedom who spent ten years living in England, and Richard Wright, both of whom were communists, and he gave me a copy of James Baldwin's *Another Country*, which caused a sensation when it was published, with its unexpurgated picture of New York Bohemia. *Giovanni's Room* was Baldwin's second book to appear in this country, and its gay theme was even more explicit. For years I would remember lines from both of these books, lines that shocked me with their erotic intensity. I liked the way Baldwin wrote about sex as a 'terrifying' desire. As time went by, I recognised just how different his was from the usual male view. There was something overwhelming in the scenarios he described, something that struck a chord inside me and that I would encounter only infrequently in personal relationships over the years.

Another book we all read in the Battersea circle was *A Star to Steer By*, the autobiography of Hugh Mulzac, the first Black man to command an American ship during World War Two. Mulzac also served as first officer on the ill-fated *S.S. Yarmouth* of Marcus Garvey's Black Star Line, and his was an uplifting story of struggle against the odds. I had first heard of Garvey when Max Roach recorded a piece of music dedicated to him, but his significance was minimised when he was dismissed as a charlatan by a *Downbeat* reviewer. *Downbeat*, described as the 'musicians' bible' was for many of us our only source of information about what was happening at the source of the music. Its conservatism meant that we imbibed reactionary attitudes along with the news, so it was eye-opening to read Mulzac and learn something of Garvey's vision and the Back-to-Africa movement.

Despite the theoretical positions taken by the Battersea circle, our 'membership' stayed almost exclusively white, and women remained in the background. We'd sup pints of Young's bitter along-side the lads but equality went only so far. We considered ourselves liberated at the time, though, because in contrast to the 'non-liberal' world outside here women were no longer sneered at for sleeping with whomever they chose.

Another Battersea figure was Steve Piper, a teacher who had once skippered a Grimsby trawler. He was a flamboyant character, who got himself banned from local pubs for his vulgar invective, but he had a fine record of activism on behalf of tenants' associations. The Communist Party was involved in the campaign against poor housing and he asked me to photograph the appalling conditions that still existed in some council and private dwellings in the area where we lived.

When it came to music, recordings of works by Shostakovich and Prokofiev and other European composers would be played in preference to folk-music and jazz. For all their enlightened and optimistic worldview, my socialist friends knew little about Black music. For me the two worlds were separate, the pubs and the beer providing a welcome refuge at times from the sophisticated and fast-moving 'foreign' world in which I had become embroiled. 'People's' music and the company of 'chippies' and housepainters ensured that my own roots were at hand whenever I needed them. The years of theoretical discussion, political action and gossip sowed the seeds for my later political awakening. Socialist ideas I first heard at The Falcon or sitting around a Battersea kitchen table would recur constantly through the years, even when I was more concerned with having a good time than with changing the world.

The last time I actually worked for an employer was when I came back from the States. His name was Alton Bowen and he was the first

Westindian to import beer and spirits from the Caribbean. His shop was decorated with huge colour enlargements of Jamaican beauty-spots and I photographed it for him so that he could show the exporters back home what he was doing. Alton was hospitable and I got into the habit of dropping by for the occasional lager-and-lime.

Caribbean Imports supplied clubs, restaurants and off-licences with Red Stripe lager, making its first appearance in Britain, and brands of rum that were hard to come by. It was common in the Caribbean community for people to buy drinks on a sale-or-return basis for 'blues' or houseparties, where entry fees were sometimes charged and a reasonable profit could be made on supplying food and drink. The demand for Caribbean products was enormous, and within months Alton was desperate for help. He asked me to come and work in reception. With little else to do, I agreed. The full-time photographic jobs on offer paid next to nothing, and nearly all involved doing darkroom work for somebody else. I'd had enough of that. So I learned to handle orders and invoices like a veteran of office practice. In the kitchen over the shop, Alton had a man brewing up strawberry syrup which he'd bottle and sell. Occasionally he'd invite me to try out various combinations of this sweetest of Caribbean concoctions, along with the lager-and-lime, and rum. We were nothing if not adventurous on Eversholt Street.

One morning I walked in to find him brandishing a small sample tube filled with a clear liquid. 'Listen, nuh, Miss Wilmer,' he ordered, 'try this for me.' I took a tentative sip and felt the shock as overproof rum surged through my veins. My eyes watered and I hastily passed back the sample. Alton hissed his teeth in impatience and called on George, the lugubrious handyman. He took a generous swig and mused thoughtfully. A decent pause ensued before he offered his verdict: 'Mmm, it not bad. Not bad at a-a-ll.' I began to view George in a new light. Years later I saw him, apparently unchanged, walk by as I stood on the *Time Out* picket-line. Twenty years of Wray and Nephews' 110° proof rum for breakfast had clearly done him no harm.

Eventually, Alton came up with someone to replace me, but not before I met a woman who would radically alter my life. Among the people who came into the shop were some who just wanted a few drinks for a party. One such customer was an energetic woman of my own age whom I'd seen at the Ronnie Scott Club. We greeted each other in some surprise and exchanged a few words. Who was that, I asked, after she left clutching a case of Long Life. 'Oh, that's Claude Tagoe's daughter,' said Alton. 'She sings.'

Another year would go by before I would get to know Stevie Tagoe and find how she hated her music being linked with her father's; (neither are their real names). I had to learn how to survive without the security of a regular wage and in a climate that was hostile towards the idea of independent women. There were pitfalls wherever you turned. A Ghanaian student named George came into the shop one day. We got talking and he asked for a date. We went out together a few times, ending up in one of the little Greek-run clubs in Essex Road where afterhours drinking and gambling flourished and interracial couples were welcome. George was a smooth-talking sophisticate with an eye for

93

the main chance. He suggested I carry my Rolleiflex and flashgun, 'just in case'. Inevitably someone wanted a picture taken and I picked up a few bob on the spot.

He found other clients for me, too. One of these had suggested I look at a room over his Kentish Town shop with a view to helping me set up a photographic business there. When I had turned up for another portrait session George had arranged, I'd discovered his 'friend' had something else on his mind. I had managed to avert this eventuality and added the experience to the 'Loss' account. The shop owner, however, was another matter, a physically unpleasant man with a red-lipped leer and a bottle of VP wine at the ready. He wore a greasy hat and ankle-length overcoat, and smelled as though he'd stepped out of a bottle of cough medicine. He was in such a state of trembling anticipation, that I barely escaped in one piece. I finally knew what was happening. George, who had shown hardly any interest in sex, was trying to pimp me. I was furious.

It took me a while to realise this, of course. I was used to sexual pressure by now but nothing so blatant. I was still quite naïve, but I was not exactly a pushover, neither was I financially desperate like other women who turn to prostitution. Why, then, should George have seen me as a potential candidate to supplement his student income? Like so many affected by racist society, I am sure that he, too, subscribed to the belief that white women who mixed with Black men had questionable morals.

Much more desperate at the time, however, was the fact that I had foolishly lent him my camera. In my anger I'd told him to take a runner when he phoned me again. Now I'd lost the essential tool of my trade. I determined to get it back by direct action. He lived with a landlady in Hendon, the opposite side of the city. Sunday morning seemed like a good time, so I got up early and crossed town by a series of buses and trains. I surprised him just as he was getting up. He stood there in pyjamas and overcoat, looking shifty. 'Give me back my camera, you bastard!' I shouted. Anxious that his landlady should witness no altercation, he swiftly demurred. I was back home with Rollei and satisfied smile in time to eat cornflakes and sausages with the last of the lodgers at breakfast. I still had his copy of Nat 'King' Cole's *After Midnight*; I felt I could hang on to it with justification.

As I moved more outside my own community, I began to realise that the photographer played an important role for people living away from their land of origin. I can't say whether we are respected any more than we are in the English community where, since the demise of the black focusing cloth and flashpowder, our status has rapidly diminished, but our skills are wanted more often. I did draw the line when someone asked me to photograph a man in his coffin – I was scared – but as my photographic technique improved, I found I need seldom be without work.

Many African students found it cheaper to marry in Britain rather than waiting until they returned home, where the cost of entertaining could be prohibitive for newly qualified graduates. Others had already gone through a form of marriage at home and wanted their union formalised in Britain or sanctified by the Christian church. I started a business doing weddings, christenings and parties for students and diplomats which went on for years alongside my more visible work for the press. I never formalised it or advertised, clients approached me constantly until I reached the point where I had enough contacts elsewhere to gracefully bow out of the 'commercial' arena.

Of the few photographers who worked in African circles, some were Africans and students themselves. One showed me the professional way to present wedding albums, and told me to always get a deposit from clients – traditionally the photographer was always the last to be paid. But I was popular partly because I was a woman: that, apparently, meant I would be more amenable to being kept waiting for hours at a wedding reception. This happened frequently, because there were many rituals at any African event of significance.

At most weddings the celebrants went through several changes of costume, a procedure for which clothes are traditionally provided by the groom and which is done to show that the bride is marrying into money. Each costume change had to be recorded, a time-consuming process, and white male photographers with other jobs to attend were seldom prepared to go along with this. The groomsmen would placate me with a constant supply of 'hot drinks' (spirits), somewhat unfairly, I thought, when other women seemed to be confined to sherry or minerals. By the time the happy pair were into their third change of dress, however, I would generally be feeling no pain. Bride and groom would open the floor (for dancing) and guests would move forward to 'spray' the couple, pressing paper money or coins on their foreheads where suction and sweat would help it to stay temporarily. It was at wedding parties like these that I first lost my English inhibitions about going on the dance-floor and forgot the traumatic rejection of schooldays. It is considered a mark of disrespect among Africans for a woman to be left without a dancing partner, and so I would frequently find myself on the floor, doing the highlife to the sounds of E.T. Mensah or Victor Olaiya, recorded on somebody's Grundig and relayed enthusiastically over the PA system, crackling atmospherics and all. Often, however, my progress on the dance-floor would be cut short by someone tugging my sleeve, asking for one more group picture. Struggling with flashgun and camera, I'd then be urged, seductively, to 'come and take rice' by one of the women who had stayed up the night before 'preparing chop'. Jollof rice was the usual fare provided for wedding celebrations, and occasionally there'd be little packages of *moyin-moyin*, fermented bean paste, which, eaten alone, I found peculiarly bland after the peppery rice. It could be quite overwhelming. My constant resolve to stay no longer than was necessary after the final photograph always broke down in the face of African hospitality and persuasion.

There were Town Hall dances, too, organised by political parties or student unions based on clan or educational allegiance. Such events were advertised long in advance and much anticipated by students, especially when leading highlife bands came over to play. At other times the entertainment was provided by African musicians living in London. There were Abraham and Akanni's Highlife Dandies and the African Messengers, originally led by my friend Bayo Martins, later by Nigerian saxophonist Peter King. Both bands featured the fluid trumpet of the diminutive Mike Falana, who was also active in several jazz groups of the period. Mike, a brilliant instrumentalist, was, sadly, to suffer a severe mental breakdown while still very young.

The atmosphere at these events contrasted strongly with the prevailing situation in white dance-halls such as the Lyceum. There African patrons were reticent, hugging the walls for security as they sipped their drink, often too shy to ask for a dance for fear of rejection. At the dances I was invited to photograph, the students shed some of their inhibitions in the safety of numbers. Many were anxious to have their presence recorded for their families back home, and I'd pick up dozens of orders for prints, as well as contacts for future commissions.

From time to time I would be invited to eat in African homes. A history of Western antipathy towards this food (or anything 'foreign') had created caution in the African kitchen, with the result that some women anxiously sought to provide the kind of food to which they felt I might be more accustomed. In most cases, though, African 'chop' was the order of the day. Hot pepper stews called 'soup', thickened with okra, *egusi* (melon seed) or *agbono*, another seed, accompanied the main starch component: *fufu*, yam, semolina or rice. I got used to the flavour of stockfish and meat cooked together, and discovered how some dishes were prepared. I learned how to eat *eba*, too, porridge made from grated, toasted cassava flour, being shown how to work it into a ball with the fingers before dipping into stew. To do this with slippery okra was a not inconsiderable achievement for someone reared on meat and two veg.

But although most African sojourners tried to maintain their own cuisine and continue links with regional or educational affiliation societies and unions, some found survival simpler if they played down their cultural background. Bitter experience of British indifference and hostility made some students almost apologetic for their 'African-ness'. 'My name is Richard' – he pronounced it 'Rish-ard' – said one of the Nigerians I met at the Marquee, all teeth and nervous smile. I didn't see why I shouldn't call him by the name he was given, so he was always *Rashied* to me, an insistence on my part that was doubtless doubly embarrassing to him, this alternative persona having been carefully created.

There was no way that I could grasp the significance of such self-effacement. I just knew that it made *me* feel uncomfortable. I liked to hear about the places people came from, about their families and why they did certain things. Take dancing, for example. Highlife music still predominated in the early 1960s, but the new *juju* style was gaining ground. Musicians such as I.K. Dairo always changed the mood of a party. A *juju* guitarist had only to play a few notes in the characteristically casual style of the music for people to break off from the upright, Western style of dancing that went with the vocal passages – 'boxing', some called it – and switch to an older, more expressive form. Women and men alike would move slowly down towards the floor, hips gently swaying to what the guitar was saying.

There was one record in particular that always brought a feeling of exhilaration to the room. 'Bɔh-bɔ, bo su-eh' people would sing along with Ghanaian highlife veteran E.T. Mensah, going down with an expressive bump on the final 'bɔh'. Roughly translated, the expression meant 'Hit it!' akin to the musical 'Do that thing!' used in Afro-America.

Just as in some other such phrases linking musical expressiveness and good times, it had overtones of sexual pleasure as well. It was the first time I had noticed the sense of elation and collective strength that comes from identifying with something of one's own. It was as if a spirit of renewal had passed through the room. People seemed to relate differently to each other—and to me.

'Oh, please,' I was told, 'it is our African thing!' as the dancers got down and celebrated *themselves*. Well, I could see that for myself, but it was precisely because of such bashfulness on the part of the students, a product of the circumspection necessary then for survival, that I learned relatively little of the specifics of that 'African thing' until I was considerably older. It was an omission that was especially poignant for me as far as music was concerned. I enjoyed dancing the highlife, and knew the names of the prominent musicians, but with jazz always uppermost in my mind, the music seemed relatively lightweight. I had yet to realise the pointlessness of making comparisons.

At one dance, organised by what was then the largest and most powerful Nigerian political party, the NPC (Northern Peoples' Congress), I met a group of Hausa and Fulani students from the Northern Region, some of whom would become controversial political figures. One of these was Umaru Dikko, eventually brother-in-law and 'third ear' of President Shagari, who was ousted in the 1983 coup. The subsequent attempt to kidnap Dikko in London and return him to Lagos to face corruption charges created an Anglo-Nigerian sensation.

The Northerners were all Moslems, most of whom did not drink alcohol. At their parties, however, there were always plenty of spirits for the guests. Embassy officials could buy drinks at rock-bottom prices and I frequently left clutching a huge bottle of duty-free gin 'for Mummy'. They often dressed in a long flowing robe known as *babban-riga*, generally white, with sumptuous embroidery down the front panel, and wore hats made from fur or a multi-coloured *malfa*, hand-woven from cotton. I met one or two women from the North at these events but, unlike the other African parties I attended, they were predominantly male affairs. Some of the men had English girlfriends with whom I became friendly. Most of them worked as secretaries or teachers and were on the quiet and refined side, in contrast to the widely-held belief that only women 'of a certain type' had anything to do with Africans.

One day I was asked to bring my camera to an NPC reception at the Mayfair Hotel. The Premier of Northern Nigeria and leader of the NPC, a man said to be the most powerful person in Nigeria, was visiting. As a direct descendent of Shehu Usman dan Fodio, the religious reformer who restored Islam to Northern Nigeria at the beginning of the nineteenth century, Alhaji Sir Ahmadu Bello, the Sardauna of Sokoto, was regared as a semi-religious figure in some quarters. Before him men like Dikko and other feudal princes engaged in law studies bowed low after striking their chest with clenched fist in a gesture of respect. The elders are blessed, they said, thus may their blessing come also to you.

I knew it was important that I photograph each individual greeting, so I pressed forward, professionally, between the long white robes. Immediately an Igbo photographer working by my side gave me a nudge. 'You mustn't get too near him, you know.' I had forgotten the Sardauna's holy stature for a moment and felt uncomfortable at the oversight.

There was another thing, too. Although we might dance together at parties and eat from the same pot, I was, after all, a woman among the most feudal of men. The Northerners, although friendly, kept their distance in a way that was quite unusual among the Africans I met. As long as I moved in their circle, I tried to maintain a degree of aloofness as well.

Umaru Dikko was the least flamboyant of feudal lords imaginable, always to be found in a corner at parties. He asked me to cover his wedding, yet the only thing I can remember about the occasion is that he had hired another photographer, too. At first I was a little piqued at what I interpreted as his lack of faith in me, but the other photographer turned out to be an exceptionally useful person to know. Jim Daubney was a middle-aged Londoner who had learnt his photography in the RAF during the war. From time to time I would hang out in his darkroom while he treated me to a stream-of-consciousness commentary on the whys and wherefores of earning a living with the camera. I learned more from him in those impromptu darkroom sessions than I had done in a year at the Regent Street Poly.

There was another reason why I was popular with African students. As a woman I might provide temporary alleviation from loneliness. In the years to come I would meet scores of African students, women as well as men, and with few exceptions the story was always the same. The wealthier ones were able to keep loneliness at bay to an extent by moving in the elevated circles of the diplomatic élite, but for practically every 'been-to', whatever their status, there had been a period of sadness and sheer human need.

Britain, for most students, was a foreign and hostile society, where saying 'Good morning' to a neighbour, so one student told me, appeared to constitute some kind of crime. The need to know colloquial English in order to join in casual conversation ensured many Africans stayed 'outsiders' throughout their stay. The traditional British reserve combined with ignorance and racist attitudes to create a barrier between most visitors and any hope of a normal existence. Anyone who looked a likely companion assumed some importance. It was a simple matter for any student I met at a dance to invite me to visit his bedsitter to 'take me some picture'. He could then offer drink and some home-cooked 'chop' and try to begin a relationship.

Nothing conveys the feeling of student misery to me more than the smell of palmoil and *egusi* soup mingled with paraffin. Most African students were only able to find rooms in shabby houses where the rooms were cramped, draughty and hard to heat. In wintertime, every chink and crack was stuffed with newspaper. Cooking and heater fumes blended and lingered, hence that unforgettable smell.

It was common for those landlords who did let to Africans to maintain that their tenants were indifferent to the dinginess of their surroundings. But the depressing conditions that many students suffered often forced them to spend their time in the well-lit and heated public libraries in preference to damp rooms for which they were generally expected to pay exorbitant rents well above the going rate. Bedsitters were used more for bed than for sitting.

For private students, unsupported by government grants, the situation was even more intolerable. Many had arrived with a hopelessly outdated idea of the cost of living in Britain. They were forced to take day-jobs to maintain themselves, leaving only the night for study. Poorly paid manual work was often all that was available, and the combination of economic necessity and mental and physical exhaustion might result in a relatively short course having to be stretched out over several years. With constant pressure from home to complete their studies and return to support dependants in the extended family, it was small wonder that students sometimes suffered breakdowns. Some, unable to live up to family expectations, never went back.

When it came to companionship, the numbers of male students far outweighed those of women from a similar cultural background. African women living in Britain were often already married or committed to a boyfriend at home. For men, the chance of meeting local women was restricted by lack of time, money, opportunity and, above all, by racial hostility. Such friendships were not entirely unknown – 'Without some of the English girls, some of us would have gone mad,' said Joshua, a Nigerian who studied at art college with my schoolfriend Liz – but the slanderous 'animal' reputation of the Black male preceded him like a plague, making it virtually impossible for the unprepossessing student to greet a white woman without arousing in her fear for her safety. It was not uncommon for a lonely African man to cross London for a night at a ballroom such as the Lyceum and go home without having managed a single dance, too shy to attempt bridging that gap between reputation and reality. It was hard for someone in such a position to form any kind of relationship, and by merely being 'on the scene' I found myself under enormous pressure.

Not all students lived in dismal conditions, of course. Some were married and had council accommodation, others lived in well-appointed private rooms, neat and warm. Some were lucky to lodge with thoughtful white landladies, whose kindness would be acknowledged over the years whenever party-time came around. On such occasions, sensible, white-haired figures dressed in Crimplene or twin-set and pearls were often to be seen mingling with young African celebrants and dealing expertly with plates of joloff rice and a glass of Martini. But such women were rare.

In the case of couples with children, the restrictions of study and housing forced a particularly cruel form of deprivation. Children were sent either to relatives in their parents' homeland, in accordance with the tradition whereby a child has not one but several 'mothers'. Or they might be fostered out, often to unlicensed families living in Essex or Kent, counties with a tradition of fostering West African children. From time to time I might be asked to accompany a parent on an infrequent visit to the foster-home, to take pictures recording a birthday or similar occasion. Some mothers and fathers did not see their children for weeks on end, but what was a lonely and solitary life for them could be equally disturbing for the children. Cultural differences and hearsay led to suspicion on the part of isolated parents, who might find themselves discouraged from seeing their own children because of the disruption caused by such visits. Children, in turn, grew attached to their foster-parents, a mutual closeness that could lead to further misunderstandings when natural parents sought to reclaim their offspring.

Few of the male students I got to know had the money to go out for the evening, to the pictures or to dinner, part of the 'acceptable' process of wooing in middle-class English society. Westindians and Africans didn't eat out as a rule – the working class didn't, anyway. As the 1960s wore on, though, women began to expect dinner as part of the deal – whatever the deal was, and *that* could be ambiguous. So, for students and lowpaid Black workers alike, an evening out was not only in many cases an economic hardship, it was culturally problematic, too. It wasn't just for immediate sexual advantage that invitations to visit a man at home were more common than trips to the cinema or restaurant. I would sometimes invite one of the students home for a meal and my mother would make him welcome. But not everyone was as friendly towards Black men as she had become. One woman said to me, sarcastically, 'Have you noticed that pretty girls don't go out with coloured men?' something that echoed the oft-repeated fallacy that only the dregs in white society would associate with them.

It was a self-oppressive idea that had been used on occasion as an excuse for treating women badly, even for divorcing a white wife on returning home, it being claimed she wasn't 'good enough' for a qualified professional. I knew all this was rubbish and vicious propaganda, but it had its effect on me. Along with the sneers of the music scene, I occasionally felt uncomfortable because of my African associations. And I began to wonder whether I was doing the right thing by spending so much time outside my own community.

On the credit side, however, was the experience of being treated like a *woman* rather than a girl, which had been my lamentable experience hitherto with the 'kind of man you might marry'. Most Africans seemed to have a definite place for women in the scheme of things, in contrast to English society where you could just as easily be overlooked. Against the hostility and disapproval had to be posed a new way of seeing that was to challenge just about everything with which I'd grown up. Other whites have the same experience: once you have been around people who encourage you to see the world 'through Black eyes', you can't go back again – ever.

At a Christmas dance I got talking to the bandleader, a shortish, balding Nigerian with a slight 'Oxford' accent who played the trumpet. Adam Fiberesima was studying at Trinity College of Music at the same time as Fela Ransome-Kuti and had written a number of orchestral works. Dag's Skyrockets was the name of the band he put together for occasional dances (his Ijaw name was Dagodo), but he was not a great lover of highlife, the West African popular music, which he said was not indigenous to Africa. He was more interested in writing extended compositions based on the music and beliefs of ritual society. He would go on to make a name for himself as one of Africa's prominent concert music composers. Through him I met and interviewed others respected in that field, Sammy Akpabot and Akin Euba.

Adam lived in a smart house in Earls Court, which contrasted noticeably with other student accommodation. He had been in England since 1953 and was a dab-hand at dealing with the English — especially middle-class mothers. Every Christmas he paid a regular visit to one of his former girlfriends who lived with her mother, an event which had achieved ritual status. Mother was known only as 'Madam', spoken in clipped 'Knightsbridge' tones.

Going to 'take tea with Mum' was often a prerequisite for the sanctioning of interracial friendships. Men like Adam moved easily into their 'afternoon visitor' role, donning blazer and striped college tie and an expression of interested acquiescence. But countless others must have been made to sweat over the necessary ritual, balancing cups of tea on knees unaccustomed to the task and making polite conversation while sneaking glances at their object of affection — and the clock.

Adam introduced me to Africa Unity House, the student centre in Earls Court founded by Ghana's President Nkrumah, and one of the few places in London where Africans could eat pepper soup, yam, *eba* and rice. On our way there one day we ran into the eminent Yoruba academic Professor Fela Sowande, who during the war years had been organist and choirmaster in a West London church and before that earned a living arranging for dance bands and gigging around London as a pianist. He was now highly respected on several counts, as a composer who had pioneered the use of African elements in orchestral works, a superb instrumentalist (and philosopher), and Adam was flattered when he agreed to come to the BBC's Maida Vale studios, where a new work of his was being recorded. Such establishment recognition for African orchestral writing was a considerable accolade and, as a consequence, worthy of Sowande's support; and yet where I was concerned, I failed to be sufficiently impressed or to take Adam as seriously as his achievements warranted.

I remember one conversation in particular. Adam answered one of my questions by suggesting the answer lay in 'the realms of the metaphysical'. His response struck me as faintly ludicrous, my first reaction being that he was using the word because it sounded impressive. It was easy for me to make this assumption, for he could be rather pompous at times, and yet the truth of the matter was that I had absolutely no idea what 'metaphysical' actually meant. Despite everything I had learned from Black people since I first started listening to music, I was still so brainwashed by racist assumptions that it was 'common sense' to conclude that few Africans could possibly know the meaning of such a word!

In the summer of 1962 John Batcheldor and I went to France with Paul from the Battersea circle and the French woman to whom he was married. Marie-France had relatives in Le Mans and we stayed there and in a nearby small village with her grandmother. Our last night was spent with the communist mayor and his comrades, who presented us with a medicine bottle of *eau-de-vie*, 'to drink on the train'.

In Paris we trailed around Montmartre, visiting historical landmarks and trying to re-create for ourselves something of what it must have been like in the Impressionists' heyday. At the Musée de Vieux Montmartre we met the curator, Paul Yaki, who wore the ribbon of the Légion d'Honneur and had been an intimate of Toulouse-Lautrec and Utrillo. We imagined ourselves back in the days of the

Moulin Rouge as we basked in his reflected glory.

On the Left Bank Paul sat at Les Deux Magots café, pretending to be an Existentialist and hoping for a glimpse of de Beauvoir and Sartre, who lived nearby. I dragged John off for a look at the Hotel La Louisiane, where Billie Holiday, Lester Young and Charlie Parker had stayed and where Bud Powell lived with his family during his exile. For English jazz fans, Paris meant an opportunity to hear American musicians in relatively intimate surroundings and I was raring to go. I renewed my acquaintance with Bill and Lily Coleman and they took us all to Pigalle to hear two of the city's many Afro-American expatriates. John and I visited Versailles with the Colemans; then Juanita, my replacement in the job at Caribbean Imports, came over for a few days. We all went to see Memphis Slim, who was playing at Les Trois Mailletz. Slim did his usual thing of saying there was somebody 'special' he'd like to announce in the audience. He'd done this before when I was there and I thought, smugly, it was happening again. I was preening myself a little when he announced 'the lovely — Juanita!' Seldom have I seen anyone so delighted. I think it made the trip for her. From then on, she was known as 'the lovely — Juanita' at all times.

Something else memorable happened that night at Les Trois Mailletz. Slim was joined on the stage by a slight, goatee-bearded American saxophonist who went on to play the *shit* out of the blues. There was a very clear division between blues and jazz players in those days, partially the creation of outside forces; pigeonholing operates as a form of control. Sonny Criss was a musician from Memphis, Slim's home town. For years, however, he had lived on the West Coast, an area then renowned for its 'cool' music which seemed to be the antithesis of the blues tradition. In his checkered sports jacket and well-cut flannels, he didn't even *look* like a bluesman.

The following day, John and I met him for an interview. He told us his mother was responsible for his 'good taste', having raised him on Memphis Slim records. It was common at this time for some 'schooled' musicians to hold the blues in low esteem. The blues form was used, of course, but for many people the music when wearing its traditional clothes spoke of bad times better forgotten. The Afro-American mood of the period was onward and upward, the pursuit of democratic rights being the major goal. Sonny Criss was a traditionalist as well as a modernist, a positive combination that placed him ahead of his time. 'In order to be a worthwhile jazzman, if you can't play the blues you can forget it,' he told us. 'The blues *is* jazz, believe me. All the rest is just embellishments, decoration.'

Just a handful of years later, roots would become a real source of artistic vitality and determination in every aspect of Afro-American culture, but the soul-jazz movement that emphasised this was only just beginning. I was getting to know the music quite well by now and had reached the point where the familiar cadences and emotions of the blues could be reassuring. Sonny's words were a comfort.

He told us something else. Memphis Slim, he said, found it hard to believe Sonny was still in his thirties because of his ideas and the way he expressed himself. For the saxophonist, interchange between age groups was an essential for progress. All the really great musicians, he said, listened to younger players, while he himself had always enjoyed being with older people. 'You have to talk to those who have had the experience, because if you discuss things with the people of your own age, you can never draw on the source of things.'

I was, I think, beginning to realise this, too. I was still young, naïve and enthusiastic, but I was surrounded by older people whom I saw as society's achievers. To me there was nothing strange about 'hanging out' with my mother's generation; they were, after all, the people who were making things happen and I wanted to move in their circle. The Swinging Sixties and the youth cult had yet to explode and shake up the established order of things.

My work put me in a unique position. As I began to interview more people, most, but not all of them, musicians, so I began to move away from the ideas my contemporaries held. At first these interviews were straightforward historical affairs, limited to 'when did you play what and with whom?' The interviewee might take the question somewhere else, but shyness and inexperience made me hold back from expressing any opinion of my own. When I wrote up the conversation, it invariably reflected the prevailing establishment view of the music.

Doing interviews was part of a continuing process of learning. As I began to question existing ideas I was able to ask things for which I, rather than 'the reader', wanted an answer. Interviewing was like taking a degree in life, and using a tape-recorder emphasised the element of study. To this day I can remember things said to me twenty years ago and the way they sounded when they were said. Without exception, though, the people I interviewed were older than me. Small wonder that I began to drift away from my peers.

9
A Brand New Bag

Flamingo was another Black magazine that arose from the ashes of *Tropic*. It had offices at Ludgate Circus in the heart of the newspaper capital, and featured an advice page headed with the receptionist's photograph. Both magazines relied on City financing and had international ambitions, but *Flamingo*, with a conventional white English publisher who dressed in a three-piece pinstripe, was in a better position to realise its expectations. Entrepreneurial whites were becoming aware of untapped Black consumer potential and a white face was more acceptable when financial backing was being sought. For over four years the magazine flourished, expanding into several editions at one stage.

Edward Scobie was Editor-in-Chief for a while, and he brought in another *Tropic* writer as editor, the Ghanaian Ellis Komey, one of whose most memorable contributions was his hilarious 'Look at the English', as seen by an African tourist – an anthropological journey around 'darkest England' written up in the language of the Victorian explorer. Wearing traditional dress, he and his companion were shown photographing astonished pastoral natives encountered in a 'desolate' Yorkshire village.

Scobie asked me to write for the new publication and I produced illustrated articles about Langston Hughes and my composer friend Adam Fiberesima. In the same issue as the latter piece appeared, the magazine printed a long piece on Rastafari. The University College of the West Indies had recently undertaken a historic study of the movement. Many Diasporean Africans had long sought redemption and deliverance by a return to the ancestral continent. The UCWI team had gone on a mission to Ethiopia and other states to examine the feasibility of resettlement for Afro-Caribbeans and the report of their historic mission had now been published. The popular belief that the religion's followers were 'disturbed' was already being rebutted as a result of this evaluation.

Twenty years before Dreads became a familiar sight outside Jamaica, I encountered a man whose appearance struck a chord of recognition. He stood outside the elegant Piccadilly Hotel, of all places, dressed in a gabardine raincoat tied with a thong. His locksed hair hung down his back. He wore sandals, no socks, despite the cold weather, and carried a long wooden stave. It is impossible to say if he were a Rastaman, but after reading this account, I recognised the significance of what I had seen.

The historical articles, by Scobie and others, continued. The history of Pan-Africanism was explored, the contributions of DuBois, Kenyatta and Edward Wilmot Blyden analysed, and the fabled Aesop turned out to have been an African slave. There were short stories and fashion, recipes and career features: I wrote one about becoming a dietician. As the circulation grew, two other editors were added, Ken Campbell, a Jamaican, and John Harold, a British veteran of West African publishing. John liked my work and although he let me do a series on Caribbean musicians in Britain, encouraged me to cover subjects outside music.

The topics discussed became more controversial. Black participation in trade unions was evaluated, and an investigation conducted into the exorbitant premiums settlers had to shell out for Motor Insurance, a shameful anomaly. As a regular readership built up in Africa, though, more sensational pieces appeared. 'Do Nigerian Men Make Good Lovers?' asked *Flamingo's* own African Correspondent. And, on the exploitation of African boxers overseas, 'Are our Fighters Used as Punchbags?' To the question 'Should Women Be Haremed?' the unequivocal response was 'No'. The letters' column was a forum for provocative debate, and in many ways the magazine was way ahead of anything 'popular' published in Britain. 'Beauty and the Beast', for example, was an illustrated blow-by-blow (literally) account of how to handle unwelcome advances. Twenty years before Western women encouraged each other to fight back, it legitimised self-defence for women.

Now that photography had emerged to take its place in the arts, I noted that other photographers took themselves seriously as artists. I still wanted to do something along the lines pioneered by Ida Kar. *Amateur Photographer* had published a piece of mine about jazz photography and I thought I might write about some of the sculptors whose work I admired. I wrote to several of the artists who had exhibited at Battersea Park, and to my great surprise Barbara Hepworth agreed to my going to see her at her studio in St Ives. It was quite an honour for she was known to be something of a recluse.

John and I took off for Cornwall on his blue Norton 650SS, one of the great British motor-cycles, which fairly ate up the miles. We arrived at Stonehenge soon after sunrise, and climbed over the picket fence, unheeded, to take pictures of each other amid the ancient stones. Albert McCarthy, who edited *Jazz Monthly*, lived in Cornwall, and we stayed at his home overnight. When I phoned the sculptor, she said she could 'give me half an hour', very *grande-dame*.

Half an hour was hardly time to even take in the extent of her collection, many of which stood, surrounded by pampas grass in the garden. They seemed to melt into the rugged landscape, each stone speaking with eloquence. We were awed at what was on view and could see why the sculptor was inspired by her surroundings. She stood, hand resting casually on one piece or another, caressing them as if they were her children — which they were — and told us how she would sometimes go out in the full moon to look at a piece by its light. She said how pleased she was to find marks showing people had touched her sculptures, 'handling improves them', and relented over the allotted time. Over tea and biscuits we asked a few questions. Being on unfamiliar ground, I was more tentative than when talking to musicians. She told us her main inspiration came from seeing people in relation to the landscape, individual forms taking on more significance there than in the city. She had brought up four children, but had still managed to work at her art every day, and before becoming restless to get back to the studio, agreed that women, whoever they were, still had to 'struggle against prejudice'.

I sent her a selection of prints, and she phoned me from Cornwall one evening. Long-distance calls were an occasion then, but I was even more surprised when she said that she wanted to buy some of my pictures. When her letter of confirmation arrived, she had ordered not a handful but a couple of hundred – and sent a cheque. She told me that my photographs were some of the best she had seen. I was elated for ages, both by her response and the size of the cheque.

Anthony Caro was less encouraging. I took shots of his children and he said he felt I was better at people than sculpture. But he went on to commission some family portraits.

Siegfried Charoux was another of my subjects, a Royal Academician, less abstract than the others. He specialised in huge concrete figures, making ironic comments on society through works such as *The Judge*, a gaping hole in place of a heart, one piece of many to be seen at various municipal sites. He was a huge, shambling man, getting elderly, with billowing white hair and a floppy velvet bow tie. I photographed him standing beside a towering concrete fisherman, and with another sculpture, of his beloved violinist, in the garden of his Hampstead Garden Suburb house. His wife Margaretha, calling him Charoux, fussed lovingly around him and his works. Both of them liked my pictures, and I was invited back on subsequent occasions. I loved the atmosphere of their beautiful, rambling house, the walls covered with paintings and air filled with conversation about art and philosophy that went over my head. They were Austrian, with the intellectual aura of a bygone age, and served the coffee and cakes that made Vienna famous. Both of them treated me as though I, too, was an artist, and after the sculptor's death Margaretha would call on me to take new pictures of his work for her Christmas cards, 'keeping up Charoux's tradition'.

I also met Ronald Moody, the great Jamaican sculptor, who died in 1984 scandalously neglected by the establishment. He, too, looked like a man surrounded by his children, his Fulham studio filled with spectacular figures carved from stone and from wood. This time, our interview was more successful, and *Flamingo* published it over three pages.

And then I got to know another photographer named Roland Miller. His ideas about photography were a bit artsy-fartsy and he didn't have much equipment or a proper darkroom, but he sought my advice and encouragement and I liked to think that I helped just a little. It made a change for roles to be reversed in this way. Roland had been born just ten days after me and this seemed a handy explanation for our unusual affinity. He came from Guyana and shared a flat with two women, one of whom, a Frenchwoman named Jackie, took an instant dislike to me. I didn't realise at first that they were married; Roland liked to surround himself with an air of mystery. He was something of a sophisticate, too, much given to the appraisal of the finer things in life. We went out for an evening in Soho and he drew me into a doorway. 'I've got a little something,' he said with a mysterious smile, and produced from his haversack a small bottle of brandy and two exquisite porcelain cups. In a shabby goods-entrance on Lexington Street, we sipped the finest of cognac from this delicate ware while hookers and punters strolled by, doing their Soho thing.

It was never quite clear what our relationship was. There was hardly any sex in it, and Roland who was slim and sensitive, with impossibly long-lashed eyes, decided to tell me one day that he thought he might be in love with his dentist, a man. He still insisted on referring to Jackie as 'a friend', but it was clear that he and I were very much drawn to each other and becoming mutually dependent to a degree. Gradually I became part of their circle, a multi-racial network of ravers and hipsters intent on having a good time. Saturday nights there were generally parties. They were sophisticated affairs given by liberal publishers and the like who enjoyed having a few Black faces along, and sometimes we went to 'blues' (Westindian houseparties) in the Grove. I got into the habit of staying overnight at their flat. Next morning we'd go to The Coleherne in Earls Court, now better known as a male 'leather' pub, but for a brief period on Sundays the rhythmic hub of the new breed of libertarian swingers who cut boldly across barriers of class, race and sexual orientation. Trinidadian Russ Henderson played piano there accompanied by drummer Stirling Betancourt and bassist Clyde Davis. The rest was open house; anyone who could play was welcome. The hard core of percussionists trundling their conga drums into the back room had to make sure to arrive early because it rapidly became impossible to push through the crowd. The musicians who jammed occasionally included respected names such as saxophonist Joe Harriott, trumpeter Shake Keane, and trombonist Eric Allandale, later with the Foundations, but at this time leading his own Trad band the Jazz Knights, an unusual choice of situation for a Black player.

As the tempo hotted up, the audience would seize bottles and play on them with openers, keys or whatever came to hand. The crowd was dominated by the legendary George, a tall man who always wore a hat and a red carnation in his buttonhole and before whom all gave way in respect. Dancing was not permitted but when the band broke into the home-stretch with their polyrhythmic version of 'Peanut Vendor', wild horses could not have kept those people still.

Even in the early 1960s, The Coleherne was a predominantly gay pub, its main bars filled with leather menace. A good deal of beer was drunk in those days and although a lot of sexual hustling went on, it never got really oppressive in the back room where a number of lesbians and gay men would make their way. It was a good place for people to socialise who were unsure of how to define their sexuality, for an 'anything goes' attitude was part of The Coleherne's attraction.

Roland and I discussed our ambivalent sexuality. I told him I was often attracted to women but didn't know how to go about things. He told me about 'butch' and 'bitch' — male terms; lesbians, I learned later, talked about 'butch' and 'femme' — the role-playing that was then *de rigueur* in gay and lesbian circles. I had experimented a couple of times, as many women had, but now 'lesbian' seemed like a label, and labels had serious implications. Everything I had read or seen about homosexuality — the Dirk Bogarde film *Victim*, books like *The Well of Loneliness* and *Against the Law*, journalist Peter Wildeblood's story of his trial and imprisonment — was negative. A picture was painted of a dreadful existence doomed to sadness and failure, and I didn't want any of that. It was common knowledge that some of the crowd occasionally indulged in 'sessions' and troilism, but I knew, without really articulating it, that in me the desire went much deeper than 'swinging'. Despite the dubious and, really, horrific predictions, I was wondering whether I wanted to *be* a lesbian myself.

There was no doubt about it, women definitely disturbed me. The Great Unrequited Love of my Youth was a woman, and she stayed on my mind for years. It had happened at school, at the cinema, too. French actress Odile Versois vied with James Dean on the screen for the honour of giving me my first post-pubertal sexual thrill; I came home feeling shaky, unable to explain what was 'wrong' with me. There was Susan Hayward in *I Want to Live* – God, I loved that film, for her. And when Althea Gibson won Wimbledon in 1957 and her opponent kissed her – on the cheek, it's true, but passionately, so it seemed to me – I'd experienced an instant *frisson*. No doubt I had picked up on general comments concerning the lifestyle of some women tennis players. There was Connie, too, my neighbour and friend from the Girl Guides, who kissed me one night before climbing over the fence and I went out and bought her the Everlys' 'All I Have to Do is Dream' in the morning. Memories were made of this, but it was not until three years after I'd left school that I ran into one of my classmates and found myself exploring the-love-that-dare-not-speak-its-name. Occasionally I'd lunge at hapless women with an approach singularly devoid of charm, until one day a friend of Roland's took me up on the challenge. But no one wanted to admit that it was anything more than part of the generalised thrill-seeking that characterised the culture of the times.

One evening we all dropped by to see Lou, one of their lesbian friends, and found her relaxing, fully dressed, on the bed with her girlfriend. I experienced instant flashback to that cellar in Paris, where women sat with their arms around each other, and I began to feel incredibly nervous. I could hardly look Lou in the eye, but I was excited and began to wonder how I would find someone who felt the same way.

On another occasion I was backstage at the Marquee when I met 'Tina', a singing star from the days of the dance bands. I had gone there with an American musician, but she brushed him aside with her eyes and turned her attention fully on me. Somewhat unsettled by her intensity, I said to someone, '*She*'s a peculiar woman.' 'Oh, Tina,' replied the man-in-the-know, 'she's been a lezzie for years.' I wanted to kick myself. I had failed to pick up on the vibes. The chance was there to talk to the 'real thing' and I'd let it pass me by.

Before I was able to make any headway towards resolving my fantasies about women, a more common disaster struck. I found I was pregnant. I had met an Angolan named João at a dance, a compact, powerful man with a commanding manner and unbelievably erotic eyes. I don't know whether there has ever been a folk-belief about 'getting a baby' from a look like that, but I'd be willing to believe that there might be. João was a Freedom Fighter, with the scars on his body to prove it, and he was in Europe to raise funds for the protracted guerrilla war against the Portuguese. His day consisted of a lengthy round of interviews, many of which would prove fruitless. I would go to his hotel in the evening.

There we would dine with a couple of newly arrived Nigerian diplomats, cod and chips and steamed marmalade pudding featuring prominently. João was always even-tempered, concerned to see that the Nigerians felt at home in the big city. I was surprised that someone so obviously fiery could stay calm in the face of the rejection he continually experienced as he went around seeking support.

He had been in Britain for some weeks when I realised what had happened. I panicked. There was no legal abortion then, and I knew that I did not want a baby. Horror stories abounded of soap and saline injections, and knitting-needle deaths. I knew one woman who had haemorrhaged, lying on the kitchen-floor, from a back-street abortion, and I was, frankly, terrified. I didn't know who I could safely tell, either, and there was no way I wanted my mother to know. A friend sent me to a herbalist at the Elephant and Castle for pennyroyal pills, a traditional remedy for the unwanted condition. I walked up and down for ages before gathering the nerve to go in. I steeled myself and the man in the white coat gave me a knowing look as he handed over the packet. The pills didn't work, neither did João's repeated calls on a friend who 'knew a doctor'. He was not one of those men who say 'I want you to have a baby for me'; he knew I was desperate, but there was little he could do. Both of us were ignorant and channels of communication were limited. He was personally penniless and his political schedule required him to move on to Paris.

In the end I asked Roland and Jackie. They knew someone who had had an abortion and she put me in touch with a gynaecologist who worked outside the law. I made an appointment to see him and João left, thrusting some money into my hand and wishing me well. The gynaecologist was a Hungarian who worked assisted by his wife. He was a slow-speaking man who lived in a luxurious house in Ealing, ran two sports cars, and had the coldest eyes I had ever seen. He told me, laconically, that the price had gone up, but agreed to do the operation 'in this case', for the fee I'd been quoted. It was just as well because even with João's contribution, I could barely scrape together the £60 that he wanted. He told me to make sure that a car was waiting around the corner when I left. 'No taxis,' he stipulated.

I racked my brains to think of someone who had a car. Few young people drove in those days, and the only likely candidate, an occasional lover, turned me down flat. John drove an old van but to ask him seemed out of the question. We had stopped seeing each other some time ago and he wanted nothing more to do with me, I knew. In the end, however, I approached him in desperation. I rang him at work and could imagine him puffing relentlessly on his pipe as he barked through clenched teeth. He had wanted us to 'go steady' and his pride had been hurt by this upstart of a middle-class woman who wanted to 'swing' through the world of showbusiness and thought herself too good for his kind. But when I explained the gravity of the situation, he immediately agreed he would help.

I told my mother I was spending the weekend at Jackie and Roland's and made my way over to Ealing, shaking with fear. The operation went smoothly and I left the house feeling woozy under the anaesthetic. John had taken time off work and was waiting, and I passed out before we got back to Fulham. Roland was working at a day-job but he came home in the afternoon to see I was safe. I lay in bed all weekend, going in and out of a haze, while Jackie fed me with soup. Then I went home as if nothing had happened. What would have been the situation if I had not had friends 'in the know' is something I dread to think. The music world abounded with horror stories of unwanted pregnancy and abortion and men who went around boasting about 'my baby in Sweden', or 'my Paris baby'. It was all so utterly sordid and unsafe and many women refused to have anything at all to do with it.

Late in October 1963 I was sitting in Lyons Coventry Street Corner House interviewing the Nigerian trumpeter Mike Falana, when one of my brother's schoolfriends walked in. His name was Michael Aldred and I had first met him when he was in short trousers. He'd been interviewing Sarah Vaughan for his school magazine, and later when Ray Charles came to Britain we'd hung out together. We had managed to get friendly with the Raelettes and their lead-singer Margie Hendrix, whose scorching responses to Ray on things like 'Tell the Truth' and 'Night Time is the Right Time' literally took our breath away. We had sat in the orchestra pit together and dug into the music, taking our cue from Margie. She was unforgettable, a sound of the times.

Now Michael was with two other people, a dreamy young woman with shoulder-length hair, and one about my own age with laughing eyes and an animated manner. She wore a pink denim suit, something I had never seen before, and she wore it with style. 'Hello,' he said casually. 'We've just been for an interview. We're all going to be in a new TV music programme.' The show in question was *Ready Steady Go!*, which was to be the greatest teenage trendsetter in history and would represent an entire era of fashion and ideas. It gave the youth of the nation their first chance to experience such dramatic performers as James Brown and Jerry Lee Lewis right in their living-rooms. The younger woman was Cathy McGowan, who would become a household name, presenting the show with Michael and Keith Fordyce. The other was Vicki Wickham, who moved from floor-manager to producer before going into artist management in America where she shaped the careers of Labelle and Nona Hendryx. Because of the emphasis now being given to the original models followed by the Beat groups, Black entertainers such as Betty Everett, John Lee Hooker and Inez and Charlie Foxx were now being regularly seen in most homes.

Not long after the programme started, I began to go along to take photographs at the Friday afternoon rehearsals before the live televising. For the first time I experienced no prejudice on phoning the Press Office. Access was a matter of first come, first served, and although I was generally the only woman there with a camera, most of the other photographers were quite friendly. The music papers wanted pictures of the new wave of British performers and I regularly shot stills of up-and-coming artists such as the Hollies, the Rolling Stones and Elkie Brooks whose brother played drums with Billy J. Kramer.

The British Beat boom was under way and few of us who worked in the music business would remain unaffected by it. It helped thrust Black music into the spotlight for the first time in a big way and caused purists like myself to revise our ideas about what was musically significant. *Jazz News* caught on to the trend and became *Jazz Beat* overnight. And before I knew where I was, I was going along on an interview to shoot pictures of the Beatles backstage during their Christmas show. Everything went smoothly until someone said something about 'I Wanna Be Your Man'. 'Oh,' I perked up, eager to show off my blues knowledge, 'didn't Bo Diddley write that?' Paul McCartney gave me a smile behind which lurked a withering glance. 'Well, no, actually. We did.' I decided to keep quiet after that.

Increasingly I began to hang out at the Swing Shop. Specialist record outlets have always presented a daunting prospect for the casual visitor, for cliques form easily and the place where Bert Bradfield first put me on the right track was no exception. Earnest-looking men would stand around for hours on end muttering about 'alternate takes' in a way that was bound to exclude anyone who might have foolishly imagined they stocked Mantovani or the Swinging Blue Jeans. The Swing Shop stood strictly for jazz, and when Bert left for France, I only got into the new clique by chance, walking in to ask for two volumes of trumpeter Fats Navarro on Blue Note. Such good taste commanded respect even if I was only a 'girl', and Len Tempan who was now in charge with his sidekick Bob Glass would share help and information even on Saturdays when the shop filled with raincoats and pipesmoke and the mere mention of Cilla Black was enough to send collectors into paroxysms of laughter.

Among those who regularly met there for a chat and a listen were several musicians of my age who had started playing the blues. Simon Prager, an accomplished guitarist, did a double-act with harmonica-player Steve Rye; they modelled themselves on Sonny Terry and Brownie McGhee. There was JoAnn Kelly, too, who played a mean guitar and could belt out songs by the likes of Memphis Minnie with a timbre of voice that belied her retiring, elfin appearance. Over the years we'd all watch each other move on into some kind of recognition.

My name now appeared regularly in the music press but I continued to experience difficulties at concerts. When the Duke Ellington Orchestra came through town again, I renewed my acquaintance with Harry Carney and the others, but instead of jockeying for a backstage position I decided to stay out front to take action shots of the band. I knew there was no point in asking for access to the pit. Male photographers were able to get in there, for only they seemed to be considered to have any serious purpose in dragging along all that camera equipment. Presumably I did it just for the exercise.

At Hammersmith Odeon (then the Gaumont), a substantial gap separates the first row of seats from the edge of the pit but I managed to tread on somebody's foot and started a minor incident. Nobody wanted to make room for me until I looked up and saw Stevie Tagoe and her mother. Immediately the older woman took pity on me. 'You come and sit here, my girl. Don't let them stop you doing your job.' In the interval the three of us began talking. It was the first time I had the chance to speak with the woman I knew only as 'Claude Tagoe's daughter'. She had always seemed rather distant but here she was being quite friendly. The Ellingtonians taped a show for BBC television, and we ran into each other again. When they left town, she phoned me to have a look at the pictures.

Stevie had only recently started singing around town. She came from a musical family, her paternal grandfather, a Ga, being one of the first jazz musicians to come out of Ghana in the 1920s. Her father, Claude, was a respected singer, pianist and occasional drummer. Some of her earliest memories included waking up to Dizzy Gillespie and Charlie Parker on the record player, and moving to two delicious numbers by singer and pianist Nellie Lutcher, 'Fine Brown Frame' and 'Hurry On Down'. As a child she had been surrounded by musicians, but Claude was not keen on her following in his footsteps. In fact, he had told some musicians not to work with her. She was forced to keep a weather-eye open whenever she sat in at clubs like the Mandrake.

We had a few drinks together and found out that, unlike most of the other women around, we were both obsessed with the music as opposed to the men who played it. It was so unusual to meet another woman who could talk about Nellie Lutcher in the same breath as Duke and Miles Davis, I was quite overwhelmed. My old friend Pam from *Coda* had dropped out on getting married, and although I occasionally went to hear music with John or Roland or Clive, hanging out with another woman was different. A feeling of relief came over me.

The other Flamingo became significant, too. Now more of a dance venue than a serious listening spot, it was still regarded in some quarters as a jazz club. Billie Holiday had jammed there once on a visit in the 1950s and it remained a focus of attention for American visitors who might sit in with whoever was playing. Word spread on the grapevine when important figures were planning an unscheduled appearance in defiance of the strict union ban that prevented Americans working without a one-for-one exchange. In this way I heard the former Miles Davis drummer, Art Taylor, play the club, an event that had a packed room hanging on his every brush-stroke and paradiddle.

The Flamingo stayed open later than other clubs, Ronnie Scott's included. It had a deep, dark-red feel to it, with a low ceiling the music clung to, and sweat soaking into the crimson walls. There was an innocuous coffee-bar in one corner, the common stimulants being charge and 'blues' (amphetamines); most people just had a drink in The Blue Posts over the road. A liberal racial policy had long made it a favourite for Black American servicemen based in Britain, and its burgeoning Afro-Caribbean clientele now made it feel more soulful than the essentially teenage Marquee.

Stevie worked for Rik Gunnell, who was running the club now in a tough, happy-go-lucky way. He managed singer/organist Georgie Fame, who was resident there with his band, the Blue Flames, and gave us free run of the place. I began to hang out there, tentatively at first, for the older clientele made it seem a little daunting. Occasionally I'd take my camera, as on the memorable night when a be-cloaked and bewitched Screaming Jay Hawkins put a spell on the audience, waving a skull with flashing eyes and gutturally mouthing his bloodthirsty lyrics. But trying to take pictures in that humid atmosphere was a trip in itself. Keeping the sweat off the camera lens was a very real problem, and to use a Rolleiflex, with a heavy flashgun held out at arm's length while a crowd of recycled Teds pushed forward, required stamina of a kind more generally associated with the rugby field. Later on, other legendary artists such as Jimmy Witherspoon and John Lee Hooker appeared at the club, their easy, deep blues stirring the crowd. Seamlessly locked together with them in mutual understanding, appreciation – and sweat – I began to get a taste of how I imagined an American ghetto nightspot might be.

Increasingly, Westindian music was making its influence felt outside Black society. Blues sung to a Caribbean 'shuffle' rhythm played on guitar was popular, the London-based label which featured the style even giving its name to a genre, as in 'I'm taking m'BlueBeats to the party'. Ska and Rocksteady followed, and the Flamingo sound system featured records such as Laurel Aitkin's 'Humpty Dumpty' and Prince Buster's 'Ten Commandments' (arguably the most mysogynist track ever cut), alongside Lord Kitchener's more traditional, and risqué, calypso, 'Dr Kitch'.

But another sound came to dominate the Flamingo atmosphere. A new wave of determination and optimism was sweeping Afro-America, fired by sounds that reached back into race memory for inspiration. Organ music was a feature of the period, with hundreds of players pouring out of the churches to bring gospel music down front for popular consumption. The organ, partly because of its religious identification, came close to the saxophone as an instrument for expressing the soul, and inevitably the two hooked up. Players such as Jimmy Smith and Brother Jack McDuff took on the role of the preacher, latterday soulmen with a message as old as religion. Westindians liked their music 'sticky', and nothing fitted that funky closeness more than a record called 'Groovin' with Jug'. It was played at the Flamingo every time the musicians came off the stand, creating a mood that was overwhelmingly un-English and which had little to do with the jazz scene as I'd encountered it elsewhere. The Blue Flames were top-class musicians, who combined these key elements and turned in an eminently danceable and listenable performance. Georgie, who came from Leigh in Lancashire, was a couple of years younger than me. He was intent on coming as close to the Black sound as possible. He had ears, too, and GIs and Westindian listeners would often bring him new records. He used two Black musicians in his group and was treated by most of the patrons almost as one of their own. He was one of the few white people doing Black music who got it just right, settling on role models for singing who suited his natural timbre and range. He could swing on the organ, too.

I wrote an enthusiastic piece about him in *Jazz Beat* and Stevie ran off copies to use for publicity. I was to be given a bottle of whisky for the privilege, said Rik, standard music business practice, it seemed. We made a distinction between the Flamingo and Ronnie Scott's, which we kept for our 'serious' listening, and it was to Scott's that we went, to a Saturday All-Nighter, to celebrate my little PR achievement. The club had no licence and, as everyone did in those days, we smuggled in the bottle of whisky, refreshing our Cokes surreptitiously under the table. It was the first time I had stayed up all night listening to music in London. We left the club as dawn was breaking, and I made my way through Soho to wait for the first Sunday bus. The music business was starting to look up.

Our devotion to music was total. When Stevie had to complete the Performing Right Society returns for the Flamingo, I helped fill in the names of those jazz composers we considered more deserving of royalties than those whose music was actually played. So while Booker T's 'Green Onions' was a regular nightly feature, we logged composer credits for writers like John Lewis, Milt Jackson and Thelonious Monk.

We both enjoyed dancing, of course, but the inventiveness, vision and sheer stamina of the 'jazz' musicians was breathtaking. Ronnie Scott liked having other saxophonists at the club and began to feature many of the leading American exponents. Long, tall Dexter, the leisurely but loquacious Dexter Gordon, and the exuberant 'Little Giant', Johnny Griffin, who played faster than anyone in history, followed Lucky Thompson. I'd met Lucky before, in Paris, where he'd played the Pettiford Benefit, and in London. But the fact that the Blakeneys were friends of his, too, provided a better introduction. I found him to be most enlightening, even if his impossibly high standards and personal manner did not endear him to the musicians chosen to play with him. For the first time I came across someone whose lifestyle and the way he held the music in respect suggested something of what was lacking elsewhere. Lucky avoided calling the music by the white-defined appellation 'jazz', with its suggestion of sexual activity. To him the spirit of the music was being ruined by the 'swine' and 'vultures' who controlled the business. He made certain the tools of his trade were kept clean and would sit in his hotel-room surrounded by dismantled instruments, each section wrapped in a separate towel. No one I'd met treated music this way. I developed the deepest respect for him and still consider him to be an under-rated giant of the music.

I continued to learn from Black people. There were exceptions, of course, but a tendency has always existed among white listeners to look back to the past and document. Black people, it seemed to me, were always looking ahead. Stevie had begun playing conga-drums and it was she who first made me aware of percussionists such as the Cuban Mongo Santamaria. I had not listened to drummers closely before. Now I began to see how the drummer was responsible for the actual shape of the music, the coachman who drives the horses, in fact.

There was Ruddy, too, a bus conductor who worked on the 159s. Like many Afro-Caribbean settlers he had friends in the States who would send him the latest 'sounds' on labels such as Blue Note and Riverside. I would jump on his bus on my way into town and get a free ride and an invitation to come by for a record session. The quality of the American pressings then was superb and the sound was recorded in a special way. US albums were especially popular for their thick card covers, too. We would prop these up around the room as we listened. What was 'head' music for most of us, Westindians regarded as dance music. Dexter Gordon, for example, was always a great dance favourite with Jamaicans, and when one of Ruddy's friends would drop by for a sip no one thought twice about dancing to Dexter's 'Doin' Allright'. As for the Blue Notes, conga drums were often added to tenor and organ, giving more texture to an already polyrhythmic sound-picture. A lot of the music was now known as 'Soul' or 'funky-jazz', uptempo blues and chants that went back to the church for inspiration. Johnny Griffin even recorded the traditional spiritual 'Wade in the Water' in a stomping, declamatory version with his Big Soul Band. Sipping on a brew, we clicked our fingers to Junior Mance strutting through 'The Uptown' or Cannonball Adderley's ostinato 'Sack O' Woe', with Britain's own Victor Feldman playing a piano vamp as though he'd been born a Holy Roller instead of a London Jew.

Ruddy knew Ernest Ranglin, too, the brilliant guitarist who worked for a while at the Scott Club. Ernest lived in Jamaica but he spent a period in England writing and producing popular records, most notably Millie's saucy 'My Boy Lollipop', which put the Ska beat into the charts. I wanted to interview him and Ruddy made the connection. In later years he'd keep me posted on Ernest's whereabouts whenever we met on the bus.

It was this kind of personal contact that helped me build a wider picture of the world in which the musicians lived. I learned how they worked and earned a living, of what was important to different individuals and, in a then indefinable way, what the music was actually about. It was something that could not be gleaned from listening to records alone. Neither could it be gathered from reading conventional opinion, for, with the exception of Marc Crawford, Barbara Gardner and LeRoi Jones, all of whom wrote occasionally for *Downbeat*, the only readily accessible writers were white.

Analysis tended to depend on Eurocentric notions of 'quality', even when the writer himself (and it was generally a man) moved with and around Black musicians. There was no way then that the critics would link Prince Buster or 'My Boy Lollipop' with, say, Eric Dolphy, or with what the 'hard men' of soul-jazz were doing. Yet for other people such links clearly existed. Black people, it seemed to me, took a more pragmatic and generous view of the music. When my attention was drawn to something the critics dismissed, I was forced to revise whatever I had learned in order to work out why it was valuable. I began to discover how the music *worked* for different people, even if I couldn't quite put this into words when I wrote about it. The whole process seemed more democratic to me.

British musicians such as the Beatles and the Rolling Stones were becoming dominant worldwide now, playing what was basically the blues. But unlike the white rock 'n' rollers of the previous decade, they made sure that their listeners knew where their inspiration had come from. They talked about Mary Wells and the Miracles, John Lee Hooker and Howlin' Wolf, and *Melody Maker* printed dozens of readers' letters proclaiming the blues as the sound of the times. Veteran harpist Sonny Boy Williamson even decided to stay behind after a European tour and work around Britain with a local group, the Yardbirds.

Betty Everett, Buddy Guy and Fontella Bass appeared on *Ready Steady Go!* and got into the charts alongside Cilla Black and the Searchers; and then it began to emerge that practically every soul singer had first performed in the church. A gospel package came to England, featuring renowned artists such as the Five Blind Boys of Mississippi and Bishop Samuel Kelsey, a veteran preacher who put on what amounted to a staged version of a Baptist service. The atmosphere was electric, with such singers as Inez Andrews performing magnificent melismatic leaps with their voices and building up tremendous evange-lical fervour, yet the concerts were poorly attended.

Gospel music did not have the same popular appeal for Whites as the blues, despite the fact that many white singers were trying their damnedest to sound as though they'd been raised on the moaners' bench. One of those who admitted to damaging her voice trying to get a 'Black' sound was Dusty Springfield, one of the most popular solo singers of the day. Dusty sang songs such as 'Can I Get a Witness?', nominally copied from Motown's Marvin Gaye yet echoing an age-old cry that went back to the beginnings of Afro-America. When the gospel package played Croydon, I looked around to see Dusty transfixed, unselfconsciously wearing her spectacles, clapping on the off-beat and cheering, doing her best to be the 'witness' the communality of the music demanded. With her were two other ardent devotees of the faith, *RSG!*'s Vicki Wickham and Madeleine Bell, the wonderful gospel singer from Newark, New Jersey, who had come over with Langston Hughes' *Black Nativity* and decided to stay.

I'd liked gospel music ever since I saw Mahalia Jackson look over her shoulder at the close of the sublime *Jazz on a Summer's Day*, when she'd finished walking 'All Over God's Heaven'. Like many other jazz fans, I had gone to see *Black Nativity*, too, several times. The show took London by storm. Through Chris Barber I had got to know some of the singers, including the leading soloists, Professor Alex Bradford and Marion Williams. Bradford was a flamboyant character, something of a hedonist. He swanned around in a grey cape and a beret and entertained people like Little Richard backstage. We hit it off from the start. I was proud to be able to help him with some publicity photographs, my printer mate John even supplying him with a nice line in business cards, free of charge.

Bradford used an impassioned shout to get over. Marion Williams, on the other hand, was majestic, 'rocking her church' with a minimum of physical movement but the promise of enormous power. Both were big stars in gospel music, but as usual I had a healthy interest in the lesser-knowns. Madeleine, who sang with Bradford's otherwise male group, was skinny and not long out of school. She had to make the most of the few solo lines she was allotted, but when the others laid out, her acid, penetrating voice cut through the theatre like a knife. The music, I knew already, could make my blood run cold, and yet I still had only a superficial grasp of what the demands for reassurance, involvement and communality were all about. I had never been inside a Black church, even.

From time to time I had seen a group of Westindians evangelising with tambourines outside Brixton Library. Through a Jamaican friend I got in touch with Pastor F. Wallen, the head of this particular 'Clap Hands' congregation (as they were known then), and asked if I might visit the church.

Pastor and Mrs Wallen were most welcoming and we talked about the financial problems that prevented them developing churches like theirs. I attended a service at the Church of God in a basement on Effra Road, where an elderly lady played piano and the Wallens took it in turns to beat on a tambourine. The pastor gave a stirring sermon, but the atmosphere seemed to me to lack the tension and drama created by the American gospel artists. To expect that it would do was presumptuous on my part and, I think now, quite offensive. The Americans were professional singers, for a start. But like most whites I had failed to differentiate between the hundreds of forms that Black Christianity takes. I had yet to realise that everything should be allowed to exist on its own terms, and not contrasted unfairly with something quite different in what amounted to an orgy of points-scoring. I wrote up the conversation with the Wallens, though, and it was published in another new magazine, *Daylight International*, 'for forward-looking negroes' [*sic*]. This had just been started by Aubrey Baynes, a pioneer in British Black publishing from Antigua, who would go on to found the newspaper *Westindian World*.

Gospel music and the blues were everywhere, all wrapped up with rock 'n' roll. Some hip white people knew what was what, but most of us were only just learning. One of the great rock 'n' roll heroes came to England, but most rockers missed him because he sang with a 'jazz' band. Big Joe Turner laid down such classics as 'Shake Rattle and Roll' in the 1950s but was originally a singing bartender out of Kansas City, where Count Basie first took the blues on the road with a big band. Big Joe *was* the blues, walking. He hardly moved on stage, just snapped his fingers, opened his mouth and shouted. And he really was massive. I took him to an outsize men's shop to fit him out with some clothes and he repaid the courtesy with an invitation to eat. To my annoyance, the 'mistress' of one of the local musicians inveigled her way into our date, proceeding to eat enormous quantities of Chinese food for which Joe had to pay. She could not make up her mind whether to flirt with the singer or patronise me, but once again I felt a hint of the 'white trash' innuendo, even though she was prepared for him to spend money on her, as well.

One memorable night I went down to Ronnie Scott's with Big Joe and Memphis Slim. Saxophonist Ben Webster was playing and the two blues giants sat in with him, bringing a rare smile of approval to his face. After a while, they were joined by another American saxophonist, Gerry Mulligan, and the place just took off. Some of the South Africans who had come over in 1961 with the musical *King Kong* were on hand. So were a handful of gospel singers, including Madeleine Bell. That night the Scott Club turned into a church, a juke-joint, a shebeen, all in one, sweeping up white people like myself in a loving and vital Pan-African embrace. I loved it, and the music, to death.

For the first time I wrote something for *Downbeat*, an interview with Joe Harriott whom I knew from his Marquee residency. He was an incisive, salty saxophonist, who, as Kitty Grime wrote 'has always played beautiful love and hate songs', but could be distant and unapproachable away from the music. I went to see him and he talked about the new concept he had developed – he called it 'Abstract' or 'Free Form' – in an equally abstract way. He had a tendency to leave questions unanswered, to make statements that sounded impressive but didn't quite add up in the end, but I did a reasonable job with the write-up and it was published in the magazine's 1964 'International' issue. It established my credentials as a serious professional writer, and from then on the editor would cable me whenever he needed something from Britain. Eventually I became the magazine's London correspondent.

That July my mother went on holiday. I decided to have a   **117** party and invite several musicians in the hope that they would bring their instruments. To my surprise, they did. The group included Harry Beckett on trumpet, Herman Wilson on trombone, Rudy Jones playing tenor, Graham Collier, bass, and John Stevens, with whom Stevie sang at the Mandrake, at the drums. Stevie and Bobby Breen played congas, and then she sang a couple of blues. Like all memorable parties, somebody called the police. Fortunately, they were easily placated, and Mum knew nothing when she returned.

At the end of the summer, I.K. Dairo MBE and his Blue Spots came to England. An important figure in Yoruba *juju* music, Dairo was the first person to introduce the talking-drum into a modern African context. In doing so, he marked the beginning of a new era in which the continent's 'commercial' music began to exhibit a more African personality. Hitherto, Nigerian, Ghanaian and Congolese (Zaïrean) highlife had dominated the urban picture. The highlife was dance-music named for the lifestyle of those who lived in the manner of the colonialists. It was danced face-to-face, sometimes holding a partner European-style. Rhythmically it was predominantly Latin-American, and although these rhythms may themselves have originated from people of African descent, *juju* music re-emphasised purely African elements. Its name was connected with healing and medicine, too.

At the start of the evening the leader sat almost anonymously in the centre of the stage, surrounded by eight bandsmen uniformly robed in *dansiki* and *filla* in handwoven green and red *as-oke* cloth. He played guitar and accordion and sang, but it was not until he flung the hourglass-shaped drum over his left shoulder that the atmosphere changed. It was a signal for the crowd to throw their arms in the air. He grinned shyly as they shouted their appreciation. In the same way that most students I knew would always at some point break away from their partner when dancing, and abandon the Western pose by bunching their loose clothes before them, buttocks pressed outwards and shaking, so people starved of homegrown sounds were acknowledging something their own.

Flamingo wanted a story and I went to see the musicians. They were staying nearby at a guest-house in Streatham. Dairo spoke little English. My Yoruba was limited to *e-karo* ('good morning'), *o-daaro* ('bye bye') and *e-se* ('thank you'), so one of the organisers suggested we go back to my mother's house where he could interpret. There, late at night, I conducted an unusual interview. The three of us sat around the scrubbed kitchen table, drinking tea. I.K. spoke mainly in Yoruba, occasionally in *pidgin*, maintaining his shyness throughout. His material, I learned was full of social commentary, attacking those who did not fulfil their civic duty. Although he would just as readily sing a praise-song, I.K. was apparently feared in Nigeria because of his influence. The organiser explained he had asked him to drop some songs during his visit, as they might be considered 'too pungent'.

Not long after I had written the story, the telephone rang. It was John Harold from *Flamingo*. 'Have you got your passport?' he wanted to know. 'Good. Come and see us. You're going to Africa.'

Despite its rota of African correspondents, the magazine was running short of material. It was an unprecedented opportunity for me. The money was, frankly, exploitative, but I knew the offer was unlikely to be repeated. I agreed and came away from the office with a plane-ticket as long as my arm.

A couple of weeks before I left, Roland and Jackie laid on a party for me. Someone brought along a woman I'll call Yvonne. She came from the Bahamas, she worked as a nurse, and we'd met once before, only briefly. We looked at each other and in an instant it became clear that we had to see each other again. We arranged to meet. I couldn't believe that a woman like her, really straight, not a 'swinger', should want me, but she did. She really did. I left for West Africa, first stop Gambia, with my head and my heart in a whirl.

10
Mama Africa

The first music I heard on clearing Immigration in Gambia took my breath away. Over the airport radio came the unmistakable thud of Honey Lantree's four-to-the-bar bass drum on the Honeycombs' 'Have I the Right to Hold You?' It seemed to me that I had left Britain to escape from music like this. I was not impressed. A Gambian I had met on the plane escorted me to the tiny corner-bar. He still sported the black homburg and winter coat in which he'd left Gatwick and was beginning to sweat. At the bar he greeted a fellow 'been-to' who engaged me in conversation over a beer. 'Streatham, eh?' he murmured with interest. 'Do you know the Locarno?'

I was puzzled at the way so many things centred on England. I had not stopped to think what colonial influence might mean on African soil, and when 'My Boy Lollipop' followed hard on the heels of 'Lead-foot' Lantree, I started to feel uneasy.

Mr Locarno kindly drove me to my hotel on the outskirts of Bathurst (as Banjul, the Gambian capital, was known then), and on the way I was reassured to spot several monkeys, a sure sign of 'Africa'. Gambia would later become a centre for tourism but in 1964 it was still a sleepy little country, a British-ruled enclave in the middle of Senegal, with an economy based almost solely on groundnuts. At the Atlantic I felt marooned and uncertain. Then the desk telephoned: I had a visitor. I came out of my room to see a slim young man running up the stairs, wearing a striped shirt and shorts and a nervous smile. Ousman N'Jie was a photographer who had shot the pictures for a couple of *Flamingo* articles. He had been asked to help me out during my stay.

Shyly, he asked if I'd like to eat at his house and I agreed, willingly. I began to feel more at ease as we made our way there. We walked past neat houses built of wood and cement blocks, others, more basic, made from sheets of corrugated iron. Banana trees hung over fences, dangling their sensuous wares, chickens and guinea-fowl dodged in and out of alleyways. Flowers I had never seen before erupted from every corner. I remember a school wall covered, grandly, in purple bougainvillea interwoven with red hibiscus. Cooking smells and the sweetness of burnt charcoal were everywhere, and everyone seemed to be occupied in sweeping, washing, cleaning. By the roadside pedlars offered goods piled high on enamel dishes decorated in bold primary colours, others walked or cycled, bearing bundles of firewood or groundnuts with the earth still clinging to their shell-like roots.

Passers-by were curious. Some made excuses to greet Ousman, obviously interested to know the identity of this foreign woman he had in tow. For my first African meal, Ousman's wife prepared fish and chips, Gambian-style. We ate off the same kind of multi-coloured enamel plates I'd seen in the street. These were turned face downwards on the plastic cloth to keep them clean until food was served. As I dipped fried fish into hot pepper-sauce, I started to feel more relaxed. For the rest of the week I ate there, Mrs N'Jie preparing potatoes, rice and millet in a different style each day. Few words were exchanged at table, just smiles and courtesies, but I felt lucky to be eating in a Gambian home rather than at the hotel, where stiff and starchy English fare was the order of the day.

Gambia was so small a country that it did not boast a newspaper of any kind, just an occasional bulletin which was posted in public places. Because of this, it was important to *Flamingo* to make inroads there as well as in the relatively more affluent neighbouring Sierra Leone and Liberia. Correspondents in Ghana and Southern Nigeria sent plenty of stories to the magazine, but material from these other countries and from Northern Nigeria was in short supply. I was given an outline of what was required, a few contacts and suggestions, but otherwise had to decide for myself what would make suitable copy. I was also expected to shoot a few cover poses of 'attractive' young women.

It was a heavy responsibility to place on the shoulders of an inexperienced 22-year-old with little real knowledge of Africa. Without Ousman's help and guidance in that first week, I might well have wanted to head for home. I was totally out of my depth and yet, because I was so obviously naïve, attracted an enormous amount of kindness from practically everyone I met.

The atmosphere in Bathurst and the surrounding area was warm and positive, the weather clement and the pace relaxed. The scale of the place was in its favour for a first-time traveller to Africa, and although I saw only the surface of things, and obviously was unable to approach any kind of understanding of what was actually happening, it was a good place to start on a voyage of discovery. One of my dancing-partners at the Marquee had been a Gambian and I asked Ousman if he knew him. Within minutes I was sitting in his office as he shook his head in surprise that I'd remembered his name, as much as anything. Gambia had yet to achieve Independence from Britain and he took me to meet the Minister for Local Government to get a quote to accompany the *vox pop* piece I was doing about the impending changes. Later, we went to an open-air night club for dancing, beer and a meal. On the way back we travelled along a road covered with huge toads making their way across. Hitting some was unavoidable, the car squashed and slithered along.

Ousman's studio was tiny, equipped with the bare essentials and a couple of painted backdrops, yet he managed to turn out excellent portraits and seemed to have more work than he could cope with. We were out walking one day when he was approached by a woman who spoke long and volubly in Wollof while he tried to placate her with gentle interjections. Eventually she reached inside her clothes and dragged out a tattered old photograph. Ousman took it without enthusiasm and put it in his pocket. He turned to me after she'd gone with an expression that photographers anywhere will recognise. 'Copying job', he sighed. I laughed with feeling at the sheer universality of it all.

We visited a new children's nursery and the country's first intensive chicken farm, and on two occasions found ourselves delayed by nine-foot pythons crossing the road. Then we did what the whole world does on a Saturday and went to a sports event. Wrestling is popular throughout West Africa and in Bathurst the excitement began in the late afternoon as the teams assembled. Groups of young men made their way to the arena, accompanied by drummers also blowing whistles and by a huge supporting crowd. Children and adults danced and strutted to the music in support of their heroes, just like the Second Line that accompanies a New Orleans parade. On the field the wrestlers presented a daunting sight, shiny with oil and sweat and constant dousing with water. The arms, legs and waists of all of them were encircled by strength-giving leather 'ju-ju'. Their performance was constantly boosted by their personal drummers, the first time I'd come across African music in a functional context. Just as in Britain, the wrestling looked far more brutal than it actually was, and there was a great degree of mutual celebration after each event.

John Harold had suggested I look up Mrs Jawara, the President's wife, whom he knew from a previous visit. A former nurse, she had just returned from the United States. I spent a pleasant evening at her house, recording her Stateside impressions for the magazine. On the night before I left, she appeared at the hotel bringing me a gift of two carvings. 'I couldn't let you leave without giving you something to remember our little country,' she said. The carvings sit on my mantelpiece still, but I have never needed them to remind me of that fairy-tale week in Gambia. Everyone had been so hospitable and warm.

Ousman came to the airport with me. I hated to leave someone who had been so comfortable to be with and on whom I had grown to rely. But I had to move on to Freetown. I said 'jerijef' (Wollof for 'thank you') and boarded the plane.

In the 1780s a committee was formed in London by British abolitionists campaigning against the slave trade to settle the 'indigent blacks', or the Black Poor of London, as they were known, on the coast of West Africa. The area chosen was Sierra Leone and the settlement was called Freetown. Later settlers included Black soldiers who had fought on the British side during the American War of Independence and whom their new-found benefactors were reluctant to return to the slavocracy of the Southern States.

The idea of repatriation as a redemptive journey to the African homeland actually goes back to before the American Revolution. There were projects to train freed slaves as missionaries, a kind of atonement for the atrocities of slavery. In the years to come, Sierra Leone was repeatedly settled by waves of Diasporean Blacks, including a group of Jamaican Maroons, the legendary guerrilla fighters who terrorised the British colonisers. There were European settlers too, including women married to men of African descent (for years referred to as 'prostitutes', in keeping with the European view of interracial relationships). Eventually the descendants of the non-indigenes, the Krios (Creoles), became dominant, and the preponderance today of European names is indicative of a heritage based partly on resettlement, intermarriage and slavery.

At the Atlantic Hotel in Bathurst a fellow guest had been Sir Samuel Bankole-Jones, Lord Chief Justice of Sierra Leone. He invited me to Sunday lunch at his home, a beautiful clifftop dwelling. We ate curry served in the British style, with side-dishes of bananas, nuts, raisins and grated coconut, and he suggested I broaden my education by attending the court. There he presided grandly, dressed in the regalia of the British judiciary, with all the surrounding pomp and circumstance. 'S-B', as people called him, could adopt the hauteur and manner of the most aristocratic member of the peerage, but away from public gaze he was gritty and humorous, with the ability to laugh at himself.

Freetown was much bigger than Bathurst, even boasting a handful of ex-London Transport buses which travelled around the historic cotton-tree landmark in the centre of town. There were bustling street-markets and a constant feast of new food to be sampled. There was much about the capital reminiscent of pre-war Britain as well as other links with home.

I went for a walk near my hotel one day and bumped straight into someone I knew. Outside the Governor-General's residence stood his uniformed ADC, all starched and pressed, blanco-ed and burnished The last time I had seen Mark Koroma had been in far less dignified circumstances. In Waterloo Station he had defended me from two men who had abused me for sharing a cup of tea with him and his cousin. Angered, I'd slapped one man around the face, and he had moved to retaliate. Mark had moved forward quickly, drawing himself up to his full camel-hair, Sandhurst-trained height. 'Don't lay a hand on that woman,' he said evenly, as a crowd began to gather. His commanding manner prevailed and the antagonists melted away, mouthing the predictable insults.

We were amazed to encounter each other again, and he came back to the hotel for tea. His Sandhurst training was reflected in his spit-and-polish appearance. As for me, I was beside myself with pride to be seen walking with someone who looked so distinguished.

In Freetown the *Daily Mail* photographer, George Shanu-Taylor, showed me around. With his help I wrote a piece on Fourah Bay College, the oldest modern university in West Africa and which has links with Durham University. I visited the House of Representatives, too, where I photographed Madam Ella Koblo-Gulama, a Paramount Chief who was Minister of State in the government, the first woman to hold such a post anywhere in West Africa. The Diamond Corporation arranged for me to fly up-country by light aircraft to one of their mines but, typically of the kind of Europeans attached to such enterprises, they had failed to take into account that most of their workforce were Moslems. The trip was arranged for a Friday, with the result that hardly anyone was on site.

One of the *Daily Mail* journalists took me nightclubbing and we danced, but I heard little music to hold my attention until I met S.E. Rogers. Sierra Leone has never been noted for its modern musicians, but guitarist and singer 'Rogie' was an exception. 'My Lovely Elizabeth', recorded on his own label, was always on the radio and sold 18,000 copies in Sierra Leone alone. Rogie wrote songs in English, Krio and Mende, but favoured the American ballad style of singers such as Jim Reeves (one of the biggest record-sellers in West Africa). He had a big, warm baritone, and a warm personality to go with it. I met him at his rambling old house on Wellington Street in the centre of the city, where he sang and played for me, captivating me with his not inconsiderable charm. A self-made man, shy but confident, he maintained: 'If the guitar is played correctly, you can get the whole world in your palms.'

Between my other assignments, writing about the State Lottery, photographing President-to-be Siaka Stevens, we got to know each other. Rogie told me intimate stories about his life and loves, and I was touched by his gentleness and consideration. He wanted to try his luck in Europe and I promised to help him with contacts in the music business. As it turned out, it took Rogie 23 years to make it to England. Denied a visa despite my interventions, he opted for California instead. But 1988 saw an upsurge in his fortunes and a successful tour of Britain.

I had another 'musical' experience during my stay in Freetown. At the Chief Justice's house I met a friend's father, who had been High Commissioner in London. He invited me for a meal and it was agreed we would accept an invitation from the local representatives of builders Taylor-Woodrow. Mr and Mrs Taylor-Woodrow-representative were the kind of overpaid English people doing a job in Africa under sufferance – feeling superior to every African they met, while maintaining an 'Oh-isn't-this-terribly-jolly' façade for the sake of business. Clearly they had little respect for my escort because he had brought along a white woman, and they despised me for being with him. They certainly did their best to humiliate both of us all evening.

Dinner was fondue, a new craze from Switzerland I had not come across before. With much tutting and clucking, and treating me like a small child, our hostess showed me how to dip my pieces of meat into the hot oil – and of course I managed to spill it all over the table. Then, as if that wasn't enough, Mrs T-W-r put on one of those 'terribly interested' faces that such people save for their supposed inferiors. I had let slip conversationally that I enjoyed music, and she suddenly Had An Idea. 'Do you like Connie Francis, Miss Wilmer?' she asked. I muttered something incoherent. 'Oh, good,' she continued, 'I believe we have some Connie Francis records, haven't we?' Looking over her shoulder I saw to my horror that they appeared to have *only* Connie Francis records. These they proceeded to play, relentlessly. Fondue has ever since then been indelibly associated in my mind with Connie Francis and indescribable misery.

So much had happened in the two weeks since I left home that I had hardly been able to think of Yvonne. She was set to leave for the Bahamas four weeks after I returned, and although I knew I had been profoundly excited by the experience of really getting close to a woman at last, I had already met two men on my African journey whom I had also found attractive. In Liberia I would meet another, only this time it would go beyond mere attraction.

Liberia has always been a difficult place for outsiders to visit, a country founded in 1821 by freed Afro-Americans whose presence in the South was a threat to the institution of slavery. Although settled spasmodically by generations of Black Americans, its creation was initially seen by abolitionists as an 'outrage' supporting slave-holding interests. Until comparatively recently, the settlers' descendants, the

Americo-Liberians, prevented most indigenes from rising to positions of prominence. My main contacts for work purposes were non-Liberian Africans, and I felt more comfortable about this, especially when it was common knowledge that spies and *agents provocateurs* lurked in every corner. The atmosphere in Monrovia was heavy, there was no doubt about it, although it has to be noted that, as W.E.B. DuBois had written, Liberia's 'chief crime was to be Black and poor in a rich white world'. I stayed at the Ducor Palace, an impressive American-style hotel at the top of a hill, but its isolation did little to hide the discomforting number of heavily armed police and militia in evidence everywhere.

I met an artist named Vahnjah Richards who had studied sculpture in Chicago. In the States he had got to know pianist Horace Silver and several other musicians, and when I revealed my own interest in the music, he took me to the city's smoky jazz room, where several of his metal works hung on walls draped fetchingly with fishnets. We listened to records and acted cool.

Van was chief sculptor in the Public Works Department and many of his works were to be found in the homes of the President and other wealthy Liberians. The tension that was everywhere in Monrovia seemed to have little effect on him. Van, who later visited London and stayed with my family on several occasions, seemed to take it all in his stride, puffing thoughtfully on his hand-carved pipe.

It was in Liberia that I learned the West African handshake. Palms meet and touch each other gently, the middle-fingers sliding the length of each other, meeting the thumb for a concluding fingerclick. In Liberia, I also learned to keep my mouth shut.

It happened when I attended a birthday address given by President Tubman at the Executive Mansion. The President, a short, bespectacled man, arrived in a motorcade, surrounded by motorcycles with wailing sirens. Like the rest of the leading members of his True Whig party, he was dressed in top-hat and tails, and the atmosphere was tense with security. Over drinks at the reception that followed, I got into conversation with a tall, slim man whose eyes were hidden behind dark glasses. A waiter came over with a message asking me to come outside. There I found my Nigerian contact. Without wasting time on details, he told me to stop talking to the man. The implication was obvious; he was an agent who would like nothing better than to provoke me into a criticism of the régime. Journalists and foreigners were easy prey for such fit-ups; only recently a Dutch pilot had been imprisoned for splashing mud up the wall of a minister's house as he drove by. His clothes had been taken away from him and he went without food for a while. Despite this, I found it hard to hide a smile when I returned to the reception. It is common for rural Africans of the same age-group to hold hands, but I hardly expected to see this in the Executive Mansion. Nevertheless, walking around hand-in-hand, were two uniformed officers with the words 'Secret Service' emblazoned on their caps. To Western eyes, they presented an incongruous sight.

For many years Liberia's economy had been almost entirely based on rubber production. In 1926 a contract was signed with Firestone in America, giving the company a lease on one million acres for 88 years. Firestone, then, controlled the entire revenue of the country, an invidious situation for the descendants of an enterprising group of freed slaves. Now, iron-ore mining had begun to provide an alternative source of revenue, and I wrote an enthusiastic piece about the new mining operations. I also did a story on a small rubber producer who ran a plantation of his own.

On one of the trips into the bush I was accompanied by a journalist I'll call Joe. He came from another African country and was constantly thwarted in his attempts to become a serious writer by the repressive and philistine atmosphere in which he was forced to work. To my great surprise I found myself falling for him in a way I had only felt twice before in my life. I had no time to think about the consequences of becoming involved with him, for I was only there for a few days more, but when I left I was in love in that hopeless way that gradually fades with the realisation that nothing on earth can be done about it. Some people call it a holiday romance. I called it magic.

In Nigeria, Africa's most populous country, I was entirely on my own. No one from *Flamingo* had made any inroads into the feudal North, whose people, politically and numerically, were the most influential in the Federation. Nigeria had been an independent state for just four years and the magazine wanted interviews with two prominent political figures about the forthcoming elections. Key issues included the balance of power between the regions, thrown together in an uncomfortable liaison by the British, and progress versus tradition. There was the position of women in the North, too, disenfranchised by custom if not by the constitution, many of them living in purdah, sometimes married at the age of 12. I succeeded in reaching these politicians through contacts I had made among the Hausa-Fulani élite in London.

One of these had been a law student and was now a prestigious Crown Counsel in Kano, though it was obvious that if he continued drinking at the rate he was going, he wouldn't hold this position for long. I accompanied him to Court one day and was taken aback at the way he was sweating under his wig and shaking. Those Northern Moslems who drank were few, but those who did seemed to succumb pretty fast.

My barrister friend introduced me to a car-dealer named Garba Mohammed, a Moslem who had made the *haj* (pilgrimage) to Mecca. Alhaji Garba was a philosophical man who went out of his way to help me, and gave me quite an education in the process. On my first night he took me to a political rally organised by the ruling NPC in the old city. Kano is an ancient walled town with a history dating back many centuries. Much of the old city has since been destroyed but in 1964 it was a fascinating maze of streets and buildings made from unbaked earth. We entered a compound through a small gap in the wall of one of these houses. Hundreds of people had gathered to watch the display by dancers dressed in the federal green-and-white. The proceedings were lit by torches and storm-lanterns and the music was insistent. A group of drummers played intensely, then other string-instrument players walked around, singing to – praising, presumably – various onlookers. It was the most absorbing of musical experiences and yet I shivered throughout. Not realising how cold it could get at night when the winds blew across the Sahara, I was wearing only a light summer dress. Someone lent me a jacket, but next time I didn't forget.

Each country I had visited so far had been distinctive, but Northern Nigeria was strikingly different. In most places the terrain was arid compared to the rain-forest and coastal areas where I had been. European dress was uncommon and, despite the relative populousness of Kano City, the pace of life was slow. An air of calm surrounded everything, greetings were exchanged in a ritualistic, timeless way. 'Sannu, ranka ya dade.' 'Lafiya lau' – 'Hello, may you live long.' 'Very well'. From Alhaji Garba I learned something of the teachings of Islam and the customs of the people. On Friday, the Moslem religious day, he took me to the mosque. From early on I had seen hundreds of people making their way across town, but as we drew nearer to the muezzin's tower, the long *babban riga* worn by each man blended into a sea of white, the oncoming tide of the faithful. Those unable to gain access to the building knelt to perform their devotions outside. A brisk policeman stopped me, politely, from passing a certain point as a woman, but I was permitted to photograph rows of men at prayer, their bicycles piled up beside them. Women were nowhere to be seen.

Flamingo wanted an interview with the Emir of Kano, one of the powerful traditional rulers. The Emir, a relatively young man, had just taken over from his father. He and Garba had been schoolmates, so arranging a meeting would be simple. Protocol demanded that we apply to the Native Authority first, however. There I met a daunting elder whose face was almost completely hidden in a dark blue turban wrapped round his head and chin. The turban, *rawani*, worn by Northerners, protects them against the violent sandstorms common in the desert regions. Powdered indigo had been beaten into his to make it shine. His teeth were stained red with years of chewing kola-nut and he talked distantly to Garba as if I did not exist. He agreed to the interview taking place, however. Garba took me to the palace, reminding me to keep my distance from the Emir, as custom demanded.

I had enquired what form of address to use and had been told 'Your Majesty' or 'Sir' would do. I opted for the latter. Alhaji Sir Ado Bayero was a soft-spoken, good-looking man in this thirties. He answered my questions with care and precision, giving the impression of putting all his time at my disposal. With a guard at his feet, he sat on a beautifully upholstered regency-style chair, dressed in a white *babban-riga* under a dark-blue cloak, an enveloping white *rawani* swathed around his neck and chin and hanging in folds. I sat a few feet away on a smaller chair.

To my surprise, the Emir said he would like to see the abolition of the custom of early marriage for girls. It was an unusual statement for a traditional ruler to make, but reflected a view that was already starting to change as women were increasingly being allowed access to education. He was anxious, however, to point out that child-marriage was a worldwide phenomenon: 'Remember all that fuss when that American pop singer – what was his name? Jerry Lee Lewis – brought his thirteen-year-old wife to England?' I did remember and felt that ever-welcome sense of universality inside the ancient palace.

At the end of our interview I asked if I might take some photographs. The Emir agreed. Mindful of the admonition to keep my distance, I cautiously took a light-reading off his face. Our eyes met and his twinkled. 'Aren't you supposed to take the light-reading off the darkest part of the subject?' he asked with a smile. Clearly he thought I was taking a reading off the brilliant white folds of his *rawani*. I laughed and explained what I was doing, asking, 'Are you interested in photography?' He nodded, and as soon as I had finished, motioned me to come and sit beside him. He banished his guard to the next room, much to that worthy's annoyance, and we embarked on an interesting chat about photography.

When it was time for the Emir to leave, he told me to be sure to photograph him on horseback, accompanied by his guards. 'I won't be able to stop for you,' he said, 'but I'll look your way for a minute.' Outside, he mounted his finely caparisoned horse. The saddlecloth was magnificently embroidered, the bridle could have been made from silver. A serious-looking retinue surrounded him, protectively. Some of the men, each dressed in matching red *rawani* and red/green *babban-riga*, carried double-ended spears or swords. There were musicians, too, blowing on ram's-horn trumpets. The Emir didn't slow down as he passed me by, but I swear I noticed a wink between the folds of white cloth.

I decided to do a *vox pop* piece on child-marriage after visiting the hospital and talking with a Hausa doctor there who told me horrific stories of mutilated children brought in after their 'wedding-night'. It was customary for men to wait until their young brides were 'of age' before having sex, but not everyone was equally considerate. Garba had translated for me during most of my interviews, now he told me that one of his friends was married to a twelve-year-old and I could talk to her if I wished. The husband turned out to be one of those who sometimes accompanied us on our evening drinking sessions, although he himself was devout and a non-drinker. At his house I met the girl he had married. She sat on a mat dressed in her best clothes, eyes painted with antimony, hands, feet and lips dyed with henna, and looked terrified at the sight of me. For myself, I was utterly embarrassed; she was only a child. Mallam Usman was a gentle, sensitive person who expressed his disgust at the way some men abused women. 'I will wait until she is much older,' he said. 'Now we are like brother and sister, just getting to know each other and becoming friends.'

Nigeria is a country of living arts. Kano's ancient market and its surrounding area comprised a labyrinth of stimulating sights and smells, not all of them pleasant. The dyeing vats, where the characteristic cloths of the region are dipped into fermented natural indigo, give off a truly remarkable odour. But the results, to be seen on the backs and brows of the desert people, are spectacular. Unlike elsewhere in Nigeria, dyeing is a male preserve, many men's arms and feet becoming dyed deep blue where the cloth drips.

A number of the buildings in the old quarter were beautifully decorated, some with broken plates embedded in the unbaked earth walls, others with relief patterns painted in contrasting colours. Everywhere rows of bricks, shaped by hand, lay drying in the heat of the sun. From time to time magnificent horsemen would come trotting down the narrow streets, their own and their horses' heads held high, bridles and saddlery glistening in the sun. Sometimes they sported splendid leggings made from soft leather dyed in the black and brilliant red, yellow and green of the Sahelian regions. In the market I found the leather-workers. They sewed sandals, boots and bridles for customers appreciative of this long-established tradition of excellence.

I came across money-changers, too, who in exchange for hard currency, offered bracelets made from nickel and brass with a trace of silver. There were healers and herbalists, hustlers and conjurers. One bearded old man tossed a six-foot python at my feet without a word of warning, much to the amusement of the crowd. Only a careful monetary intervention by Garba saved me from continuing embarrassment. And then I rounded a corner to come face to face with a giant, wearing skins and a skirt. His bulging arms were covered in leather *kambu*, imparting strength, and a *guru*, another amulet, encircled his waist. Drummers surrounded him as he entertained. His speciality consisted of flinging a treacherous-looking hoe with a triangular blade in the air, catching it skilfully. As a *pièce de résistance*, put on for me, he allowed three men to climb on his back, drums and all, lifting a fourth with his unburdened right arm. Quite a show.

As we walked through the old quarter, people muttered the word '*baturia*'. The constant low-key commentary annoyed me and I asked Garba what it meant. 'European' or 'white woman', he explained. I wanted to know how to say 'Black man' or 'Black woman', to have something in reserve. He thought for a minute, then shook his head. 'We don't really have a word for that,' he said. 'We are "the people".' His reply came as a shock. I'd never looked at things that way before. Now when I asked for a translation I noticed he would say ' "women" means "*mata*",' rather than ' "*mata*" means "women".' After a lifetime of thinking of Africans as 'foreigners', I realised it was now I who was the 'other'. I couldn't get it out of my mind. Theoretically I knew that Whites were in a minority worldwide, but it took these exchanges with Garba to show me the arrogant way in which we evaluated everything in terms of our own perspective. Travelling to Africa taught me there was more than one way of looking at any given situation.

Although Northern Nigeria was such a feudal and, in terms of what I was accustomed to, alien society, I felt more at ease there than I had done since leaving home. I kept meeting people connected with students I had known in London and this helped me to get some kind of grip on contemporary politics in the region as it related to the rest of the Federation. The British, however, had played off the people of each nation against one another during colonial days, and in Nigeria this process helped intensify tribalism after the Federation became independent. Traditionally, the colonialists had preferred the company of the Hausa and Fulani aristocracy to the Obas and Obis of the south. A mutual interest in horses helped foster the belief that the feeling was reciprocal. I did wonder whether by responding positively to the aloofness I encountered I was unwittingly following in the footsteps of my colonialist predecessors.

I celebrated my twenty-third birthday in Kaduna, the regional capital. Alhaji Hassan Hadeija, a businessman friend of Garba's, laid on a small party for me. He invited an English couple I had got to know and everyone was terribly polite to each other. But as soon as they left, the Director of Information sank loudly into a huge leather pouffe and kicked off his slippers. 'Thank goodness they've gone!' he said with feeling. 'Now we can relax.' More soft drinks and some gentle dancing

129

followed, then a man called Ibrahim came up with the coup of the evening. From beneath the folds of his voluminous *babban-riga* he produced an album of Dizzy Gillespie and another by Duke Ellington. I hadn't realised until then how homesick I was.

Hassan Hadeija was an intimate of Alhaji Sir Ahmadu Bello, the Sardauna of Sokoto and Premier of the Northern Region, whom I had photographed in London on a previous occasion. *Flamingo* wanted an interview with him. He took me in the Premier's entourage to the airport where Sir Ahmadu was arriving with the Federal Prime Minister. There he set wheels in motion.

The Sardauna, who was a traditionalist opposed to the emancipation of women, had a reputation among his opponents for being unapproachable. I soon found out this was untrue. He spent the entire day receiving visitors and discussing grievances in the time-honoured fashion of the benevolent despot. Hassan arranged for me to talk to him in his relatively spartan modern concrete home, where friends wandered casually in and out all day. I discovered that he was a hard worker who seldom got to bed until 2 a.m., rising just before dawn. Our interview was fairly bland and inconsequential, Sir Ahmadu parrying significant questions with the skill of the veteran diplomat he was. As I had been told he would, he skirted around the question of women's rights. (Years later, in another of life's ironic coincidences, I would get to know Terry Hunt, guitarist and driving-force behind Jam Today, longest-lived of British women's rock bands, and discover she had gone to school in Kaduna with one of the Sardauna's daughters.)

When I left, the Sardauna gave me a copy of his autobiography, signed with a flourish. I had been hesitant before, but now I was determined to seek out some of the women who were striving to find a voice for the disenfranchised in Northern politics. Hassan arranged for me to meet three such women. One was a supporter of the NPC, the Sardauna's party, the others members of the opposition NEPU (Northern Elements Progressive Union). Malama Ladi Shehu was a Christian who worked as a teacher and felt she could raise women's consciousness through education. And then there was Hajiya Gambo Sawaba, a Moslem, who was already a legendary figure in the struggle for women's rights. Hassan sent a message to her, telling her to meet us at my hotel.

At the appointed time she strode into the foyer, alone. She crossed to our table in a swashbuckling manner, making every head turn. She kicked off her shoes and sat with her legs wide apart, then helped herself to a cigarette. Hassan treated her with the utmost respect, and a group of his friends sitting in on our interview were clearly not a little in awe of this unusual woman. I was rather surprised at the friendly relationship that seemed to exist between her and them, NPC supporters to a man. Later I learned that she, like his other political opponents, was free to visit the Sardauna at will. Open discussion was, confusingly, a feature of this conservative regime.

Hajiya Gambo came from Nupe in Niger Province. 'Sawaba' was not her real name, but the NEPU slogan which, translated, means 'after suffering, peace comes'. It seemed fitting for someone who had been jailed on seven occasions since 1959 for gathering together groups of women to teach them what was happening on the political front. (In all, she was imprisoned seventeen times.) The interview was conducted in Hausa and English, with Hassan acting as interpreter. I suggested that he tape our conversation, too, so that when it came to writing it up, I could use our actual words rather than his approximation of what had been said. Our conversation was punctuated with gales of laughter all round, but what Hajiya Gambo had to say was deadly serious. She spoke in a husky voice tinged with sadness, all the while gesticulating extravagantly with her cigarette.

It is unusual anywhere for women to speak their minds openly when men are present, but she appeared to have no inhibitions. The Sardauna had told me that he had referred the question of women's suffrage to the Moslem experts and was awaiting their verdict. NEPU women, said Hajiya Gambo, pushing her headtie casually over her eyes, would continue to pester the government whatever that verdict might be. She said, 'We are not being denied the right to vote on religious grounds, it is because of the age-old attitude of Northern men towards their women. The non-Moslem women in the North are more progressive than their Moslem counterparts because the latter are always pushed into the background. Consequently, Christian women will become more progressive here, and, being a Moslem, I resent this.'

Opponents of women's suffrage claimed that by clamouring for the vote to be made a constitutional reality, NEPU would defeat its own ends. They pointed out that as most NPC supporters had four wives, these women would vote the same way as their husbands, thereby increasing the NPC's already substantial majority. Hajiya Gambo laughed derisively at this suggestion. 'It is not only NPC men who have four wives, you know, and who's to say that women will necessarily vote the same way as their husbands?' Her own situation reflected the trend away from orthodoxy. Her husband had married four wives, as permitted by Moslem custom, yet he supported her all the way, even during her incarceration.

At one point she had even threatened to take Sir Ahmadu Bello 'and the whole of his government' to court unless the franchise was extended to women. As far as she was concerned, the case was cut and dried, and it was on that note that our conversation ended. She tossed back her head and admonished, in English, 'Remember Sawaba!' A triumphant smile came over her face. 'You're looking at the first woman premier of the North!'

Despite the numbers of women who lived in purdah, Northern Nigeria differed considerably from some other Islamic countries. Several of the women I met moved around freely, their behaviour creating little comment despite the Sardauna's condemnation of women being seen in the street. In Kaduna I spent some evenings in the company of Irene Faruku, a teacher, and her husband Mohammed. Both were Hassan's friends and held progressive views. Irene prepared *tuwo*, the Northern staple made from pounded guinea corn, and the four of us sat down together, conversation ranging freely over the matters confronting Moslems in the Federation and women in the North. It was, I should imagine, comparatively unusual for women and men to eat together, although I realised that as a *baturia* I had certain advantages not normally accorded my gender.

Another woman I met told an amusing tale of polygamy. Polygamous marriages are like any other relationship in their diversity.

In some, the women become friends, in others they make an accommodation. In this case, no love was lost between the four women. Increasingly, though, dissatisfaction was setting in. Eventually a meeting was held where each revealed that for some time the husband, a distinguished local figure, had failed to pass their *girki*, the two nights where, under Islamic law, each woman is said to be 'in charge of the cooking', taking it in turn to look after the house and sleep with her husband. They concluded that he was seeing 'outside' women and resolved to teach him a lesson. They lay in wait one night and saw him come home with a woman from the town. Immediately they set about him. The other woman they sent naked into the night, later relenting and allowing the driver to take her home, but the husband was badly beaten. Unable to show his face for days for fear of the ridicule that would attach to his trouncing, he could not, under the circumstances, chastise his wives, either. For a while, at least, he became a dutiful husband.

The story was told with great relish and I felt a vicarious sense of mischief at being invited to share such intimate revelations. The conservatives of the North projected an aloof and puritanical view of themselves. There was something reassuring about knowing that behind every *babban-riga* and all the hauteur some aspects of life had a distinctly familiar ring.

I could not leave Nigeria without visiting Lagos, although it was not strictly on the agenda. However, I had gathered so much good material that I reasoned I could get away with stretching my ticket a little. I got in touch with Adam Fiberesima, my composer friend, and arranged to spend a weekend with him.

Adam organised a party, where I met the sculptor Ben Enwonwu and several other prominent Nigerian artists, then took me to the Nigeria Broadcasting Corporation, where I was able to interview composer Akin Euba and Chinua Achebe, author of the African classics *Things Fall Apart* and *No Longer At Ease*. Before leaving for London I went to the Lagos Museum. As I looked at the beautiful Benin bronzes and terracottas from ancient Ife an awful realisation dawned on me. With a handful of exceptions, all these works of art were reproductions. The originals were in collections in Europe and America. The museum's director expressed his unease at this iniquitous situation. The fight to reclaim African history was on.

Back in England, Yvonne told me she had extended her stay by several weeks in order to be with me. I wasn't too sure about this lesbian thing after my experience in Liberia, and I wasn't too happy. I wanted to think about what was happening to me. When she eventually left I felt a sense of relief. Stevie came with me to see her off at the station *en route* for Liverpool. I felt more secure with friends than with lovers.

11
Change is Gonna Come

People always want to know: 'What did Coltrane *say*?' 'What was 'Trane really *like*?' All I can reply is that I really don't know. I look at my interview with him, a simple, straightforward piece of reporting, and all it does is remind me that I was there. Because Coltrane was to die prematurely, at the age of 41 in 1967, some people are resentful not merely of the fact that I can't tell them more but also that it was I rather than they who had the opportunity to meet someone whose influence went beyond music. Coltrane made a point of treating fellow musicians as equals, instituting an egalitarian approach that would have a considerable impact on collective ways of working. Through his own example, he demonstrated that women had a place in the music, too. His attitudes reflected the developing concern for mutual and self-respect that occupied Afro-America during the 1960s. Coltrane is still a symbol of dignity and self-sufficiency. My abiding memory is one of quiet strength.

I am saddened that I was not better equipped to enquire more deeply into the saxophonist's philosophy and politics; but at the time I met him I was terribly inexperienced, groping my way in an alien world. Yet it was through meeting Coltrane and other musicians that I not only learned about the music but discovered a new way of looking at the world. In the process, I developed into a fairly accomplished interviewer.

Women have always been good listeners; that's been one of our ways of getting by. Conversations seldom take place between men and women as equals, but consist mostly of a man *telling* a woman about this, that or the other. A lifetime of that and you could go crazy. Many women do. However, turning the usual process to an advantage is one form of resistance. My ability to do this is, I think, one of the reasons why I have been successful as an interviewer, since most of the people I talked to were men. Anyway I never wanted to be the type of interviewer who provokes someone into an explosive statement. I preferred to let the other person do the talking, nudging here and there. Later, when I became a little more self-conscious about my technique, I developed tactics to use if the proceedings were flagging. By and large, the simple process worked for me.

When I grew bolder, I did occasionally use aggressive tactics but seldom felt happy doing so. Occasionally it happened by accident, as when I went to see Thelonious Monk. After years in the backroom, barely making ends meet, he was achieving the recognition his innovative piano-playing and composition deserved. His name was spoken with reverence in music circles but he was notoriously taciturn. He confined himself to monosyllabic remarks or, if you were lucky, one-liners, and to the best of my knowledge, was only interviewed on a handful of occasions.

Working for *Jazz News* I had got to know another photographer named John Hopkins and when Monk came to London in 1966, he suggested we do a big piece on him together. 'Hoppy' saw photography as a way of getting to meet the people who interested him. As I was still basically a writer, he felt I could act as the entrée to Thelonious. We determined to sell our story to one of the big 'glossies' that flourished in the 'Swinging Sixties'. Monk was staying at the Park Lane Hilton with his wife, the redoubtable Nellie. Her sustaining role in his life has been often acknowledged, and Kitty Grime had suggested she might be the more interesting person to interview. It was an idea I kept in mind.

It was an unbelievably awful day, pouring with rain, and Hoppy and I arrived drenched to the skin. I trundled my battered old portable Grundig tape-recorder into the foyer and we must have looked pretty disreputable because the house detective pounced on us as we were tidying up. We were only allowed up to Monk's suite after producing some credentials. There the pianist slumped, bearlike, in a chintz-covered armchair, a floppy fur hat on his head.

Monk's middle name was, I ventured, alleged to be 'Sphere'. 'Sphere?' echoed Hoppy with delight. 'You were made very early on, namewise – all you had to do was find a hustle!' I used that as the first line – divine – of the article. Monk, however, was unshaken by this enthusiasm. It was common knowledge that he had nearly always lived with his mother, so I asked him whether women had been a great help in his life. 'Uh-huh,' he agreed. I suggested that many musicians had said they would never have survived in the music without the help of wives, mothers and other women. Did he agree? 'Uh-huh.' How, I wondered, had his mother helped? 'Well, she never figured I should do anything else. If I wanted to play music, it was all right with her.' Unusual? 'Yes, I think so.' And Nellie? 'She's the same way around, man. Whatever I want to do . . . do what I want to do.'

He gave his answers in a detached, uninterested fashion. To enliven the proceedings, Hoppy chimed in with a few 'socially aware' comments on the New York police, who had denied Monk his Cabaret Card (work permit) for some time. Monk stayed unmoved. He had said something about the sound of New York City, too, so I asked him how did it actually sound. All of a sudden he was on his feet, demanding, 'How do you expect me to describe to you right here how New York sounds? How does London sound? Can you tell me how it sounds, huh?' He paced up and down, growing increasingly exasperated. But he also did a lot of talking.

I had got quite a bit on tape, but still didn't feel there was enough material for the grand feature-spread we had planned. We decided to follow the Monks to Birmingham the following day where the pianist was playing a concert with his quartet. Backstage, he was affable, the ice having been broken, but he had little more to say. I decided to follow Kitty's suggestion and try talking to Nellie. It was a shrewd move. She had some telling observations to make about the business of being a genius who had to earn a living like anyone else. 'He's no more impressed with himself than he was in the dark days,' she said.

We sold the story to *King*, the British equivalent to *Playboy*. (In 1966 the 'girlie' magazines were regarded as a sophisticated outlet for jazz writers.) I also sent it to *Downbeat*. When it appeared there, as a cover-story, it created quite a stir. Trumpeter Art Farmer told me his drummer had called him to say, 'hey, there's this *wild* piece on Thelonious!' I was in New York City again later that year and when the musicians found out that I was 'the chick who did that story on Thelonious', most of them were a little surprised. I still dressed in unobtrusive clothes and hid my shyness behind a smear of blue eye-shadow and the palest pink lipstick. I did not give the impression of being particularly worldly. At first I had been a little ashamed at annoying Monk. Now I had to admit feeling vindicated at having stirred him from his customary lethargy. Monk did most of his talking through his music, but the people who loved him for 'Straight, No Chaser' or 'Evidence' also wanted to know about the *man*. The piece certainly put my name on the map.

Through doing interviews I learnt that people with a positive racial viewpoint never made disparaging remarks about other musicians. Over the years I did meet individuals who would badmouth others, and as a journalist, of course, I sometimes enjoyed being handed a wicked quote on a plate. But I actually used such comments less and less as time went on. And I always felt that 'put-downs' only reflected badly, ultimately, on the speaker.

I developed a 'confidential' style of writing, basing my approach on the work of writers such as Max Jones, who seemed to be on good terms with the musicians. This meant occasionally writing about 'names' with what was, in some cases, a presumptuous familiarity. Among jazz fans, of every race, there has always been a feeling that 'everyone' *knows* about Monk, Duke, Louis and Bird, implying an intimate bond between them and us that does not, in its true sense, exist. It's there, though, in the sense of there being an alternative community, and whenever a death is announced there is often for many music lovers an acute sense of personal loss. But I did get to know an enormous number of musicians, eventually being able to number several among my friends. Some writers deliberately kept away from the players. They felt it was important to keep their 'critical' faculties intact, so as not to be swayed, as they saw it, by personal considerations. I felt the opposite. If you knew someone personally, it was less easy to write irresponsibly about what they were doing. It was not good enough to make a reputation for yourself at the expense of someone else's means of earning a living, although that was the method the popular music weeklies encouraged. There, ego was all, and style the major consideration. Had it not been for my close contact with the musicians, though, it would have taken me far longer than it did to reach these conclusions.

For a long time I vacillated between pen and camera, never being able to decide which tool suited me best. I became British correspondent for an American Rock monthly, *Hit Parader*, and did stories on everyone from John Lennon to Jimi Hendrix. 'Stay funny as a bunny,' were the latter's parting words to me on the day I rescued him from a crowd of vociferous fans and drove him home in my old Ford Popular, to his considerable relief. Jimi was a gentle soul, a far cry from the racist 'wild man of pop' image with which he was sold. British Rock music was sweeping the world and I enjoyed the opportunity of meeting such star-names as Stevie Winwood and the Hollies, while remaining as much into 'jazz' as ever. Photographically, though, I felt I could do better than continuing to cover the occasional wedding. When I looked at the standards of photography in the musical papers, I knew I could. Hoppy helped to convince me. He was the first photographer I came across who was concerned to present musicians in a dignified way. When he shot pictures for the feature on Monk, he went about producing an exhaustive coverage. He never settled for the easy 'action' shot. For a while I followed humbly in his footsteps. This is not to imply that he was arrogant in any way. Hoppy believed in Peace, Love and Sharing.

I was embarking on my first attempt to change consciousness and perception through my pictures, although I certainly didn't know that was what I was doing at the time. It just seemed normal to shoot pictures that showed who the people were rather than merely what they did. Ronnie Scott and Pete King, his club manager, generously let us into the Gerrard Street basement to take pictures, and we were always busy and on the scene. The jazz magazines paid so little money that the 'big' photographers never bothered with them. Our work was received with gratitude and neither of us were particularly fussy about where it appeared. Getting published was the important thing. We used available light at all times, selling reportage-style pictures to anyone. We even managed to get documentary stuff into *Crescendo*, the dance-band magazine – the editor, Tony Brown, was encouraging – until one day the publisher flung back a picture at me with the retort that it was 'too black' and unprintable. When I protested, he waved a crude, direct-flash mug-shot at me. There was no modelling whatsoever on the face, but plenty of eyebrow detail. '*That's* what our readers want,' he told me. 'You can see every hair, every pore. We don't want all this *arty* stuff!' From the facial hair angle, I had to admit he was right. But the Thelonious Monks of this world, it seemed to me, were about a great deal more than the beetling of their brows.

As far as I could tell, Hoppy and I were the only photographers who cared about anything other than earning a living. Most people churned out the same old poses over and over. Nobody complained as long as the picture was in focus, but there came a point when you realised there were only five angles you could get on a trumpet-player. In those days before bromides, paste-ups and PMTs, the subs or the editor prepared layouts; there was no studio or anything like that. Pictures were sized crudely, marked-up by sticking four pins through the print at the corners of an imaginary rectangle or square. The holes were then joined on the back in pencil. All 'unnecessary' details were automatically excluded, tight 'head' shots being the order of the day. We had a hard fight on our hands.

Hoppy was an amazing person, ahead of his time in everything. Like me, he had started out a Louis Armstrong fan – his virtuoso 'Cornet Chop Suey' was in both our record collections – but he moved on to newer sounds before I did. In New York he had met and photographed William Burroughs, hung out with Allen Ginsberg; at home he helped set up the London Free School and, with others, founded the hippie newspaper *International Times*. He was the first English person I knew who cooked 'real' Indian curries at home, and the first I heard speak about LSD, DNA, THC, psychedelia, lightshows and video. His energy and personal lifestyle were immensely attractive, although I could not completely identify with the outrageous hedonism and contempt for material possesions that being a true hippie entailed. But it was he who was my entrée to the fringes of the new counter-culture that developed in the wake of the era of 'never-had-it-so-good' capitalism.

Saxophonist Ornette Coleman and his drummer lived at Hoppy's during a lengthy European sojourn in 1965; his enthusiasm for music led him to record, totally without experience, another American saxophonist, Steve Lacy. Years later he told me he had felt as at a loss for words with Ornette as he had done with Burroughs. Because I seemed able to relate easily to the visiting Black musicians, he thought I was the one being adventurous. 'Getting close to those guys was something I could never do,' he said. 'No one did things like that.' To me, though, it was Hoppy who was always ahead of the game. It was he, after all, who provided a personal introduction to Albert Ayler, Cecil Taylor, Sun Ra and Frank Zappa. And it was through meeting these musical revolutionaries that I started writing for *Melody Maker*.

In the 1960s Black Americans became, as Louis E. Lomax put it in *The Negro Revolt*, 'more tribal'. This meant a conscious coming together as the Afro-American nation, and when I went back to New York in 1966 and 1967 I became aware of the changing mood. Historically, most musicians stayed away from politics. The precarious nature of work made speaking out or the espousal of causes inadvisable, although a notable number of musicians, many of whom were in the artistic vanguard, were among those Afro-Americans who converted to Islam in the period following World War II. Generally speaking, musicians viewed themselves as a libertarian élite who were always 'ahead of the game'. But the tribal mood of the period, especially in the wake of the assassination of Malcolm X and with the increasing loss of Black life in Vietnam, intensified to the point where pragmatism among artists gave way to the adoption of a more committed position.

All this would not have been obvious to me yet had I moved only with the older musicians, but Hoppy, whose interest was cultural rather than political, insisted I get to know the people who were playing the 'New Thing'. Black commentators LeRoi Jones and A.B. Spellman among others had been writing about musical revolutionaries like Albert Ayler, Cecil Taylor and Archie Shepp, but I had yet to hear how they sounded. Hoppy had met some of the new musicians at the Newport Jazz Festival and now he gave me telephone numbers for Taylor, Sun Ra and a trumpeter named Bill Dixon who had organised the new music's first 'statement of intent', the October Revolution in Jazz of 1964. He also put me in touch with Elisabeth van der Mei, a Dutch woman who worked at Atlantic Records and was a vital force in stimulating outside interest in the new music. She took me to hear a rehearsal band led by saxophonist Joe Henderson and trumpeter Kenny Dorham at the Dom on St Mark's Place, the main drag of the East Village, and introduced me to people as yet unknown, such as saxophonists Gato Barbieri, Marion Brown, Benny Maupin and Robin Kenyatta. She supported several musicians emotionally and materially, too, and at her apartment I met bassist Norris Jones, later known as Sirone, who had just arrived from Atlanta.

It was Elisabeth who helped me get to know Cecil Taylor. A fearsomely talented pianist who had already played Europe and recorded, he occupied the same 'alternative' cultural space as people such as Allen Ginsberg, painter Larry Rivers and film-maker Shirley Clarke during the period before many Black artists moved away from Bohemia to 'work on the building' back home. His music was hard and uncompromising, with no set key signatures or barlines, but devastating in its intensity and freshness. His audience was limited, his critics merciless, a degree of rejection that caused him to withdraw into intellectual obtuseness and 'weirdness'. I ran into Cecil several times before I succeeded in pinning him down with a tape-recorder. He lived in a dingy loft above an equally grimy warehouse not far from Herald Square. The fashion for loft-living was to come later; Cecil lived there out of necessity. He seldom worked and I had just missed one of his rare residencies at Slug's, home of the new music on East 3rd Street between Avenues B and C. Cecil was acerbic and cynical. He knew what it was to be 'in vogue' with the arbiters of artistic fashion. He had, he said, felt their 'emotional fibres': 'They're very gentle, they look so pale and anaemic, but they're very bright and they're very witty – and they can't do much of anything, really. They can think, but they don't *live*.' He hissed the words, 'There's no fucking *blood*!'

He gave an impromptu recital to enable me to take some photographs, an exercise which produced an Embarrassing Incident. The loft was deadly grey and I needed more light. I asked Cecil if I could let up the blind which needed a downward jerk to get started. 'I don't think it's been down for years,' he said, just as the huge sheet left its moorings and fell on my head, enveloping me. I stood there covered in filth and choking. 'Has now,' said Cecil blithely and hit the keyboard, hard. He proceeded to play as though his life depended on it.

What I didn't know then was that most of the people involved in the New Music were playing as though their lives depended on it because, indeed, they did. The music had always been of vital import-ance to Afro-Americans, a lifeline into the mainstream as well as a means of earning a living. Black men and women escaped from the ghetto through playing the horn or singing; now people were begin-ning to see the music in political terms. The idea that Blacks kept on creating new forms of music to protect the culture from the ravaging of whites who codified, copied and plundered was just being espoused. I did not, however, hear the view of the music as a repository of the oral tradition expounded until I met saxophonist Archie Shepp.

Archie was a university graduate who had read history and Marx and worked as an actor. He wrote plays and poetry, too, and had contributed some startling polemical articles to *Downbeat* which was still reeling from the response to its unaccustomed liberalism. Archie incorporated the flavour of older forms into his tenor playing and was developing an unusual style on the horn, with arrogant, sarcastic overtones.

138   In person he was 'militant' but not antagonistic or without

humour. He spoke with devastating candour and put me straight on a number of misconceptions. It was common then for whites to refer to positive discrimination or the expression of Afro-American nationalism or autonomy as 'Black racism'. I inadequately slipped into the habit in one of my questions. 'Racism?' he parried. 'It's difficult for a Negro to be a racist because we have no power . . . Racism implies power. I mean, you aren't seriously suggesting that Malcolm X ever kept white children out of Negro schools, are you?' I took his point.

I was staying next door to the Blakeneys, and several musicians came by to see me at their apartment. One of these was Milford Graves, an as yet little known drummer who would become, through example, one of my important teachers. Milford discussed how American musicians had taken the drum too far from its African origins, and how he intended to bring it back. He told me of various sticking techniques that had been overlooked by Western drummers more concerned with show business than depth of meaning. I had never heard anyone talk about such things before.

Not all the committed musicians I met were involved in the New Music. Saxophonists Jackie McLean and Jimmy Heath were traditionalists but clearly 'outspoken', and pianist Randy Weston, who played a little like Monk, had actually moved to Africa and was putting down permanent roots in Morocco. It was Randy, in fact, who was the first to clarify for me the distinction between separatism and autonomy. The goal of the Southern-based civil rights movement had been integration; now, said Randy, many Black people saw that as another part of the American lie. Painstakingly he explained that he should have the right to choose to live apart from Whites or side by side and not be indicted for either choice. When it came to the music, the injustice accorded the innovators had been so profound that acknowledging and proclaiming their contribution was essential, he said, even if to do so meant excluding the individual white artist, however worthy. As he put it, 'I don't care if so-and-so *is* a great jazz musician, it's immaterial.' It gave me great pause for thought. To Randy, his antecedents and peers were about far more than the music they played. He saw the jazz musician as the bearer of a certain tradition, forged in the African furnace, and carried throughout the Diaspora as living history. Not for nothing had he chosen to make his home in the continent paced out by griots, the oral historians of the African nations.

Older musicians were part of the avant garde as well. Sun Ra was one of these, a composer and pianist from Alabama who used Egyptian and astrological symbolism in his philosophy and purposely kept his early background a mystery. African dress had yet to be adopted by Black Americans to any degree – Milford Graves was wearing a rather fetching ski-pullover when we first met – but Sun Ra had anticipated the movement by getting loose-fitting tunics made up for himself and his Arkestra using sparkling remnants of something theatrical. Several of the musicians who lived with him at his Sun Studio wore spangled bandanas wrapped around their heads; reedplayer Marshall Allen, with his fairish curls tumbling over his headtie, looked like a Mexican *bandido*. Sun Ra himself sported a turban with a star at the centre. They looked like space-age African hippies – which, I suppose, they were.

Sun Ra showed me a copy of J.A. Rogers' *Sex and Race*. I had first encountered this book, which claims African ancestry for many historical European figures, when another musician, Prince Lasha, brought it to London. I knew it was hard to come by but Sun Ra had a great deal of unusual literature. He produced his own poetry and instructive pamphlets and studied anything connected with the theory of Egypt as the origin of the human race. To my eternal shame, I have to admit that like most white people then, I was sceptical about this. Sun Ra talked in metaphors, using language hard for an outsider to fathom. He liked to indulge in a little bit of the harmless put-on, too, but what he had to say tended to stand the test of time. Twenty years ago, though, I was yet to read Cheikh Anta Diop, the Senegalese historian devoted to the reconstruction of Africa's place in history. Diop was one of the scholars who traced the origin of civilisation to Egypt, but I thought Sun Ra's theory was a quaint idea, popular only among some older Blacks intent on finding something to replace the history slavery destroyed. By inference, I said so when I wrote up our conversation.

I saw Al Douglas again, but found we had little to say to each other. He was on staff at a major network TV show and doing theatre work and barely had time to sleep. But New York was packed with musicians and I renewed a brief London acquaintance with trumpeter Howard McGhee, who had been a close associate of Charlie Parker. Howard had just started a big band for musicians who enjoyed playing for the fun of it, and I went along on their gigs with him and Sandy, his wife. They treated me like an adopted daughter for a while and generally we'd end up back at their place for a meal and more music, usually with other musicians in tow. I saw at first hand the realities of trying to make a living from something you loved but which was not necessarily fashionable.

Paul Jeffrey, who played saxophone with Howard's band, took me to Brooklyn one night to hear Wynton Kelly playing at the Blue Coronet, a neighbourhood bar. It was the first time I'd seen Wynton since that night in London when I could think of nothing to say. Any embarrassment vanished when he sat down to play. He was one of the most exciting pianists of his generation, someone who, for me, epitomised what the music was all about. Drinkers clustered around the bar, some talking loudly, but the atmosphere only encouraged the trio to swing. With their everyday banter and casual way of showing their appreciation, the audience were, in fact, making a statement, saying this is *our* music. It was different from the more serious rooms of Manhattan.

I went back to Harlem, too, to Minton's and Count Basie's bar, where the beer-mats echoed Congressman Adam Clayton Powell Jr's slogan, 'Keep the Faith, Baby!' and to see Langston Hughes. When he had visited London in 1964, he had held a party for a select group and invited me, too. Now I found him playing host to Ernest Cole, the brilliant African photographer who got himself classified as 'Coloured' to document life in South Africa under apartheid. His startling photographs, many of which have become icons, were soon to be published in *House of Bondage*, and Langston, characteristically, was helping him find his feet. The three of us talked for a while and had a few drinks, then I left them to discuss more relevant matters. Langston, who was to die the following year, always seemed to have as much time for others as he did for himself.

I still didn't know what to make of the avant garde music. Coltrane's extended collective improvisation, *Ascension*, released in 1965, had heralded changing times but I, along with other listeners, found it hard to listen to. Coltrane, however, was building on an obvious past. He represented a musical breakthrough that was comparatively easy to understand. But the rest of the new music did not *swing* in the accepted sense, the main reason why it did not appeal immediately to many in its traditional community audience.

A lawyer, Bernard Stollman, had recorded most of the musicians who appeared at Bill Dixon's October Revolution and started a label called ESP. That was where most people heard musicians like Sun Ra, Ayler and percussionist Sunny Murray for the first time. I went to see Stollman and staggered back to the Blakeneys with a bunch of new albums. The record I liked best was Albert Ayler's *Spirits Rejoice*! and I played it on the Tannoy system whenever Egg and Barbara were out of the way. Ayler was a saxophonist who wrenched tremendous emotion out of music and listener alike, using simple marches and church tunes as his material and taking the music back to places where, as Archie Shepp remarked, it had not been for a long time. It was powerful, no doubt about it, and totally iconoclastic. But I didn't know whether I liked it.

Elisabeth van der Mei sent Albert to see me. He arrived with his brother Donald, who played the trumpet, and I found myself caught up in the world of 'that old-time religion'. Albert was not just an extraordinary musician whose playing was suffused with yearning, he was an extraordinary person who spoke about spiritual matters in a way I had never encountered before. He even looked unusual, his beard growing out of an unpigmented patch on his skin, half black and half white. I noticed he had patches of white hair on his head as well.

When we talked, Albert had a lot to say about 'love' and 'feeling the spirit'. He hinted that time was running out both for himself and those who did not take heed of his musical message. He was melancholy, but he talked in an easy matter-of-fact fashion. Still, I felt uncertain about what he was saying. In subsequent years I would encounter many devout Afro-Americans raised in the church and develop a greater awareness of the philosophy and speech of the 'saved'. Now I was out of my depth.

He signed my copy of *Spirits Rejoice*! with the words 'Love to All, Best of the True', and we went up to Harlem to take some photographs. On the subway, the brothers stood slightly apart from me. Both were immaculately groomed, dressed in matching olive-green checked suits of the kind everyone wanted in those days. With their candystripe shirts and slimline silk ties, they looked like a couple of hip executives.

The next time I saw Albert was in London. He had brought his band over to Europe and been the hit of the Berlin Jazz Festival. Now he was to tape a BBC television programme at the London School of Economics. The whole event was a disaster; everyone was stunned or shocked by the music. Donald and the sound technicians were in perpetual dispute over the positioning of microphones. The crew and some local musicians laughed out loud at the music, others were overcome by its passion. Eventually I would come to regard Albert Ayler as one of the most profound artists to emerge from the music. At the LSE, though, I was still a bit puzzled, even though I wanted to like him.

But South African pianist Chris McGregor was ecstatic when the Aylers said they wanted to stay around for a while. I introduced them to Chris and his wife Maxine, who had not been in London long, and Albert and Donald moved into their flat, drummer Beaver Harris joining them. They played together and the Americans expressed a desire to stay on and work with Chris in England. But their concert promoter dismissed the idea. He said it would be 'bad for their image'.

My old barber friend Johnny Millington had taken over the Fiesta Restaurant and Stevie and I took the Aylers there for a meal. We gave him advance warning that we were headed there with a bunch of cats in tow, and he prepared a special meal for us. Business was slow, so he joined us at the table. After we had finished eating, Beaver started playing rhythms on the table with his hands. Stevie joined in, matching him lick for lick and anticipating the changes of rhythm. Then she began to change up the rhythms herself. Beaver's superior air was replaced by one of delight when he realised he had someone who could play. 'All r-i-i-*ght*!' he said. Albert nodded quietly.

Someone suggested we go round to Hoppy's to see if he had something to smoke. We set off, but Stevie's old car broke down on the way. Albert and Beaver joined me to give her a push-start, but the sight of two Black men and a white woman together was like a red rag to a bull to the Westbourne Grove police. We had done nothing untoward, had hardly had a drink, in fact, but were pulled over nevertheless. We were quizzed, and harassed, the Americans being asked to explain themselves. They had already had a bad experience with Immigration officials on their arrival, and I was expecting them to explode. Sensibly, they played it cool, but Stevie and I were fuming. I never saw Albert again, as it happens. Given what seemed to me then his other-worldly nature, though, I've relished the sheer ordinariness of that last memory which had him and me pushing that old 'banger' down the road together.

I did speak to the saxophonist once more on the phone when I was in New York the following year. He was friendly, but preoccupied, and we were unable to get together. He died three years later in mysterious circumstances which have yet to be adequately explained.

Back in New York I ran up against heroin. I had come across addicts before, of course, but mainly in London, where drugs could be obtained legally, by prescription. 'Scag' was the fashionable bebop drug, though its use was by no means confined to the musicians' community, the media just made it appear that way. I came to realise that equating narcotics abuse with the music could be seen as deliberate propaganda, aimed at keeping Black people 'in their place' by linking the music with 'immorality'. Nevertheless, it was common knowledge that among the survivors of the bebop period were several who had served prison terms under the punitive federal system. From time to time a respected musician would return from rehabilitation to the accompaniment of encouraging noises from the music press. Behind the scenes it was a different matter. Cynics speculated on how long so-and-so would 'stay clean', the names of the three-time losers being cited as 'told-you-so' examples of 'once an addict, always an addict'.

A number of musicians I wanted to meet seemed to be hard to locate. Other writers told me not to bother because it would be imposs-ible to pin down someone with a 'habit', musicians could be unhelpful and discouraging if I mentioned certain names. In some cases, though, I persisted. The implication was that addicts belonged on the scrap heap. I did not agree. There were a couple of people I felt merited wider exposure, brilliant instrumentalists whose names seldom appeared in music publications although privately, other artists paid tribute to their contribution.

I went to see a man I'll call 'Freddy' who lived in a sleazy Broadway hotel in the West 80s. As far as I could make out, his wife was also an addict who supported them both by hustling. Freddy was one of the greats on his instrument, but after completing a jail term and reneging on several 'return' gigs, he was hardly working at all. The room where they lived was filthy, the tables and window-ledges covered with spent matches and Coke bottle caps in which they had heated up the crystalline scag to dissolve it. Had I subscribed to the prevailing moralism, I should have felt contempt for this man, but I didn't. We took an immediate liking to each other and I saw him on several occasions. We went for a walk by the river, where he posed for pictures with his horn, then breakfasted at a coffeeshop nearby. He was friendly, entertaining and witty, the only telltale sign of his habit being his hands, swollen like big brown boxing-gloves. Away from the claus-trophobic hotel-room, I found it hard to associate him with its squalor.

'Larry', who lived in similar circumstances, was a drummer. Despite a heavy 'Jones', he was continually sought for his sensitivity and drive. The fact that he never missed a job showed there were no hard-and-fast rules where dope is concerned. It took me two weeks of phone-calls to persuade him to see me, and when he did finally turn up, two hours after the appointed time, he started nodding off between questions. But Larry loved music and he told me enough to enable me to write a feature that did him proud. Some years later he entered a drug programme and emerged clean and triumphant. He became involved in religion, renouncing all artificial stimulants and working with children whenever his heavy schedule allowed him. Freddy, sadly, didn't make it. He moved to Las Vegas where he found work in a showband, but died just as he began earning a decent living.

My attitude to drugs was ambivalent. I seemed to get along with people who were addicted, probably because I did not moralise or condemn. And yet it used to break my heart to see the way that some really fine people lived. At first I was fascinated at the reason why anyone should allow themselves to get into such a state of dependency. It was some time before I realised the extent to which narcotics were pumped into the Black community as a deliberate means of pacifica-tion. It was not until six years after meeting Freddy and Larry that I saw white dealers standing openly beside 'needle-park', their briefcases bulging with money, while Black dope-fiends took all the risks and hustled each other. People used to say that their old blue needle-tracks were a souvenir from the struggle, like the numbers tattooed on the arm of a death-camp survivor. It was a provocative idea but when I saw such dope-dealing scenarios being enacted, it began to make sense.

I had already decided to do a book when I made my third visit to New York, in 1967. I would expand on some of my earlier articles with fresh interviews and put these and new pieces together. My plan was to build up a representative picture of the 'Jazz People' by talking to individuals with a particular aspect of the collective story to tell. There would be a blues singer in there, Big Joe Turner, and an older musician whose creative fire continued to burn, Buck Clayton. Archie Shepp and Cecil Taylor expressed the militant mood of the 'New Negro', and I got to know saxophonist Jimmy Heath, too, a Coltrane contemporary who was raised on bebop but was beginning to adapt the newer ideas to his style. I wanted someone who had grown up in the shadow of Charlie Parker, too, and emerged his own man. Jackie McLean was a natural for that.

But I also wanted a spectacular 'How I Beat Narcotics' story. I persuaded a reformed addict to tell me his tale for posterity, feeling confident enough in our relationship to ask him some intimate questions. His unexpurgated story had already appeared in *Melody Maker*; now, late one night, he went through it again for me. At the time, I never gave the morality of this any thought. Newspaper stories, though, were one thing, a chapter in a book was permanent. The story stunned people in England when they read it – 'harrowing', 'painful', these were the stock responses – and yet I now question the good sense of having exposed him in this way. Although he never expressed a view, and indeed, repeated the story elsewhere, I have come to believe that what I did was mistaken. To reveal the tragedy of a single individual, at the expense of a people constantly threatened by forces that seek to muzzle protest and action was an ignorant act on my part. The story *was* true, and at the time it felt like a real scoop. Now I regret having done it.

On my trips to New York, I learned how to be a better photographic technician. My bread, as they say, was short, so I sought out other photographers to save on darkroom expenses. Chuck Stewart was one of these, a man who had shot hundreds of record-sleeves, including many of Coltrane's sessions for ABC-Impulse. Unlike most of the music scene's visible photographers, he was Black, which gave him more of an entrée with the musicians. 'We think of Chuck as one of the fellows,' Clark Terry told me.

Chuck shared a studio with two other photographers, also Black, located in midtown Manhattan. It seemed pretty smart to me, compared to the cramped way most of us worked at home. Faced with the new stainless-steel developing tanks, though, I panicked. Everyone I knew still used plastic ones, but the guys couldn't believe this piece of news and snorted with derision, secure in their modern, upmarket environment. They took the task out of my hands for the meantime, but I was too embarrassed to ask for Chuck's help again. And I never did get the knack of loading those tanks.

Another man from whom I begged space knocked me out of the way with impatience when I proceeded to print at my usual slow pace. Heated, I wanted to escape as quickly as possible, and told him the initial prints would do for *Melody Maker*, overinked as it always was. He rounded on me instantly. 'You're *not* going out of here with prints like that!' he said fiercely. 'I pride myself in being a good printer and you should, too.' Swallowing my annoyance, I watched him, dodging and burning in, getting the very best from my negatives, and in doing so had one of the best printing lessons I've had in my life.

I continued to see quite a lot of the Blakeneys, but in 1967 they were no longer as devoted to the music as before. Barbara, in fact, seemed to be following the British beat groups with almost as much enthusiasm as her teenage daughter.

We went to the Village Gate one night to hear Mingus, and I renewed my acquaintance with the unruly genius. He was in one of his offhand moods, in notable contrast to the music he played that night. Working with just a quartet, an unusual setting for him, he exchanged smiles and nods of encouragement with his old friend, trombonist Britt Woodman, their music warm and evocative of Ellington. Mingus did give me his phone number so I could call to arrange an interview.

I arrived at his apartment to find him in his shirt-sleeves, a flat throwing-knife in his hand. On the wall hung a couple of cheap wooden plaques he had won as 'Best Bassist' in *Downbeat* readers' and critics' polls, and he wanted to show what he thought of such useless awards. The broad-bladed knife whistled across the room and lodged itself with a thud in one of the plaques. Then Mingus poured himself a substantial vodka — 'None for the press,' he said belligerently, though with a twinkle — and we sat down to talk about the record company he had just formed. When the interview was over he relented, tipping the remainder of the bottle's contents in my direction.

I played back the tape the next day. To my dismay, nothing had registered. Mingus had given me a brilliant interview, full of vivid observations and controversial statements, and I'd failed to depress the 'Record' button. I was heartbroken, but there was nothing else for it. With the courage born only of youth, I picked up the phone and asked if I could see him again. I daresay he was too taken aback to refuse, and the following day saw me back at his side. This time I met Sue Graham, his wife, a Village sophisticate who was to inspire and support the turbulent genius for the rest of his life. The three of us sat around, talking and joking 'just like normal people'. At the end of it all, Mingus handed me an order-form for a couple of his new albums. These included the legendary *Mingus at Monterey*. 'Write your address on here,' he commanded, and arranged that the records be sent, free of charge. It was a typically generous gesture from a volatile, much-misunderstood man.

As I became more interested in what everyone now called the New Music, I noticed that the drummers got as much attention as the horns or the keyboard players. I had written a longish feature for *Downbeat* on Sunny Murray, the most prominent of the new percussionists and a major innovator, now I wanted to do a more substantial interview with Milford Graves for *Jazz Monthly*. When he asked if there were any money involved, I was taken aback. My *Melody Maker* stories on him and Sunny, on Albert Ayler, Sun Ra and Cecil Taylor were the first interviews with the new revolutionaries to appear in Britain. But the MM was

145

a popular music weekly with a large circulation and paid accordingly, while the small music magazines were a different matter entirely. Run on a shoestring by enthusiasts, they all paid a pittance – when they paid. Milford was not to know this, of course, and I explained the situation as carefully as I could.

What he was doing was questioning why anyone should be allowed to make money out of his music when he was unable to support himself and his family by it. The exploitation of Blacks across the entire music spectrum was a reflection of the history of the African people in America. Increasingly Afro-Americans saw no reason to help Whites enrich themselves at the expense of their labour and history. Milford was a cultural nationalist who had little time for white people. He could see I was serious, though, and agreed to talk to me again. He had just joined forces with pianist Don Pullen and they had started their own record label. He gave me the first of their albums, the cover hand-painted by himself, and I was impressed when he outlined their plans for self-sufficiency. I admired his personal confidence and self-possession, too, and it was because of this, as much as the music, that I became involved with the New Music and what was, in essence, a Black way of seeing.

To ask a writer to subjugate their own ego went against the established order of things. But that was what nationalists like Milford and most of the younger musicians demanded of any white person who sought to get to grips with the New Music. Few were prepared to make the sacrifice initially, reasoning that an interest in the music was some-how proof that they could not harbour racist ideas. It wasn't easy to abandon the traditional white view of the music, but I found the confrontational mood instructive. Just as in Northern Nigeria I'd been 'baturia' and the Hausa 'the people', now I realised I was 'the other', admitted into aspects of the Black reality only on sufferance.

The new musicians had a mission. They spoke of their desire to erase the image of their forebears as unthinking hedonists, numbed with narcotics and unable to control their own destinies. It was a positive view. And as far as personal interaction was concerned, they were no longer especially flirtatious, a considerable advantage after the sexual pressure that had intruded too often as I went about my pro-fessional business. As for me, my politicisation was developing. I was moving on up.

With the popularity of British rock music in the United States, the exchange restrictions that operated against Americans playing in Bri-tain were eased. Now there was the opportunity to hear any number of celebrated musicians. But for me, as for most serious jazz fans, the regular visits by the Duke Ellington orchestra remained the high spot. Whether there was new material on offer or just a new look at the old standbys, 'Rocking in Rhythm' and the like, Duke was the artist supreme. Harry Carney would call as soon as the band hit town, and Clive and I would be greeted like old friends backstage. I'd occasionally go on the road with them, too. And yet there remained something magical about Duke's music and the people who played it.

I had dinner with Cootie Williams one night and got to know a little about the melancholy master of the 'growl' trumpet. He and the saxophonist Johnny Hodges stayed aloof, surrounded by an air of mystery which they had built up around themselves since their early days on the road. They wrapped themselves in heavy coats with astrakhan collars and carried themselves like lords, effortlessly producing elegant women to accompany them on out-of-town trips, often to the chagrin of the various jobsworths. Over a steak and a bottle of wine, Cootie told me what women had meant to him over the years. He had known filmstars, he told me, and named them. 'All great jazz musicians, every one of them, have had many loves and girls in their lives. People don't read about these things in books, but a girl *is* jazz music. They throw something into the mind to make you produce jazz.'

It was on one of the annual Ellington jaunts that I met Joan Spalding, a London-born social worker who looked after pensioners in the Welsh valleys. Joan loved jazz and had spent a fleeting period on the halls in her youth. To an outsider, though, she was the least likely of jazz fans, a tiny, shortsighted woman alone, middle-aged and marooned in the middle of Abergavenny. She was, however, one of an uncountable number besotted by the music with no one to talk to. Sneakily she snapped her fingers to Oscar Peterson at night and knocked back sweet sherry while her neighbours were watching *Crossroads* and drinking their cocoa.

By being in the right place at the right time, Joan got to know some of the Ellingtons, then, through a typical kindness of Harry's, found herself in the presence of the Great Man. She persuaded Duke to see my photographs, and rang me from Bristol in the middle of the night to say so, sounding in her enthusiasm like a cross between a schoolmarm and a naughty little girl. 'He's expecting you to ring him at the Dorchester tomorrow,' she said. '*Don't* ring before two.' I rang and to my surprise was granted an audience. When I arrived, Duke was breakfasting on steak and salad, and discussing the merits of cooking brandy and ice with a *Sunday Mirror* reporter. He liked my pictures and bought some, and the reporter took one for his paper.

But I was far from being the only beneficiary of Joan's thoughtfulness. Her own isolation made her aware of others whose business or family commitments made an active engagement with the scene impossible, and she formed a tape correspondence circle called 'The Jazz Loners'. In many cases she would decide what people should hear, tape it and mail it with a command to give the music a listen.

She had an almost pedantic attitude about what constituted 'good jazz', not unusual among collectors, and as a result her leg was pulled unmercifully from time to time, but only by friends. She'd be egged on to believe that some dire Sid Phillips tapes were actually remastered Gennett rarities or some such, but it was always done with good grace. She was adored by everyone who knew her, me included. Tapes, books and records would arrive out of the blue with no excuse other than that they were 'good for you'.

She arranged her regular London eye check-ups to coincide with the Ellington visits, booking herself into the Washington Hotel where the musicians would stay. There she'd soak up the ambience just like a kid. Her dedication was rewarded when Johnny Hodges, never the most approachable of musicians, shared a few Bristol Creams with her and gave her an interview on tape for the Loners. The musicians enjoyed her company, and she was the recipient of numerous confidences, but she remained in awe of them, afraid to push herself forward in case she was 'in the way'. I explained that years on the road had taught them to differentiate between the sincere and the time-wasters, but she was never completely convinced. 'Tell Joan she's always welcome,' said Harry. 'Never let her wait outside the stage door.' But she remained lonely. I promised to enlarge photographs of Harry and Hodges for her and make frames embedded with old saxophone keys. I gathered together some parts but never completed my plan. A call came from one of the Loners to say she had died of a barbiturate overdose in unexplained circumstances, and I went down to Wales for her funeral, a sad affair far removed from the New Orleans style send-off her devotion to the music deserved. I will always be grateful to Joan for her unstinting generosity and the constant encouragement to listen to music that might have otherwise passed me by as I moved on into the new areas the musicians were opening up.

Increasingly attention centred on Americans who came over to tour as soloists with local bands. As always, I seemed to get along famously with some of those who sparked off dislike or resentment among the British musicians. Don Byas was one of these. Byas was a veteran expatriate, a saxophonist who had moved to Europe after the War. A tough, wiry little man who played with a sturdy tone and great passion, 'He and his horn know just about every big railway station in Europe,' someone once wrote. He was what is usually described as a 'muscular' player, and was known to be a 'hard man', alleged to have pulled a knife on more than one occasion.

In the course of an interview, we put a substantial dent in a bottle of vodka, and Byas made it clear that he fancied me. He was a renowned cook, and about to prepare dinner, so why didn't I stay and share a meal with him? I had another appointment so I made my apologies, saying I might return later.

After I left, I weighed up the situation. I did fancy a meal with Byas, but not an entanglement. I was heavily involved elsewhere and just not interested, even though I was attracted by his rather Mephistophelian demeanour. I did go back, however, and discovered that his reputation was fully deserved on one count at least. The smothered cabbage he served up that night was one of the best meals I have ever tasted. As for the other, we finished most of the vodka and I told him about my lover. He could do little but express his regret. He kissed my hand and I left.

Now I wonder what kind of racism he must have encountered during his visit to provoke him into the anger for which he was known. The local men always liked 'their' Black visitors to be easygoing. Should any individual be bold enough to question the status quo or stand his ground, however, he was no longer seen as such an affable proposition.

The friendships I valued most were, in the main, ones with no sexual dimension. Only then did I feel that what I had to say was as important as anything else I might have to offer. One of the most memorable of these had an inauspicious beginning. Rex Stewart was a trumpeter best known for his work with Duke Ellington. A superb soloist who developed the 'half-valve' style which provides a dramatic,

148

choked, effect on the horn, he had made several extended visits to Europe. He, too, was renowned as a cook – he was a Cordon Bleu graduate – but he had a reputation among the white jazz fraternity for being somewhat spikey. As he would explain later, he was not about to be anyone's 'nigger'. I was a bit apprehensive, though, when I turned up late for an interview. I knocked and he refused to open the door of his hotel room. 'Our appointment was for 2 o'clock,' he said firmly through the panelling. 'You're twenty minutes late and I'm not prepared to see you.' Chastened, I explained that the interview was scheduled and I'd be in trouble if I didn't produce it. He relented, and our talk was brief and courteous.

Some days later I saw Rex backstage at the Royal Festival Hall. He was sitting in the bar surrounded by veteran critics who were prodding him with queries about old records and the whereabouts of other aged horn players. Some of them were becoming a little worse for wear in the process, and Rex was bored. In the middle of it all, he leaned across to me and his eyes twinkled. Did I know any good French restaurants?' Fortunately, I did. 'Good,' he said, 'let's go.' To the chagrin of the assembled company, he left with me in tow.

This was the first of several entertaining evenings of good food, fine wine and intelligent conversation. Rex was a sophisticate, who had worked as a journalist and disc-jockey as well as musician. He had an informative, easy writing style, and wrote a series of reminiscences about other musicians that were full of important insights. After his death these were turned into a book, *Jazz Masters of the Thirties*. His descriptions of people he had known from the heyday of Swing music had a ring of authenticity missing from the work of other writers from outside the musicians' community. In a piece on Tricky Sam Nanton, a key figure in the Ellington Orchestra, he revealed that the trombonist was 'a scholar, a fierce nationalist and devoted follower of Marcus Garvey in the 1930s'. He also described musicians by colour – Nanton was 'gingerbread' – something no white writer would have done. Not that this had not been the case in the past. When the Afro-American musical *In Dahomey* came to London in 1903, the first to tour outside America, reviews commented on actors 'ranging in colours from ebony to a faint shade of olive', but by this time no jazz writer would have dreamed of making such a distinction. Rex did. Skin-shades had considerable influence in Afro-America, especially during the period with which his articles were concerned; then colour would have had a considerable bearing on how an individual made out. Just by mentioning this he increased my own race awareness. Later, when more Afro-Americans expressed the desire to be as 'African' as possible, many with light skins suffered unfairly for the way the 'yellow-complected' had often prospered in the past at the expense of their darker relations. A couple of drummers I knew were told they 'weren't Black enough to play no drums', in fact, something that was enormously hurtful. When I heard that I thought about what Rex had written.

During his stay in England, the trumpeter did several articles for *Melody Maker*, writing laboriously in 'music copyists' caps' on foolscap-sized American legal pads rather than borrowing a typewriter. We exchanged many views on the writing process, Rex paying careful attention to my ideas and offering observations of his own based on years of experience. He was fascinated with what made other people tick, he said. Rather than buttonhole an individual and draw them into conversation, though, he found it more productive to sit back and observe. It was this habit that gave such insight to his writing. It hit a chord with me because I was learning something new every day just through sitting back and listening.

Rex gave me any number of insights into the music business and explained how racism affected every Black artist, no matter how famous. As he put it, a slow movement towards recognising jazz musicians as 'people' was being countered by another in which a sensationalist press, hostile to Black achievement, caused the public to automatically link musicians with drug abuse. He explained: 'A caption associating musicians with dope will sell newspapers because this follows the line that is apparent in all Anglo-Saxon thinking about jazz music.'

There are those who considered Rex bitter and cynical, and like many artists of his generation he had been hurt by the injustice accorded the music's creators. To me, he was nothing but generous. When he went back to the States, he dropped me encouraging notes. I had expressed my doubts about having anything worthwhile to offer and he wrote to congratulate me on something of mine he had read: 'How quite un-English you seem to be. . . . I trust that this note proves to be *lagniappe* for your shrinking little ego! All the best, you sparkling specimen of Youthful English Womanhood on the move, from your erstwhile acquaintance.' I treasured his remarks, and felt more encouraged by him than I had by just about anyone to date.

A few months after meeting Rex I was involved in an unpleasant episode which I did nothing to provoke. I got into a physical fight with a Famous Musician. Because my protagonist was and is such an important figure in the music the incident is still talked about and I take time to explain what happened only for the reason that historically women have been blamed for many events and situations for which men were actually responsible.

Stevie and I were backstage at a concert, sharing a drink with a couple of musicians, one of whom was a blues guitar pioneer. Everyone was accompanied by friends, apart from the Famous Musician, and I watched him roving around making several attempts to barge into other conversations. Then he lurched over to our table and leered. He said something insulting and Mr Blues dismissed it: 'Don't pay him any attention, he's not worth bothering with.' I had noticed a slight animosity between the two men on stage, FM doing his best to distract attention from the guitarist during his solo-spot. It was something he often did. It had earned him a reputation for clowning, although I have yet to meet anyone who worked with him who found the experience of being publicly belittled amusing.

I went to the Ladies, emerging to find FM blocking the narrow corridor. I told him to let me through and he immediately abused me, verbally and physically, grabbing me between the legs and squeezing. I was enraged but managed to get past him. Back at the bar, Mr Blues asked what had happened. I gave him an edited version and he apologised for his colleague's behaviour. But the mood of the evening had been spoilt, and we decided to go home.

Before leaving, though, I had to speak to another musician. I found him in a nearby large dressing-room, being interviewed. Motioning at him across the room, I backed away, only to collide with a huge punch aimed at my backside. FM had come up behind me, cursing. This time I had had enough. 'You do that again and I'll punch you in your face!' I told him.

At this point, Stevie came into the room. FM made a grab for her, screaming about 'Fucking bitches!' I gazed in astonishment as he pulled her down by her hair to waist-level. There were three other men in the room but they just froze, open-mouthed. I grabbed FM's arm and tried to drag him off, but he was a heavy man and wouldn't be shifted. He was limbering up, drunkenly, with his other fist, so I had no other option but to punch him myself, in the face. With a bull-like roar, he turned on me and sent me flying across the room where I bounced to the floor down a stack of aluminium chairs. In a second he was astride me, fist raised to strike. One of the onlookers was a local musician who had been drinking. FM was his hero, yet even in his sozzled state, this was too much for him. He helped Stevie pull my assailant away. He staggered to his feet but I had gone beyond fury by now. I had never really hit anyone before but now I punched him, as hard as I could. He went sprawling, blood spurting from his nose and his lip. I know I could not have accomplished this pugilistic feat had he been sober, but that left hook stayed notorious for ages.

As FM lay on the floor, I looked around and saw Mr Blues standing quietly in the doorway. 'You women get out of here,' he told us and we meekly obeyed. He shut the door and waited until the other man rose to his feet. Then, apparently, he knocked him down again. 'That's for hitting those women,' he told him. I found it ironic that the 'countryboy' whom FM had so despised should act the 'gentleman', while two other men, one of whom I had once regarded as a friend, looked on and did nothing while we were being attacked.

On my way out, I bumped into the concert promoter. I was incoherent and shaking, my shirt sleeve soaked in blood. I shouted at him about what had happened, holding him responsible for conditions backstage. That night, apparently, FM turned up at Ronnie Scott's Club, waving a knife. He was looking, he said, 'for those fucking bitches to cut their ass!'

The truth of the incident was obvious to everyone else in the room, but experience had taught me that women were generally 'in the wrong' when anything untoward happened backstage. I was worried that I might be banned from future events. I took a deep breath and phoned the promoter. To my surprise, he was fairly apologetic, implying that this was not the first time he had had trouble with FM.

As the years went by, I assembled an interesting little mental dossier concerning FM's appalling behaviour towards women. He appears to delight in indecently assaulting women when their male partner is in the vicinity. Not so long ago, he allegedly punched a woman in the face at a reception in South America, much to the astonishment of the other musicians on the tour. I kept tabs on him mainly for my own amusement, but partly because of the continuing – and tedious – need to justify myself.

Women, Blacks, gays and other 'minorities' are always being forced on to the defensive when we are abused. So often responsibility is placed on us to 'prove' that something negative has occurred. For a long time I felt uncomfortable whenever the FM incident was raised, although, interestingly, I was seldom disbelieved when I told my side of the story. Over the years I came to realise that most musicians, at any rate, aware of FM's reputation where women are concerned, drew the conclusion that he must have 'asked for it'. Only recently a longtime musician friend confided that I had long enjoyed the reputation of being 'the only chick to give him the hiding he deserved'.

At the time, however, it was Rex whose response gave me the biggest boost. 'Congratulations and thanx for the beaut of a story that is going round here,' he wrote. 'What did you use, a left or a right? . . . Actually, I do not blame you. I like and respect you for doing a good job in a man's world.'

In 1967, believe me, that was praise indeed.

Part Three
Feel the Need in Me

See how I'm walking
        See how I'm talking
Notice everything in me
        Feel it
Feel the need in me

Detroit Emeralds

12
Pretty Mama, Where You Been So Long?

When Yvonne left for the Bahamas, I had cried a few crocodile tears at the station. I wasn't too sorry to see her go, for we had begun to get on each other's nerves. I laughed it off when she told me that I would soon find another woman to 'look after me'. I was still not prepared seriously to consider being a lesbian, with all the ostracism that way of life clearly entailed. Casual sex between women was just one of the new items on the menu for some of us growing up in the 'permissive' Swinging Sixties, something that many of us indulged in but no one treated with any more significance than all those farcical dates with incompatible men met in pubs or at parties and unceremoniously dumped after dinner or a passionless, pointless one-night stand. Involvements were strenuously avoided; there was a whole world out there to explore and none of us wanted commitment any more than we wanted a family. Or at least that's what we said.

Stevie and I spent a great deal of time together, hanging out with visiting Americans and listening to music. We began to discover more about each other and our very different backgrounds. Both her parents were Afro-British, her father's father one of the first jazz musicians to come out of Ghana, but the central figure in her family household was her maternal grandmother, a no-nonsense white East Ender of iron will. Gran, who had married three husbands and outlived them all, had braved Dockland racism back in the 1920s by befriending visiting Black seamen. When their ships docked in London, there were many British-born people whose existence was enlivened by the humour, kindness and alternative view of the world these visitors brought. She and her sister threw parties, removing doors and windows from their Custom House home as a precaution against damage by resentful neighbours. There was a network of such pioneering elderly women who married African and West Indian seamen decades before the *Empire Windrush* docked. Accompanying Stevie on a trip down East to flesh out her Barbadian family-tree – her maternal grandfather had perished at sea – I was proud to meet several of these rugged fighters and the tough old seadogs who had settled here with them, sixty years on and not out.

Gran cooked rice and peas, English version, with the roast at the weekend, a bottle of hot sauce on the table the only hint of the Westindian legacy. The food was delicious, but in contrast to our own family dinners full of chatter and laughter, the mood was frequently sombre. Conversation was discouraged and there was an uncomfortable air at times that we were lucky to have something to eat. This feeling, more moralistic than grateful, was occasioned in part by Gran's age, partly by history.

Stevie's lifestyle and way of dealing with the world were totally different from mine. As I began to realise how hard she and her family had worked for what they had, I recognised that, despite what I had been led to believe was a less than privileged existence, we had really had it pretty easy at home. At Gran's I met other Black Britons, some with one white parent, most of whom had carved out a solid niche for themselves notwithstanding the often inauspicious circumstances of their youth. They spoke a particular kind of language, figuratively, that bore little superficial relationship to the ideas of the people I knew who were born overseas.

Stevie had the ability to create a homely ambience out of very little, and I was increasingly attracted by the warmth and comfort of her small flat near the Brecknock, which she illuminated with glowing pink lights and the choicest of sounds. She cooked wonderful meals for the Ellington musicians when they came to London, pork chops, rice and peas, and was always listening to, and learning from, the consummate soul sisters Sarah, Ella and Lena. Dakota Staton's *Late Late Show* was another classic album that was seldom off the deck. She was singing in earnest by now, sitting in around town, her musicianly approach earning genuine approval from the Ellingtonians and others in a world notoriously chary of 'decorative' female singers.

Then she got a job in Newcastle with the houseband at La Dolce Vita, the largest and most prestigious of the clubs in the north east where many a name artist had their start. Originally set for two weeks, she ended up staying for months. She wrote to me frequently with hilarious and hair-raising tales of her encounters with the stars who topped the bill each week, Dusty Springfield, Cy Grant, Helen Shapiro and Lonnie Donegan to name a few. She was beginning to develop an appreciative personal following among the Geordies who admired her duets with the Guyanese singer and percussionist who was the bandleader. She had just started playing conga-drums seriously, too, taking the occasional feature spot, and she was a stylish dancer. The audience really warmed to her personality.

One week, Sandie Shaw was the featured act. She had just topped the charts with a cover of a Dionne Warwicke record, but her fame stemmed from her winsome looks and habit of singing barefoot. Technically speaking, she was strictly limited. It happened that one of Stevie's specialities was the tongue-twisting number in the age-old Rap tradition, 'The Clapping Song', written and recorded by Shirley Ellis. It was a fast-moving number for which she had worked out an intricate song-and-dance routine with the pianist. Sandie Shaw also featured this number, but the complexities of it were beyond her capabilities. She played it safe with a couple of well-rehearsed choruses, avoiding the dangers of stretching out into a polyrhythmic and lyrical minefield. In an autocratic manner, her manager sent a message to the bandleader, requesting that 'the girl' leave out the song for the week. Stevie was not pleased, but she acquiesced.

Ms Shaw, in the meantime, failed to endear herself with the club's employees during her stay; thus she inspired no feeling of loyalty. By the end of the week, Stevie had no compunction about teaching her a musical lesson. With the bandleader temporarily off the stand, she persuaded the pianist down front. Together they stomped, danced and sang 'The Clapping Song' and did it to death. The crowd was ecstatic, Ms Shaw and her manager sweeping out in a huff. Stevie phoned to tell me the story and I realised how much I missed having someone close to · talk to. At the time Sandie Shaw epitomised for us all that was fake about popular music. We both knew Stevie belonged in another league. I missed her enormously yet she discouraged me from going up there on a visit. When I did finally receive a summons, I understood why. The first night in Newcastle we got back to her digs as the sun was rising. It was to a dawn chorus in Jesmond that our relationship developed into something else. She had been, she said, waiting for me to slow down for a minute and think about something else rather than hanging out with 'the guys' before she would tell me how she really felt about me.

The early days of our relationship were spent on the road as much as in each other's homes. Stevie was just starting to carve out a niche for herself in cabaret and I was growing increasingly dissatisfied with the kind of work I was doing. Weddings and graduation portraits were not what I'd planned for myself when I read books such as *Without Assignment* and envisaged a career in Fleet Street. Travelling around the country with a musician was an enjoyable – and educational – way of escaping from what was turning into a hack career. Although I didn't realise it at the time, it had been pretty nerve-racking for Stevie to leave the relative security of an office job and go on the road for the first time. She had grown up in a showbusiness environment, surrounded by musicians and entertainers, and she knew from her father's precarious existence of the hardships and insecurity of the life; but still it took an enormous amount of courage to face audiences who could sometimes be pretty cold. Manchester was a major centre for nightlife then and she acquired a rather sleazy agent there who booked her with little regard to her specific talent. The audiences she encountered could be ignorant, too; like most artists then, she worked a stultifying string of night clubs, pubs and working-men's clubs in the north and Midlands where the clientele was more often interested in bingo, beer and the coarser, cruder comedians than someone reared on the vocabulary of Billie and Bird.

It was rare to come across good musicians in working-men's clubs, and the night clubs where she would play week-long residencies were often not much better. She would be forced to struggle with pianists who couldn't read her musical arrangements, drummers who couldn't keep time. On more than one occasion she actually cracked the skin of her middle-finger, drawing blood, from the intensity with which she'd had to click to keep time and prevent the drummer from slowing down.

She was glad to have me along for company, and I dutifully helped to carry her conga-drums when she proudly acquired a set of her own. She had an engaging on-stage personality and an unusual singing style, soulful but with little vibrato. But because she was Black, she was constantly running into prejudice. Sometimes it was racism of the most vicious kind which sent her home in tears, other times it was unintentional. All Black people have experienced the 'ACPLA' syndrome, ('all coloured people look alike'), but I would like to have a quid for every time she heard the comment, usually intended as a compliment, from white people who told her how much she reminded them of

157

Ella Fitzgerald or Shirley Bassey, generally the only Black female singers they knew. She gritted her teeth and came back with a snappy response, but would retaliate by ordering a double Scotch for herself and me, whenever the transgressor offered. Then she'd give me a nudge, we'd drink up and leave.

I was reminded of this many years later, when I took a friend to Ronnie Scott's to hear Arnett Cobb, the bluesy saxophonist from Texas whose legs had been badly damaged in a car accident. I had just introduced them at the bar when a white man came rushing over to embrace Arnett in an over-familiar way. 'My son heard you in France,' he enthused, slurring his words. 'He said: "You've just *got* to see this guy! Out comes this really old *spade* on crutches, can't hardly walk at *all*, went on to blow the place down!" ' He stood back a few seconds for his words to sink in, then clapped Arnett on the shoulder: 'You *must* let me buy you a drink.' The saxophonist smiled amiably. 'Oh,' he said, 'I believe I'll have a triple brandy. And,' his outstretched fingers gently squeezed our elbows, 'my friends will have the same.'

It was not surprising that Stevie would befriend those people who took her at face-value and avoided the references to race that so many whites feel compelled to make in the presence of Blacks. I sometimes wondered at the sheer ordinariness of some of her companions, until I began to realise she had chosen to mix with generous and open people who respected her musicianship and saw her as a person of some stature.

Another showbusiness pitfall is the way in which some people assume that because artists are up there giving of themselves, they somehow belong to the public, even in their moments of relaxation. At a smart Newcastle restaurant Stevie stood on the stairs, waiting for her cue to go on. She had just had some stage-clothes made and looked stunning in an elegant gold outfit. Strings of iridescent beads emblazoned the top, dangling from a backdrop of gold sequins. A man on his way to the Gents said admiringly, 'That's a beautiful dress,' then, to my utter amazement, he reached out his hand and tweaked, not a bead, but one of Stevie's breasts. She slapped him down and turned away. But I was shocked at the presumption of punters. What happened to her had its parallel in my world, too. If you were 'out there' as a woman, it was often seen as being ultimately for the benefit of men.

It was partly because of the belief that female singers were 'easy' and always on the look-out for a date for the week, that Stevie began to dress and make-up at the digs. As soon as her act was over, she'd collect her coat fom the dressing-room and be on her way out of the club before some of the musicians were off the stand. Her attitude was often misunderstood; other artists stayed behind to drink with the patrons. We had other things to do.

During the day, places of interest were on the agenda, but when the gig was over, we'd explore other aspects of whatever city we were in. Manchester, with its nightlife, was our favourite. You wouldn't think there was much to be found at the Salford end of Upper Chorlton Road in the 1960s, especially if you believed in *Coronation Street*, but whatever there was, we managed to find it. There were after-hours clubs where musicians jammed, and late-night Indian and Chinese restaurants where culinary outrages were wreaked on undiscriminating locals after the pubs closed. Gradually we were discovering different kinds of food, but if we sometimes came up with a loser, we survived. Our stomachs were strong and so were we. Once we bought cheap whisky at Yates' Wine Lodge, a penny-pinching move we regretted the following day. In Moss Side, where such legendary Black clubs as the Lagos Lagoon flourished, we found a woman who cooked rice-and-peas in her front-room. We went looking for curry goat at a late-night Westindian café and got stopped by the law. 'What are you doing here?' asked the policeman, ever mindful that strange women in Black areas could be there for *one thing* only. Stevie replied she was working in Manchester. 'This isn't Manchester, this is *Moss Side*,' said the guardian of the law pointedly, although he did allow us to get our goat before moving on from his patch.

Relying on agents for work was a haphazard and often frustrating procedure. Stevie let A Manager take care of the headaches for a while. Peter was well known on the London jazz scene and had moved down to Bristol. He suggested that she do the same. Work had been sparse but when a New Year's Eve engagement at a smart Country Club turned up, I went along for the ride. The club was deep in the countryside, and Peter drove us there, the three of us crammed in his sports car. He was a mess of nerves, almost putting us all in a ditch on the way, and we blundered around the countryside in the dark, getting lost. We arrived at the gig quite shattered.

As soon as she saw the set-up, Stevie began to have second thoughts about having brought me along. Tactfulness was not one of my virtues, and a couple of drinks was all it needed for me to speak my mind if I were riled. The other guests were dripping with jewellery, sarcasm, too, and I failed to acquit myself with the requisite wit and style. 'What a *charming* dress!' drawled one ancient relic of Empire, fawning over 'the artiste' and pointedly turning her back on 'the artiste's friend' whose dress, clearly, left a little to be desired. 'Oh, yes,' she came back, quick as a flash, 'I had it specially made – in Paris.' It was one I'd seen her buy off-the-peg in Manchester, but one-upmanship was the name of the game in this setting. She saw me start to bristle, Scotch in hand, and she balked. 'It's not going to work,' she muttered, and shooed me up to the room. There, in the prettiest of country bedrooms, I lay on the bed and stared up at the oak-beamed ceiling as I listened to them ring in the new. I could hear Stevie's voice below and I fumed. No drinks for me and no dinner, while the rich got sloshed and enjoyed themselves at my lover's expense. I felt cheated at being excluded, although I knew I didn't want any part of people like that. My mood was broken by the sound of an exquisite Spanish guitar. At first I thought it must be a record, but when I realised the guitarist was accompanying Stevie's singing, I propped myself up on one elbow. Despite myself, I was enraptured. When she finally staggered to bed, exhausted and reeking of the good times I'd been denied, I wanted to know: who was *that*? 'Oh, Julian Bream,' she said. 'We were swinging!'

But the chance to jam with one of the world's acknowledged greats on the instrument was an isolated highlight in her West Country sojourn. The promised gigs failed to materialise and Peter kept her dangling on the end of the phone. Showbusiness requires a brave face at all times, but her savings were dwindling and eventually she had to confront him. His reply was a classic: 'Starving's good for you. It'll give you more soul.' She came home.

Out on the road, Stevie carried her portable record-player and a hip collection of records. Duke Ellington, Clifford Brown and Ernestine Anderson (*Welcome to the Club*) provided the aural backdrop to the process of getting to know each other and falling in love. For me, Nancy Wilson's album *Yesterday's Lovesongs, Today's Blues* is redolent with memories of that era. I have only to hear the young Nancy swoop, Dinah Washington-style, on to 'The Best is Yet to Come' to be carried back to a time when even our tragedies could be turned into fun. Whether the best did actually lie around the corner is debatable, but then we were too busy being 'sophisticated' nightclubbers to notice.

Our mothers went into the semi-oblivion mode adopted by those parents of lesbians and gays who are not overtly hostile to their offspring's lifestyle. It's easier for them to pretend you are 'just close friends', although in their hearts they know what's happening. Sex between consenting males had not yet been legalised and homosexuality was still seen as an evil or, at best, an unfortunate disease, which was often 'treated' with electric-shock therapy. Many people who were lesbian or gay even confided in each other that they wished they were straight. For gay men to be 'out' in those days was not even an option, given the legal penalties that existed, and most lesbians pretended that they were indeed 'just friends'. Life was, in fact, a constant game of duck and dodge – duck the questions and dodge the issue. Staying in the closet was destructive for most of us, although we didn't know it at the time; but the alternative could mean losing friends and family and constantly chancing verbal and physical attack. As for Stevie and me, we were young and in love and, actually, pretty blatant about it, given the dangers of discovery.

One of the problems for us at first was that we didn't know any other lesbians. A lot of people on the music scene were gay but, without exception, stayed in the 'closet'. Singers would be asked about boy-friends or girlfriends and they'd invent someone to placate interviewer and public. I knew that a number of the people around *Ready Steady Go!* were 'of the life', but no matter how many hints I dropped, I never managed to get invited to any of their parties. We did know a few gay men, most of whom were involved in showbusiness in some way. There were dressmakers and drag queens, and on one daring occasion we went to a male bar in Manchester, where we clung to each other and with a mixture of amusement and exctement watched the clientele dance. We developed a friendship with Benny Wise, (not his real name), a nationally known comedian, who was working the same Manchester circuit. Benny, who had hosted a major TV series, was outrageous, one of the few people we met who didn't give a damn about being gay. 'Men are pigs. Pigs,' he told us. 'You're right – if I was a woman I wouldn't want anything to do with them. What they do, what they want in the name of sex – pigs.' His act was quite vulgar, but at the time we thought him hilarious. A tough Jew from the East End, he could give as good as he got, with a routine that consisted of setting up someone in the audience to shout insulting remarks. He would then proceed to demolish them in a way that might well have been crude but to me carried him head and shoulders above the homophobes who surrounded him and us. By drawing attention to his lifestyle, he was asserting his right to be gay.

One night, the drummer at a working-men's club was being particularly obnoxious to Stevie. Benny saw what was going on and told her not to worry, he'd fix the so-and-so. He waited until the drummer was playing away like a superstar. Standing in the wings where he could not be seen by anyone else, he suddenly unzipped his fly and shook his cock menacingly at the smarmy troublemaker. It may have been an unconventional way of dealing with the situation but it certainly worked. Seldom have I seen anyone so bumptious so rapidly cowed. 'You've got to watch out for that man,' he spluttered as he rushed off stage red-faced. 'He's a dr-r-r-eadful person!' We thought Benny was great.

The three of us stayed at an old pub in the centre of Manchester, a favourite with artists, and it was there something occurred that gave me considerable pause for thought. Whenever the figures 'one in five' or 'one in ten' are trotted out for the percentage of lesbians and gays in the population, heterosexuals tend to question the proportion. Some of us question it ourselves until we started to consider our own experiences. Only we know the frequency of approaches by apparently 'straight' people who want to be turned on by someone experienced. These incidents generally take place behind the safety of an alcoholic haze and can, if the need arises, be conveniently forgotten the following day. Something like this happened to Benny at the hotel. A frequent visitor there, he was often involved in after-hours drinking-sessions organised by the landlord and his wife. They loved being in his company and enjoyed the cachet of being friendly with someone who was a household name. One night on his way to bed, Benny found the landlord following him upstairs. 'Jokingly' the latter put his hand on his butocks. Benny told him to go away, saying he couldn't be bothered with someone who wasn't gay. That should have been the end of it except that two nights later he brought home a sailor. It was a house-rule that no overnight guests were permitted, but Benny was always allowed to have visitors, provided he was discreet about it. This time the position had changed. The landlord knocked at his door and ordered the sailor to leave. The following morning Benny, too, was told to pack his bags. Hell hath no fury, etc.

On the road we got to know a couple of drag-queens, sometimes admitting we were lovers, generally letting it just be assumed. On stage, these men could be sad or hilarious by turns, but they seemed to revel in the insults and coarse badinage that was the stock-in-trade of the Northern circuit. Backstage, though, it was a different story. Both of them smoked and drank heavily, were nervous and self-deprecatory. One covered his nervousness with bluster but they really were stereotypical queens for whom life was probably a lonely existence. I wanted to be friendly with people I took to be kindred spirits, but when I saw the tension and lack of self-confidence, the shabby clothes and the nicotine-stained fingers, I knew there was no way I wanted to be like them.

At the hotel conversation sometimes centred on 'So-and-so and her girlfriend', a well-known singer who was known to be 'lezzie', but we were no nearer to finding friends of our own kind. Back in

London one week we decided to find out about the lesbian clubs that we knew existed. There was the Robin Hood off Westbourne Park and the Gateways, the legendary membership-only club in Chelsea. Stevie, who always made major decisions, went on an expedition, leaving me at home. The Robin, she decided, was not for us, too many drugs and the threat of violence in the atmosphere. She persuaded someone to sign her in at the Gateways, and rushed back, bubbling with excitement: 'You'll never guess who I saw!' Sitting at the bar she'd found Maggie Nicols, a singer who was one of the tiny handful of serious woman around the jazz scene. Maggie, who was then into what she calls her 'first lesbian period', had worked as a dancer at the Windmill and started to hang out at Ronnie Scott's Club around the time when Americans Zoot Sims and Stan Getz started to play there. I had known her for some time, a shy, sweet-natured person who was completely devoted to music. By some quirk of fate, I had even 'stolen' a man from her one night, something completely unintentional on my part, but an event that made me feel guilty for years. I never dreamed she too might be a lesbian – a word never used then, by the way; we were 'gay'. Now I insisted that Stevie take me along to the club.

The Gateways was situated at the corner of Bramerton Street, an address whispered collusively for years between women throughout the country. It was run by a married couple called Ted and Gina, with Gina's girlfriend keeping a tight rein on proceedings from the door. A smallish room in need of decoration, it had a jukebox for dancing and pictures of some of the regulars painted on a wall studded with small pieces of mirror. I looked around nervously, unable to relax and feeling painfully ill-at-ease. I always felt clumsy in company then, rather over-weight and, so it seemed to me, unsuitably drssed, and it was no different down here than it was in the outside world. Stevie on the other hand, was an extrovert. She soon struck up a conversation with a woman who worked as a traffic warden and her girlfriend. I had only just started driving, but had already acquired the mandatory dislike of the species. I felt a little more sympathetic when she told us she had started out in the police force but lost her job when there was a raid on the club and she'd looked up to find her station officer staring at her in disgust.

It is difficult for women emerging from a movement that has legitimised sexual relationships between women to imagine how it used to be as recently as the 1960s. There was nowhere to meet, no forum for discussion, nowhere to relax or dance apart from the 'Gates', with its overpriced drinks putting it beyond the reach of many women except at weekends. One of the club's main attractions was drinking, and with women's wages being even lower then, comparatively, than now, some people would save for weeks for a night out in Chelsea. For all its reputation as a wild den of hedonism and seduction, it was a rather quiet place for most of the week. Accustomed as we were to the jazz scene and the nightspots of the north, it seemed remarkably tame.

Groups of women, many of them in male attire, sat at the tables that seemed to hug the walls for security. In those days before unisex clothing became official, these 'butches' were actually making a statement with their dress. We, too, wore trousers by now and, like

Left
Aged about 11, with my mother

Below
My father (centre) with my
mother's parents, 1930s

Bottom
Putney High School, the sixth form.
Liz Spiro (centre), 1959

Left
First box Brownie musician portrait, 1956. Clive, aged 11, has Louis' autograph

Below
Clark Terry and typical 'jobsworth'. Davis Theatre, Croydon, 1958

Bottom
Teenagers still, posing with Sonny Terry (left) and Brownie McGhee, 1958 *(Paul Oliver)*

Visitors to Streatham

Above
Jesse Fuller cooks breakfast, 1960

Left
Mum takes tea
with Herbie Lovelle, 1959

Left
Sister Rosetta Tharpe
shows Ottilie Patterson that
high note

Below
With Little Brother Montgomery,
the picture they wouldn't print
(Pam Bavin)

Bottom
Muddy Waters and Otis Spann
(Terry Cryer)

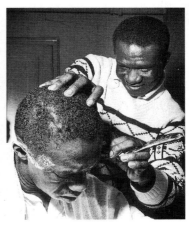

Top
Clive (right) with Coleman Hawkins
and playwright-to-be Steve Gooch, 1960

Left
With Sam Jones and 'that' bass, 1960

Above
Haircut and shave for
Art Blakey. John Millington, 1961

Top left
Henry Coker backstage, 1959

Top right
Rex Stewart, 1966

Above
Memphis Slim and Pam Bavin.
Roundhouse, Wardour Street, 1961

Below
Adam Fiberesima

Right
Lucky Wadiri

Bottom
With Harry Carney. BBC-TV, 1963

New York, 1962

Top
Edgar and Barbara Blakeney,
Herbie Lovelle, Leonard Gaskin

Above right
Langston Hughes

Above left
Gene Ramey and fellow bassist Al Lucas

Top left
Priscilla and John Batcheldor, 1969

Top right
Roland Miller

Above
Nigerian students and their
landladies, 1960s.
Janet Coleman (top, third from right)

Top
At work, Nigerian wedding

Above
Demonstration, Notting Hill Gate,
c. 1967, John 'Hoppy' Hopkins (right)
(Graham Keen)

Left
With Mike Eghan.
Ghana Radio, Accra, 1970

Opposite page

Top
Polo Barnes, Preservation Hall,
New Orleans, 1971

Bottom left
Kunle Mwanga, Liberty House,
New York, 1971

Bottom right
Carol Blank, Brooklyn, New York, 1982

Confronting the *Evening News*, 1978

Left
Carole Spedding; Jill Nicholls (top right)

Above
Confronting aggravation *(Mark Rusher/IFL)*

Below
Music for Socialism, Battersea, 1977.
Gary Herman, Dave Laing

Top
Maggie Nicols (right).
First 'Reclaim the Night' demonstration,
London, 1977

Left
Maggie Murray

Above
Penny Valentine

Above
Friends in the
Lydia D'Ustebyn Ladies'
Swing Orchestra, 1984:
a long way from 'Perdido Street'

Left
Camping it up with sisters
and tie, 1983:
a long way from Bramerton Street
(*Joanne O'Brien/Format*)

Below
James Baldwin, Archie Shepp and
Peter Guralnick at the *Sorrow Songs* opening.
University of Massachusetts,
1986 *(Chris Hardin)*

Bottom
Thirty years on, with Herbie Lovelle
and Earle Warren.
Sweet Basil, New York, 1989 *(Phil Schaap)*

every self-respecting lesbian of the day, never went out without ironing in a razor-edged crease. But we distanced ourselves from those women whose D-A hair-dos and square-shouldered style screamed their 'deviancy' – 'collar-and-tie jobs' as they were unkindly dubbed by some – and who, it seemed to us, *asked* to be abused in the street. It could be hurtful enough to be recognised as a lesbian and insulted or spat at, without actually drawing attention to yourself in this way. I was really surprised at women who wore men's clothing in contrast to the tailored slacks and crushed-velvet flares that we favoured, topped off by elaborate, Indian silk dresses worn as shirts, or embroidered *danşikis* and *joromi*, gifts from African friends.

Frightened of attracting attention, I took years to pluck up courage to buy an ordinary shirt anywhere than a chainstore. Even then, I reeled in embarrassment on my first venture into the hallowed halls of Moss Bros to pick out a stylish red-checked Viyella. An elderly male assistant, trying to be helpful with collar-size, asked discreetly, 'Does Madam wear a tie?' No doubt he had countryside point-to-points in mind, but I immediately thought I'd been 'spotted'. To me, a tie meant two things only. For heterosexuals it labelled me as 'queer' and that was dangerous, while within the role-playing world of the ghetto it would have given me a strictly 'butch' identity. I had no wish to be identified as either. I was a woman, not a freak, and to prove it I still found men attractive and sometimes went out with them. Stevie did likewise.

The clientele at the Gates was strictly members-only. Like all gay clubs, management was constantly aware of the possibility of losing their licence and consequently did not suffer troublesome customers gladly. Unlike the rougher places where lesbians met, the Robin and the nearby Raven, fights were abruptly stopped, the perpetrators removed and immediately banned. Drunkenness was another reason for banishment. It took an enormous amount of grovelling to be allowed back in after behaving with anything less than the requisite amount of self-control. Everyone was supposed to be able to hold their liquor. From time to time there were police raids. The club was not alone in the gay world in being singled out for this treatment, but generally these clumsy, 'jack-booted' intrusions were a quite unjustified invasion of privacy in which some members of the force seemed to delight.

When it came to music, the jukebox featured a few interesting records, Motown and the like, alongside such forgettable 'bubblegum' items as Tommy Roe's 'Dizzy'. But 'The Clapping Song' was on there, too, and we annoyed some people by playing it over and over. Once we got over the shock of the fact that all the women around us were actually lesbians, we took to dancing in earnest. There were numbers such as the Isley Brothers' 'This Old Heart Of Mine' ('been broke a thousand times') and James and Bobby Purify's 'Do Unto Me' ('girl, as you'd have me do to you'), Soul music with a singalong beat. Engelbert Humperdinck's 'Release Me' summed up the favoured style; it stayed on that jukebox for years. It wasn't really until the 'smoochies' such as this and Dusty's 'You Don't Have to Say You Love Me' that the majority of women took to the floor.

We missed the soulful sounds of the Flamingo, the organ-and-tenor groups, the Ska and Rocksteady beat, but we did our best to show that we, at least, knew how to dance to the few rhythmic tracks on offer. I was never much of a dancer, though I like to think that what I lacked in style I made up for in enthusiasm. Stevie, on the other hand, was an expert. She chastised me for my shyness and encouraged me, attracting a good deal of attention from other women in the process. Everyone would try to have a partner for the final dance of the evening, but in contrast to what an outside observer might imagine, relatively few of those last dancers ended up between the sheets. For those in love, a crowded night out there was an occasion for celebration; for the majority, though, a feeling of ennui was inescapable, and resignation to one's lot the commonplace.

It was only at the weekends that the room became packed. Then the cry sometimes went up 'The Army's in!' a generally scathing reference to those isolated women in the forces who would journey from various parts of the country on their weekend passes. For the more snobbish patrons who felt that associating with the masses was beneath their dignity, it was the signal to beat a retreat. Lesbianism was illegal in the forces then as it still is, if only for 'other ranks' (officers, oddly, were immune from the suggestion of possible 'perversion'). For a great number of women, however, the comparative anonymity of service life made it a good place to be gay – until you got caught. Self-oppressive hatred operated there with a vengeance, tales abounding of lesbian sergeants who reported clandestine sexual activity to avoid attracting attention to themselves. There were even some officers who 'had their way' with younger women then shopped them when the loving went sour.

The membership war was a constant. For months after we'd paid up we were interminably quizzed about fees before being allowed into the club. For some unaccountable reason, the management took a dislike to us, something that may not have been unconnected with the way we avoided the claustrophobic cliquiness of the place and leapt readily on to the dance-floor, trying to get others to join us. We tried to get other women to talk to us, too, with relatively little success.

Conversation was not one of the Gates' big attractions; posing rated higher. If you did try to talk to a stranger, it was automatically assumed you were 'on the pick-up'. Sometimes we would run into Maggie Nicols but away from the music world, a veil of embarrassment often came down between us and we found little to say to each other. From time to time a few other Black women appeared, a couple of whom had the same complexion as Stevie and, I assumed from their East London accents, similar backgrounds. I noticed them eyeing her with suspicion, however, and when we did try to strike up a conversation, they made it quite clear that this was their patch and anyone in their company not for sharing.

It was confusing at first; after all, here we all were, escaping from the hostility of the outside world. We came to realise that the majority of favoured regulars earned status by flocking around Gina and her girlfriend like groupies, supplying them with drinks and hanging on their every word.

Much is made of the democratic nature of the gay and lesbian

world, the fact that people from all classes and backgrounds mix together. Although it is true that many of the women who move in the ghetto would not generally meet socially under usual circumstances, it is an enforced democracy rather than one that is worked for or chosen. And although there is much that can be learned from this proximity of soldiers and solicitors, the media and the mechanical, outside a political context it does not necessarily lead to constructive exchanges. Conversation at the Gates tended to be strictly limited, and whatever might have been the potential of all those women who made their regular pilgrimage to the shrine of Sappho, heavy drinking and cynical banter generally took precedence. For those without friends or a partner, finding a soulmate was as remote as a trip to the Moon. The best to be hoped for was an infrequent back-to-my-place, with a hangover and nothing to say to each other next day. Younger lesbians speak of the Gates with fascination. Some older ones who knew it in its pre-feminism heyday express nostalgia for its clandestine intimacy and the sense in which we all shared this awful but dreadfully exciting secret. Like other gay legends, the Apollo and Le Duce, the Chelsea rendezvous had been aggrandised in popular memory to occupy a revered position in gay history. But for many of us, who went there because no alternative social arena existed, it was none of that.

Ever since time began, women have fallen in love with other women, who then leave to go off with men. They may do it because of a particular man, but generally it is because of social pressure. The idea of relationships with bisexual women has always been dangerous for lesbians because they know they could easily be hurt in this way. The ghetto provided safety from this possibility, but in exchange it offered the proximity of all those potential lovers. The frustrations of life outside the ghetto and the way that love with women was proscribed made these newfound sisters all the more attractive. This, combined with heterosexual society's insistence that we were lesbian purely because of the *sex*, led to an atmosphere of sexual aggression with which many of us, in our heart of hearts, did not actually feel in tune. The scene did provide solace and friendship for many but in the ghetto other oppressions replaced those of the straight world. The freedom to be oneself was not necessarily the experience of everyone who went there.

Yet because what we were doing by walking through that door was *declaring* ourselves – what some would call 'coming out' – there was about the whole exercise a sense of terrible excitement. It revolved around bravado and ritual. Getting ready to go there was a ritual, the crease in the trousers, the eyes made-up just so. Parking the car was a ritual, as near to the club as possible to avoid the voyeurs and the challenge of passers-by. Gaining entry meant mustering bravado. And for what? To spend time in a place where you could, supposedly, be yourself. For many, including me, the tension didn't let up once you were safely inside. Just to walk down those stairs to a sea of faces turned expectantly upward, checking out the arrival of talent, was an unnerving, and for many, unbearable experience. Some never came back for a second helping.

There was excitement, it's true, and a sense of daring in being among others who indulged in the-love-that-dare-not-speak-its-name, but from the moment the street door opened, women were forced on to the defensive. Not only were you constantly under threat of attack and insult in the world outside, the word 'lesbian' hurled like a poisoned dart, hurtful and destructive, there was constant confrontation in the ghetto as well. Women had to be tough to survive there. Role-playing that echoed male and female stereotypes was mandatory; everyone was 'butch' or 'femme', and if you were neither you kept quiet about it for fear of being regarded as odd. People who did not want to be tough or adopt an attitude were ostracised by others and made to feel outcasts.

Many forced arbitrarily into the butch role because of their physical appearance, adopting male names and mannerisms, were in reality incredibly gentle women. One such who worked behind the bar at the Gates had her hair cropped shorter than almost anyone dared in those days. She wore braces and waistcoats years before the film *Annie Hall* popularised this lesbian fashion and made it safe for other women. She was a real sweetie, generous and caring, but even she would take on the combative stance from time to time, dotting her conversation with barbs and cynicism as she pulled pints and drank one-for-one with the customers.

When the Gates shut at 11 p.m., the only alternatives for those who wanted to stay awake were begrudging male bars which admitted us in handfuls or unlicensed dives in Soho and the Grove (Ladbroke Grove) frequented by pimps and prostitutes. There Coca-Cola was the strongest stimulant available; if you wanted to get high you had to make your own arrangements. With a group of friends I went to one of these Soho dives one night, a truly filthy spot down an alleyway which encouraged the outcasts and dregs of society – people like us – and fell over a woman jacking-up in the toilet. The only attraction of such places was that women could dance together. On occasion we would end up at the infamous Burlington in Hammersmith, where the dancing dykes were one of the main attractions for a seedy male clientele. It was quite common for women's liaisons to be overseen by voyeuristic men. At the Gates, above the jukebox there was even a portrait of Ted, the co-owner, and it remained there until after he died, an incongruous sight in a women's bar. The occasional gay male guest was permitted if the owners were in a receptive mood, but they themselves often invited men friends along for a drink. These, it is true, kept a low profile, but I was stunned one day to run across the father of someone I knew. What's more, I had done a story on him while I was working at *Tropic*. He greeted me with amused surprise and I felt I had to ask after his daughter. But, as with the other habituées, it was clearly not the done thing to have a long conversation.

Although discovering the lesbian ghetto had an enormous and far-reaching effect on my life, music remained just as important. John and I had remained friends and we still saw each other from time to time and would go to The Bull's Head on the river at Barnes, one of the better-known London jazz pubs. Stevie would come along, too, sometimes Steve Piper and Priscilla, to whom he was married. There were some legendary sessions at The Bull's Head, such as the Sunday lunchtime when pianist Jaki Byard and trumpeter Freddie Hubbard sat in with Tubby Hayes, South London's saxophonist hero, and Hubbard burned the paint off the walls with his playing.

We regularly went to The Coleherne in Earl's Court, too, and before long Stevie became one of the hardy group of conga-drummers who lined up each week to sit in. At first there were some in that blasé and musically hard-bitten audience who expressed surprise on seeing a woman approach the ancestral instruments. All doubts and apprehension vanished as soon as she started to play. She had a firm, resilient beat, which gave an uplift to any musical proceedings, and within a short space of time she had built up a strong personal following. 'Play, sister!' the cry went up from her fan club when she made her appearance. Longtime Westindian settlers, people who never dreamed they would swing and sway to a woman's beat, would stand up when she took over, laughing and cheering her on.

But not everyone shared this delight. There were two particular conga-men, kings of the skins, who bristled with resentment whenever she stepped forward to play. It would not have mattered if she had been unremarkable; then they could have patted her head and looked on paternalistically. The fact that she was such an accomplished percussionist was what disturbed them so much. Up until then, the competition had been pretty routine; now they were forced to look to their laurels. Deliberately, they would delay handing over the drums until the crowd's demands — 'Let the *chick* play!' — grew obvious. It is customary for sitters-in to await the resident musicians' pleasure, yet holding out on someone with known ability was at odds with the pub's jam-session policy. When she did finally get to the skins, one of the aggrieved pair would position himself close behind her, nudging her unnoticed in the crush, doing his best to disrupt her time-keeping. The other musicians expressed no such resentment, they were either oblivious or turned a blind eye to what was happening. The crowd were oblivious, too, especially as her persecutor kept a smile on his face as he muttered loving imprecations in her ear, things like: 'Get off the drums, you bitch!' It was the first time I'd encountered this kind of anger.

Ronnie Scott's Club became more and more like a second home as Stevie and I made friends with some of the musicians and waitresses who worked there and took to hanging out into the early hours. We were privileged to see some of the great names in the music, such as saxophonists Ben Webster and Coleman Hawkins, and for the first time we found ourselves on something like an equal footing with some of the musicians, a number of whom were women. Outstanding among these was saxophonist Vi Redd, who holds the distinction of having the longest continuous stay at the club. Vi, who comes from California, is a pretty mean singer, too, the kind who makes you want to get down and party the minute you hear her launch into a blues. One night, however, she became exasperated at an unresponsive audience. 'I go to church on a *Sunday*!' she snapped, raising her eyebrows at us in despair. It was a revelation to encounter a woman who could play with such fire and technical command. I reviewed her performance for *Downbeat* and said so.

Two other Scott Club regulars we got to know were the expatriate American singer Joy Marshall and Blossom Dearie, also an American, who played piano as well as singing her idiosyncratic collection of witty songs, some of which, like 'Sweet Georgie Fame', were penned by herself. Joy had problems with audiences, too. She was a strong, musi-

cianly singer, who suffered unfairly from comparisons with Sarah
Vaughan, to whom she bore a slight physical resemblance. One night
Joy was singing her heart out to a half-empty room, a man slumped
across a table at her feet, gently snoring. In the middle of a poignant
number she jerked her thumb in his direction and gave us that same
despairing look. '*Jazz fan*,' she announced, laughing mirthlessly. Show
business was not always a bundle of laughs, I was learning.

Joy was also a deeply unhappy person. When she died from an
overdose of sleeping pills, it was traumatic for Stevie, who had been
particularly close to her. The funeral brought us together with people
like Tubby Hayes, with whom Joy had lived for a while, and the
amazing vocal improviser Annie Ross, whom I'd admired from afar for
years. Sadly, the music world brought us in touch with death in a way
that was unknown to most other people of our age. The rigours of life
on the road, the disasters, frustrations and sheer injustice that so many
talented artists suffered all combined to add to the terrible death toll
that the music business endures.

Stevie went back to her mother's house for a while following a
fire at her flat. Her brother was an accomplished guitarist who had just
started work at a music publishing firm after a spell on the road playing
the blues. The pianist from that band, a brilliant musician, also worked
at the firm and often stayed at the house. His name was Reg Dwight and
from time to time we would meet at the breakfast table. One day in
1968 he asked me to take some publicity photographs; he had just cut a
record and was planning on being a star. He had decided to change his
name for this new singing career, he said: professionally, he was now
called Elton John.

Reg was doing a lot of song-writing by now, cutting demo-discs
at the music publishers, and Stevie and I thought we might try our hand
at the business ourselves. She had worked out a couple of choruses and
a middle-eight at the piano, and I had written some words. It was a witty
little number which we called 'Screwy' (as in 'I'm screwy for you'), and
was in similar quizzical vein to some of the things that both Georgie
Fame and Blossom were doing in their then current mutual admiration
society. We thought we might persuade one of them to record it. There
was good money to be made from even the B-side of a single, as we
learned from other song-writers we knew. Blossom kept the song for a
while then returned it, regretfully. She liked it, she said, but there was
no way that, as a woman, she could do a song with a title like that. It had
never even crossed our minds that there was a problem.

When it comes to sex, the general impression of the jazz scene is that it
is a society where anything goes. In reality, it is a rather conservative
world, particularly in its expectations of how women should behave. So
although there is just as much lesbian and gay activity among musicians
as in any other sector of society, it tends to be ignored or, when
'discovered', explained away as being circumstantial; and few indeed
have been the artists, or for that matter, listeners, who have made such
personal preferences known. When a British bass player began to
review records in *Gay News* in the 1970s, an outraged collector wrote to
one of the record companies to advise them of this horrific situation;
they replied they were grateful for the publicity, to which his response

was that he intended removing all their albums from his shelves. A public display of affection between the same musician and his male lover on a TV documentary about his work attracted abuse in the jazz press as recently as 1985. Around the same time, a gay man wrote to Gene Lees' *Jazzletter* proclaiming his astonishment when he met other gays who enjoyed the music he loved. He had thought he was completely alone. 'Blowing a masculine stick/Avoiding the faggot's trick', in the words of one jazz poet, the musician lives in a society where machismo is expected as the norm and women's sexuality is largely ignored.

Behind the scenes, it was a different story. As I became less diffident about my sexual lifestyle I found that, despite the official rejections of homosexuality that abound in the jazz world, there was, privately, a considerable degree of sympathy and understanding. To well-travelled musicians used to encountering women who loved women in the business, lesbians were not some rare, freakish species. Such women, men would tell me, often shared their heartaches with them when they were out on the road. Some of them shared solace, too. They could be considered bisexual and therefore not too threatening to the male ego; but as a way of life, lesbianism was not as foreign to most American musicians I met as it seemed to be to some of my cultural contemporaries. There were one or two who were hostile, others who suggested a little mutual participation, but in the main I found that those who were sure in their own sexual identity were respectful. They were far more sophisticated and worldly about 'the life' than most Englishmen I knew and I felt less hesitant about sharing my secret feelings with those of them I considered my friends.

There was another reason for the understanding that I encountered. Oppression creates a particular kind of awareness, the ability to grasp what is taking place in any situation with a speed and shrewdness that leaves the oppressor bemused. Gay men and lesbians have developed intricate strategies for survival, in the same way that people of oppressed races have done – indeed as women everywhere do in their relationship to men. The degree to which this is necessary differs according to the severity of the oppression, but exclusion can produce a particularly enlightened sensitivity.

It does not necessarily follow, though, that various oppressed minorities will easily identify with each other. For a start, the white gay world has always been notoriously racist, Black people being pursued for their 'exotic' quality above all. Homophobia is common in Black societies, 'homosexuality' being called 'the white man's disease', as if love for one's own sex were not a familiar way of life throughout the Third World. In Africa, particularly, relationships of an obvious gay nature have traditionally been refuted. Yet in practice they have always existed. Kenya's Jomo Kenyatta, after all, is on record claiming that clitoridectomy was introduced (by men) to curtail lesbian activity in polygamous society. Same-sex love occurs in the harem, the nomadic encampment, among male warriors and the women who marry other women widowed in war. It is only the question of a declared sexual identity that is recent and thus, to many, so startling. As a sympathetic friend from Northern Nigeria (not gay himself) once said to me, 'The only difference between us and you in Europe is that you talk about it and we don't.'

The question of owning a gay cultural identity would become important to me, too, later on as I began to realise that whatever happened in my life was not unconnected with my gender, sexuality and, indeed, my race. Identifying in this way would be a positive move, even if doing so brought with it a new set of problems and complexities. At the beginning, though, being a lesbian was something I 'just happened' to be.

By gradually 'coming out' to a considerable number of people, I was also coming out to myself, and that was important for the sake of self-esteem. Because of the 'official' attitudes that prevailed, however, I tended to keep a low profile away from intimate one-to-one exchanges. As long as Stevie and I stayed together, little was said to our faces. As time went by, we realised that most people assumed we were lovers, although as far as our public behaviour was concerned, this was purely speculation on their part. We could well have been 'just friends', and it must have been quite confusing when we turned up individually or together with various male friends in tow.

Assumptions about lesbians also tended to equate us with a libertarian approach to sexual matters. Stevie was delighted when one of her idols, a distinguished American singer, took up residence in London with her husband. They spent time together, socialising, shopping and exchanging ideas. One day, however, she arrived at their flat to find them wearing their night-clothes. There was an air of expectancy and she felt quite uncomfortable. After a while, it was suggested that they all go to bed together. When she refused, the atmosphere became evil. 'You're a lesbian,' they told her; 'why not?' She left in dismay, with words of abuse ringing in her ears. On another occasion, a thwarted pianist said to me, 'Why not? It's always a gas going to bed with a bull-dyke; the cats knew that from way back'. Although women's sexual needs might be denied in the main, it was automatically assumed that a lesbian must be over-sexed. After all, why else would she want to do it?

In 1967, the year Vi Redd appeared at Ronnie Scott's new premises in Frith Street and Engelbert's 'Release Me' went into the charts, the Sexual Offences Bill partially legalised male homosexuality. It was the year I made my third trip to New York and Stevie and I celebrated our second anniversary. There was an increasing awareness in the general (heterosexual) public that gay people were not quite as rare as they might have imagined. Not entirely unconnected with the liberalising of the laws that affected gay men was the beginning of a late-night gay disco scene, exclusively male at first.

One of the first such places to open was the Sombrero in Kensington High Street, whose basement, Yours and Mine, would, we learned from a man friend, occasionally allow women through its hallowed portals. We took to going there occasionally, after the Gates shut up shop for the night. As elsewhere, the doormen were reluctant, but once inside our presence created no waves.

The difference between the Sombrero and the Gateways was noteworthy. For a start, there was space — space to talk, to relax, to be seen or not seen. Above all, there was space to dance. The room featured far hipper sounds than the Gateways, and the dancing was flamboyant and extrovert, none of that hang-dog shuffling that bedevilled so many lesbian encounters. It was stylish, clean and modern, and providing you ordered the mandatory salad, provision of which was the club's way around the late-night licensing law, you could dance up to 2 a.m. This was something that had been unimaginable for gays up till then.

But the self-oppression and denial that characterised the gay and lesbian community in the days before the Women's and Gay Liberation Movements, persisted. It was reflected in the self-deprecatory talk that prevailed when people were not blustering, and it led to enormous emotional dislocation.

At the Sombrero I ran into some of the people around *Ready Steady Go!* They included a singer who went on to become a very big star indeed. The first time there was some consternation. One man was embarrassed to see me and began to pretend that he knew nothing about the club. Plenty of straight people went there as they did to the Gates, after all, spending a night out with friends and dancing, and there were many who were just dabbling their toes in the water to see how it felt. It seemed pointless to explain that I knew we both 'went the same way' if he hadn't realised it by now, but I felt cheated and disturbed by his evasion. Whether it would have been more comforting to acknowledge that we had gayness in common is unclear. Certainly I found little reflection of my own desires and ideals whenever I talked with people like these. But as so many conversations were cynical and deeply dishonest, it really was quite hard to tell.

One weekend, Stevie was booked to play a country club somewhere in Hampshire. She came back with the news that the owners were a couple of queens and that I had a standing invitation to visit with her any time. She'd met some women there, too, a lesbian couple who lived together, and had had a thoroughly enjoyable time.

'Johnny' and 'Frank' who ran the club were warm-hearted, gregarious people, respected throughout the local community despite the retinue of sailors and 'boys' who were drawn to the club like bees around a honey-pot. They had inherited two sitting tenants when they acquired the premises, and these genteel elderly ladies continued to live there, apparently oblivious to the exact nature of the musical-beds that went on after nightfall. Frank, who was as camp as a row of tents, had worked on the boats as a steward. He and Johnny were adept at nursing their lodgers whenever they were under the weather, and they'd send them up tastefully prepared meals on a tray each night, while drink was consumed in large quantities downstairs and there was an awful lot of amnesia next morning. Nothing was more amusing than the sight of a hairy overnight guest clutching a towel and leaping into the bathroom for safety, narrowly avoiding a clash with little Miss Foulsham, green eye-shade in place and stout stick in hand, toddling out for her morning constitutional.

The boys kept open house for people they liked, and we were always welcome whether Stevie was working or not. Drag artistes also appeared there in cabaret, one notable playing the piano and offering a never-ending flow of 'palare' (gay slang). 'Let me varda your lallies,' he'd accost some boyish young punter, who'd love it, whether he understood it or not. (It means: 'Let me look at your legs.') The subject of his attention could even be in female company, and still react the same way, indicative to a certain extent of the way so many heterosexual people are fascinated with the gay world. 'Bona eek,' our man would sing to the tune of 'Baby Face': 'You've got the cutest little bona eek,' and 'Nice face!' we'd all chorus back, ' 'omi' (homosexual) style.

It was cheerful enough and the boys were generosity itself, steak dinners appearing for both of us as a matter of routine. On some visits they'd introduce me to revellers who wanted their photographs taken, and remembering my past dance-hall successes, I contrived to come back to London, pockets bulging with money.

'Henry' and her girlfriend were hospitable and friendly, too, but I found their role-playing relationship challenging in its openness and because of this, overpowering. Henry was an entrepreneur who had moved from frozen foods into publishing. 'Drag' was becoming increasingly popular and she decided there might be a readership for a regular magazine on the subject and its history.

She commissioned me to be 'her' photographer, and took me along on an interview with the amazing Mr Jean Fredericks who hosted the annual Drag Ball at Porchester Hall. Stevie and I went with Henry and her lover to the event and once again I experienced the breathless *frisson* that goes with the love-that-dare-not-speak-its-name. It had nothing to do with the bevy of transvestites who paraded up and down in astonishing parodies of women. Rather, it was the fact that we found ourselves seated next to someone I recognised. It was Tina, the famous big-band singer who had once given me the eye backstage at the Marquee. I felt embarrassed, pointlessly, for she would hardly remember that brief encounter, but to my astonishment I felt an element of retrospective 'fancying', of opportunities lost, and didn't want Stevie to sense my confusion. The irony of it was that they actually knew each other already. We were living together by now and Tina lived nearby with a woman known as her sister. Whether she was sister or lover was never discovered, for the singer was nervous and totally 'closety'. Now it was she who was anxious not to be judged as a lesbian. We all thought it terribly funny.

All this was forgotten when the cabaret act appeared. A male and female stripper were featured and Henry pushed me forward, camera in hand. At the side of the stage where I had photographed so many African dances and met my Angolan lover João, I watched with fascination as they stripped down to spangled G-string and pouch. To my amazement, the woman's breasts remained firmly erect as she lay on her back; I knew nothing of silicon implants. Sharing the steps was another photographer, a man wearing a golden wig and a flamboyant creation in bright orange satin. He peered at me over his flash-gun. 'Ooo,' he said, 'you're a *real girl*.' 'Er, yes,' I replied apologetically, 'but I am gay.' Evening-Gown reeled back in horror. 'Oh,' he tossed his head, disparagingly, '*I'm* not gay. I'm a *bank manager*.'

The early days of my relationship with Stevie seemed simple. We continued to date other people, for I thought that was something that people in showbusiness did when they were on the road. Most men seemed to do it, after all. We knew plenty of men with money, Africans in business, as well as well-heeled musicians, many of whom were mature, experienced people who took sex as it came and were unperturbed by platonic encounters of the kind on offer with us. We could drink as much as they did and knew how to have fun, and sometimes these evenings would end up in exchanging confidences about our respective 'affairs' or 'old ladies'.

It was simpler to keep things light, for although we were in love, I don't think that I, for one, imagined at this point that a lesbian relationship could last. We did know some women who had stayed together for years, but they seemed uncertain and isolated, with life-styles that had little in common with ours. Even before I became aware of the ghetto's potential for destructiveness, the idea of two women living together into old age seemed unlikely. Gradually, however, we grew closer together, our loving friendship shored up by what we had in common – the music in particular, and the very real business of leaving the uncertainties of youth behind. It was not until we had been together for four years and set up home together that I started to realise I had cut myself off from the possibility of freedom. I don't think I even spelt it out to myself, I just knew I wanted to explore how far I could go on my own. I had seldom been to the Gates without Stevie, but now I began to go there when she was away on the road.

As gay men and lesbians we have chosen those particular words to describe ourselves because we do not want to be defined as 'homosexual', a term suggesting that our relationships revolve around sex alone. It is ironic, then, that on the 'scene' many of us were forced to become sexually aggressive in order to be accepted – simply because of the way the outside world, which invented that word, has made us see ourselves. The situation has altered somewhat with the raising of consciousness and the passing of time, but back then, people would adopt a predatory pose when all they really wanted was a drink and a dance.

Not surprisingly, I, too, adopted a predatory style and routine. It was not enough that I had a relationship with someone I loved and with whom I had so much in common. I had discovered a whole new world and, despite the fact that I didn't care that much for some of the women I met in the ghetto, something drove me to spend more time seeking out other lesbians. In truth, I was still painfully shy; it was only with an effort of will – and a not inconsiderable amount of alcohol – that I gathered the nerve to approach other women. But men had accustomed me to sexual conquest being a part of everyday human relations and I found myself bolstering my ego by making a play for women rather than trying to make friends or find people with similar interests. As women we had never really been taught how to value our friendships, anyway. Friendship was something that men had; women just got along, marking time until being 'noticed' – or so it was said.

And yet, because of the role-playing, I found myself to be ill-equipped and inept on the scene. I realised I found boyish women attractive, slim garage workers and girls in the army, yet because of my height and the way I carried myself, I was classified 'butch'. 'Femme' women often wore skirts and grew their hair longer than long, and there was no way I was going to dress like that again or wanted someone who did. Jeans, tailored slacks and Viyella were liberating after years of being trussed up in pencil-slim skirts and high-heels, but Stevie and I still wore make-up, because if you didn't you were definitely 'diesel' or mannish; we felt above that and acted accordingly.

But however you felt about yourself was immaterial as I discovered when I went out on my own. I hadn't planned to do anything other than have a look round, but things changed in the predatory milieu. There was one tallish woman called Cheryl, a bit of a 'Sloane', who wore her blonde hair long and carried herself with great poise. In a drunken moment one day I told her I found her attractive. Her response was to toss back her hair and snort with incredible disdain. 'Don't let the hair fool you, darling!' She meant she was 'butch' and I was definitely out of line. Another time I gave someone a lift into Soho and suggested we might get together. She apologised, saying she could only relate to really 'butch' women. It was all terribly confusing and bore no relationship to who and what I actually was.

When Stevie discovered my infidelities, she was upset but forgiving. In those days before feminism and gay liberation politics we had no ideas about acceptable alternatives to monogamy. It was *wrong* to be unfaithful and that was all there was to it. I did feel guilty, but was continually fascinated by all those women out there in spite of the fact that I didn't much care for being in a ghetto.

I was somewhat surprised when she, too, had an affair while working in Germany. It was with a saxophone player, a man, and so less of a threat, but a complete surprise none the less. It was me, after all, whose behaviour suggested I was less than dedicated to our relationship. But I think that the failure of my liaison with Al Douglas, though I always shrugged it off, did stay with me and make me feel that I didn't have what it took to stay on. Stevie met him briefly once in New York and found his rigidity and old-fashioned attitude unbelievable. I had to agree, yet I retained a fondness for him, if not for the ideal of love with a man or marriage. It took a long time for this to evaporate, though vanish it finally did.

It was late in 1972 when I arranged to meet Al in a Manhattan bar to talk of his time with Coltrane. Stevie and I had been lovers for over six years but she'd gone back to London, leaving me to research for a new book. I was feeling alone and uncertain and joked that I seemed to have lost my interest in women. His relief was tangible. 'That's a *good girl!*' he said cheerfully, patting my thirty-going-on-thirty-one-year-old shoulder. That really did it for me.

Part Four
I'm a Road-Runner Baby

I'm a road-runner, baby,
Got to keep on keeping on.

Junior Walker

13
Bringing It All Back Home

In the summer of 1968, when Black Power and the student revolts had America and Europe in ferment, I went back to Africa with my mind set on music. On the day I arrived in Morocco, Edward Blackwell fell off a motor-cycle and broke his shoulder. Blackwell was a drummer from New Orleans, one of the great originals on his instrument. By reintroducing the dancing-beat of the marching bands into a modern jazz setting he had brought new vitality to the music. He was riding pillion around Rabat's Medina with a Moroccan musician when he had the accident which kept him away from the drums for the best part of a month. It was tragic for Edward, a musician who lives to play, and a severe disappointment for me, looking forward to hearing one of my favourites in an African setting.

I landed at Rabat, the Moroccan capital, at night, and succumbed once again to Africa, the gentle warmth and the way all the senses are stimulated by the continent. I nearly succumbed to officialdom, too, called back into Immigration when the word 'Photographer' was spotted on my passport. '*Oh, je fais les photos pour les mariages, les bébés, les familles,*' I managed in faltering French. All smiles, and I was waved on my way.

Waiting to meet me with a broad grin and a huge, enveloping African embrace was a man who stood almost 6 feet 8 inches tall. He wore bebopper's shades and a flowing Ghanaian *batakari* embroidered in yellow and green, and looked like any of the Senegalese travellers milling around the airport. He walked slowly, with a casual, African lope, his massive feet relaxing inside bright yellow Moroccan *babouches*. The only thing that betrayed his American origins was a faultless pair of navy-blue trousers in mohair, refugees from a suit made for less clement climes. He was Randy Weston, a pianist from the Bedford-Stuyvesant section of Brooklyn, who had made his home in Morocco. We had been corresponding for the past year and I planned to write about his decision to explore his African roots, something other musicians only talked about doing.

As we drove through the wide streets of the modern administrative capital and past the mud-brick walls of the old Medina, the smells of the evening took over my consciousness: charcoal burning for cooking, spices for *cous-cous*, the heady perfume of flowers that gave up their secrets at night. I was overwhelmed and felt quite emotional. 'It's funny,' I ventured hesitantly, 'although I'm a European, I feel like I'm coming home.' 'That's not surprising,' said Randy; 'we like to think that Africa is the birthplace of all mankind.'

For the past year the pianist had made his home in Morocco. We had met in New York and he had told me of the emotional impact of his previous African journeys and how inspirational the experience had been. He spoke of meeting people he felt he had known all his life, faces and mannerisms familiar from Bed-Stuy and Harlem, of hearing speech patterns and rhythms that reminded him of Afro-American language. Growing up Black in America he had experienced the Diasporean dilemma of dual allegiance. He had fought for his rights as a citizen, yet was torn between that American identity and an awareness of kinship and solidarity with others of African descent. He had been bombarded with the notion that all connections between the two cultures had been severed, but refused to believe it. Early grounding by Westindian parents who instilled race-pride in him from the beginning made him realise that he had to go and find out the truth for himself. He did so and made the connections, thereafter devoting himself to clarifying that discovery for others. The music he wrote was based on African rhythms, and he made a point of playing at places such as the United Nations.

He had made up his mind about repatriation when he attended John Coltrane's funeral service and heard the white pastor intone how many jazz musicians he had buried. 'I thought to myself, "Well, you're not going to bury me." ' Riding the subway and walking down 5th Avenue no longer held any attraction for Randy, and when the Moroccan government responded to a concert he gave with two Berber drummers by offering him a tour of the country's hotels, he had no hesitancy about going back there with Blackwell and bassist Bill Wood.

Randy saw no conflict between basing himself in Morocco, and the probability that his ancestors had sub-Saharan origins; to him Africa was a continent without boundaries, offering opportunities to develop and learn away from the frustrations and strictures of American racism and the pattern of one-sided cultural support the system engendered. For a pianist there were particular problems, but if the country was a little short on adequate instruments, receptivity and warmth relegated this to merely a slight inconvenience.

Villa Weston, his house in Rabat, was surrounded by bougainvillea, lemon and lime; at night the air was scented with jasmine and orange blossom. Furnished in the sparse but functional Moroccan style with plenty of rugs and leather cushions, it was home also to two of his teenage children, Pam and Niles, his secretary Leslie, and a cook. Food was prepared in Moroccan style and eaten from deep earthenware bowls, *cous-cous* and various *tajines* constantly stretched to accommodate visitors. Blackwell shared Randy's vision of finding peace in Africa and had his family with him as well; they and Bill Wood, later known as Vishnu, lived elsewhere. At home the men wore Yoruba *agbada*, freeflowing robes that reached the ground. For the first time in his life, said the pianist, he had found relaxation. And if work was infrequent, he could console himself with the thought: 'I struggled in America for almost thirty years so I can certainly struggle in beautiful Africa for as much time or longer.' Rabat was not the most historic of Moroccan cities, but I was a little disappointed when Randy announced we were leaving for the more cosmopolitan port of Tangier. I had hoped to go down to the South, to see Marrakesh at least, but the intermittent work situation could only continue for so long. We took the train northward,

Khadeija the cook coming too.

The United States Consul installed us at the American Legation, a distinguished old building decorated with tiles and intricately
carved woodwork just inside the walled Medina. Like most Moroccan
houses, it was built around an inner courtyard where palm trees and
oranges blossomed, the different areas linked by tiled corridors and
terraces. The Blackwells moved into their own quarters there, Frances,
who came from Georgia and spoke with a slow Southern drawl, and
their children J.E., Harry and Near-in. ('All these people givin' their
children such far-out names,' said their mother, 'I reckoned Near-in
went in the other direction.') Frances was white and her marriage to
Blackwell in the 1950s had landed them in a New Orleans jail under
Louisiana's miscegenation laws of the time. She had lost none of her
folksy humour, however. On my way out one day she asked me to look
for a cobbler to repair Harry's shoes: 'Look at them, their tongues
hangin' out like thirsty dogs!'

As time went on, I got to know both of them well. Blackwell —
everyone, Frances included, called him that — was a legend in jazz
circles. His appearance in London with Ornette Coleman the previous
year had been significant for me. Blackwell was Ornette's original
drummer and I was beginning to realise the way that percussionists
had been overlooked, their contribution to the music underplayed by
Western-oriented critics. He'd been embarrassed when I suggested an
interview and I was surprised at his modesty, but we'd got together
none the less. We had dined at an Indian restaurant, where he stunned
the waiters by taking out a felt-tipped pen and drawing drum-patterns
all over the tablecloth to demonstrate a particular point of percussion.
When it came to his instrument, his modesty vanished. Everyone said it:
'Blackwell *knows*.' Randy was set to play two concerts during the Tangier
Festival, one a private affair in the home of a London art-dealer. But
there were tensions in the household, occasioned partly by the different
expectations each of us had of a stay in a foreign society, mainly because
money was scarce. I contributed most of my spending money to the
common cause, which left me unable to move around freely. On top of
this, I felt isolated from the main activity. Randy and Bill would stay out
late, socialising with Moroccan musicians, but I was never invited to join
them. I'd been brought up to believe that women should never take the
initiative in a strange situation and it would have gone against that
education to ask to be taken along.

Tangier, with its constant influx of seafarers and tourists and a
history of sexual exploitation by Europeans, could still be a little daunting for a woman from outside the society at this time. Most men and
women dressed in *djellaba*, and the veil was a common sight in the
streets. Male protection was an advantage, so I palled up with a gay
Venezuelan, who took me around the bazaars where we could relax and
drink mint tea without being importuned by opportunistic young men.
The hippy era was under way and the Venezuelan, who dressed in a
flowing pink *kmiss* tied round the waist with a brilliant wool *mejdoul*,
looked like a romantic Sheikh of Araby. He was busy raising funds for
the forthcoming concert and dropped names with a profligacy that left
some people believing that members of the aristocracy would be on
hand to patronise the event. He was not the ideal companion with

whom to discover the city – indeed on the night of the concert he made a half-hearted attempt to abscond with the funds – but I was beginning to feel increasingly left out of whatever it was that was happening. The other women in the Weston ménage were reluctant to do much in the way of exploring, and with him at least there was no sexual pressure to combat.

The Festival of Folklore was a highlight of the year for Tangier's artistic community which included, as it had done for centuries, a substantial sprinkling of foreigners. For years following Independence the Moroccan government had played down the significance of folk-culture in an ill-conceived attempt to woo the West. Now they were really going to town, putting on a series of events in Tangier's largest theatre. During the festival I met a Moroccan dancer called Ouakrim Lahcen, and he took me and some of his friends to see the Gnawa, Black Guineans who live in the south of Morocco. With several small boys in their retinue, the Gnawa men dance accompanied by drums and a guitar called *hajhouj Gnawi* and an impressive array of iron-clappers (*karkaba*); these are held out before them as they move forward and beaten rhythmically together. It was deafening but truly hypnotic. Years later I could still hear those rhythms and visualise that line of men dancing forward, warriorlike, shaking their heads, their feet stomping in staccato patterns which interacted with the clap of their *karkaba*. The audience were almost as loud, eating, drinking and shouting throughout the performance, ignoring the 'them' and 'us' implied by the concert stage, adding their own equal part to each rhythm in the African tradition.

The highlight of the festival was the appearance of the legendary Guedra, Berber women from Goulemine in the south, who danced traditionally for the entertainment of travelling caravans. The women were wrapped in startling indigo-blue sheets, their hands, arms and feet patterned in henna, their lips stained red by chewing walnut bark. Bouchara, their leader, can be seen on postcards for sale all over Morocco, her long hair intertwined with jewellery and coloured threads, her henna-ed wrists weighted with silver bangles. Because their dancing used to take place in tents, the entire performance is done on their knees. Accompanied by a large, Black woman beating an equally substantial *tabla*, Bouchara moved into the spotlight, swathed completely in veils. Only her hands were visible, her expressive fingers the main focus of the dance. Around her the other women ululated in the Arabic fashion, an eerie, compelling effect that succeeded in hushing even that voracious and celebratory audience.

The Berber musicians and dancers were staying in a Tangier school and Ouakrim took us to see them. A cooking-fire had been lit on the concrete floor of one classroom, but Ouakrim persuaded a group of men from the Haha region to stage an impromptu sword-dance. Daggers flashed dangerously in the air, slicing close to ears, hands and noses, accompaniment being provided by the tambourine-like drum *al bendir* and the *al ghita* flute. One man kept time metallically with two rods on a wheel-hub, raised off the ground on the toes of a pair of shoes.

Randy taped some of the music, then sat down to talk with Bouchara. He could always enliven or defuse any situation with his charismatic personality and deep, booming laugh, and the two musicians gravitated to each other immediately, two obvious 'stars' in any language. They exchanged views in a mixture of French, Moroccan Arabic and Berber, talking as if they had known each other for ages. Whatever was said, they were in solid agreement. 'Mama knows,' said Randy, turning to me, 'Mama *knows*!'

Relations between Randy and me became increasingly strained. He was under enormous pressure because of the number of people he had to support and the dawning realisation that Africa could not provide as much work as he needed. He had asked me to help him with his autobiography and I'd agreed, but I was accustomed to allowing interviews to move easily from one topic to another, rather than exerting the discipline needed to establish historical continuity. We taped a fair amount of material, but I felt that an autobiography would take more than a year of discussion and told him it was not going to work out.

We managed a trip to Chaouen, a fairytale village in the Rif Mountains, as yet unvisited by many tourists. In a café where the local Jbala musicians played, we enjoyed huge bowls of bright yellow lentil soup. The Jbala violinist played his instrument in the African fashion, bowing it between his knees like a cello. Dancing to the music was a young boy, his slim waist swathed in a bulky cloth belt, balancing a copper tea-tray and glasses on his head as he moved. Randy worried constantly about his children and so wherever we went, the whole ménage came too. I managed to take a few pictures, but surrounded by so many people, it was not an auspicious atmosphere in which to attempt the kind of documentation I had in mind.

Randy generally got by on a mixture of good humour and optimism, his resonant, expressive voice and declarations of love for Africa papering over any cracks that appeared in the day-to-day social fabric. On one occasion, though, his frustrations rose to the surface and he took them out on the people nearest to him. A meeting of all the women was called, at which he complained that the house was a mess. Frances and I exchanged glances, Leslie, Pam and another visitor looked embarrassed. To myself I reasoned that Khadeija had a job to do, so what business was it of ours? I kept my allotted space neat and clean, and, after all, why shouldn't the men be equally responsible? There was silence as everyone tried to think of something to say. It was J.E., Blackwell's 7-year-old, who broke the silence. He had noticed a slight physical peculiarity of Our Leader's, and pointed, as only a child of that age can do: 'Hey, Randy, your ears are all kind of curly on top!' That broke up the atmosphere; everyone stood up and left and our failings were never mentioned again.

From time to time the musicians rehearsed, Blackwell chomping at the bit, frustrated by his injury, an old army jacket slung around his shoulders. His entire chest was encased in plaster and he constantly complained that ants had crawled inside his cast, reaching in with a drumstick to scratch. He played as much as he could, but increasingly Niles (later known as Azzedin) was growing stronger on the conga-drum, the instrument he had started playing in earnest since coming to Africa. Blackwell was not the only one who was frustrated, however, and I was relieved when I ran into two women from London, Rachel and Carolyn, waitresses from Ronnie Scott's Club.

Rachel, an American, wanted to go to Chaouen. She had lived there for two years and knew everyone in the town. I'd felt cheated by my brief glimpse of this mountain hideaway and wanted to go along, but I had this financial problem. I rushed back to the Legation and confronted Our Leader. I need some money, I told him, and to my surprise he produced some. We took a bus with goats tied on the roof into the mountains, passing through Tetouan. The approach to the village was breathtaking, the mountains rising up behind it in a misty pattern of mauve and green. Young boys met us as we climbed down from the bus and offered us fresh figs as we made our way to the central square. I thought I had never seen such a beautiful place.

Rachel knew someone who owned a hotel. He was delighted to see her again and gave us a meal and a room. We met only men on our visit, but there was none of the sexual pressure I'd experienced in Tangier. We were whisked into a long, smoke-filled room with a low ceiling for huge kidney kebabs and invited to tiny rooftop cafés for tea. Such easy hospitality was symptomatic of the calm before the storm of the full-scale tourist invasion which would dehumanise social contacts between the cultures in places like this. We smoked some powerful *kif* before retiring, and I awoke to the strains of Oscar Peterson. I couldn't believe it; here I was in this tiny hotel in the Rif Mountains, and Oscar was playing a concert. I made my way gingerly across the beds to peer out of the tiny window and the music grew louder. It was 'Night Train' and I was baffled. I craned further upwards and trod heavily on Rachel's arm. She awoke with a scream and a shout. It was only then I realised I was listening to somebody's radio.

Back in Tangier, Carolyn and Rachel moved into a hotel in the Medina. I'd visit them at night and then, too stoned to walk home down the tortuous alleyways, would fall asleep on their rooftop under the stars. I loved the Medina at night, the shadows, the strange smells and the music, but was forbidden because of my race and my gender to know what went on behind closed doors. That chance would come later.

Towards the end of my visit, Randy appeared in concert at the American School. Niles was set to play regular drums in Blackwell's place, but at the last minute he could stand the frustration no longer. He threw his tuxedo jacket over his cast and announced he was making the gig. Before the concert, a Moroccan painter came by with some "erbes' for the musicians. Yacoubi's concoction was famous, having something to do with *kif* but including other elements wrapped up in a paste made from honey. Despite the prevalence of *kif* and the way that most foreigners smoked, drugs were low on my list of priorities. All the same, I decided to sample this offering. On the way to the concert I asked Blackwell what kind of effect the herbs were expected to have. He mused for a minute then said: 'Have you tried LSD? If you had you could compare them.' Oh, Christ, I thought, that's all I need. I'd been waiting all month to hear one of my heroes in concert again, and now I'm going to be stoned. Sure enough, when we got to the concert, I began hallucinating. The stage changed shape before my eyes and I felt totally dislocated, floating. The odd thing was that I was able to write a constructive, detailed review of the music while it was in progress, something I would never have been able to do on alcohol, even though my head felt as if it was on Mars.

Randy (as I said in the review) is one of the purest non-commercial composers on the jazz scene. He opened the concert playing 'Marrakesh Blues', a piece based on Berber themes he had recorded in the regional village of Imin Tanout. 'Berber music,' he explained to the audience, 'is the purest minor blues,' and sure enough, the insistent blues theme the four musicians developed had overtones of Mississippi as well as Morocco.

Then he turned out the lights for a new piece, 'Night in the Medina', an eerie, Arabic-inflected melody evocative for me of those nights I spent curled up under the stars. This, he said later, was his first attempt at playing a slow number in Africa, and he kept the audience spellbound. Blackwell sat this one out while Niles carried his conga drum into the audience. Spearheaded by Randy's lyrical piano, the trio kept the people quiet until the final almost inaudible tap of the conga. But it was an adaptation of Nigerian Bobby Benson's highlife number, 'Niger Mambo', that was the highlight. Blackwell was featured on this, his long-awaited chance to express his phenomenal way with the drum. He started out the rhythm on cowbell, the crowd giving a shout of astonishment when they realised he planned a one-handed solo. His pattern was simple, effortlessly alternating from cowbell to tuned side-drum. Then he switched from side-drum to bass drum and snare, making the skins shout and setting up a polyrhythmic conversation with himself that drove the crowd over the edge. As the applause and the shouting erupted and the people rose to their feet, I looked at Frances sitting beside me. She had tears in her eyes. She shook her head and turned to me, bursting with pride: 'Blackwell usually sounds like four men; tonight he just sounded like three!'

After the concert, we went for drinks at the house of the American Consul, then Ouakrim drove me back to the Medina. This time we didn't stop at the Legation but plunged into the alleyway and inside a darkened doorway. In a beautiful old house, with tiled walls and soft cushions on the floor, we found some of the Guedra and their husbands seated beside local painters and a Moroccan film-director of some eminence. The women, regarded as courtesans in the past, poured tea and passed sweetmeats. Today they are seen as 'international figures' and thus exempt from traditional censure. The atmosphere was relaxed and casual, with no overtones of intrigue or sexual anticipation. *Kif* was passed, too, and I found myself in a dream. I was in danger of developing a vision of Africa that was impossibly romantic.

14
Power to the People

It is not always easy to remember how a certain understanding develops, but sometimes the words come back over the years like a hurricane. Just as John Donne's poem 'No Man is an Island' said more to me about humanity than going to church ever did, Elaine Caulker put a new world-construct into words in one sentence.

Elaine was from Sierra Leone, her father the former Ambassador with whom I had shared the memorable night of fondue and Connie Francis in Freetown. She lived in London and occasionally worked as a radio presenter for the BBC's African Service. After a spell of teaching in Algeria, she had come back by way of Italy and its classical sites. The cultural contrasts were fresh in her mind, resurrecting for her the duality of her own situation, African-born, English grammar-schooled. She spoke about walking around places such as Florence and Rome, marvelling at their beauty, but being forced to ask herself, 'How much of this was built on my back?'

What she said echoed something I was beginning to hear increasingly expressed: the understanding common to all people of colour of how the White world had benefited from centuries of their material and physical enslavement. The matter-of-fact way she said it had an added effect. Every time I stopped to consider rights and privileges I had taken for granted, I could hear Elaine's words in my head. The idea of palaces in Florence and Venetian churches shored up by centuries of slavery was a powerful image.

Elaine was a person who moved in white circles with ease. She was married to a white man and represented the 'acceptable' African face in our midst. She knew the language and played by the rules, yet she was as angry as someone from a far less privileged background might be. She knew her colour was important, just as Stevie did, and by being in their company I began to see how everything was affected by this realisation. 'Every Black person has two sides,' said Elaine. 'You are your history on the one hand and you are yourself on the other. You have to make up your mind which one you are.' Though their backgrounds were different, both Stevie and Elaine identified with people who grew up under the colonial heel or in the lynchlaw Deep South where the magnolia trees, as Billie Holiday sang, had 'blood on the leaves, and blood at the root'.

It was hardly surprising that I should have reached this awareness, for practically all my work and much of my social life revolved around Africans and people of African descent. Working as I did as a freelance, jobs and contacts led on one from another, and at one point I had as many African names as others in my address-book.

As the Sixties wore on, so the global Black consciousness movement grew, affecting all people of colour. Even those who might have seemed by their behaviour to support the status quo became involved in self-help programmes in every field and in attempts to wrest control from white entrepreneurs. In Paris, Memphis Slim formed United Black Artists, a booking agency that sought to promote various branches from the same root, and added saxophonist Johnny Griffin to his rota of artists. Pride and self-respect became the cultural watchwords. Debate still raged in Africa as to whether women should wear wigs and men affect three-piece suits, but the music, as always, provided the best indication of what people had on their minds. Now at African parties they seldom played records by the ubiquitous Jim Reeves or Bluebeat favourites such as Keith and Enid's 'Worried Over You'. James Brown became everybody's main man, and 'Say it Loud I'm Black and I'm Proud' a new national anthem.

There were still very few Black journalists and photographers in London, and my skills, contacts and knowledge made me useful to a number of Black publications. In 1966 I started taking photographs for the Transcription Centre, a service started by art historian Dennis Duerden to produce cultural radio programmes on the Arts in Africa and supplement the limited material available from the BBC's African Service. It was a short step from there for me to work for the Service itself, taking photographs of such bands as E.T. Mensah's when he toured the country. I became a regular at Bush House, home of the BBC's External Services, where Jomo Kenyatta's son was one of the producers. Occasionally I'd contribute views to one of the music programmes.

South African journalist Maxine Lautré ran day-to-day operations at the Transcription Centre. Visiting artists as well as residents used the Centre's Mayfair offices as an unofficial base and she would help organise contacts and publicity for them as the occasion arose. She had come to London with the African jazz group the Blue Notes and their white pianist Chris McGregor, whom she later married. She was a tall, good-natured woman who bubbled with enthusiasm and for whom nothing was too much trouble. We became friends and through her I got to know the work of African painters and writers who might otherwise have remained hidden for me. Practically all these artists were male, with the notable exception of Ghanaian Ama Ata Aidoo, whose early collection of short stories, *No Sweetness here*, made a lasting impression on me.

Elaine, who occasionally reviewed books, was beginning to write herself. She expressed the common distaste for the syndrome that continue to plague artists of colour, when some European critics, ignorant, guilty, or both, praise Black work regardless of its quality: 'You can never know your actual worth as an artist.' The finger was pointed often at Heinemann Educational Books, seen by many as the colonialist guardians of African literature, but one of the few outlets available. At times the Transcription Centre's visitors could have come from a Who's Who of their African Writers Series. It was there I met people such as Ghanaian poet Kofi Awoonor Williams, and Legson Kayira, who'd walked to America from his home in Malawi — names immediately recognisable from those orange-jacketed paperbacks. I also met Ulli Beier, who wrote about African art and had helped to stimulate a

185

legendary artists' community at Osogbo in Yorubaland. Ulli, a large bearded Austrian who swept around wearing a *dansiki*, had just written *Contemporary Art in Africa* and needed photographs of some paintings. I found myself focusing my venerable Rolleiflex on some disturbing drawings from the pen of the Sudanese Ibrahim Salahi, and upon some varnished gouaches, unceremoniously propped against the railings of the Beier residence, done by Twins Seven-Seven, whose fantastic mythical figures would earn him an international reputation when shown in New York galleries.

Akin Euba, the composer I knew from my visit to Lagos, turned up at the Centre one day and I photographed him in front of a pair of beautifully crafted talking-drums. I also photographed two renowned poets, the Azanian (South African) Mazizi Kunene, living in exile in London, and the Ugandan Okot p'Bitek, who wrote the acclaimed epic 'Song of Lawino'. There were always Azanians on hand, including the brilliant pianist Dollar Brand (later Abdullah Ibrahim) and his vocalist wife Sathima Bea Benjamin. They made a brief appearance at Ronnie Scott's Old Place, as the original Gerrard Street premises were now known, soon to be followed by the Blue Notes, who carved out a comfortable niche for themselves on the London scene. Even given the freedom from chords and time-signatures that characterised the New Music, the Blue Notes' unorthodox version was to have an enormous influence on local ideas.

Flamingo was in its death-throes, having been taken over by a dubious colonial entrepreneur of limited publishing experience and marked reluctance to pay his contributors. I squeezed in a couple of swansongs, stories on two important Nigerians I met at the Transcription Centre. One was Jimo Akolo, a Northern Yoruba painter who had studied with Dennis Duerden at Ahmadu Bello University in Zaria and would end up heading the art department there himself. The other was Wole Soyinka, later to receive the Nobel Prize for Literature.

Wole, who already had a reputation as an unconventional artist and sophisticate, caught me up in his ambience. He was in town for the production of one of his plays and made short shrift of the interview. Instead he swept me along on a shopping trip, purchasing a pair of elegant soft-leather boots and unceremoniously dumping his discarded pair on the floor of the shop. Then we went for an Indian meal. Wole ordered two bottles of Mateus Rosé with our chicken curries, something I thought was terribly daring.

From time to time I would approach one of the white newspapers or magazines with an idea for a story on one of the artists who were household names at Bush House and in African circles, but generally met with incredulity that anyone would be interested in reading about Black endeavour and achievement. Newspapers such as the *Guardian* would run the occasional piece on Baldwin or Soyinka – even LeRoi Jones on one occasion – but that generally meant they'd had their 'Black story' for the next month or two. Music remained the exception; Ellington and Basie could always be sure of some coverage, especially when Princess Margaret graced one of their concerts. The prevailing media belief was that Black people had nothing to say.

A distinct, if unvoiced, understanding existed among those white people who had recognised the wealth of the African cultural heritage and whose lives had been enriched by that discovery. We knew that we shared an almost forbidden secret, for our views were neither echoed nor welcome elsewhere. At concerts and Transcription Centre openings and around Bush House, our delight was expressed unobtrusively, in a refined, middle-class English way, for we knew we held an unfashionable position and were relieved that we could at least recognise each other. Many of us were indeed from such a class background, nothing like the hip and flashy people around the jazz scene, and uniting us was the realisation that to support Black creativity meant being treated with amusement or disdain by our peers.

And yet self-doubt frequently lingered. It has often been common to describe those whites who mix with Black people as 'outsiders' in a way that implies inadequacy, and for a while, I, too, wondered what it said about me that I felt so at home with African people. I'd look at others in a similar position, the men especially, often quiet, shy, lacking in the sense of aggression that 'masculinity' demanded, and speculate as to why the assertive artists and intellectuals in the African community had time to spare for such apparently insignificant personalities. As time went on, I realised that for the sensitive there was a fellowship to be found here that was missing in relationships with our more competitive peers. I found a sureness of place as a woman – as they did as men – that didn't need to be constantly underlined as so often required by English society. Such unquestioning acceptance held enormous reassurance, too.

But it was not until I was approached by an agency that did not express incomprehension about my focus of interest that I began to feel less of a freak. For a long time my byline appeared in publications throughout Anglophone Africa, courtesy of Africa Features. I collaborated with others, too, working as photographer on stories by Jumoke Debayo, a Yoruba actress and presenter turned journalist, and Sam Uba, an Igbo exiled from Nigeria through the Civil War. Sam worked as a sub on *The Times*, a rare berth for an African journalist, and survived as a stringer for various agencies and by playing the Fleet Street games. The agency tended to be more interested in 'glamour' shots of eligible women students than the in-depth coverage I'd done for *Flamingo*, but working with Sam I did manage a few foot-in-the-door exposés of dubious Black characters who milked their own communities.

And then I met Margaret Busby, a Ghanaian-born graduate who, like Elaine Caulker, had been through the privileged end of British education. She had just started a small poetry publishing firm and was an obvious candidate for an Africa Features profile. Now she told me that she and her partner Clive Allison were about to bring out a novel – the first for their firm – a tale of Afro-American guerrilla warfare so hot that no American publisher would touch it. 'Oh,' I said, 'Is that Sam Greenlee's *The Spook Who Sat By the Door*?' Margaret was amazed: 'How did you know?' It was through one of those coincidences with which my life seemed to be riddled. Leslie Moëd, who had worked for Randy Weston in Morocco, knew Greenlee, who came from Chicago's Southside. His struggle to find a publisher was a formidable one. He came to London for the launch of the book early in 1969 and I was flattered to discover he knew my work, which was by now appearing frequently in *Downbeat*. 'This is not a novel, it's a Chicago blues. Hope you dig it,' he wrote in my copy of *Spook*. Margaret was now a fully-fledged publisher and worthy of a spread in *Drum*, the picture-magazine founded in South Africa, now with West African editions. John Harold from *Flamingo* now ran the London office and encouraged me to come up with ideas. He called my piece 'The Girl By the Spook by the Door'.

Spook would later become required reading in American High Schools but its revolutionary theme seemed like political sci-fi in this country then. At the time of its publication 100 Black students carrying rifles and shotguns had just taken over the Student Union building at America's Cornell University to protest racism. This followed the example of the Black Panthers, who, two years earlier had marched into the Sacramento, California, State Capitol Building with guns at the ready, maintaining their constitutional right to bear arms. In prison, George Jackson was writing the final letters that would be published in *Soledad Brother*; Malcolm X's *Autobiography* was already a classic. But Britain, for the most part, was still getting over the 'kitchen-sink' realism of *Saturday Night, Sunday Morning* and angry young men who used four-letter words.

I had not thought of myself as a political person since the halcyon days of the Young Communist League, but as the musicians I met expressed themselves on racial issues more vehemently, I became unavoidably caught up in what they were saying. The Battersea group ensured that I knew something of what was taking place in socialist circles too, as I rushed hedonistically around the country, following Stevie on gigs or having fun with visiting musicians. When the Americans were poised to invade Cuba, we had all joined in the demonstration outside the American Embassy, but when horses were used on the crowd at the Vietnam protest in the Battle of Grosvenor Square some years later, there were few whose attitude did not harden.

The events of 1968 caused me to develop a different perspective on what was taking place in Afro-America. Inevitably, I began to delve deeper into revolutionary literature. I read Che Guevara and *The Wretched of the Earth*, in which Fanon suggested that for spiritual liberation it was necessary for blood to be shed, and I pinned up pictures of Lenin and Ho Chi Minh next to a drawing of Coltrane. I started to haunt radical bookshops, learning about the New Left as well as the Black revolt. I kept my distance from direct involvement, though, being more interested in knowing what was happening than actually getting blood on my hands.

Musicians, who had always 'bitched' about the ignorance and lack of impartiality of critics, now began to talk openly of the role Whites had played in misrepresenting and suppressing the music. This attitude was further fuelled by the perpetual irony of seeing white people making a mint out of singing the blues. This phenomenon that began with the rise of rock 'n' roll increased in visibility with the worldwide colonial expansion of British Beat. There were few Black people, whatever their generation or political views, who allowed this particular indignity to pass without comment and yet, with a few notable exceptions, the local jazz fraternity took the view that this outspokenness was but a passing phase. Some writers, among them the most respected for their knowledge of music, insisted that such expressions had nothing to do with art and ignored what was happening under their noses. But Malcolm X had irrevocably changed the way Afro-Americans felt about themselves, and the changing political attitude was having a considerable effect on the music. The politics behind the music just could not, it seemed to me, be ignored by anyone who had anything to do with it. As the poet Jayne Cortez would say to me later, 'After Malcolm had said what most Black people were thinking, you could never have the same relationship with a white person again. . . . You either had to stand up and say "yes" or you had to go back and start shufflin'.'

In Britain, however, it went virtually unrecognised in the jazz community that something unusual was happening. As a group, musicians generally had other, creative, priorities, and had tended to express themselves in a circumspect manner to avoid damaging their work opportunities. Now that some Black artists were being more outspoken, they were dubbed 'extremists' by their detractors. Yet had these Doubting Thomases merely flicked the dial towards popular music, they would have heard equally 'extreme' records, such as the Temptations' 'Message to a Black Man.' The entertainers and tribunes alike were only echoing what was being said in the streets.

Marion Brown, a saxophonist from Atlanta whom I had met on my second visit to New York, began sending me books he felt would enlarge my appreciation of the New Music and help understand where it was coming from. In his letters he spoke of going back to his birthplace in the Deep South, and reviving roots and childhood memories with his uncle, an oldstyle fire-and-brimstone preacher. It was a revelation to me that the two acknowledged extremes of the musical spectrum should exist within the span of two generations. Marion epitomised the new intellectual musician, who cared for the music and the image its practitioners projected, but he missed the grounding he had received when living closer to nature. He recalled blues players bringing their music into the dirt streets where he grew up, 'some blind, some blind alcoholically', and realised how in his hatred for segregation and his desperation to get away from the South he had been blind to the significance of such a fertile cultural environment. As for me, I was thirsty for knowledge, and people like Marion held the key to discovery.

Books became vital. Like other whites with a toe in the waters of Black culture, I read Eldridge Cleaver's *Soul on Ice*, written in prison. The author, a convicted rapist, wrote about taking out his hatred for the oppressor by attacking white women, a stereotype he played for all it was worth, much to my dismay. I was tired of hearing white women involved with Blacks being called 'prostitutes', and I was equally tired at the way women were used as receptacles for all kinds of wrath. He was, nevertheless, a compelling writer, who made hairs rise on the back of white liberal necks, mine included. Cleaver would be discredited later as a callous opportunist who embraced political views as it suited him. He had become a Black Panther in prison soon after the party was formed, and for a while was its Minister of Information. I'm sure many of us fell for his 'sexual mystique', yet as a self-styled 'Ofay-watcher' he articulated a pungent critique of white society. The book was for many whites the first inkling of how deeply rotten was our world.

In London people came out in their thousands when the Rev. Martin Luther King was assassinated. Those American musicians who lived in Britain at the time joined in the march through the city held in his tribute, and performed on the steps of St Paul's Cathedral. P.P. Arnold, who once worked with Ike and Tina Turner, beat a tambourine and sang gospel to Alexis Korner's guitar. Jon Hendricks read a poem. Dakota Staton sang accompanied by saxophonist Peter King (the English one), with the iconoclastic Philly Joe Jones, a two-year London resident, on the drums. Julie Felix, a singer in the Joan Baez mould, played guitar, and speeches were delivered by Dr David (later Lord) Pitt, Fenner Brockway, CND's Canon Collins and others. The mood, tinged with sorrow, was one of commitment to racial unity. It reflected British solidarity with the American civil rights movement and had little to do with what was happening as major cities there went up in flames and insurrectionists chanted Rap Brown's slogan 'Burn, baby, burn!' In America, the time for autonomy had come – but in Britain, the mood was still one of liberal democracy.

James Baldwin, always a controversial figure since his attack on the venerated Richard Wright, was under attack himself now, too. It was not enough that he had written with such grace and power about sexual love – he shuddered at its 'terribleness' and I shuddered with him – he did not fit the new picture. His exile in Europe made him a target for people such as Cleaver, and he was pilloried for his 'inability' to be heterosexual. 'We shall have our manhood . . . or the earth will be levelled by our attempts to gain it,' wrote Cleaver. For the time being, Baldwin's tenderness counted for little in the face of such unequivocal militancy. One of the first songs of social awareness I remember was Big Bill Broonzy's 'When Do I Get to be Called a Man?' It enlightened me early on to the specific nature of the humiliations for which the Black male had been singled out throughout history, and helped me to understand the preoccupation with the recognition of manhood that marked this turbulent decade. Separated though I was from the struggle, Cleaver's challenge struck a chord in my heart. In the more chauvinist manifestations of this celebration, however, I was unable to offer unequivocal support. And I was deeply disconcerted whenever homophobia reared its head.

Among the literature that Marion sent me were the newspapers *Muhammad Speaks* and *The Black Panther*. Reading them enabled me to grasp something of two vastly differing ideologies, although I found it hard to come to terms with their unbending stance. Like other white liberals of my generation I'd been brought up to believe that integration between the races was the key to universal democracy. Now I read in the Nation of Islam's manifesto that the Muslims considered that to suggest friendship could be possible after 400 years of enmity was hypocritical on white people's part. If the proponents of 'integration' were sincere, said Elijah Muhammad, let them prove it by dividing up America with their former slaves, and the Nation demanded a separate state or territory for resettlement. I'd heard some of this from Randy and Archie before, but here it was written on paper and consumed by a grass roots readership, Marion assured me.

As well as their respective manifestos, the two papers carried news of the work they were doing. The Nation owned a chain of bakeries, food shops and fish-canneries, and reported the views of neighbourhood tradespeople as well as prominent figures. When they interviewed James Brown, he said that Black ownership of land was the only way to achieve Black stability. He suggested he and other stars contribute a percentage of their earnings to the Nation. The Panthers, on the other hand, were Marxist-Leninists who referred to Black people as the 'lumpen'. They operated a Free Breakfast programme for children, actively nourishing the future where working mothers were unable to provide.

For a while I was attracted to the macho ethos and style of the Panthers. They were easier for me to deal with by comparison with the Muslims, who spoke of white people as 'devils', and they seemed to be deadly serious in the face of attack and infiltration by counter-revolutionary elements. There was, I am sure, a degree, of sexual attraction in it, as well. I might be living my life as a lesbian, but that did not mean I could not appreciate strength and beauty whenever I saw it. The Panthers *were* beautiful in their black leather jackets, berets and shades – just like Fidel and Che. And when one of my friends went to Algiers and found herself hanging out with Archie Shepp, poet Ted Joans and the exiled Cleaver, I did feel a pang of envy.

Stevie and I had just moved into a flat in Balham, when a musician called George Conley came to stay. George, who would later take the name of Kunle Mwanga, went on to become an important force in the New Music, managing and helping to shape the careers of saxophonists Anthony Braxton and David Murray and the revolutionary group, the Art Ensemble of Chicago. At this point, though, he was still playing the clarinet and had come to England to renew old acquaintances. As a GI based in Britain, he had got to know Georgie Fame at the Flamingo and was one of the people who introduced the organist to the hip new American sounds. George could see I was serious about the music from the way that I wrote in *Downbeat*, and we had been in correspondence for a while. It was he who introduced me to the music of Chicago's radical collective, the AACM (Association for the Advancement of Creative Musicians), for me until then just names in a magazine article. He talked enthusiastically about the seriousness of musicians such as Anthony Braxton, Joseph Jarman and Roscoe Mitchell, and left some of their records behind when he moved on.

He also left a copy of *The Cricket*, a Nationalist music publication edited by Amiri Baraka (LeRoi Jones) and two other important writers, Larry Neal and A.B. Spellman. The masthead details were printed in Swahili, the adopted *lingua franca* of the new Black nationalism. The tone was puritanical in places and highly critical of some important figures in the new music, castigating them for embracing reactionary values, and I found it hard to digest. But it also contained a long letter from Albert Ayler, written before his mysterious death. It was addressed to Mr Jones (Baraka) and to Elijah Muhammad. The saxophonist spoke of having a vision. The language was straight out of the Bible in places, allegorical and redemptionist in tone. I did not know what to make of it, but would return to it from time to time to see whether there could be a message to help me understand more contained within its passionate lines.

Increasingly the musicians of the New Wave were finding an audience for their uncompromising music in Europe. Several moved to France for an extended period, and I began to go over to Paris from time to time to listen to what they were doing. Our Balham flat became a base for some of these passing through London, the virtuoso reedman and composer Anthony Braxton staying with us for a couple of months and so becoming a good friend. It was an exciting period when we never knew who would turn up on the doorstep, but despite the way in which the musicians became the heroes of Paris students and the New Left following the political events of 1968, they occupied an ambivalent position. Like Al Douglas they would laugh uproariously when they found out that the French too ate chitt'lins, albeit in the guise of *andouillettes* – but that was often as far as the laughter went.

By 1970 the racial climate in France had changed considerably from the tolerant one that had seemed so attractive to expatriate Blacks of an earlier generation. Following the war in Algeria, open hostility was directed against North Africans and anyone with a dark skin not dressed conservatively. And the Black man/pimp: white woman/whore stereotype persisted wherever interracial couples were found. Taxis in Pigalle were a problem. My aid was enlisted to hail a cab by a musician *en route* to a concert; he skulked in a doorway while I stopped it. 'He'll think I'm one of them Algerians,' was his jocular comment, but his enforced acquiescence in the situation was painfully evident.

Despite their enormous popularity with the students which involved nationwide tours of the various Maisons de Culture and the like, the musicians could be seen as participating in minstrelsy in yet another guise. The more they chanted Black Power slogans, shook fists and blew frantic sheets of sound, the more they were lionised. Archie Shepp became a national name in France, as Sidney Bechet had been a generation before, but as time went on and the revolutionary fervour died down, many found themselves as unwelcome as the Algerians had become. The racism that had surfaced in Britain jazz circles became the French experience, too.

The Art Ensemble of Chicago, who were part of the AACM, took up residence outside Paris during this period. Fontella Bass, who had had a successful career as a pianist and hit-maker ('Rescue Me'), was married to their trumpeter Lester Bowie and sang with the Art Ensemble on some occasions. I met her and her children before a concert in Paris, along with the other musicians. She was a beautiful, warm woman, who came out on stage like a graceful African queen, then went on to sing the weirdest collection of lyrics, the band creating a continually changing tapestry of colour behind her.

As her final notes died away, a whoop came from the back of the hall and I looked around to see a flurry of 'Black solidarity'. A group of Americans visiting Paris came striding down the aisle, filling the theatre with shouts of pride. A tall man headed the onslaught, long navy coat swinging open, dark shades perched on his nose, hair protruding in an Afro 'bush' from under his beret. The women clasped Fontella to themselves, the men slapped fives and jived. I was still reeling from the music's intensity, now I looked at this group of

Chicagoans and envied the intimacy they shared.

Just like those white men who had envied me for getting close to musicians in a way they could not, so I found myself gazing wistfully at this display of camaraderie. It wasn't that I wanted to 'be' one of them; rather, that I knew I was not. Moments like this made me realise I could never get close to the music the way that a person 'of' the culture could do. Too much history had gone before for that to be possible; the music was about much more than the notes. To sit in the audience and absorb, though, was enough. I would not let the realisation of my 'outsider' status deter me from appreciating the music and working however I could for the cause.

15
When the Dust Hit
my Shoe

I was never a hippie – too young for the first wave, too old for the second – but when I set off for Turkey and other points East at the end of the Love 'n' Peace era, I was invariably wrapped in an old Afghan sheepskin. Cheap package travel has almost put Samarkand and Ulan Bator within the traveller's grasp today, but, until the hippie trail opened the way, few young English people thought of going further than Ramsgate or Rouen. Hoppy, for example, had been to Albania and Russia, and that made him some kind of celebrity. But to explore the world was a goal for both Stevie and me and we used our work to do this whenever we could. There was a period when I would drop anything at a moment's notice to go along on one of her gigs.

My old mate John Batcheldor had got together with Priscilla Piper following Steve's untimely death from leukaemia, and on New Year's Day 1969 they were married. I went to their wedding with Janet and the next day left with Stevie for Istanbul, following the route of the old Orient Express. It was not her first trip to Turkey; she'd already done the American bases, now she was set to play one of the country's leading hotels. In Belgrade we left the station during a stopover, returning to find the train gone. With no mutual language of enquiry, we attempted to find out what had happened. Our throats began to grow dry as we shivered in the thick snow, trying to decide what to do. Everything we had was on the train – drums and cameras, my Afghan coat – and we were inadequately dressed for the weather. After what seemed like an hour, and several prayers later, the train rolled back into the station. It had been into the sidings to divide in two sections. Luck was with us: the half that returned said 'Istanbul'.

We took an overnight bus to Izmir, the ancient port of Smyrna and the third largest city in Turkey. It was a hair-raising journey and, despite constant ministrations of lemon cologne, we arrived feeling ill and distinctly dishevelled. At the Büyük Efes Hotel the manager gazed with dismay at the apparition before him. A poster which showed a singer in thigh-clinging gown was displayed in the lobby, and he kept looking from Stevie to the photograph and back in disbelief. On opening night she set his mind at rest, but came back complaining to me about the attitude to the dancer who opened the show. The Efes' clientele were a blasé élite whose idea of good manners was to leave their food on their plates and yawn wearily at anything that wasn't foreign. The waiters reflected this attitude, but Stevie was having none of this. She struck up a conversation with Nalân, the dancer, and Feride, her mother, who was there as a chaperone. A few nights of this and Feride, invited us to a restaurant for dinner. On the way she bought a small bunch of flowers, explaining that later she was going to a 'married'. Feride, nicknamed

'Farah' on a visit to London, spoke a little English, and we had begun to pick up some words of Turkish. Bold as brass, we invited ourselves to the wedding. Music was provided by a traditional band of violin, clarinet, guitar, *darbuka* (the hand-drum held under the arm and alternately snapped and hit with the fingers), and regular drumkit. The clarinettist played an old Albert system instrument which seemed larger and had a tone deeper than the more common Boëhm system used in the West. Some things he played made me think of Albert Ayler.

Ramazan, the violinist, was also Master of Ceremonies. The dancing had been going on for some time when he indicated that we should join in. I was petrified. Highlife and bluebeat I could handle, but the Turks, it was obvious, expected a virtuoso display. 'You've got it!' I hissed at Stevie, and knocking back another *raki* for confidence, she blithely took to the floor. It was lucky she was such a good dancer, for her enthusiasm ensured we would be remembered. Tourists are rare in Izmir at the best of times and because it was winter there were few other foreigners to compete for attention. As a result we experienced friendship and hospitality wherever we went.

Through Farah we got to know a network of entertainers who lived in Ikiçeşmelik, the less distinguished section of town. We discovered, too, that although the 'belly dancer' has come to symbolise Turkish culture for many, those women who earned their living this way were often regarded as being of easy virtue. As we got to know all of them better, various women would visit us at the hotel, much to the surprise of the English-speaking Turks there, who would stare at us with incomprehension when we rejected their offers of dinner in favour of friendship with women they saw as 'cheap'. But such prejudice had its roots in class snobbery and when we were hassled in the street as we made our way to Farah's one day, Ramazan materialised from out of an alleyway and whisked us away to a café to be protected as 'ladies'.

I began writing down Turkish words phonetically. It never occurred to me to buy a dictionary and when I wanted a translation it was easy to check with someone at the hotel. One of the first words we learned was *seviçi*. Farah had guessed our relationship and we soon realised this translated as 'lesbian'. She loved to share gossip and scandal and would tell us, nudge-nudge, that this one or that one was *seviçi*, having us constantly in stitches. One afternoon a man took us to the Kultürpark to hear some music. Each table was equipped with its own Samovar, and we drank glasses of tea, listening appreciatively to the impressive line-up of folk-artists on offer. After a while a tall, well built woman emerged to play the *darbuka*. She was one of the 'ones', according to Farah, and Stevie kicked me under the table.

Then another group from England joined the show at the hotel. Lead singer with the Rag Dolls was Hazel, an American, the others being Pam and Elise from Jamaica, and an Indian named Lonnie who sometimes sang on back-up tracks with Americans-in-England like Doris Troy and Madeleine Bell. Lonnie, who was pretty and slight, created a stir when he apologised for their strained vocal quality. 'We've been sick,' he explained, and the audience tittered, *sik* being the Turkish for penis.

Wherever we went, people insisted on sharing with us sexual

gossip. One man even took us to look at the state-run brothel, where men urinated in troughs outside and masturbated openly in preparation, and the women, guarded by armed police behind barred gates, shouted abuse at us when they saw our faces. The potential for sexual adventure there seemed enormous, as Lonnie, more than anyone discovered. He was constantly pursued by men, something he found disconcerting, for although he enjoyed the attention he was not particularly interested in sex.

When the Efes engagement was over, Stevie got a spot at an Istanbul club called Goldfinger. No less than fourteen acts shared the bill. We practised our Turkish on one of the singers and realised from the look of slight disdain on her face that we had acquired decidedly 'provincial' accents. At Goldfinger, an afterhours spot for other entertainers, Stevie was the only foreign artist, sharing the bill with jugglers, clowns and singers who wore ancient costumes and made up their faces in fearsome style. Standout attraction for me was Nil Demirhan, a singer of great depth and charisma whose voice went inside me, like listening to someone sing gospel.

The job came to an end when Stevie ran into work-permit problems, but the traumas caused by this were nothing compared to the situation in which we found ourselves one afternoon. We were staying in an old hotel that caters for artists near Taxim, the smartest part of the city. The Rag Dolls were there, too, and the Manhattan Brothers who came to England from Azania (South Africa) with *King Kong*. Employment was haphazard for everyone, and we took it in turn to cook for each other. We'd dress up our little room with bunches of flowers, and do interesting things with lamb chops and yoghurt. Friendship in adversity was the keynote, with Hazel the only one to strike a sour one, often at loggerheads with the other Rag Dolls.

We went out for Sunday lunch by the sea and walked back into a scene of turmoil. The American Sixth Fleet was about to dock as part of a NATO exercise, and the Left was demonstrating against this. The nationalists were out in force, too, and the two factions clashed around Taxim Square. All around us people were rushing by, several with blood pouring from headwounds, stick-waving demonstrators in pursuit. Then we heard shots from the direction of the square. We were frightened that we might be taken for Americans and attacked, and finding ourselves outside one of the embassies we waved our passports desperately in the air. We were waved away. Then, as the crowd swung towards us, we ran for our lives and threw ourselves under a bush.

For the first time in my life I knew the meaning of the phrase 'bite the dust'. Others threw themselves on top of us, knocking all the breath from our bodies. We stayed down for a while, then crawled to our feet, and I wiped the grit from my face. In the background was the constant wail of sirens and we could see ambulances ferrying the injured to hospital as more bruised and bloodied demonstrators continued to run down the street. Eventually we managed to make our way back to the hotel. We found Hazel in a terrible state, with Pam doing her best to comfort her. She had rowed with Lonnie and Elise some hours earlier and they had stormed off into the street. Now they were missing. Hazel was in tears, promising she'd never get angry again if they returned safe and sound. For an hour or more we paced anxiously, too, our own cuts and bruises forgotten. Then the two missing Rag Dolls strolled in.

'Hello,' said Lonnie casually. 'What on earth's going on?' To his astonishment, Hazel embraced first him, then Elise. It turned out they had spent the afternoon in the cinema, missing the demonstration completely. Ambulances and sirens continued into the night, and the following day we read in the paper that at least six people had been killed.

Jazz People, my book of interview, had been completed around the time I went to Morocco, but I could find no one to publish it. Before leaving for Turkey, I gave Margaret Busby the manuscript, hoping she might have an idea. I phoned her as soon as I got back and she said Allison & Busby would like to do it, providing I lengthened the text.

I had already come to the conclusion that there would never be time to work with Randy Weston on his autobiography, so I used the material we had taped to write a chapter on his Moroccan experience. I had another interview I particularly liked, too, done in New York with the gregarious Billy Higgins, the drummerman-for-all-seasons I always sought out for his impeccable playing. And then there was a talk with flamboyant singer Babs Gonzales, one of the 'characters' of bebop. Babs, a hustler from the tip of his slicked-forward hair to the Dutch clogs he occasionally wore — 'some of these drummers over here are so bad I reckon they got to hear me any time I stomp my foot' — knew how to flatter white people who liked to think they were hip. He'd address me as 'Lady' (after Lester Young) or 'dude' and hold out his palm to be slapped when emphasising a point, a cultural mannerism most Blacks made a point of keeping for themselves. But Babs was far cuter than he sometimes seemed and he surprised those who viewed him as an illiterate buffoon by writing his autobiography, *I Paid my Dues*, typing it and publishing it himself. There he listed me among his 'expubident' people (his own word meaning original, down-to-earth), all part of the game. From Babs, though, I learned how street-people survive.

I did a new interview, too, with the articulate Eddie 'Lockjaw' Davis, who earned his nickname from his rock-solid saxophone embouchure. Jaws, whose laidback, declamatory solo on Count Basie's 'Whirlybird' is one of my favourite pieces of waking-up music, was another indispensable teacher. A native New Yorker who did not suffer fools gladly, he was a complex individual who could act tough like a Chester Himes character, but was hospitable and generous with information if he liked you. On several occasions I went out on the road with him, an invaluable exercise in observing professionalism at close quarters.

In May 1970 *Jazz People* appeared. I took the title from Baraka's epochal *Blues People* and hoped that, although it was gentle in tone, I had provided a sociological context at least for the characters in my drama.

Words cannot describe how it feels to hold your first book in your hand. It was laid out just as I'd wanted, a full-page portrait preceding each chapter. The reviews were positive but almost without exception I was taken to task for selecting Blacks only as interview subjects. The fact that this was done routinely elsewhere, that the music's history dictated no other approach, went unnoticed. My crime lay in pointing out why I felt such selectivity was important. That was enough for the bigots. There was, predictably, more of the 'what's a white girl doing here?' the sexual angle undoubtedly contributing to the sneer I detected in certain reviews. It seems safe to surmise that the critics in question might have expressed greater objectivity faced with a man who reasoned along similar lines. Readers, though, like the book, and I took the attacks as par for the course. Heady, halcyon days, when that was my only worry.

Stevie was becoming increasingly interested to meet her Ghanaian family. Her father had gone to Ghana during Nkrumah's regime, moving on to Nigeria after the coup that deposed him in 1966. Her brother and sister showed little interest in their African connection, but as I was anxious to get back to West Africa, too, we found a place on one of the student charters that summer. I still worked for *Drum*, which gave me some contacts in Accra, and we knew two Ghanaians from Bush House who worked there in broadcasting and film. Margaret Busby and some other friends were going to be there as well, and all of us arranged to meet up. I'd also managed to secure some industrial photography work to help pay for the trip.

Stevie's great-grandmother, a Ga, had several notable sons. Mr Mensah was one of these, a former High Commissioner in Canada, and the one family member she knew how to contact. He was the half-brother of her grandfather, the first jazz pianist to come to Britain from the Gold Coast, as Ghana was known at that time. Another son was Mr Ayitey and it was with his daughter Rose that Mensah arranged for us to stay.

As soon as she made contact with her family, Stevie was told her Ga name. Her father was Nii-Amah, and, as his first daughter, she was Naa-Dedei. She liked her name, it had a gentle sound to it, and her day-name was Afua, Friday being the day of her birth. She and Mr Ayitey liked each other at once and she called him her grandfather. He was a tall, thin man with a bald head, and as they got to know each other she would amuse him and his family by kissing him on top of his head. Word soon spread that a respected daughter had come home and wherever she went people would stop in the street and greet her, 'Naa-Dedie!', explaining their relationship with a bewildering degree of detail.

Rose lived in a modern house in Larter Biokoshie, a suburb of Accra not far from Mamprobi, where her sister ran a tailoring business in their father's house. Jimmie, Rose's husband, was a medical lecturer who was away teaching during the week, and Rose spent her spare time in the garden. 'Jimmie has come back!' she announced one day with great excitement. 'He's brought a grasscutter and I've put it in the fridge.' We were confused by this but forgot what she had said when Jimmie appeared and we sat down to eat. Stevie took the dishes into the kitchen, later. There was a scream and the crash of plates breaking. There indeed in the fridge was the grasscutter. It was large rodent not unlike a hare without ears, highly regarded as a delicacy, and a species of which we were ignorant.

198   Although we had gone to Ghana on our respective journeys of

discovery, as dyed-in-the-wool freelances, we wanted to work as well. Mike Eghan, an old friend from Bush House, was now with the Ghana Broadcasting Corporation. With seven shows weekly, he was the country's leading disc-jockey and he arranged for us both to be on the radio. Mike was a great jazz enthusiast, perturbed at the way Soul music had started to dominate the listening of young Ghanaians. He hosted a weekly programme, *Jazz in Perspective*, in which he discussed the contributions of the Afro-American greats with another veteran broadcaster, George Williams. George came from Sierra Leone and the fact that, like many people on the West Coast, he had a European name frequently puzzled Afro-Americans with a mind set on the 'purity' of the African heritage. I sat in on a couple of shows, giving *Jazz People* a plug in the process. It was challenging to be limited by the choice of records available. Jazz enthusiasts were few and far between, and those who had American albums were reluctant to lend them for airplay. We had to make do with a few 78s from the station's library and albums from Mike's personal collection. But it was fun.

To our dismay, most of the musicians we encountered, even the radio band, had a minimal grasp of what jazz was about. What's more, despite Mike's educational campaign and proselytising, 90 per cent of his requests asked for James Brown, 'Soul Brother Number One', as he was now universally known. Saxophonist Jerry Hansen was an exception. A strong, solid player, who fronted the leading dance band, the Ramblers, he preferred the well-tailored big band sound 'because it entails workmanship'. At the Star Hotel he invited Stevie to sit in with the band. She was nervous, already realising that Western drummers had a different concept to Africans, but she was eager to be part of the music, too. When the boisterous audience became unusually silent, she was worried, wondering whether she had insulted any tradition that discouraged women from playing the drums. Then the applause started. People ran forward to place money on her head. One woman, grinning beatifically, showered her with coins, shouting: 'Play, sister, play!' Right then, she said, she knew she was home.

In common with most Ghanaian musicians, Hansen had a day-job. He ran an optical repair business in Adabraka and hired out the band bus for day-trips. A personable, sophisticated man, he invited us to go on the road one night and we squeezed into the Mercedes-Benz bus with fifteen musicians and the substantial PA. We sped along the country's eighteen miles of highway, then settled down to a steady pace on the smaller roads through the bush. On the way we were stopped by a police roadblock looking for unlicensed drivers, occasioning an exasperated cry from the bandleader, 'Hey, constable! Can't you see we're the Fabulous Ramblers?'

After two hours' drive we came to Ada, a small town in the east near the border with Togo. As soon as we arrived, the bus was surrounded by an enthusiastic crowd. As Stevie remarked, there was no problem about finding the gig in this town, the gig found the musicians. The dance was held in the courtyard of a private house, desks from the local school being appropriated for use as tables, with fairylights and bunting strung from the trees. Expensive perfume hung on the air as well-dressed women wafted by, and bonded whisky and gin were on sale at a third normal prices. The townspeople, it transpired, earned a healthy revenue from cross-border smuggling. The Ramblers stuck mainly to highlife, with soloists like trumpeter Prince Boateng, who also played in the National Symphony Orchestra, outstanding. But what the crowd really wanted was Soul Brother Number One and eventually Hansen played some James Brown numbers.

It was the same wherever we went. With radio receivers at every street corner, Mike's and other request programmes fulfilled the insistent demand for 'more popcorn music', and the voices of local James Brown imitators were to be heard over loudspeakers perched on top of patrolling cars, extolling the virtues of patent medicines. The opposition party, the National Alliance of Liberals, adapted his most famous song as a slogan, printed T-shirts proclaiming, 'Say it Loud — I'm NAL and Proud!' Even when we travelled 450 miles inland, 'There Was a Time' was pumping out of the village radio set as we arrived. Jerry was unhappy at what he saw as a decline in popular standards. 'I'm purely for the sound side,' he said. 'The shouting of James Brown is a little too much for my taste.' The experience with the Ramblers was an eye-opener, especially given those Africans we knew in London who clung to their Blue Note albums with the dedication of jazz enthusiasts everywhere. One journalist we met was highly amused that we had travelled 4,000 miles to go on the road with a *dance band*. 'Here bands travel all the time and no one ever thinks of it,' he said. 'Sometimes they crash and get killed, sometimes they marry on the way, sometimes they abscond with the money. It's nothing new.'

There was nothing new about his attitude, either. Musicians in Ghana, an important integral element in traditional society, continued to have a functional role to play. Yet those who tried to make a living out of the music in contemporary urban society at this point tended to be dismissed by the élite and maligned as drifters and hustlers. It was an uphill struggle for people like Mike, seeking to acquaint his listeners with the innovations of artists in the African Diaspora.

Mensah came to see us one day to tell Stevie about the regular family meeting. This was held every month, presided over by the head of the family, at which land disputes and other such matters were discussed. At the next meeting, Mensah explained, she would be presented to all her relatives. It was an impressive occasion, with many a speech, and each person present making certain that she would be made to feel welcome. She was deeply moved by the reception she was given.

I flew up to Kumasi one morning to photograph a dam being constructed by British engineers. It was a gruelling day, during which I got soaked in rain and covered in dust and mud. It coincided with a major ceremony, too, the installation of the Asantehene, the ruler of the Ashantis. Travellers had come from far afield for this momentous occasion, and all the return flights to Accra were hopelessly overbooked until the following evening. The site engineer, an Englishman, arranged for me to stay in Kumasi and as we drove towards the main hotel, I realised I was a little short on local currency. Was there a cheaper hotel, I wondered? 'Not that *I'd* stay in,' said our man from Epsom, pointedly, before I realised the firm would pick up the tab. Nevertheless it was disquieting to arrive in the hotel's plush lobby, carrying only camera-bag and tripod, covered from head to foot in red mud.

He and his wife were to come by later to take me out for a meal. I survived censure and ridicule by banging the dust from my trousers on the balcony railing outside the window. Then, remembering a trick I'd learnt from one of the oldtime bluesmen, I hung them up in the bathroom and ran the hot shower, filling the room with steam. I completed the job by 'ironing' them under the mattress while I caught forty winks. My T-shirt I wore inside out, hiding the worst of the brickred stains.

Mr and Mrs Epsom turned out to be like the Taylor Woodrow couple in Freetown. They were hospitable enough, lending me their chauffeur the following day for a bit of sightseeing, but when I lunched, English-style, at their house, I had to endure Mrs E's complaints about the inability of local cooks to do anything useful with vegetables. I poked at my stringy meat and two veg and thought of succulent crab and garden-egg stew cooked on a charcoal stove in the garden at Rose's. I thought of little parcels of *kenkey*, fermented corn dough, delicately steamed in banana leaves, of juicy grasscutter and groundnut soup, and sighed at the predicament of those expatriates in Africa who were unable and unwilling to enjoy what was on their doorstep for the asking.

Stevie and I took the bus to Ho in the Volta Region where an old friend, Dr Seth Cudjoe, was the officer of health. Seth, a medical practitioner who decided to read psychiatry when he was in his sixties, was a man who bubbled over with crosscultural references and information. He talked of the similarities between some Afro-American religious experiences and the spiritual root from which they descended, and explained the physical processes that occur in spirit possession. As a musicologist, he had written several key papers on the music and arts of the country, and when on my return I did a rather pompous article about the disturbing preponderance of soul music in Ghana he wrote to me agreeing with what I had said. He like Jerry Hansen was perturbed, he said, in his case at the extent to which Western music preoccupied the youth. To him this could only prevent the development of a valid alternative based on African tradition.

We decided to go to the north, travelling by bus, and taking Kwamla, a cousin, along for the ride. We stayed overnight in government rest-houses in the regional capitals, Kumasi, Tamale and Bolgatanga, eventually reaching a small town called Navrongo, a few miles from the border with Upper Volta (now Burkina Faso). There we were surprised to see completely naked farmers tilling the soil. On our way to the market we found ourselves following one woman, naked except for a grass string tied around her waist. Woven bag in hand, she, too, was shopping. A man in Western dress parked his shining white car and came down the path towards her, neither giving the other a second glance as they passed.

In Bolgatanga a group of men invited us for a drink. At a place called the Bull we sat with a local chief and a couple of 'unattached' women, all of them Moslems. The chief, who was drinking heavily, had one half-closed eye. At one point in the proceedings he leaned across the table and started telling one of the women that he knew her mother. It was obvious in what sense he used the word 'knew', and to my astonishment she turned to us and gave us a wink, muttering under her breath, 'Any more out of you and I'll close the other one for you!' It was far from the usual picture created by Westerners of submissive Moslem women. Back at the rest-house we sat outside for a while, listening to the sounds of the night. The air was thick with the singing of crickets and frogs, a rich, throbbing sound that refused to let up until morning. Then, from a distance, drums began playing. After a while, another village seemed to be answering. How strange, we thought, just like something out of a book or a film. The difference was, this was real. It was moving and quite unrepeatable, uniting us with the earth and with history in a way that could not be explained in words.

Travelling on the buses, we stuck to bread and bananas for sustenance, with the occasional guinea-fowl egg if we found them. As soon as we settled in a town, though, we moved on to the local cuisine. In the Upper Region, the prevalent oil is shea butter, a paste made from the fruit of the wild shea tree which serves for cooking and cosmetic purposes alike. Its rather rancid smell hung on the air, something which neither of us particularly liked. Nevertheless, when we spotted a group of women stirring large steaming vats of stew, we plucked up courage and placed our order. We were shown into a tiny room through a hole in the wall, and sat down at a bench surrounded by curious onlookers. To my everlasting shame, and the spectators' amusement, I washed my hands in the drinking-water and drank from the dish supplied for washing.

We had asked Kwamla to come on the trip because we felt he could interpret and ensure that our questions were answered. Most Africans speak at least three languages, but he was a long way from home as well, often out of his depth. On occasion then, we preferred to move on our own. Back in Tamale, we went out to explore, leaving Kwamla headed for the abattoir, where vultures hovered overhead and meat was sold in African stew-packs: bundles of roughly butchered flesh, bone, skin and stomach, spread on banana leaves. He lit a fire in the courtyard and by the time we came back had cooked up a coastal style stew flavoured with tomatoes, onions and pepper. We fell on it ravenously.

While we were away, Kwamla had made new acquaintances. He introduced us to two Black Americans in Nigerian dress who had adopted Yoruba names. In California they had worked three jobs for a period to pay for this trip and it was obvious from their attitudes that they had not worked their fingers to the bone to come to Africa and sit down with no whitefolks. I took the rejection in my stride – I was a guest in the culture, after all – until one of them started to yell for the waiter. In his raised voice – 'Steward!' – I heard the cry of Empire and flinched. But it was when they sent him to the fridge for the good old American standby, tuna-fish sandwiches, that both Stevie and I found it hard to suppress a smile. 'Can't deal with this local food,' they told us, shamelessly, in front of Kwamla. 'You never know what you're eating.'

The following day I decided that I could not face another evening with the Americans protected by nothing stronger than beer. Back at the room I had a small bottle of *akpeteshie*, gin distilled from maize, the Ghanaian equivalent of American moonshine. It could be a lethal brew for the unaccustomed but I developed a taste for it soon after we arrived. The *akpeteshie* was in a bottle labelled Paramount Gin, the legitimate local tipple, and I returned with it to the table. After a hefty swig, I handed the bottle to one of the Americans. She carefully examined the label. 'Oh, Paramount Gin,' she said, 'I believe I'll pass on that.' Her companion was not so reluctant. With the air of someone determined to get something for nothing, he knocked back a substantial slug. He was ill-prepared for the impact and his eyes bulged as he struggled to retain his equilibrium. You could almost see the rough liquor coursing through his body. 'Hmm,' he finally managed, and I saw comprehension dawn in his eyes. I had not really planned this upset but it worked. When next we met, in Accra, he was actually friendly and greeted me with respect.

To be with Stevie on her journey of self-discovery was an enormous privilege for me. Although she was aware of her Ghanaian family's existence, she said they had been little more than names on a piece of paper until she stood at the airport, jostling suitcases with other Ghanaians returning home. Randy Weston had called the rediscovery of roots a spiritual process, now as she stood under the mango trees in Mamprobi, wearing a *batakari* brought from the North, her skin darkened by the heat and the sun, it seemed to me that she was becoming, by the minute, more visibly an African woman. The way people responded to her drumming, too, urging her on and loving her as she played, was an enormous boost to her confidence. It was a vindication of her dedication to music after the routine way she'd been under-valued in night clubs by punters only out for a thrill.

Just to sit down and drink *pito* (millet beer) from a calabash meant something different to her than to me, I realised. It was just like the music. But even in Africa with its centuries of history, I was surprised to encounter a degree of deference and desire for white patronage. Thus on several occasions, when she sought explanations for cultural phenomena, it was to me, the European, that the answer might be directed. This happened most poignantly during the Hɔmɔwɔ, the Ga's harvest festival, and their most important annual event.

The day began with a large meal of *kpepele*, the traditional festival food made from maize, with Mr Ayitey. Then Kwamla and his brother Roger took us to meet Tawia Adamafio, an important figure in Ghanaian politics who had worked closely with Nkrumah. He was a relative who had not seen Stevie since he visited her home when he was a child and was delighted that she was returning the compliment by visiting him. He said that she could not go back to England without meeting the wulɔmɔ, the 'high-priest' or spiritual leader of the family clan. He insisted that the brothers take us to his house in the heart of Jamestown, the Ga quarter of Accra.

The wulɔmɔ, a servant of the gods, who advises Ga people in times of trouble, sat on a raised platform at the end of a row of male elders, dressed completely in white. At first I was reluctant to enter, reasoning that this was a purely African affair, but Roger and Kwamla insisted and a space was made for the four of us to sit. The wɔlɔmɔ stayed aloof and silent, as coconut-shells were filled with *akpeteshie* and handed to each of us 'Do we drink it in one?' I asked Roger hastily. He nodded and we did; then, to my horror, the vessels were swiftly refilled. By now I was feeling considerably groggy. The next thing I knew, Stevie was up on her feet, pumping the *wulɔmɔ* hand, both of them laughing and talking in English. A few of the elders looked on askance, but the *wulɔmɔ* offered a speech of welcome to her as a long-lost daughter. The events of the rest of the evening remain hazy, but I remember missing my footing and slipping into an open drain in the dark on leaving the house. With shoes soaked in sewage it was an unedifying end to the day, but equally unedifying was the response that Stevie received from her cousins when she sought an explanation of the cultural significance of what had occurred. Kwamla giggled, unable to provide any answer, but Roger, sitting beside me on the bus, gave me the information that Stevie wanted to hear. She was greatly upset by this. It was all so unfair, she said, as we made our way drunkenly through the maize fields to Rose's house. I had to agree. For her, it was a day of enormous significance. For the first time in her life, she said, she felt like an African.

Towards the end of our stay, we heard that Guy Warren of Ghana was playing a concert. Warren, later known as Kofi Ghanaba, was a legendary figure, a drummer who lived in London for a period during the 1950s before going on to America. Now he was back home and reputed to be living as a recluse. That he was playing in public was quite an occasion. The concert was sparsely attended, but it took the unexpected form of a duet with the British rock drummer Ginger Baker. Baker, whom I knew slightly, had recently broken up with the leading band, Cream. He had always been highly regarded by African drummers, and along with the legendary Phil Seamen, his teacher, was acknowledged by Africans as one of the few English drummers to grasp African rhythms. He had left England to escape from drugs and the pressures of the music business, attempting to drive across the Sahara alone in his Jensen, an epic and somewhat foolhardy journey which was later the subject of a television documentary. Now he was recuperating at Warren's retreat, but looked exhausted. He gave a creditable performance under the circumstances, but when he saw us, all he could think of was being pursued by the press. 'Oh, God,' he said with a sigh of despair, 'what are *you* doing here?'

Like Baker, Stevie had several invaluable opportunities to learn more about her instrument from African drummers. Whenever we went into Accra we would travel by *tro-tro*, lorries on which the fare was threepence (*tro*) or sixpence, depending on distance. At the point where the *tro* stopped in Ga Mashie Street we often came across a group of Ga men with a couple of drums. On several occasions she joined them, to the delight of the crowd. At no time was there any suggestion that a woman had no right to be playing the drums, the criticism she feared since those days at The Coleherne. And when she met Robert Ayitee, Director of Dancing and Drumming at the Arts Council, he sent a master drummer to Apeguso in the Volta Region, where he arranged for Ewe craftsmen to carve a pair of fine instruments for her. Approbation comes no higher.

We returned home with these two magnificent specimens, filled with trepidation at what the Customs might demand for their import. The only saving grace might be that the drums were only shells because Stevie preferred to fit them with Western heads, more convenient for tuning in a colder climate. In their present state, we reasoned, they could not be classified as musical instruments. We need not have bothered. Our charter flight passengers had packed the plane with parcels and suitcases bulging with food. At the airport, several cases split open, and the luggage conveyor was awash with dried fish and bunches of palm-nuts. It was a sorry sight for those people whose mothers had sent them back to their studies with a reminder of home, but turned out favourably for us. The Customs officials took one look at the mess and turned their backs on the entire proceedings, waving us through with disdain. It was just as well, for we arrived home exhausted but happy, with hardly a penny between us.

Part Five
Behind the Sun

I'm going down in Louisiana
     Baby, behind the sun

Muddy Waters

16
Feel Like Going Home

It was one o'clock in the morning and guitarist Larry Johnson and I were waiting for the 'A' train in the middle of Harlem. An elderly man, ragged and drunk, was falling about the platform, shouting, whooping, and generally carrying on. Other travellers, worn by the day, averted their eyes. They acted as though there was nothing to see. Larry's angle was different.

'Don't look at him,' he commanded, 'listen to what he's singing. Most people would say he was drunk or crazy, but listen to that *sound*! What he's doing goes back to slavery days, the whoops and the hollers and everything. That man is living history.'

The old man was living history, all right. In his throaty hollers and cries I heard echoes of field-recordings cut in the 1930s — Southern chain-gangs, driving steel, chopping logs. But that Larry, a 'country' bluesman from Georgia, was pointing this out was crucial to my wider understanding of why Afro-American music is about much more than art or earning a living.

When the Art Ensemble of Chicago dubbed what they played Great Black Music, they meant it was rooted in the collective memory, taking in African drumchoirs and church on a Sunday. Recognising this continuum meant the music could be seen as a nourishment, a statement of impregnability. It helped, too, in rescuing it from the sidelines of 'entertainment' or 'cultural phenomen' where it had been relegated by racist comment and scholarship. Remaking the past to make the future was the new task in Afro-America. Archie Shepp had articulated the significance of this for me, but now Larry was underlining Archie's intellectual analysis with a point of view that came from the streets.

'People like him are one of the reasons I can't stay away from Harlem,' he continued, his eyes still on the old man. 'That's where I get my inspiration — from my own people. Not from some secondhand white man making a million out of our music.'

For some time I had realised that the various aspects of the music — the sacred and secular, the blues, jazz, and now what was taking place in the avant garde — were linked in ways other than the obvious chronological one. The split between the purists and moderns seemed ridiculous when I got to know the world the musicians came from. People who had grown up together might go separate ways, one staying home to play backbeat for dancers, another making a name in the international arena. Back home, though, they both ate from the same cookpot. The first time I heard trombonist Dicky Wells he was playing a phrase from one of the earliest blues records in my collection. Even talking to Sonny Criss all that time ago in Paris I was made aware of the importance of seeing jazz and blues as part of the changing same. No matter how the upwardly-mobile of previous decades had disparaged the blues as 'that slavery shit' (Miles Davis's words) or radicals rejected the spirituals, both lay at the heart of everything, backbeat and bebop alike.

But racial issues were becoming increasingly polarised and the significance of a music that built on itself in this way was something many white writers were reluctant to consider during this period. Younger Afro-Americans frequently rejected the word 'jazz' because of the way it had been used historically to downgrade the music. 'Black music' was the preferred term, though some established critics flinched from using it, deciding that to acknowledge the source of the music made it exclusive. Given the prevailing social climate, to call something 'Black' could damage the mainstream credibility of the eager young white commentator, in fact. There were exceptions. Archie Shepp directed me to a pivotal work by a white writer, *Black Talk*, which influenced my way of listening. Its author, Ben Sidran, himself a musician, set out the case for the Afro-American oral tradition as an alternative to Western literary values. It was an idea that was being continually espoused.

As I started to travel to America frequently during the 1970s, I carried Elaine Caulker's worldview with me. And an awareness of the continuum as well, instilled in me by artists such as Larry Johnson, Randy Weston and Archie Shepp, all making their own discoveries and locating themselves in history. Wherever I journeyed I met instrumentalists and singers who had structured the music, the legendary as well as the little-known. From Eddie Durham, the first electric guitarist, to the Rev. Claude Jeter, mellifluous lead-singer with the Swan Silvertones gospel group, my work provided an entrée into closed, secret worlds. In Memphis I stood in the studio, smoke-stained and funky, where Al Green, Jeter's spiritual descendant, cut some of the most sensuous Soul tracks of the 1960s and 1970s; in New York I met Otis Blackwell and Doc Pomus who wrote the pop songs of my youth (Blackwell was the writer whose demo-discs Elvis Presley had copied). In Hollywood I spent the night at guitarist Steve Cropper's house, learning how he'd worked with Otis Redding to make the sweetest Soul music this side of heaven. And in all of them, Black and white alike, I found an awareness of tradition and their debt to the past. No matter how far fame might have taken the individual, each one acknowledged they were standing on the shoulders of giants. Non-musicians helped me to come to grips with the continuum as well, among them Southern women who had stood up against the full force of American might to assert their right to vote. It was a never-ending voyage of awakening on which I was befriended by preachers and poets, revolutionaries and renegades.

I woke up one morning and decided I wanted to do all the things that any young jazz-lover dreamed of: to go down to the South and look for the blues, to visit the churches I'd seen but never dared enter, make the pilgrimage to New Orleans and 'Second Line' with the marching bands. I could not wait until I was able to do it in style, and Stevie agreed I should follow my instincts and go.

Marion Brown, who was teaching in New Haven, Connecticut, said I could visit his uncle, the fire-and-brimstone preacher in Atlanta, and stay there with one of his friends. I had a standing invitation to visit Como, Mississippi, as well, and renew my acquaintance with guitarist Fred McDowell, a perennial favourite with the British blues community. Kunle was back in New York, where he had opened an arts and crafts shop in the Village; he had put on an Eric Dolphy show there and exhibited some of my pictures. I knew Jane Welch, too, who worked in the New York office of *Downbeat* and occasionally wrote about some of the younger musicians. She kept me fully informed.

Almost as an afterthought I wrote to Paul 'Polo' Barnes, a New Orleans clarinettist with whom I had exchanged a series of letters in my teens. Polo, who had abruptly ended our correspondence when I attained the grand old age of 16 – I was a young lady now, no longer his 'flower girl', so it wouldn't be right – had once worked with King Oliver and Jelly Roll Morton. To my delight, the events of the intervening years had alleviated his fears about the potential danger in such unsafe interracial correspondence. He invited me to stay with him and his wife. I bought an airline ticket and a Greyhound bus pass and took off via New York for the Crescent City and the great unknown.

To learn more about the music by going to the roots was important to me, but I had another reason for making the trip. When I first started out taking pictures, another photographer surprised me by saying he was bored with musicians: 'There's only five angles you can get on a trumpeter.' As a novice I was surprised by his blasé attitude; I couldn't imagine anything more fascinating than a lifetime of shooting the artists in action. As time went on I realised how right he had been.

Few photographers, it seemed to me, told you more about the musicians than who they were when they were playing. Dennis Stock, who worked for Magnum, was one of the exceptions; his *Jazz Street*, with its intimate portraits of Louis Armstrong in particular, at home and backstage, was my primer. My other hero was Herb Snitzer, whose work was to be seen everywhere when I first began reading the American magazines but had now disappeared from view. Both of them gave the musicians a context, shot them with feeling. I wanted to photograph their lives. I knew musicians and I knew there was more to all of them than playing the horn. I remember a conversation with Lockjaw Davis that increased my awareness of the need to depict the life away from the public arena. Musicians had families, interests, concerns, and I wanted to show who they *were* rather than what they did.

White musicians got stereotyped as well, but it was clear that the perpetuation of stereotypes that characterises jazz photography was a racist procedure. To hang on to the visual cliché meant to be involved in reproducing images of musicians in terms only of what they *could do for us*, rather than what they were doing for themselves. I decided I did not want to be part of the process which began with eye-rolling images of minstrelcy and would reach another nadir in the way the dread-locked artists of reggae would be *consumed* in the music press. I determined to find individuals who would let me follow them through their daily routine, photograph them at home and with their loved ones.

New York in 1971 felt very different from before. Whatever I had absorbed of political views on my previous visits, these had really been far too short to recognise the real depth of Black discontent and determination to fight racism. By now, attitudes of resistance were deeply entrenched throughout the community, reaching musicians from earlier eras as well as the new wave of free-wheeling radicals. 'You don't have to make me mad at you,' said Larry Johnson. 'I've been mad at you since I was born.' Everywhere Malcolm X's ideas were emphasised, his picture on the walls of the homes I visited. Some musicians, it was said, had joined the Black Panthers, others the Nation of Islam. Many had adopted African or Islamic names, some like Kunle (George Conley) finding a substitute similar to their 'slave-name'. African clothing and jewellery were commonplace, and stores in the Village such as Kunle's Liberty House, as well as those in Black neighbourhoods, imported garments and art works from Africa. Along with the *dansiki* and carvings of Shango, Yoruba god of thunder, once-disparaged traditions had begun to re-emerge and reclaim places of honour. Braided hair and the headtie, the *gele*, symbol of status among West African women but reduced to an insult in former times ('handkerchief head' meant accommodationist), were revived by Black women to wear as objects of pride.

Drums were everywhere, played in the streets, in the parks, carried as cultural statements, and other non-Western instruments were in evidence in many bands. One musician even disassembled various woodwind in order to rebuild them in a new, Black-defined form. The recognition of Black English as a nation language became important, and people who had previously reserved one form of English talking to whites now used Afro-American expressions and idioms in situations where before they would have been taboo.

I was looking forward to seeing Jane Welch again, but found her caught up in the paranoia that surrounded some of the younger musicians, unable to work and convinced that their music could change the world if only they had the exposure. She was hanging on to her *Downbeat* job, dismayed by the publication's reactionary policy. She did put me in touch with several people she felt could use some publicity, but she suggested that I might find it easier to deal with the older musicians, avoiding the righteous hostility I was bound to encounter among the new radicals, many of whom were now separatists. I'd known the editor since my first visit to New York and considered him a friend, but Jane warned me that this would mean nothing. Attitudes in Chicago where the magazine was published were hardening as musicians became more politicised, she said, and I should look elsewhere for a market for my more radical interviews.

I stayed with Kunle and met several AACM musicians who had moved to New York. People such as violinist Leroy Jenkins who played with the Revolutionary Ensemble were open and friendly, and I renewed my acquaintance with Anthony Braxton, who was earning a living playing chess rather than music. But it was obvious from the response I encountered elsewhere that the anger of centuries was coming to the surface. No longer was it possible for most Blacks and Whites to talk freely together – if indeed they ever had done. Now every exchange had obvious political overtones.

In Atlanta, Marion's friend Clarence Hubbard met me at the bus station. As we looked for a taxi outside, a serious young *Muhammad Speaks* newspaper-seller moved quietly between us. His head was shaven and he wore a neat suit and bow tie, his eyes betraying not a flicker at seeing a brother with a white woman. Overlooking my presence entirely, he held out a copy of the paper to Clarence, its bold green masthead proclaiming its contents. Clarence took it automatically, reaching into his pocket for change. 'Peace, brother,' murmured the Muslim. 'Peace,' Clarence echoed. I would see this scenario enacted on countless occasions, outside bus stations, storefront churches and bar-rooms, distinguished always by the quality of patience. The word of Elijah Muhammad, the Honorable Messenger, was to be found in what white people had been led to believe were the most unlikely of homes. Alongside the Bible, underneath wall-hangings depicting the martyred King and the Kennedys, his *Message to the Black Man in America* endeavoured to enlighten people of what was happening to them and why.

Clarence worked in a photographic lab and lived with his mother in the north-west section of town. His bedroom was packed from floor to ceiling with records, and he was obviously glad to have someone to talk to about music. Housing in Atlanta was still quite segregated, and I felt a little uncomfortable when we went out for a drink. The bar was on Auburn Avenue, the main Black thoroughfare, later Martin Luther King Drive. It was, I was curious to note, patronised by several outrageous transvestites. When we left, they followed us out, and I was equally surprised to see several white men cruising in cars, looking for sex. What kind of sex was unclear, but they provoked adverse comments from passers-by. The anger I had heard expressed at the way the community was used and plundered by Whites was suddenly real.

Marion had gone back to Atlanta, inspired by memories of itinerant musicians peddling their wares in dirt roads, in sections with such evocative names as Buttermilk Bottom. All that was disappearing now, as the city became one of the burgeoning commercial centres of the New South. In Underground Atlanta, the tourist section, Clarence took me to hear Piano Red, the original Doctor Feelgood, after whom Aretha Franklin named one of her songs. Willie Perryman, to give him his proper name, was the brother of Speckled Red, who had taught me the ribald 'Dirty Dozens' in London. He played for tourists on a stylised honky-tonk piano, a far cry from the authentic troubadours of Marion's childhood recollections. There was the Paul Mitchell trio, too, contemporaries of Marion and Clarence, with the superb Allen Murphy on drums. Their polished act for a dinner-crowd who ate fondue was more representative of Atlanta today.

I don't know what I expected, but Marion's uncle was not the hellfire-and-damnation thunderer I had anticipated. The Reverend Emory Crolger was a small man, refined and withdrawn behind gold-rimmed spectacles, and clearly ill at ease during our interview. His was a world which excluded outsiders, designed that way for survival. He was polite enough and invited me to his little wooden church on the outskirts of town, but I was disappointed when no instrumentalists materialised to accompany the small congregation. Another preacher took the sermon, asking for children to come forward and witness, but the atmosphere was rather restrained. Whether this was due to my presence I don't know, but when service was over, the Rev. Crolger was kind enough to arrange for one of his colleagues to take me to lunch. Over candied yams, meatloaf and greens, this elderly man flirted mildly with me, rather to my surprise.

New Orleans is generally regarded as the most African of American cities. It's not just the humidity that has you soaked to the skin minutes after taking a shower; there is an African way of walking and talking there that makes the idea of cultural retentions immediately apparent. I did get to a funeral on that first visit, and the people who followed the band, 'Second Lining', strutted and waved their umbrellas aloft just like Ashanti dancers I'd seen in Ghana.

There was another thing, too. Whatever the alternative theories advanced for other, simultaneous, birthplaces of 'jazz', New Orleans remains the most significant city in the early development of the music. I felt as excited as a child as the bus drew into the city. I didn't care that Canal Street was a wide modern thoroughfare or that Bourbon Street was strictly for tourists. I was on my way to meet someone who personified everything I'd dreamed about when I first walked into the Swing Shop.

Polo was just as I'd imagined. A bespectacled, brownskin septuagenarian, he carried himself with old-fashioned dignity and spoke with a soft, Creole inflection. He and Alma, his wife, greeted me as though I were a long-lost daughter, and settled me down right away. Polo insisted I call Alma 'Mother' and himself 'Daddy Paul', fond terms of respect for the elders.

Something about the clarinettist made me think of another era. It had nothing to do with his calendar age, more with the way some things seemed to have stood still in the Crescent City. He had extravagant manners that would not have been out of place in turn-of-the-century New Orleans, and talking to him conjured up those pictures of the pioneers in *Shining Trumpets* and *Jazzmen*, serious in their starched shirt-fronts and derbys. Mother was more of a realist, and once we got to know each other she would wink at me whenever her husband launched into one of his pedantic monologues. She took a somewhat jaundiced view of the expense he incurred in carrying on a correspondence with people all over the world, chiding him gently for devotion to fans he had met in his years as a professional musician.

But Polo was immensely proud of the music – not 'jazz', he told me, that was a white man's word, just 'music' – and I imagine he felt it a duty to answer each letter and request for a picture.

The Barneses lived in a white wooden house on North Dorgenois in one of the Black sections of town, quiet and surrounded by trees and lawns. The rooms led off each other, separated by curtains rather than doors, each boasting a magnificent chifferobe, the heavy piece of furniture familiar throughout the South. Ornate and veneered in cherrywood, their drawers bulged with fresh-laundered linen and the artifacts of a lifetime.

Polo and I sat in the backyard one day to talk. I taped an interview with him while he fingered the small E-flat clarinet he used to play for parades. He differentiated between 'Dixieland' and traditional New Orleans music. To him, the first had become a performer's exercise – 'a real *show*, like *clowns*' – in contrast to the traditional music he played where 'they was more interested in making *you* play, making *you* dance'. 'Dixieland', he added, at no prompting from me, was also a white man's word, adopted to draw attention to the South and obscure the involvement of the actual people who developed and structured the music.

History manifested itself in many ways on this visit. The language of the blues was, of course, foreign to most Europeans, but so strong was the desire to emulate the jazz tradition that people like Ottilie Patterson automatically took the classic lyrics on board without a second thought. 'That mean ol' Frisco' and 'that lowdown Santa Fe' became almost as familiar as British Rail, the thinly veiled metaphor of 'Somebody's diggin' my potatoes/Tramplin' on my vine' an evocative way to describe infidelity. One of the earliest New Orleans numbers that all the Trad bands had in their repertoire was 'Make me a Pallet on your Floor', and one day at the Barneses, Polo, discussing a possible visitor, announced how he'd 'Just make me up a pallet on the floor.' I could not get over the fact that he was saying something I'd been hearing for years, without thinking. Commonplace, yes, but to me, history was talking.

Neither could I get over the fact that I was staying with someone who grew up on the coat-tails of King Oliver and Buddy Bolden. And after years of listening to more contemporary sounds, I was delighted to find I could still enjoy the kind of music that these people had pioneered. Polo would sit at the kitchen table practising the alto saxophone he played on special occasions, and I'd watch him, a professional to his fingertips, still committed to intricate phrasing and clear articulation. Before leaving for work in the evening, he would take his clarinet out of its case, clean it and check all the reeds. From time to time he'd put on the peaked cap with its insignia of interlinked birds he had worn as a member of the Eureka Brass Band. Poor health had made marching in parade bands a thing of the past for him, but he kept his cap on the wall, a reminder of the part he played in one of the city's most celebrated cultural institutions.

At the time, there were moves afoot among some Black radicals to try to stop the parades. Similar protests were taking place in other areas of endeavour, and in New Orleans where marching bands are a way of life for many, the older musicians were accused by some of perpetuating the accommodationist mentality with their 'Uncle Tom' music. The musicians, old and young, did not agree. To people who had grown up with the 'Second Line' it was part of their heritage, and Polo made it clear he was well aware of the historical and cultural importance of what he did, one of the reasons he spent so much time with pen and notepad in hand.

Twice weekly, he took the bus into the French Quarter where he held down a job at Preservation Hall. The hall was a hangover from a period when art gallery owners made their premises available to keep traditional music alive, following the demise of the famous Black dance halls. It features in countless tourist advertisements, but in its contemporary manifestation it was a far cry from the intentions of the music-lovers who had provided the new working environment. For a start it was dirty, with no facilities for musicians or patrons apart from a couple of squalid toilets and a Coca-Cola machine. The musicians sat propped in the steamed-up window, displayed like a bunch of ageing icons for tourists. A handful of chairs along one wall were occupied by some of the musicians' contemporaries, who had followed the music for years, but most of the punters had to sit on the floor. Overcrowding and short sets encouraged a rapid turnover, with equally short breaks for the musicians, many of whom were getting on in years.

Polo introduced me to some of his colleagues, notably the celebrated trombonist Jim Robinson, now pushing 80, who had played in France with the United States Army during World War One and whom I'd once seen in London. There was trumpeter Dédé Pierce, whose wife Billie played with him and the trombonist, in the city's tradition of fine women pianists; Sweet Emma Barrett, one of the first women musicians in jazz to record, and drummer Cié Frazier, Polo's cousin. At first I was so overwhelmed at coming face to face with such 'legends' of jazz, people I'd known of for as long as I could remember, that I failed to reflect on the circumstances under which they were working. But after a couple of visits realism took charge. I looked at the five- and ten-dollar bills piling up at the door and began to ask questions. Records by the featured artists sold well at the Hall, but Polo said royalties were never forthcoming. The musicians got a session-fee for each date, just as a night's work paid union 'scale', the minimum, no matter how many people packed into the room. Occasionally the band got tips for playing requests such as 'The Saints', but it was hot, gruelling and undignified, the 'oldtimey' atmosphere cultivated by the proprietors invidiously rooted in earlier social conditions. The musicians, I learned later, called it 'The Plantation'.

New Orleans was wide open for music, Bourbon Street packed with bars that dispensed something for everyone, but some of the Hall's regulars were disabled through age and would have been unlikely to find regular employment elsewhere. Whether it was a source of pride to them to be working, or whether they put a brave face on things in the light of financial necessity, I cannot say. As long as I was a guest of the Barneses, though, I felt it was only polite to accompany Polo to wherever he was playing, whatever I thought of the venue.

I visited the city on several occasions and eventually was able to refuse to go to the Hall as a matter of principle. I badly wanted to write of the shameful state of affairs – one man likened his role there to a 'circus performer' – but I did not feel I could do so as long as Polo and the other musicians I knew were living. Now I can say that many New Orleanians are among those equally dismayed that this relic of former inequities continued to exist in the city.

Paul Lentz, a journalist from Buffalo, New York, took me on a tour of the nightspots. He was involved in setting up a venue for traditional music that would present the artists in more tasteful surroundings and take patrons away from Preservation Hall, and he wanted me to hear some unsung local heroes. Paul was one of the most laidback people I had ever met. He was made for New Orleans, the 'Big Easy', and the city was made for him. We went on a sightseeing drive and I wondered why the speedometer never topped 20 mph. Then I realised there was no pressure to go any faster. Life was laid out for enjoyment in New Orleans, it was no wonder so many outsiders moved there to set up home away from the rat race.

To my delight, I found that Roosevelt Sykes, the blues pianist with whom I'd spent so much time in London, was one of these settlers. He had married a woman from Gulfport, Mississippi, and together they were bringing up the two small children of one of her relatives. Roosevelt and Mercy Dee embarrassed me at times with their hospitality, and it was with them that I stayed on subsequent visits. Mercy Dee would cook and leave food on the stove. There were pots of beans, greens and hamhocks, platters of fried chicken, fish and bright yellow cornbread, and in the Southern manner guests were left to help themselves while she sat with her feet up, watching TV. They took me fishing one day in the rain, to Lake Ponchartrain, thirteen miles wide, across which, legend had it, Buddy Bolden's horn could be heard on a clear night.

I had hoped there might be a parade while I was there and left word with several people to keep me informed. It says a lot for the way New Orleanians feel about their music that no less than three of them called with the news that an army officer had died, requesting a musical funeral. I met Freddie Kohlman and Chester Jones, another drummer, at the funeral parlour and was surprised to see trumpeter Wallace Davenport, once Ray Charles' musical director, among the assembled musicians. All kinds of people played the parades, I discovered, and as I was taking pictures, another trumpeter, this time from England, came over to say hello before taking his place in the Onward Band line-up. With the Second Line made up of children and adults of all ages, I followed the hearse to the cemetery, the band playing funeral dirges such as 'Just a Closer Walk with Thee'. On the way back, their mood changed abruptly and they broke into a jubilant stomp, the Second Line strutting and posturing with hats and umbrellas. They played 'Rock Around the Clock' as well as 'The Saints' and the beat was quite irresistible. Polo had told me, 'They'd play with so much feeling that even a little baby in your arms would jump like *that* to that music!' I was surprised I managed to take any pictures at all.

I wanted to see Fred McDowell who lived in a small Mississippi town not far south of Memphis, but I thought it was best to head straight for the city. Someone had given me an old phone number there for Gus Cannon who wrote 'Walk Right In' in 1917, a song revived countless times. If he were alive he would be around 90, but I gave him a call on the offchance. To my surprise, he answered the phone: 'Come on over.' He produced his banjo and strummed a few chords. 'Too old to play,' he laughed regretfully. It was a sad moment, but I took a shot of him that at the time I thought was a classic.

When I called, Essie Mae McDowell told me to catch the bus to Como. As I travelled away from the relative security of Memphis and into Mississippi, it was hard not to think of the state's history of brutality and racial murder. Mississippi had such an evil reputation that some Black people would even refuse to acknowledge having been born there. Fred met the bus and nobody gave us a second look as he carried me to his house, a brand new mobile home he had bought since working the folk-blues circuit. Nevertheless, I remembered a producer who had once recorded him there telling me he had woken up the following morning to see a hoarding advertising the racist John Birch Society outside his hotel. If it was that kind of area I was taking no chances. Bearing in mind that racial incidents in the South occur after dark, I ate Essie Mae's fine chicken dinner and made a point of leaving their home before night fell, for their safety as much as for mine.

Chicago was blues city, being one of the first stopping places for migrant Southerners, especially those from Mississippi. The music flourished in the areas Blacks settled, the Westside of town and on the Southside where I stayed with Anthony Braxton's family. I was anxious to meet up with some of the blues musicians I knew from London, and Bob Koester, who ran Delmark Records and recorded the AACM musicians as well as the blues, took me to see Buddy Guy whom I'd last seen playing on *Ready Steady Go!* With Little Brother Montgomery and his wife, I went to see Muddy Waters, who was appearing at one of the city's more elegant nightspots. Backstage, we found Muddy drinking champagne, relaxed and affable. He had just recovered from a serious road accident and was glad to have a visitor from England, remembering me from his earlier visits there.

Downbeat was published in Chicago, and as their longtime London correspondent I paid a courtesy call to the office. I wanted, too, to use a typewriter for some stories to send back to England. Long-established, the magazine enjoyed a reputation as the world's leading publication on the music, so I was taken aback when I walked into a dingy office in a creaking old building with decor out of the 1930s. But the owner and publisher were friendly enough until the time came when they asked whom I intended to hear on my visit. I'd noticed that Gene Ammons, one of the grits 'n' greens saxophonists, was making a rare appearance at a place called Roberts. 'Roberts?' echoed the owner. 'Didn't that close down some time ago?' No, I told him, it was on 63rd Street. His face took on a strange, wary look. 'Er, it's . . . er . . . rather *Black* around there,' he ventured. 'I know,' I told him, 'I'm staying on the next block.' And I got one of those looks.

Back in New York I found myself stranded, for Kunle had lost his apartment. Blackwell had come back from Morocco and was playing with Ornette Coleman again. I called on him and Frances in their lower East side apartment and ran into saxophonist Dewey Redman, who also worked in the group. Ornette had a large, spacious loft, they suggested, why didn't I ask him for a place to stay? I knew Ornette, of course, from when he first came to England and stayed with Hoppy, but I certainly did not think I could ask such a favour. Dewey and Blackwell insisted, and Dewey picked up the phone to speak to Ornette. 'Tell her to come on over,' was Ornette's response.

I spent the next five weeks in an enormously privileged situation. Ornette lived on Prince Street in the heart of SoHo, an old warehouse district south of Houston Street, which was just being opened up by artists. He rented the street-level space as well, where he rehearsed and put on concerts, eventually turning it into an art gallery, Artist House. Eventually greedy landlords and prejudice forced him out, as SoHo became an overpriced location for the upwardly mobile.

Ornette made few public appearances but was accessible to anyone who sought his help or advice. He refused work unless it paid an amount he thought commensurate with his reputation, which was considerable; however, he was always working at his music and held open house for other artists. People such as Braxton and Leroy would come by to gossip and play pool, others would take advantage of Ornette's luxurious sauna, or the washing-machine. During my stay he had a birthday party, at which people such as Archie Shepp and trumpeter Freddie Hubbard mingled with the British rock group Soft Machine and Village Bohemians like film-maker Shirley Clarke, who directed *The Cool World* and *The Connection*. I came home to find Ornette in conference one evening with John Lennon and Yoko Ono, another night Nina Simone.

Staying with Ornette, I should have been in the ideal position to take the kind of photographs I wanted, documenting the everyday life of one of the most prominent figures in the new music. There was only one problem: he disliked the camera and would grow restless whenever he saw me take pictures. It was part of the dedicated photographer's credo that you got your picture no matter what, but I did not feel it was right to impose on Ornette. He was generous to me in so many ways. When he played the Newport Jazz Festival, an event which ended in riots, he flew me up to Rhode Island with the rest of the band and arranged for me to stay in their hotel. I do have pictures from Newport and in rehearsal, but more typical, I feel, is a silhouette of him on the phone at 9 o'clock in the morning. Taken from quite a distance as I rolled out of bed, it shows more of the bakery wall opposite than it does of the stripped-to-the-waist Ornette. It was, I felt, a fair comment on our relationship.

I was finding out there was more to the learning experience than coming back with a story or pictures. I was on this voyage for enlightenment, not to collect any trophies. Many times I would find myself in a situation where to pick up the camera would destroy all rapport or create a crisis of confidence. Increasingly I sat back and listened.

It was a long time since an interview with Ornette had appeared anywhere, though, and in touch with *Melody Maker* at home, I told my editor, Richard Williams, where I was staying. He said he wanted an article. Ornette was evasive, with a lot on his mind, and I felt uncomfortable when I tried to pursue it. He lived at the time with a young woman, Mary Franklin, just 22 and burning with righteous passion. She had little time for white people and accused me of taking advantage of Ornette's generosity when I attempted to do an interview. I was torn between what I felt as a human being and the desirability of getting a piece on Ornette into a popular music paper with all the attendant exposure. There was, too, the ever-pressing need to 'come back with the goods' and show that I, as a woman, could do it. In the end Ornette agreed to a talk. Under the circumstances, though, I never felt really happy about the outcome – even when Richard ran it as a major feature over two weeks.

Mary was one of the most determined women I have ever met. If I spoke to a musician in her presence, even over the phone, a challenge was waiting. What, she would ask, did I plan to get out of the encounter? Was it appropriate for a white person to write about the music? These were questions being asked of Whites elsewhere, of course, but because I was living at Ornette's, there was nowhere to run. I began to wonder whether I did, in fact, have any right to be involved in the music which its exponents had begun to describe as being a political statement.

Ornette stayed aloof from all this, adopting an amused attitude. But I knew from what he told me and things I'd overheard him say that he did not disagree with this view. It was painful to undergo such a challenge, but invaluable in moving towards an understanding of what had to be done.

I'd been so sure I was doing the right thing in writing about the music. I'd actively challenged racism wherever I found it since those days when my mother slammed the door on African students and I'd been called a slag in the streets. Now self-examination became a constant. There were many who recoiled, hurt, when Malcolm X said 'all whites are racist'. But in New York I read his *Autobiography* at last and began to understand what was meant by that statement. Malcolm's integrity was unquestionable and he expressed himself unequivocally in a way that provided answers to many a disturbing question. What he had to say was reflected in the attitudes of street people as well as intellectuals. Malcolm's question, addressed to a group of older women: 'Have you ever known *one* white man who either didn't do something to you or take something from you?' ached inside me, pricking my conscience before I made any decision.

Eventually, Mary's hostility towards me would become tempered. We never became fast friends exactly, but I felt we had reached an understanding. But whatever my personal relationship with individual musicians and others in their community might be, the question of social responsibility now took centrestage. Like other whites permitted inside the musicians' circle, I was constantly forced to examine my motives. It wasn't enough to be there for the music, we had to take the whole package on board. To know something of the history, being aware of Malcolm, Rosa Parks or Huey P. Newton, meant little. You had to live it as if you meant it as well. The music magazines still ignored the Black viewpoint, refusing to encourage Black writers. As the years went by, I did my best to enlighten white editors, but the majority remained oblivious to the benefits of providing a wider cultural diversity of opinion. As for my own work, I hoped that its sheer extent and my unequivocal support for the music reflected my commitment. But however political my writing was becoming, inside I was still the fan who waited for Big Bill's autograph and missed the last bus home.

Ornette was kind, but he would make fun of me, too. It was as if he knew I was still a kid for the music at heart. I guess I was pretty wide-eyed around him, and I found it hard to talk to him like any other 'ordinary' person. To me he was 'Ornette Coleman' and I was, after all, but a guest in the culture.

The three months I had spent in the United States this time had whetted my appetite for more and made me concentrate on becoming a better photographer. Stevie joined me for another stay in New York later that year. She, too, was inspired by the city which had music coming out of its ears. Shortly after our return, I received a call from Liz Bailey at the Victoria and Albert Museum. She wanted to mount a jazz exhibition, featuring photographs and memorabilia as a background to a series of concerts. She came to see me and had a look at my recent work. After a while she paused and said, 'I don't think we need look any further; I'd like to do a show of your photographs.'

To say I was taken aback is putting it mildly. Here I was, only really just beginning to find my feet after years of playing about, and I was being given the chance of a major exhibition. And yet I did not feel I had enough strong pictures to show. I had tried to do 'Day-in-the-life' sequences on people like Horace Silver and Elvin Jones in New York, following them around as they cycled through the park, went shopping or, in the case of bassist Richard Davis, horse-riding, but the results were still glorified snapshots. I wanted to go South again, too, and I wondered whether the idea could be postponed. She agreed to put it on ice for a year.

I still did not have it quite right. The traditional approach to the subject, shooting pictures that would sell, was ingrained. I needed to earn a living and it was hard to move away from the straightforward 'blowing' shot. I had to learn how to make something for *myself*. Something that told a story as well, and could explain more of the music's mystery.

17
On the Road Again

There's a famous book called *The Movement* which documents, pictorially, the civil rights struggle of the 1960s. It opens with a picture by SNCC's Danny Lyon of Highway 49, sweeping down through the Mississippi hills from Jackson to Yazoo City, leading into the heart of the Deep South. It was a road that the Freedom Rides took on a journey which was, for many young Northerners, the route to the shocking discovery of America, the dual and divided society. In 1972 I found myself on that road, often treading fearfully, mindful of those images of that period of social upheaval.

To a significant extent, my picture of the South had been formed by that book: the campaign for voter registration, the struggle to integrate the schools – the National Guard and federal troops, guns at the ready – the sheer viciousness of the redneck police. To counteract this I had Frederick Ramsey Jr's *Been Here and Gone*, a celebratory documentary of life in the 'rurals', where African cultural retentions abounded and music was a means of surviving harsh social conditions. On one of my journeys I would meet the revered Fannie Lou Hamer who, as a leader of the Mississippi Freedom Democratic Party, was able to speak out and act in a way that would have meant death to a Black man. I'd sit in jukejoints and bar-rooms, too, where people partied in a distinctly African way and a dance was a 'country drumbeat' rather than hoedown or hop.

Now that I had got over the realisation that I was never going to be a fearless newspaper reporter, I started to look more seriously at the work of the great photographers, many of whom I'd first encountered on the bookshelves of Margaretha and Siegfried Charoux. I had never paid much attention to the pioneer Farm Security Administration photo-journalists, people such as Walker Evans and Dorothea Lange, who gave middle-America its first look at how the other half scrapes a living. But it was W. Eugene Smith, the former *Life* staffer, who set the standards for a committed approach to documentary photography who was my main inspiration. And, because I still thought of the craft as an aggressive, macho business, I was fascinated by war photographers such as Larry Burrows and Don McCullin. My brother gave me a copy of Robert Capa's *Images of War*, and in New York I bought Smith's Aperture monograph, which included his war pictures, too. And then I found a copy of *The Sweet Flypaper of Life*, which I had first seen on a visit to Langston Hughes. The poet had woven a text around Roy De Carava's evocative photographs of Harlem life, and this and the Smith became my primers. The humanity of both photographers and their dignified portrayals of everyday Americans had a considerable influence on me, and I found myself unconsciously producing pictures that echoed theirs in composition, subject and line.

When Stevie and I caught the Greyhound bus for the South, we did so forearmed with a long list of contacts. We did not, as some might imagine, bowl up at a grocery store in some Mississippi cotton town demanding, 'Take me to your blues.' The South didn't operate like that. Years of diligent study amid the pages of serious music magazines had familiarised me with the worldwide network of blues fanciers, and making connections was easy. My early good fortune in being befriended by Paul Oliver, the pioneer of blues scholarship in Britain, was crucial to an understanding of the atmosphere that strangers in search of the blues could expect to encounter in the South, still medieval in some of its ways. It was one thing to pluck a Muddy Waters album off the shelf in a record shop in Soho, another to go hunting for one of his contemporaries in the jukejoints of Clarksdale. The civil rights movement and the 1954 *Brown* v. *Board of Education* decision outlawing school segregation had begun to break down centuries-old patterns of separate development, but it was only ten years since snipers had tried to take out James Meredith as he made his way to study at the University of Mississippi, quaintly known as 'Ol' Miss', several hundred United States marshals at his side. Had we attempted to nose about, without any information to go on, it could have been dangerous – as recently as the early 1970s – both for us and the people we wanted to meet. We were women, after all, and I was white. When Paul Oliver had taken his wife with him on a field trip, he told me, it meant potential danger for their Black contacts. They were forced to meet outside town at night in the cotton fields in order to visit jukes where the music was played. The historical connection of white woman/Black man was like a red rag to a bull where many white Southerners were concerned, and any suggestion that we were just hanging out, with no 'legitimate' purpose, could be all a bunch of bored rednecks might need. Stevie's racial descent could help smoothe the way in Black circles at times, but as soon as she opened her mouth, she was an obvious stranger. And the diehards hated strangers as much, if not more, than 'uppity' local Blacks.

Over a period of ten years I travelled to the South and saw tremendous changes take place. Even in Mississippi, some interracial couples began to live openly together, although marriage between the races was not legalised until 1987. 'Things has changed,' guitarist Eugene Powell told me in 1979. 'Folks is living like *people* now.' Yet on those first visits we trod carefully as we went in search of the blues, moving on at the first sign of trouble. The events which had permanently upset the status quo were still fresh in local minds, and we realised that travelling together, we looked like a couple of 'integrationists'. The vicious fate that had befallen Freedom Fighters Schwerner, Goodman and Chaney and Viola Liuzzo was a chilling thought to carry along on the journey.*

Several of the people Paul Oliver had met and recorded on his

*Michael Schwerner, Andrew Goodman and Black Mississippian James Chaney were murdered near Philadelphia, Mississippi, in 1964; Liuzzo, a Detroit housewife, shot dead the following year as she returned from driving demonstrators to the rally in Selma, Alabama, ending the historic march from Montgomery. They were among many hundreds killed during the Southern struggle for freedom, but their names stuck in my mind because three were white.

field trips had moved away from the South, some to new careers in music; others were dead. A series of recently published blues books helped to locate musicians still active, if only sporadically, in their communities. One such book was Bruce Bastin's *Crying For the Carolines*, which dealt with the music of an area which had tended to be overlooked in favour of the deep blues of the cotton states, shot through with its African shamanic mystery and power. The guitarists of the Carolinas, Virginia and Georgia expressed themselves in an intricate finger-picking style, relying on virtuosity rather than passion for effect, and their repertoire, like Jesse Fuller's, was by no means confined to the blues. Like most people who learned about the blues from recordings cut selectively by white entrepreneurs, I had been transfixed by the poignant Mississippi sound of Muddy Waters and John Lee Hooker. Josh White was a finger-picker, one of the first blues players I heard, and I'd seen the Rev. Gary Davis, probably the most accomplished, when he came to England, quite stunning, if past his prime. But the musicians we came across on this journey were a revelation. I carried Bruce's book with me like a Bible.

Bruce had spent a period teaching in North Carolina and relied on local enthusiasts for his contacts. He put us in touch with a young white guitarist, Danny McLean who lived in Rocky Mount, the town where Thelonious Monk was born. Danny was one of the slowest people I'd ever met, or so I thought until I realised I was still operating on New York time. I'd told him on the phone what we were after: to meet some of the people he'd recorded for the local radio station, hear some music and take a few pictures. He was kindness itself, even if I'm sure he was a little bemused at the fact that 'y'all girls' were interested in that oldtime finger-picking. Like everyone we met in the South, he was used to blues fanciers being male. But he gave up a lot of time to guide us carefully around.

He told us about a man known as Guitar Shorty, who lived in impoverished circumstances, subject to the whims of the tobacco farmer who 'generously' rented him a shack which let in the rain. Agricultural work for people like him was sporadic, and he supplemented his meagre income by playing on the streets of nearby Elm City, landing not infrequently in the town jail when he was drunk. We called at his house, its roof sagging dangerously over the porch and a well alongside the outhouse, but the guitarist was not at home. Instead we went to a jukepoint, a small wooden building that housed a 'piccolo', the local name for a jukebox. There we met a man named Willie Johnson who could play a little guitar. Danny had a vintage steel National in the car, and he handed it over to Willie. The men in the joint viewed us with amicable curiosity, but a couple of teenaged girls looked on with undisguised hostility. It did not take long to realise that, white woman or Black stranger, the fact that we had entered their territory meant trouble. It probably suggested we were there looking for 'lowlife' sex, generally speaking the only reason apart from labour recruitment anyone white would visit this kind of establishment. But the atmosphere gradually relaxed as Willie played, and the two young women started to dance. To my surprise, the steps they were doing echoed movements I'd seen in Ghana just a few months before. The idea of African retentions was no longer a matter of armchair speculation; here it was, a living reality, four hundred years away from the motherland.

Towards the end of the day we found Shorty, who had been drinking the day away with a group of friends in the middle of the tobacco fields. They were all somewhat the worse for wear, but when Danny produced another instrument, Shorty grabbed it. A small, stocky man with huge hands calloused by years of hard labour, he shrugged off the alcoholic haze to coax intricate figures from the guitar. Danny called him a 'real free-form guitarist', a comment on his cavalier approach to conventional form. But to say, as he did, albeit fondly, 'He don't play *nothing* right!' was nonsense in the face of the extraordinary technique that Shorty had invented for himself.

It had been a hot, hectic day, and my head was ringing through excitement and drinking on an empty stomach. But Lena, Shorty's wife, and Stevie took to each other straight away, and we cemented the first stage of a friendship that would be renewed on subsequent visits.

But getting to know Shorty and Lena and other blues people we met on our journey, meant becoming involved with a harsh way of life that was often desperate, hardly romantic. Excessive consumption of alcohol was a feature of most of our encounters with bluesmen, not confined to musicians, but part of a way of life which set them apart from the wider community and made them regarded as outlaws. Fun it might have been for us as young fans and visitors, but the reality was grim. 'Everyone knew' that the blues came out of poverty, but I was shocked at housing conditions in the community we visited, a state of affairs that would be repeated elsewhere as we went in search of the blues. Once, when I showed a picture editor a shot of a bluesman on a broken down porch like Shorty and Lena's, he accused me of setting it up. 'I've been all over America,' he said; 'people don't live like that.' I had to tell him they did.

Bruce had given us a phone number for Baby Tate, an electric guitarist whom he and his colleague Pete Lowry had recorded in the neighbouring state of South Carolina. I'd written to him tentatively, saying I was a friend of theirs, now I telephoned and left a message that we were coming. We arrived in Spartanburg late in the day, the rain pouring down. We had no idea if we would be welcome, and the taxi driver tried to discourage us from crossing the tracks to the 'Colored' section of town. But a thin, wiry man, very Black, was sitting there on the porch, waiting. 'You looking for Tate?' he queried from behind dark glasses, and we knew we'd hit gold-dust.

With Tate it was another situation right from the start. He was a man who carried himself with dignity, even after a night when the whisky flowed freely. Bruce and Pete were remembered as friends and he produced his own copy of *Crying for the Carolines*. But he'd also been in England during the War and was eager to reminisce about his Service experience. Stationed near Poole in Dorset, he had acquired a local following. He played often in pubs and for dances, travelling back to camp on a hay-wagon. There were other startling tales, too, like the time he was caught off-limits by the military police, *in flagrante delicto* in an air-raid shelter. He drove us to the store to buy hamburgers and whisky, refusing our money, then we settled in for a night with the blues.

225

If there has to be a 'most unforgettable' night in my life, I suppose this was it. Everyone has their own imaginary picture of what it would be like to experience something they hold most dear as I did the blues. Sitting around with a bottle of bourbon, listening to Tate's rugged music, fulfilled mine. The rain coursed down relentlessly, beating a polyrhythmic patter on the porch outside and seeping through the roof at one point. My copy of *Crying for the Carolines* bears a waterstain to this day, a permanent reminder of the first time I felt the blues in my bones.

Tate and Tillie, his wife, drank heavily, and so did we. She was an extrovert who got us all dancing together as Tate reached into the collective history of Africans in America, the way Black people had been doing for centuries. When he found out that Stevie played drums, he produced a washboard and something to beat with. He even got me playing his harmonica, something I hadn't done since I realised there could only be one Sonny Terry. Whenever Tate laid aside his shiny red instrument, Tillie dropped one of his records on the deck of the battered old record-player. She played 'Late In the Evening' over and over, the grooves turning grey under the light of the single bare bulb in the ceiling. Eventually we settled down for the night, enveloped in a creaking bed that sank to the floor. As we fell asleep, I heard him gently chastising Tillie to 'leave those peoples alone'. But sleep did not last long. We were wakened several times as the stylus crashed back on the record and they argued, her voice raised, his quiet and firm. Then the door burst open, and the room was flooded with light. The nature of their discussion became clear. Tillie had decided their visitors needed feeding. She had gone into the kitchen to fix something to eat, and now she swept in, thrusting two steaming plates under our noses. We had no alternative but to struggle to a sitting position, not easy in that bed, and eat. It was well past three in the morning but she had prepared pork chops, potatoes and gravy. It was a generous gesture but Tate did not approve of his guests being disturbed. He jumped into his car and drove off. Then, to our astonishment, we heard him return with the local police officer. There and then he had poor Tillie carted down to the cells to sleep it off for the night. He was worried, we heard him say, that in his state of exhaustion, he might get violent. The police officer took it all in his stride, for it was an apparently not uncommon occurrence.

The next morning we found Tate, sobered up, on the porch. He apologised for the disturbances in the night and said he had done his best to see that we slept soundly. We sat there exhausted but happy, to be greeted by an early-morning visitor who dropped by. 'These folks is from *England*,' Tate announced proudly. 'Oh,' said our man, very rural, 'd'y'all come on the bus?'

We left Spartanburg, promising to return. But it was not to be. Six weeks later, Pete Lowry phoned us in New York to say Tate had died, the result of a massive heart attack. We were stunned, and I felt like I'd lost someone I'd known a long time instead of just for a day.

From the Carolinas we went to Atlanta and New Orleans where we stayed with Polo and Mother and visited Roosevelt and Mercy Dee Sykes. Stevie had taken piano lessons in her youth but her teacher had not been encouraging. Now she had started playing again, and Roosevelt showed her a blues in thirds, simple but effective, with plenty of scope for improvisation. We rented a car and drove towards Mississippi, en route for Chicago.

In Mississippi our contacts were less reliable than they had been in the East, but I decided to use a brief meeting with Skip James as an entrée.

Nehemiah 'Skip' James was a complete original. He was responsible for putting the Bentonia blues style on the map and I, like other outsiders who heard him in concert after his 'rediscovery' in the 1960s, had been awed by the high-pitched, almost plaintive quality of pieces such as 'It Must Have Been the Devil'. I knew that a contemporary of his, Jack Owens, played in the style of the region, so we headed for the little town in Yazoo County on Highway 49. At the grocery store we asked if anyone knew of his whereabouts.

We were directed along a series of dirt roads to a large wooden house in the middle of spinach fields. A man in a stetson came out to meet us, a wary look on his face. His eyes showed no expression at our strange accents, but when I mentioned Skip James he invited us inside. Jack Owens and his wife Mabel had once run their place as a roadhouse, catering for Saturday night trade. Now, although they still sold beer and soft drinks from a massive refrigerator and occasionally cooked, he was not anxious to pick up his guitar for strangers.

Three other visitors, one a woman, sat beside a huge stove made from an oil drum, drinking away the afternoon. One, Jacob Stuckey, turned out to be the nephew of the man who had taught 'Skippy' to play. I recognised his name and we were in with a chance, although no one knew quite what to make of us until I produced a bottle of whisky brought along to break the ice on such an occasion. Before long, Jack fetched his instrument, a new Yamaha, and started to play. He allowed me to take some photographs and then, as the mood mellowed, the others began to reminisce about their hometown hero. Raife Brown, the older of the two men and a contemporary of Skip, puffed on his pipe. 'That Negro could hit that guitar till it be trembling,' he recalled. 'I seen him outplay himself till he cry like a baby.' Jacob agreed: 'Skip James put all the stuff out that I know about the guitar.'

'If your mind is on something, you play it [the blues] to yourself,' Raife continued. 'I seen Nehemiah James late at night in the woods over yonder; he play that "Lonesome Children" and cry like a baby. That's a wonderful Negro, born and bred round here in this vicinity.' After a while a harmonica player, a younger man, came by. His name was Bud Spires and he and Jack had once cut a few records together. Now they sat facing each other, their thighs interlocked so that Bud, who was blind, could take his cue from the older man's touch. They played together until well after nightfall, minor-key tunes such as 'Good Morning Little Schoolgirl' and 'Catfish Blues', and the eerie Bentonia classic, 'The Devil', stomping in time on the wooden floor which was covered with beaten sheets of metal cut from oil drums. Theirs was the deep blues in truth, haunting, lonely, a sound I will never forget.

Eventually Bud stumbled away across the fields in the dark

and Raife, who had stayed silent for most of the afternoon, relishing his pipe, the whisky and music, enquired, 'Where were you ladies planning on spending the night?' There were no motels in the area and we had counted on sleeping in the car, but he invited us back to his house, saying he knew his sister would like to meet us.

We followed Raife's car through a maze of dirt roads to his house, a wooden shack on the far side of the town. His sister was out, and her daughter did not look too happy to see us, but she settled us into a huge wooden bed with four posts carved from mahogany and covered in ancient quilts. The atmosphere was stifling, for we were in the windowless middle room in a house that was far bigger than it had seemed from the outside. Presently, the door was opened and in came Raife's sister, Ruby Lee Blanche. She sat down on the edge of the bed to give us the once-over. 'I heard we had visitors,' she said warmly. 'I had to see what you looked like.'

She had been, she said, to an emergency meeting of the Voters' Registration group, an organisation set up during the period of civil rights activity. A local man, returning from Memphis with a white woman in his car, had been shot dead by police and the community was organising a boycott of all the white businesses. We had the uncanny sensation of being involved in something that up to now we had only read about in newspapers. Musicians in New York said lynch-law still prevailed in the South; here was the proof.

In the morning we met the rest of the family. Ruby Lee's daughter Bobbie had three children; after her initial hesitation, she was friendly. As Ruby Lee cooked us breakfast – cornbread, fried tripe and chicken – I asked where I could wash my hair. I'd expected to find a well nearby, but learned that they had to purchase their water by the barrel. There was plenty of water around, rivers and streams, but the white landowners saw no need to dig wells for the convenience of Black tenants if they could make money from supplying this most basic of facilities. It was, said Ruby Lee, another battle in which the Voters' Registration group was involved.

She said she would fetch me some water and I was embarrassed. I told her I could fetch it myself. Later, she told me that was what most warmed her towards me; she had never come across a white person who would fetch and carry for themselves if a coloured person was standing by. While I was sitting on the porch drying my hair in the sun, a police officer drove past and stopped to examine our car which was parked near the road. The combination of Stevie and me, she with an Afro hair-do, and our rented car which had California number-plates, seemed to us to spell trouble. Given the recent events, we felt it might be safer for Ruby Lee, Raife and the others if we went on our way. They tried to persuade us to stay, but we felt it wiser to leave. Sure enough, as we made our way out of Bentonia, the police followed us to the city limits.

The Mississippi Delta is deep blues country, where the flat, alluvial plain given over to cotton production stretches for miles. There, in Leland, we stayed with the mother of Leo Smith, a trumpet player involved in the New Music who had been one of our house-guests in Balham. Leo's stepfather, Alex 'Little Bill' Wallace was an occasional blues guitarist himself, but he could not understand what women like us were doing looking for the old country blues. Because of the way that we dressed, in T-shirts and shorts because of the heat, he thought we were just out of school. He was taken aback to learn we were both in our thirties, even more so when we went out to find James 'Son' Thomas, a guitarist who, to judge from Wallace's disparaging attitude, represented the low side of life. Leo's family lived in a pretty house with modern amenities; Son's home was a shack in need of repair, its cardboard ceiling stained with the rain. He worked in a store on Main Street moving heavy furniture, and dug graves whenever the need arose. A lifetime of hard labour showed in his gaunt frame and tired eyes, but he found time to occupy himself in artistic pursuits other than music, moulding heads out of clay dredged from the bed of the nearby stream. A storm was brewing as I took a few photographs of him on the porch, one of which would cause that picture editor such disbelief. Another portrait is often cited as one of my most successful. I think viewers who like it, who are invariably white, do so because it reminds them of something Walker Evans or Dorothea Lange might have shot in the 1930s, not because it necessarily makes them consider the continuing realities of life for some in the Black Belt South. They speak of its timeless quality, and the irony of the adjective escapes them. People from outside the culture, I have found, generally read into such images something not necessarily there.

It was not hard to produce similar images wherever we went, for in this area of plantations and tenant farms, as elsewhere in the South, some people continued to have to struggle for the bare necessities. In Greenville, one of the few large towns in Mississippi, we were introduced to Eugene Powell, another guitarist. His wife was severely disabled and he cared for her on his own, doing the best he could on a minimal Welfare check supplemented by food stamps and occasional dealing in scrap. He was a good acoustic guitarist, a cousin of the famous Chatmon family of bluesmen, and had recorded as Sonny Boy Nelson in the 1930s. There had been several opportunities for him to go on the road and perform for the new blues audience that had grown up during the previous decade. But he refused to leave Carrie, who had set him up financially when he was younger, footloose and fancy-free and, as he boasted, followed by women from town to town. 'They tries to get me to go, but you don't throw somebody away just because they wore out,' he said gently.

I knew some chords on the guitar and Eugene encouraged me, showing me a few Mississippi runs. An ancient piano, painted white, stood on the porch, and Stevie started to work out a blues, using the chord changes Roosevelt had taught her. Some keys stuck and refused to play, but she coped. Eugene joined her, handing me a venerable Gibson guitar, a slim Kalamazoo model with elegant f-holes cut in the soundbox, and persuading me that I could play along with them. I felt ridiculous trying to 'second' someone who had played with the Chatmons, but he insisted. He was eager for company and didn't want us to leave. He made up a bed for us and we went and bought food at the Chinese grocery store on the corner and cooked dinner for us all in return.

Our finances by now were severely depleted, for wherever we went we paid the people who played us their music, and bought groceries for those who allowed us to stay in their homes. Southern hospitality was all very well but not something of which to take unfair advantage. I was dismayed to learn how some blues enthusiasts would turn up on musicians' doorsteps and expect them to drop whatever they might be doing in exchange for what I can only call the cachet of white patronage. I even heard the argument that what the blues musician was doing was passing down knowledge from a 'universal' tradition that is the common heritage of 'us all', that music should not *belong* to anyone, in fact. But those who adopted this attitude blithely ignored that they were being entertained by people who earned a living this way, and were learning from them in the process. While we formed good relationships with some of the people we visited, in other cases the ambivalent situation of blues people faced with the materially better-off white student was unavoidable. There were enthusiasts who chose to pretend no such conflict existed. Joni Mitchell, though, was not so arrogant. When she met veteran Furry Lewis in Memphis, she wrote a song about it, eloquently describing her discomfiture: 'Why should I expect that old guy to give it to me true/Fallin' to hard luck/And time and other thieves/While our limo is shining on his shanty street.' But not everyone could see it that way.

There's a middle-class tradition, too, that to offer money to someone less well-off is somehow insulting. Well, I have yet to see a poor person who wasn't pleased to have cash in hand, whether impoverished for individual reasons or because they belonged to an underprivileged sector of society. Of course there are ways of doing it, and in intercultural relationships, finding the right way sometimes takes a bit of effort. Eugene had plenty of stories of 'this white boy' or 'that one' who had passed through for a merry afternoon of music-making, leaving nothing behind but a memory. As for that Gibson guitar, in need of repair but a classic instrument, he'd held on to it despite several offers. I told him never to sell it, but the last time I saw him, was dismayed to find it was missing. Shamefacedly, he admitted he'd sold it to another 'white boy' one day when he needed the money. This 'music lover' had offered him a tenth of its value and got away with it when times were tough down Greenville way.

As I travelled around the South, sometimes in the company of other white people, albeit lovers of music, I began to realise that white Americans, although they would never admit it, still considered they had the right to walk into Black homes at will. Information abounded in the enthusiasts' community concerning those who were 'amenable' and those who were not. Guitarist Buddy Moss, one of the great Georgia bluesmen, was said to have pulled a gun on someone who sought to record him. When we did meet, though, in Atlanta, he could not have been more courteous and charming. He insisted on playing a delicate country blues into my tape-machine for me to 'catch' it, then took Stevie and me out for the rest of the day. Buddy was a proud man, with a reputation for having an 'attitude', which meant that he was not about to kowtow to the white man.

The South was strong on tradition and acknowledged for its oldstyle manners, but that meant the perpetuation of *all* the old values. When we first went there, we greeted people such as Eugene and Carrie by their first names, not giving a second thought to what that implied. We were, after all, of the generation that first dropped formality with older people and we were only being as friendly as we'd been at home. Gradually, however, it dawned on me that the polite form of address in the South was Mr This or Mizz That. To call the elders by their first names was disrespectful; there was a tradition of that – Uncle Ben, Aunt Jemima – just as there were songs protesting 'call me by my rightful name'. I consciously changed the language I used, addressing older people in a formal manner that was becoming unusual at home, even introducing my travelling companions as 'Mr or Mizz so-and-so' when I remembered.

However hesitant I might be about pushing myself forward, I realised that merely by being white I raised the issue of inequitable power relations and often placed other people in a difficult situation. It could be argued that I had no business to be interfering in the Black community in the first place, but the music had made me want to see and hear, to experience and know. I knew that the people I was meeting were part of history or very soon might be.

As on our visit to Ghana, Stevie was involved in the process of reclaiming her personal history. She was as excited as I was to explore unknown territory and the experience had a far-reaching effect on her. She encouraged me to take photographs and interview the people we met, spurring me on whenever I was discouraged by frustration or fatigue. I could never have accomplished what I did without her or learned as much as I did, for she had a way of endearing herself to others which made both of us welcome when my shyness intruded.

Americans have little time for people who are backward in coming forward, and my reticence, due in part to my English upbringing as much as woman's experience of being denied access to whatever I wanted to do, was open to misinterpretation. Not Stevie, she was in there all warmth and enthusiasm, cocking a snook at convention just as she had with the Wɔn ŋ-tse in Accra.

We went back to the South on several occasions together, meeting blues musicians too numerous to mention, and staying with Shorty and Lena in their tumbledown house near Elm City, NC. But it was in Atlanta that we relaxed, hanging out with Clarence and Allen Murphy, driving around listening to music and partying. On one of these visits Allen cut a record with the Paul Mitchell trio, and invited us along to the date. He was a big man, solid and dark, with a rumpled face and laughing eyes that had seen it all. As a singer, he was sensitive and expressive, employing relatively little vibrato in contrast to the expectations of his physical appearance. The heavy Southern Soul style was in vogue, and the producer, an intrepid young white entrepreneur, obviously wanted something nearer 'that old-time religion'. 'Hey, Allen!' he shouted. 'You're not sounding *Black* enough!' The look he got told him everything he needed to know about 'Soul'.

It was in Atlanta, too, that the Rev. Emory Crolger took us to one of the city's big churches, renowned for its singing. The minister invited us to join in the service, the choir's annual event. All afternoon the congregation welcomed a stream of choirs from other churches, and for over three hours we listened with growing awe to dozens of people unknown outside their own neighbourhoods who could each have 'made it' singing commercially whenever they wanted. The standard of singing was quite extraordinary, although Atlanta had always been a major stopover for the great gospel groups (Marion Brown's mother took them in as lodgers) and as choir followed choir, it only seemed to get better. But I can still see the woman who brought me the nearest I've been to experiencing spirit-possession.

She was slight and mid-brown, her hair tied back at the nape of her neck. Her choir wore maroon robes, she was in a skirt of the same colour and a lighter, lilac-hued blouse. She opened her mouth to sing, and then, just as with Madeleine Bell all those years ago in *Black Nativity*, the sound seemed to go through me like a knife, hitting me just under my heart and hurting. I was sweating and I felt myself starting to sway. Already two or three people had been seized by the spirit and had to be restrained, then carried, exhausted, out of the church. Now the noise around me seemed deafening. The congregation had been clapping without let-up, and the church reverberated with the rhythm. It was like being inside one huge drum. We had been there for a long time and I began to feel faint, so I told Stevie and we decided to leave.

As we walked out of the door an old man got to his feet and started to sing. His voice quavered with age, shook with emotion. With a handful of notes he went back deep into history, right to the depths of the sorrow songs. It was like being grabbed from inside and caught up in the siftings of centuries. Stevie turned around, hypnotised, and went back inside the church, but I could not take any more. I sat on the steps and everything around me went blank. I did not want to cry in front of Black people, but inside, my heart felt torn in two.

It was late in the afternoon and stifling, and we walked back along Auburn Avenue in a daze. We could find nothing to say to each other but we had each, I know, been taken somewhere we'd never been before. The mood was shattered abruptly when we walked into a domestic incident. A couple were arguing on a balcony nearby, a woman threatening a man with a carving knife while others edged around behind her and wrested the knife away.

That finally did it. The tears started to course down my cheeks and I didn't care who saw them. We got back to Clarence's and fell asleep, wordless, for the rest of the day. It was a long time since I'd been a believer; I'd turned my back on the church long ago. Unbidden, though, an ancient expression came into my mind, something about being washed in the Blood of the Lamb. I felt I knew how that might be.

18
The City That Eats
People for Breakfast

On a Sunday afternoon in spring, I stood in a large crowd sprawled across 7th Avenue in Harlem. We were waiting to hear Milford Graves, the drummer, one of the outstanding figures in what was now universally known as the New Music. Beneath the burnt-out shell of a supermarket, casualty of the recent nationwide uprisings, the red, green and black banners of Black Nationalism fluttered from lamp-posts and storefronts. A sea of expectant, and predominantly young, Black faces clustered around a stage surmounted by a backdrop proclaiming: 'It's Nation-Time!' Singers, poets and dancers, all wearing African clothes, performed for the crowd, accompanied by a band with a woman guitarist. Then it was Milford's turn. He flung his coat and fur hat to the ground, leapt behind his multi-coloured drumkit and proceeded to play as though his life depended on it.

I remember being stunned by his technique as much as his presence and aesthetic audacity. He wove an amazing collection of polyrhythms into his cultural cloth, but his speed was such that even from a few feet away I could not always see what he was doing. He accompanied his playing with neo-African whoops and hollers to the delight of the crowd. It was the first time I'd seen Milford play and I realised then that most white analyses of the music have never had very much to do with where it is actually going and why. The general feeling among the hardheads and cynics out there in the street about what Graves was doing was, 'Well, it certainly ain't Kool and The Gang, but whatever it is, it's ours.'

It was a powerful education for me both musically and politically. Not only had I never heard such sounds in my life or, indeed, seen anyone play with such daring, but the response Graves received gave the lie to the notion that what the post-Coltrane musicians were doing was over the heads of everyday Blackfolks.

Given the way that the New Music had been abandoned by the critical establishment, and how certain writers had prospered over decades at the music's expense, it was hardly surprising that some people shunned Whites who wrote about the music. I was upset when I ran into one of the emergent young saxophonists in the street and was refused permission to photograph him in rehearsal. To do so, he said, would mean him colluding in another aspect of exploitation. Soon afterwards photographs of him appeared in several European publications, taken by people I knew had only a passing interest in the music. I felt the same way I had that time Miles came to London and insulted me, then befriended the Editor who'd refused to print that picture of me and Little Brother Montgomery with his shirt undone, inviting him to socialise for the rest of the night.

In the main, however, the musicians weighed up each individual on their respective merits. As Kunle said: 'Well, at least you come over here and search out the music; very few of the writers do that.'

The people who encouraged me were, without exception, outspoken fighters for justice, many of whom I met through Jane Welch. Milford Graves was a cultural nationalist, which meant he had little to do with white people at that time, trombonist Clifford Thornton had been a Black Panther, yet they, along with other such 'militants' as Cecil Taylor, Archie Shepp and Andrew Cyrille, had faith in me and what I was doing. Clifford was one of the first Afro-Americans to greet me with the 'Black Power' handshake. This would later be used routinely to express interracial solidarity (or abused, as when a Black person was bullshitting a white) but at the time it gave me a feeling of warmth. It was a sign of being 'accepted' at a certain level, even if you knew that as a white person, you could not expect to be really trusted. He worked in the African-American Music Department of one of the universities, and would take time out to write me long letters, providing a political context for some of the things that were said elsewhere out of emotion and rage. Archie invited me into his home, Andrew wrote to me often. They encouraged me to listen and learn and keep on.

I made a point of contacting Milford, Cecil, Archie and Andrew whenever I went to New York. Milford no longer played any commercial gigs, confining his activities to the Black community. He reasoned that it was possible and productive to play free music for the 'people on the block', provided there were enough references and familiar handholds for them to make the switch from straightforward backbeat and funk. Every time I saw him, he won over his listeners to music that downtown was considered totally weird and way-out. He gave me his phone number and whenever I called him would let me know where he would next be playing. Most notable of these appearances in various community settings was at the Harlem Cultural Centre where, accompanied by two reedplayers only, he offered an explosive exercise in percussion that went far beyond anything I had ever imagined could be done with the drums. Each time the people responded to his pre-playing rap which located the music firmly in the tradition, then thrilled to his intensity and skill.

Cecil was elusive. Few people ever knew where to reach him, but for some reason he had taken a liking to me. My mother had come with me once to the Berlin Jazz Festival and we had ended up drinking with Cecil. Apart from the fact that Mum, then well into her sixties, sailed blithely through the following day when I could hardly raise my head off the pillow, the most memorable thing about the trip was when Cecil informed me later that Mum and I 'were the only *real* people there'. We found we had plenty in common.

Cecil was choosy about the company he kept. He was an intellectual, a sophisticate, and although he surrounded himself with dancers and people who spoke an entirely different language, he had little time for the bullshit that accompanied the 'names' of jazz around the circuit. He was a hedonist who liked to party and was just as likely to be discussing what Miles Davis was wearing or the latest Gladys Knight record as talking about what Terry Riley or John Cage was — or was not — up to. He liked wearing silk scarves and expensive sheepskin; even in the dark days when we first met and he was supporting himself with gruesome day-jobs, he had managed a pair of elegant leather riding boots. Later, when his hairline began to recede, he'd swathe his head in Indian cheesecloth, knotted at the side, when playing.

I always got the impression that Cecil felt he could talk to me on a level he had to avoid with other people who expected quotations of stunning import. There was a group of friends with whom he seemed to feel equally comfortable, and he would summon us to meet in one of the bars in the Village that had music, and the conversation would always take an unexpected turn. Cecil did not hang out on the block with 'the brothers'. He preferred the ballet or disco, but whenever he showed up at Boomer's, the musicians' Village hangout on Bleeker, the pianists who played there, Bobby Timmons or Cedar Walton, would be engaged and pleased by his interest. When he started to work more often, he would take a crowd of friends to eat after the concert. In this way I heard the wonderful Mary Lou Williams at the Cookery – 'The *only* person really saying anything on piano,' said Cecil. Later, they would appear in concert together.

No one could be more different than Milford and Cecil, yet their dignity and sense of self helped me persevere with their essentially difficult music. Both men had enormous energy and played as though the music was as serious as their life. Mainstream listeners sheered away from what they were doing, taking the music into areas where the beat and the key were eliminated, but knowing them personally made me listen intently to them and others who were equally revolutionary in their approach to rhythm and form. They were my teachers: one word from them could open up a new way of seeing.

By contrast, Archie Shepp was more of a traditionalist in his playing. His public image was of an unbending Black Power advocate, but at home he was warm, and outgoing, a family man, who taught other musicians whatever he could and sought out older players to learn from them. Whenever he spoke of his important male predecessors, he always used the prefix 'Mr', and it was he more than anyone who made younger players aware of the need to look into the past. Archie had worked as an actor, too, and had a dramatic way of presenting his analysis of the situation of the Black artist in America. He was usually quite amenable to speaking out on behalf of the musicians' community.

When the American edition of my book *Jazz People* was published, I asked him if he would come along on a radio interview I was doing. He agreed. He appeared wearing a tie and smart brown pin-stripe suit, but I noticed to my surprise that he had on one of the saddest pairs of shoes, split at the sides, and did not appear to be wearing any socks. Some whites in New York at this time were just about terrified of any Black person who wasn't visibly shuffling, and Archie, the actor, rather enjoyed adopting a pose of jocular menace. When we arrived for the broadcast, his manner had the desired effect; to my relief, no one bothered to look at his feet. The interlocutor opened the proceedings with a routine question, Archie looked him dead in the eye and said: 'It has reached the point where it is impossible for a Black man to be honest with a white man in America today,' then went on to analyse, eloquently and with a good deal of charm, the invidious situation of the Black artist in a way that made complete sense to the listeners. He said more than I could ever have hoped to, more than my little book could manage, and I was grateful to him for giving *Jazz People* a plug in the process.

We rode back downtown together and went for a beer. I thanked him and said I would like to interview him at length on some occasion. I had just been reading Lee Lockwood's extended *Conversation* with Eldridge Cleaver and wanted to do a similar exercise with Archie, in which music and politics could be woven together.

I started going to Cooper Square regularly. Sitting in the disarray of the music room beneath a poster of Jimi Hendrix and another showing athletes John Carlos and Tommie Smith giving the clenched fist Black Power salute at the 1968 Mexico Olympics, we did a series of question-and-answer interviews which I'd hoped might make at least part of a book. In doing so I was able to discover the answers to questions that continued to puzzle me and work out some solutions for myself. I felt I was getting to know a little more about the new 'militant' musicians. Whatever their politics, they were a lot more complicated than was suggested by the simplistic Pantherish image with which they were sold in Europe.

I began to consider who else would be a good subject for the book of 'Conversations'. Ornette, I knew, didn't like talking, and I had already done a long piece on Cecil in *Jazz People*. Elvin Jones, the drummer who had worked with Coltrane, seemed a good candidate. If any percussionist was a household name in America, he was – for he had a considerable following in the rock world as well as his chosen field. He was an articulate, friendly man and we already knew each other quite well. I began to talk to him regularly, too, then went to see a literary agent with a proposal. His attitude stunned me. 'Why Elvin Jones?' he asked. 'He's only a drummer.' That was one connection I didn't pursue.

Increasingly, I was discovering more Afro-American literature, as publishers vied with each other to bring out new books, the 'Blacker' the better. Poetry, I was coming to realise, played an important role in the fashioning of the new consciousness, just as the music did. The fact that so many pieces paid tribute to John Coltrane, 'The shaping spirit/limit of the whirlwind', made the work of these new writers more accessible to someone immersed in the music as I was.

At Kunle's I had encountered the work of Sonia Sanchez, whose books *Homecoming* and *We A BaaDDD People* were vivid and powerful manifestations of what many Black women were saying. Like Amiri Baraka, she rubbed America's nose in the mire of its oppression. And she chastised and challenged Black backsliders caught up in the pursuit of negative values. Sonia wrote verse fired by dynamite that could leap right off the page and sounded like saxophones wailing. Years later I'd get to know her and find a genuine revolutionary, fuelled by the search for the truth, full of loving and caring.

Baraka had long left the Greenwich Village Bohemia he inhabited when he wrote for *Downbeat* as LeRoi Jones. Now, as the guiding light of Kawaida, the new Nationalism, much of what he wrote was angry and violent. But he expressed contemporary ideas about the music which were unavailable elsewhere. Having earned credentials as one of the Beats, he was not as hidden as the other radical poets. His *Black Music*, an anthology of previously published pieces, was a primer for anyone who wanted a Black handle on the new music.

Just by introducing outsiders to inside words, Baraka revealed more of the music's mystery. Someone I know called him one of the 'language warriors', and for many white people the first time we came across words such as 'heavy' was when he wrote about Albert Ayler. Heavy meant 'significant', 'powerful', not as in its later perversion. The way whites messed up the language was another source of constant annoyance. There were even poems about reclaiming the word 'uptight', which had been appropriated to mean the opposite of its original intention.

Some of the things Baraka had to say were painful for Whites and most of the critics refused to have anything to do with them. It was said that his views went beyond music. But his urgency and that of other Black writers hit a chord within me. It was for a deeper understanding of where the music was coming from and what it symbolised as it went on its way that kept me returning to such writing, daggers, javelins, and all.

As the decade went on, several musicians moved into warehouses or lofts, doing their own building work and providing alternative venues for the new music. At the turn of the 1970s, though, the main places where the post-Coltrane musicians could be heard were Slug's and the East in Brooklyn, and the East, a Nationalist venue, categorically stated that admission was limited to people of African descent. Slug's was situated on the lower East Side on 3rd Street between Avenues B & C, and I would go there to hear Sun Ra and his Arkestra, who held court there each Monday and attracted a wide ranging audience of musicians and other artists. The area around the bar was rugged. Some musicians even refused to go there, but with no money to spare for taxis, I generally walked back in the early hours to where I was staying. My love for the music was total and I remained quite unscathed.

Many of the young musicians lived on the lower East Side, one of the cheaper sections of town, but some more established players did, also, people like Mingus and Wilbur Ware, another of the music's formidable bass players. Billy Higgins had told me how Wilbur could quieten a room full of loudmouths with a solo; Eric Dolphy used him as the yardstick to describe a similar silencing act by Al Douglas. His supremacy was often acknowledged.

When I went to interview Wilbur, he was living on Avenue B with Helen, his wife, and a beautiful Egyptian cat called Selah. They stayed just a block from the Blackwells and I would go over to see both families quite often. Avenue B was in the heart of drug-country, and I became a dab hand at negotiating my way past peddlars and addicts. I soon learned how to watch out for myself at any hour of the day or night.

Some time after we met, Helen split up with Wilbur, but I continued to drop by Avenue B to see her, and we became quite close in the years to come. I took to going by to see her on Sunday mornings. She played Art Tatum and Billie Holiday for breakfast and cooked

Southern style, fried chicken, cornbread and greens. I missed Stevie when she couldn't be with me, and I certainly missed my Mum. Helen dispensed cinnamon toast and comfort, and her stream of East Side survivor philosophy made me feel I had a home as long as she was in New York.

She worked with alcoholics in the Men's Shelter on the Bowery, a gruelling vocation that was not without its rewarding and amusing moments, although to learn how many distinguished musicians had served time on Skidrow was as harrowing as it was instructive and sobering. Such exposure to the raw realities of the city certainly led to my greater awareness and understanding of the impossible stresses faced by the creative spirit in conflict with Mammon, and helped me towards self-knowledge later. But it was a shock to someone who had grown up in Streatham.

Helen was another white woman who had seen the world through what we fondly imagined then to be Black eyes, and even after Wilbur had gone, it could never be the same way again. She expected to be shunned by the musicians' community following their break-up but it was not the case. She stayed living on Avenue B for some years, an integral part of a ramshackle community getting druggier with each day but not without its humour and soul. She was respected as a survivor herself, and when she walked down those bottle-littered streets, people would shout greetings from the doorways and stoops. They knew she had paid her dues and it showed in the respect she was given, in an area fraught with everyday danger.

The lower East Side was chock-full with artists. One musician I knew lived in a squat with his family. Holes gaped in the brickwork and the electricity was long gone. But he spraypainted the walls with luminous pictures, creating what became a fantasy gallery when illuminated by candles at night. Creativity was in the air. It wasn't necessary for someone to be holding a paintbrush or a horn; creativity came from the way they used words, their manners and gesture, the philosophy and artifacts each one developed to deal with their lives.

But creativity of this kind, was not confined to people of colour. Helen decorated her apartment with 'stained glass' made out of pieces of plastic and fantastic *objets trouvés* from the street. She sewed herself smart new outfits for important occasions, and when Stevie came to New York and landed a gig in the Village, ran up a stunning tie-dyed *buba* and *lappa* for her for pennies. She had started out as a painter of horses, but allowed her painting to lapse when she met Wilbur: 'There could only be one genius in the family.' The possibilities opened up by the women's movement helped her go back to her first love. She went to art classes and found herself some commissions, then moved to horse-country, Kentucky, to continue her revitalised career. She avoided the drug-scene in 'Alphabet City', which got more out of hand with each minute, and the arsonists preparing the homes of the poor for gentrification, an even worse evil she would have been glad to have missed.

Leslie Moëd, from the Weston ménage in Morocco, was another source of strength. We had not seen eye to eye in Tangier, but over the years she, too, provided many a refuge from the strains and stresses of dealing with the city that eats people for breakfast. She gave me a place to stay and shelter from the storm.

New York, I discovered, was really a collection of villages. As I began to run into acquaintances on the street, I started to feel quite at home. Music was very much a part of everyday life and musicians held in great awe elsewhere were treated with an odd mixture of familiarity and respect by white and Black people alike. Familiar faces, many of them Black, would turn up wherever the New Music was being played, giving the lie to the suggestion that its audience was exclusively white and enabling me to appreciate how much the music meant to people outside the musicians' own social circles. Not everyone could afford the price of a ticket, but at home such fans played Coltrane constantly.

The level of violence in the city was apparent, but as one person put it, 'If New York was as violent as people say it is, we'd have all killed each other by now.' I began to make friends. Saxophonist Frank Lowe and his artist wife Carmen lived around the corner from Leslie on St Mark's Place, the hub of East Village life, and I'd often go by there for breakfast.

To my great delight, Nellie Lutcher appeared at the Cookery, and I was able to talk with her one teatime. The *New Yorker* called her 'unflappable' and she lived up to that description the night I saw her, responding with humour as plates crashed to the floor in the kitchen and shrugging off the tendency of admirers to singalong, anticipating all her best lines. I was not alone in remembering the irrepressible glories of 'Hurry On Down' and 'Fine Brown Frame'; to my amazement, a couple of genuine *nuns* sat glued to her every note and nuance. Only in New York, I thought, could this happen.

The city was full of musical surprises. Fred McDowell came up from Mississippi to appear at the Gaslight, a famous folkclub. Sharing the bill was Bonnie Raitt, yet to emerge as a star of the 1970s. Bonnie loved the blues and played them with no little skill, proud to be working with Fred and picking up tips on his evocative Delta slide. She was halfway into her set when she was joined by another, invisible, guitarist, echoing her phrases with long Spanish lines of his own. It was spellbinding. She shaded her eyes and peered across the room. 'Hey', who *is* that?' Heads turned, everyone wanted to know. Anonymous behind shades in a darkened corner, casually strumming the guitar on his lap, was José Feliciano. Taking her higher, lighting her fire.

But it was at Midtown in the heart of the music publishing district that I met the sessioneers and song-writers who had structured the popular music of my youth. I continued to see the older musicians, Buck and Dicky, Buddy Tate and Gene Ramey who now worked as a bankguard, and each Wednesday Earle Warren came down from the Bronx to check out work opportunities on the Union floor, the New York version of Archer Street. We'd meet for a drink, then he'd take me back to his family house for dinner and record-sessions that went on into the night. We sat over vodka martinis with another man at the China Song on Broadway one lunchtime: 'This is Henry Glover,' Earle announced casually. 'He wrote "Drown in my Own Tears".' Another time he was busy rehearsing a reformed version of the Platters and we went by Tony Williams' apartment, the original silky-voiced 'Great Pretender'.

Then there was Abdul Razaq Yunusa, the Hausa diplomat, who seemed to have every Soul record ever released. I'd known him since he first came to London, shy and unable to cook, rattling around on his own in a great big diplomat's house. I'd shown him how to prepare rice and pepper stew, now he returned the favour, taking me to the Apollo in Harlem each week. He'd buy me lunch at the United Nations canteen whenever I wanted, a valuable adjunct to my regular survival diet of beans and rice. He had his family with him in New York, but his wife was a quiet young woman from Northern Nigeria who stayed home, and it was obvious he had been longing for someone with whom to share the sounds of the city.

The Apollo was the most famous theatre in Afro-America, the launchpad for countless careers. Comedian Pigmeat Markham, a huge, shambling man whose catch-phrase 'Here come de judge!' briefly entered the popular mainstream, introduced some of the acts wearing his sloppy tramp's outfit. Wednesday was Amateur Night, when the crowd made their decision known in no uncertain terms. A trombonist would perch on the balcony or hang from the side of the stage blowing raspberries at dubious contenders. If someone was really atrocious, the 'hook' – literally that, on a pole – would appear from the wings to drag off the luckless individual. Most whites would not go to Harlem during this period of racial polarisation; Vicki Wickham, from *Ready Steady Go!* was one of the few who did. For a while she wrote a regular column for *Melody Maker* while working in management, and over the years provided useful contacts and a comforting reminder of English ways when the city's abrasiveness started getting me down. She, too, visited the Apollo when someone like Gladys Knight was appearing, but whites who were there were obviously into the music, and our presence provoked little comment. Although Abdul was an African, when we stood at the bus stop outside together, we'd be ribbed as obvious foreigners. But the hostility that so many whites feared did not materialise.

White attitudes during this period were not only ridiculous, they could actually be pretty dangerous. One night I accepted a lift from the parents of a young white musician. They were headed for New Jersey and I was meeting a trumpeter at one of the clubs Uptown, just on their way. As we drew near the Club Baron where he was playing, they grew increasingly nervous. People stared in at our white faces, and they began to ask was I sure I knew where I was going. I pointed at the club's obvious awning, and they swerved across the street in a wild U-turn, narrowly missing a group of people who were crossing the road. 'Are you *sure*?' they insisted, simultaneously throwing open the door. Hardly waiting for an answer, they sped off at speed, leaving rubber on the road and me in a tricky situation of entirely their making. I could have done without that lift, I decided.

Stevie turned up in New York wearing army fatigues and carrying a rucksack, unaccustomed clothing for her, but hitting the mood of the times just right. Army gear may have been 'in' among the smart set, but in places like Harlem and the lower East Side you had to dress 'heavy' to show you meant business. I routinely dressed that way to provide some kind of safety out walking and on the subway at night.

Our first port of call was Ornette's. Musicians coming to town would check in with him as part of the ritual of establishing themselves, but I wasn't thinking along those lines when we went round to Prince Street to see him. Hospitable as ever, he sent out for some cognac, and Stevie began the process of becoming known as a drummer who meant business. She got to know all the major percussionists: Milford, Elvin, Andrew, Blackwell, Rashied Ali and others. She also met Dennis Charles, one of the legends of the early days of the New Music, who seldom played in public during this period. Without exception they were open towards her and expressed an interest in the fact that she played. There was none of the hostility towards her as a woman that had been exhibited by the lesser mortals who had tried to make life a misery for her back at The Coleherne. We actively looked out for opportunities for each other and when I met some young bloods with a percussion workshop in Bedford-Stuyvesant in Brooklyn, suggested they might like to hook up with Stevie. They invited her over to see them: 'Bring a drum.' She was without an instrument of her own but when she mentioned this to Rashied, who had played with Coltrane, he offered her one of his congas without hesitation. She ran into Beaver Harris again, too, with whom she'd shared tabletop percussion exchanges on Albert Ayler's visit to London. Beaver was working with Archie Shepp who practised what he preached by making room for less-exposed artists to join him whenever he made a recording. Thus she appeared on one of his albums.

At a record-date on another occasion, I was included in the control-room repartee to the surprise of a visiting saxophonist. 'Of course you are really on privileged terms with the musicians, you know,' he confided. 'It's a male world, and wives have got to understand that. If you're a wife or woman or whatever, you don't be jumping in when the cats are involved in something.' And it was true. Women were expected to take a back seat in the music world there as always, and our experience did not necessarily reflect the reality of those women musicians who lived there and were trying to break into the hallowed circles of the élite. One woman I knew played creditable saxophone in the freewheeling 'outside' style of the day but had to give up working with men. Every session turned into an excuse for sexual frivolity. Worn down by not being taken seriously, she left to join one of the first women's rock bands.

But years of survival in the music world ensured that we both knew the score. We automatically knew when it was safe to voice an opinion and when it was best to keep quiet.

It was impossible not to be affected by the negative circumstances of some in the musicians' community. Just as not all the people we met in the South lived in an impoverished way, so the fortunes of New Yorkers varied widely. Most of the musicians I'd known in the past earned a reasonable living. Buck Clayton and Buddy Tate, for example, owned houses impressive by British standards, others busy with session work lived in fashionable apartments. But as I spent more time in the city, I met people who struggled each day for survival. Pianist McCoy Tyner told me, 'Music's not a plaything, it's as serious as your life,' and I began to recognise the depth of commitment that kept some artists from seeking a regular paycheck in order to stay free to create. 241

The Japanese jazz audience was growing and I did some work for their monthly, *Swing Journal*. But I was disappointed at the editor's attitude to the less than 'successful' musicians. He went to interview one particular figure, a 'legend', but felt unable to write up the story when he found his hero living in straitened circumstances. The magazine was shored up by pages of glossy stereo advertising and presented an impossibly bourgeois image of the music. Photo-spreads showed musicians at work and play, making tea or writing scores in impeccable domestic surroundings. Exposure of this kind was impressive. Kunle waved an issue of the magazine at me which featured a day-in-the-life of bassist Richard Davis: 'Who else would do a piece like this on a *bass*player?' But our-man-down-on-his-luck didn't fit into this picture of gracious living. His music had given so many hours of pleasure; it seemed wrong not to give him his due because his lifestyle failed to echo the aspirations of Tokyo's 'Sta-prest' jazz coffee-house set.

It would be wrong to suggest that our trips to New York were without trauma, but we developed friendships with those musicians who showed us respect and found it more pragmatic to say 'later' for the others. As Kunle put it, 'You can only deal with the people you can deal with.' We regularly took the subway to Brooklyn to see Billy Higgins, the consummate drummer at home in any musical setting. Stevie was welcome to jam with him and Wilbur Ware, no mean recognition, and we would take bottles of vodka to party with them, attracting a crowd of neighbourhood women who came by armed with good smoke and an inexhaustible fund of stories of streetlife. Billy is one of the most good-natured people in the business, but even he had had enough of the ebullient sisterhood on the occasion we drunkenly took over a skipping-game from children on the block. Shaking his head in despair, he went off with the other men to do their own thing.

But another important friendship had an inauspicious beginning. The previous year Ronnie Scott's Club had played host to a big band co-led by Kenny Clarke, the father of modern percussion, and I went by the hotel to interview saxophonist Billy Mitchell. He sat in the lobby joking with the other musicians, offhand with me as I attempted the occasional question. My patience wore thin in the face of monosyllabic replies, and I started to bristle: 'Don't you bloody patronise me!' The words were out before I knew it. 'Patronising? *Me*? I'm not patronising you.' 'Yes, you are,' I said crossly, face reddening uncontrollably. 'If you didn't want to do the interview you should have said so. As I'm here, I'd like you to show me some respect.'

I can't say Billy was chastened, but his manner changed and the interview proceeded. I relaxed. It was only a short piece but the subs picked out a line from my copy to use as a head and it came out as 'Prickly Billy'. 'Prickly?' he queried later, feigning hurt. 'Well, I guess I asked for that!' Now in New York, he was in charge of the Jazzmobile Workshop, a project that operated each weekend in Harlem. Established professionals took classes, the musicians ranging in age from 15 to 50, and one afternoon Stevie and I went up there to hang out and take photographs.

On the wall, beneath the legend 'Drugs the Horror Trap', graphic photographs of narcotics abuse jostled for space alongside pictures of Coltrane, Malcolm X and Martin Luther King. Coptic

242

crosses and other African symbols were on display, and the mood of the Workshop was onward and upward. The teachers included Joe Newman, the trumpeter who'd grown up in New Orleans with Papa Celestin and come to Europe with Basie, and Freddie Waits, the drummer, who used a pile of books as a practice-pad for the rudiments in this otherwise modern and well-equipped school.

When the session was over, Billy took us for a drink at the Braddock, one of Harlem's noted oldtime hotels. We drove to his house on Long Island where his wife prepared a fine turkey dinner, then to a local nightspot to hear Lucky Thompson who had just returned from his European exile. Billy was attentive throughout, and refused to leave us until he made sure that Lucky would see us home. 'Prickly' would stay a good friend, but from this experience, I developed the courage to challenge, something few women are brought up to do.

So many of the musicians were angry. Their stories sounded unbelievable at times to outsiders, but as I spent more time in their society I witnessed the most extraordinary outrages that many experienced. Every musician had a family, was part of a community routinely abused and exploited. It was hardly surprising that responses to the most straightforward enquiry could be cynical or barbed. But even in the music press, not normally known for its reticence, writers were expected to tone down the 'militant' line.

To stay in the States, I continued to write. I shot publicity pictures for some of the musicians, wrote a couple of liner-notes for recordings, but *Melody Maker* remained my main outlet. I was fortunate to have an editor, Richard Williams, who shared with me a belief that stories of the lesser-known musicians were just as interesting, often more so, than those of the people who usually got all the coverage. Richard was happy to accept my judgement and that helped my confidence.

Everywhere I looked I came across heroin, eating its way into the Black community and decimating the lives of the young. White people used it too (one OD'ed on the doorstep of the building where I was staying) but the people I met talked continually of its devastating effect on Afro-America.

A friend took me to Harlem in search of 'Frankie Smithers', a pioneer of early rhythm 'n' blues. We found him standing aimlessly in a crowd of hopeless street addicts and accompanied him back to a house where heroin was part of the daily routine. I brushed aside some 'works' from the table, feigning nonchalance, and set up my tape-recorder for an interview. I got the story I wanted but did not go unmoved by the experience.

Frankie lived off and on at a rehabilitation centre, where he was trying to cut down his habit. I went back there one day to ask some more questions and he latched on to me like a saviour: 'I'm glad you came, you're my passport.' He meant he could tag along with me when I left and go in search of some dope.

Asking someone why they use drugs has always seemed to me akin to the way men ask prostitute women why they earn a living that way. It's hypocritical and reeks of smugness for the questioner to imagine that they could never find themselves in a similar position. This time, though, I was deeply saddened. As we walked down the street I could not prevent myself asking. Frankie's expression glazed over and a faraway look came into his eyes. 'To forget the past and some of the future,' was his reply.

Travelling back on the subway some nights later, I sat opposite a young Black woman, an addict, nodding off. On her knee was a baby which teetered precariously each time the train took a corner. The car lurched abruptly and the baby shot forward. I leapt to my feet, prepared to catch it, but the mother held it back just in time. I sat back, shakily, watching the pair of them and thinking of Frankie. I'd heard talk of working for enlightenment and preserving the Afro-American nation and it turned over and over in my mind. This baby represented the future. I looked along the car where others like the mother were stretched out, sleeping, as the world thundered by. 'Wake up, Black man!' the nationalists urged the people in darkness. It angered me deeply and I understood why the separatists called us 'white devils' and others sought to kill those they held responsible for premature death, disease and decay in Afro-America. Harlem, long seen as the cultural capital of Black America would experience a revival eventually; now it seemed on the surface, anyway, a broken-down, exhausted ghetto. 'A rat done bit my sister Nell/And Whitey's on the moon,' wrote the poet Gil Scott-Heron, summing up the inequality of American society. The rhetoric of Black Power was dismissed without a second thought by other jazz writers, but I could relate to it one hundred per cent.

Everywhere I went, Americans were divided by race. Furthermore, in contrast to the country's 'official' image, I found the Americans to be disproportionately people of colour. 'Don't ride the subway at night!' other whites warned me, and indeed there were desperate addicts and others down there who could make it an unsafe place to be, but I saw more Black people returning from shiftwork than anything else. It was abundantly clear from a trip on the IRT or BMT just who did the low-paid jobs and travelled the poor people's way. It began in the line at the Bus Station where I joined Service personnel and others headed South to be with their families, continued on a short trip back to Manhattan from Newark: 'Quit playing that radio!' the driver ordered one young man on the crowded bus. 'Why?' he countered. 'Ain't no white people here.' I gazed out on the passing landscape with a smile. No one gave me a second look. It was the only time in my life I'd be likely to 'pass'; it was just so unlikely someone like me would be on that bus.

Colour dictated expectations, achievement and mobility. Schooling was integrated and the invidious 'Colored Restroom' signs taken down, but the division persisted. When I fell through a step in Mississippi and broke my ankle, I was amazed to find the doctor's surgery segregated, twenty years after *Brown v. Board of Education*. That the music existed despite this and continued to grow in the face of all attempts to dilute and steal from it was crucial. I determined to do right by the musicians, however hard it was staying the course. But just because the new developments had some popularity, it did not necessarily follow that people would want what I wrote. Writers I'd met on previous American visits were unsympathetic towards the New Music and what they saw as the intransigence of militant Blacks – 'They can say what they will about the Uncle Toms but I wish we had them back,' was a comment from one well-established critic – and many people back home felt intimidated by what musicians now had to say. Richard Williams, however, was open to every suggestion and I found another ally in Philippe Carles, who edited the French *JAZZ Magazine*. Philippe always put the music in a political and sociological context, for he'd met the Frankies as well.

What I'd seen in the South had permanently coloured my vision. Looking for musicians would always lead me, literally, across the railroad tracks that divide communities in two. It is not until you have actually crossed over those lines that the true meaning of the expression 'wrong side of the tracks' sinks in. In the South the white part of town in generally cooler, shaded by trees; the 'Colored' section, roofs unprotected, simmers under the beating sun. There is no better illustration of the dual American society, but people at home didn't know this. Furthermore, had they known the reality of Afro-America instead of the music alone, it did not necessarily follow they could relate this to what I was saying. Some were annoyed when I wrote about Americans of whom few people had heard. But what I was doing was relatively unusual in music: attempting to document a movement as it was happening, rather than waiting until it solidified into a safe and unthreatening 'style'. It would be interesting to speculate whether those who resented my work would have had a different attitude had I been a man, for at times I detected a definite sexual inference behind the sniping. It might have been different, too, if they did not regard me as 'one of their own'. Since I was always around the scene, I was a natural target when it came to expressing frustration. Their protests, what's more, were racist in form, taking no account of the history of the music, of where it came from and why.

In particular I remember a surge of anger around a piece I wrote about a bassist called Hakim Jami. He was playing tuba with Sun Ra when I met him, but he was dismissed by some locals as, so I am told, 'an unknown tuba player in an unknown band'. And yet Hakim, without being aware of it himself, was, for me, a teacher. His words encapsulated what the music meant to 'the Brother – and Sister – on the street' in the fiercely culturally conscious post-Malcolm period. Simply because he was not a well-known musician, his devotion to music was more impressive. He lived in a coldwater walk-up on the lower East Side and his lifestyle epitomised the degree of dedication that existed in the musicians' community.

What he had to say about the significance of Coltrane and the philosophy that grew out of the saxophonist's example was a lesson in itself. I learned more from an hour or so listening to Hakim in those stark, comfortless surroundings than I could in a year of listening to records. But the musicians back home didn't thank me for that. There was innuendo and comment wherever I turned, and when I wrote polemical pieces about the continual need to acknowledge sources, *Melody Maker* received letters requesting I be relieved of my space.

I stayed in the States for six months in 1972, most of it in New York. A teacher named Barbara, who was friendly with one of Ornette's musicians, put me up for a while. Being in the South had inspired me to try the guitar, and now I began to learn chords from her 19-year-old daughter, a 'drop-out'. We'd sit around in the daytime, drinking wine and smoking dope, playing strum-along numbers and knocking ourselves out. Stevie had gone back to London to fulfil her working commitments and I started to wander around the Village thinking misty-eyed of the Dylan days. New York suited my style. It was abrasive, sure, but there was an openness and enthusiasm that was missing in England.

I began to wonder whether it would be too late to put down roots there. Living in close proximity to places such as the Gaslight and Folk City made me occasionally yearn for another life that might have been if I'd stayed behind on my first visit. It was a momentary fantasy, though, and one I indulged in occasionally to escape from the turbulent musical revolution with which I was involved for most of the time.

I started going by to see Larry Johnson who, at 40, rated as a 'young' bluesman. He played gospel records to wake up with and give him a righteous feeling, and played acoustic guitar in the finger-picking style of the south-eastern states. One wall of his apartment was covered with photographs of his mentor, the Rev. Gary Davis, now departed; he even had 'The Rev.'s' white cane and banjo. Larry was 'downhome' and rooted, preferring Harlem life to the coffee-house circuit. When it came to politics, though, he was as defiant and unbending as anyone out there. He showed me some fine Georgia fingering and told me to get serious about playing. It was something I never did in the end, for the camera and typewriter had turned into my horns.

19
Higher Ground

For many Black women, the presence of 'outside' women in their community has always been a source of resentment. Indeed, the expression of hatred of white women, especially those who go with Black men, can be seen as a way of expressing hatred of racism. White women, whatever their commitment to equality and justice, have traditionally been seen as upsetters, driving a wedge between people whose relationships had suffered as a legacy of slavery. It was a reaction with which I was long familiar, but which became expressed more openly in the uncompromising atmosphere that developed around Malcolm X and the politics of Nationalism.

The break-up of family that began on the auction block, the shameful tradition whereby white women were encouraged to pretend rape to entrap 'unruly' Black men, these were still burning issues in the 1970s. Some Black men, criticised for having white partners, had left them for more politically appropriate women, but the idea of 'support the man', was almost universally held, going far beyond the hardline separatists. Good intentions on the part of individual white women could not alter such deep-held perceptions, I was well aware, yet as I became more familiar with New York custom, I encountered several Black women who, despite their commitment to varying levels of autonomous expression and action, were willing to take me into their confidence — to a degree. Not surprisingly, all were artists in their own right.

Carol Blank was one of these, a painter, who lived in an area of Brooklyn that ought to go down in jazz history. Situated just across the East River from Delancey Street in Manhattan, the population of Williamsburg was divided between Hassidim and Puerto Ricans. By the late 1960s, though, a handful of adventurous Afro-Americans had braved the empty lots and torn-down façades near the waterfront to set up a small artists' colony. They took over a row of derelict storefronts, and Carol was one of these pioneers. Years before the gentrification that would eventually put this location beyond the reach of those who first spotted its potential, musicians were among those who crossed the Williamsburg Bridge in search of modestly priced accommodation. Coltrane used to rehearse in one particular building; Jane Welch told me musicians still lived there, among them 'Trane's own Rashied Ali and two other drummers, Art 'Shaki' Lewis and Roger Blank. It was here that I met Carol, who was married to Roger, and found another New York 'mother' to see me through when the city messed around with my spirit. Carol was part of a group called 'Where We At: Black Women Artists'; and when I first knew her, painted dramatic canvases in symbolic Ethiopian style. Through her I became familiar with many other visual artists, contemporary and historical. It was she who encouraged me to seek out James VanDer Zee, the veteran Harlem studio proprietor who had been Marcus Garvey's personal photographer, and to talk to Franco the Artist (Franklin Gaskins) whose idiosyncratic brushwork decorates the steel shutters along Harlem's 125th Street. She introduced me to all kinds of 'regular Blackfolk', too, around her kitchen table.

Carol was what Black people call '*down*'. She was never at a loss for a snatch of survivor philosophy, and had endless patience with and understanding of, human frailty. We were around the same age but, unlike me, she viewed the onset of age and grey hairs with eager anticipation. She could not wait, she said, to move into the role of community elder. Physically, she was not the 'earth mother' type. She was skinny and lithe, with dazzling, thoughtful eyes, and walked with a strut that said 'Brooklyn!' and no questions asked. She and Roger were raising two children, struggling with ill-lined pockets, but she'd always bounce back and find a canvas to paint on and something tasty to throw in the skillet. Eyebrows would raise occasionally when I'd turn up at their house during the period when Black musicians were organising autonomously, but I was always welcome there whatever the political climate.

I'd decided to write a book about the New Music, spurred on by Chris Albertson, another European refugee (he came from Iceland), whose biography of Bessie Smith had just been published. Martin Davidson, too, a friend from England, said it would be a pity if all my *Melody Maker* pieces ended up in the dustbin. I began to seek out musicians in earnest, but this time I wanted to talk to women as well, those who worked as singers or instrumentalists, and those involved with male musicians, sharing their lives and aspiration. Being around Carol and Shaki's wife, Aura, a singer from Azania, had a lot to do with this. So, too, did my growing awareness of the way women's contributions to society were marginalised.

Women's role in the music had always gone unacknowledged in written history, although in conversation male musicians constantly paid tribute to those without whose support survival would not have been possible. Clifford Thornton wrote to agree: 'As far as Black women are concerned, I think we're all waiting for some kind of exposition detailing the role and function of women in the music . . . women have been important to the preservation and furtherance of this culture. We know there have been many.'

Graciella Rava, a friend of Cecil Taylor, had interviewed a handful of 'wives and old ladies' for Philippe Carles' *JAZZ Magazine*; this apart, what I was planning would mark the first appearance of any alternative version. The women's movement was growing, but the jazz world remained as conservative as ever. As for Stevie and me, we were teetering on the brink of identifying ourselves as part of the movement, after years of struggling to make it in a male world and really, though we said so ourselves, doing pretty good.

My exhibition *Jazz Seen* was planned for the summer of 1973, but before that Stevie and I spent another two months in the South. Back in New York we took over the Blakeney's apartment while they were holidaying in Blackpool. It made a change from being dependent on others, and allowed us to repay hospitality. Stevie got into cooking 'soul food' with a vengeance, using tips picked up in the South. The 'slave food' once despised by some among the upwardly mobile, was making a fashionable reappearance; a smart Afro-American restaurant, reputedly run by the Mafia, had opened up on Second Avenue. Ornette took me and a group of others there to dinner one night. He ordered chitt'lins which were served up with great aplomb; I thought of Al Douglas and smiled to myself.

Our finances were strictly limited but that was no hindrance. With the resourcefulness that had kept Black people nourished for 400 years, Stevie turned out mouthwatering dishes from the cheapest ingredients; chicken wings, candied yams, corn fritters and buttermilk pancakes. There was Verta Mae Grosvenor's *Vibration Cooking* to follow as well, with hilarious tales of what happened when musicians such as Beaver and Archie mixed watermelon and whisky, a no-no, and a scathing attack on New Yorkers who would rather open up an impersonal bottle of whisky than make you a sandwich. No one could accuse us of such meanness, and the Horatio Street apartment became a regular watering-hole for old friends such as Cecil, Art Farmer and Blossom Dearie, and new ones like Chris Albertson, Frank and Carmen Lowe. We spent some hilarious times, too, with guitarist Sonny and singer Lynda Sharrock, who had just put a crazy band together, mixing freedom with funk and beyond. I bumped into Ornette at one of their concerts. 'Do you think they're serious, Valerie?' he asked me. I looked at him – was *he*? He seemed worried; on the verge of his own involvement with electric music, he clearly wanted to know.

Sonny was another person who helped the various strands of the music to fall into place. To me, he and Lynda, with their wild blend of voice and guitar, Milford Graves occasionally on hand at the drums to take them higher, epitomised the 'You never heard such sounds in your life!' of the avant garde. But Sonny turned out to be a stone fan of street-corner music, who had sung in doo-wop groups as a kid. It was he who introduced me to the *a capella* songs from the vaults by the Nutmegs and the Harptones, gooey teenage material I'd resolutely resisted as I opted for Bird on the one hand, Howlin' Wolf on the other. But the ease with which I, still a purist, was persuaded to play their recordings alongside Coltrane's and Archie's, merely served to illustrate the strength of the continuum, whether consciously realised or not.

That such different styles of expression co-existed side by side was educational at another level, too. Gradually it led me to realise that there *was* no such thing as 'the Black experience', some imaginary homogeneous state of mind. To suggest so, indeed, was a racist simplification, as I once learned to my own everlasting shame. In 1968 I'd reviewed a Supremes show for *Downbeat* and taken them to task for not sounding more 'soulful'. 'Get back to church, baby!' I'd castigated Diana Ross – so hip and so clever, I'd thought at the time. But my heart pounded when I stumbled on those words twenty years later in the autobiography of her fellow Supreme, Mary Wilson, and read of their hurt and dismay. How ignorant I had been in my 'hipness', and how intolerant of the expression of humanity in all its beautiful disguises. But I had to move with the Sharrocks and their doo-wop pals to learn this, with Larry Johnson and his waking-up gospel. The lesson was well learned in the end but it didn't come easy.

249

The book began to take shape in my mind and as ever, I concentrated on tracking down lesser-known individuals who had a 'community reputation'. Trumpeter Earl Cross was one of these, another in the Williamsburg colony. He came up with a quote on dedication that was a classic: 'I would like to walk down the street looking like a trumpet, if possible!' Roger, Carol, and Shaki and Aura 'pulled my coat' to countless aspects of the art of Black Survival that might otherwise have gone imperceived by me, the outsider – 'I want to have more than a bandstand relationship with the musicians I play with,' said Roger, reflecting the degree of commitment to self-knowledge and democracy that I encountered wherever I went. I already had a title for the book, taken from something McCoy Tyner had said to me during an interview. I would call it *As Serious As Your Life*, and avoid using the word 'jazz' in the title.

Chris put me in touch with an editor who was a feminist. She knew little of the music's specifics, but her suggestions for chapter outlines were invaluable. Mary was a lesbian, too, who wore denims and Western boots to the office, and openly displayed a picture of her lover on the wall over her desk. I was amazed, but impressed, and began to feel myself wanting to express a new kind of identity.

There'd been a gay and lesbian centre, the Firehouse, near Ornette's when I was living there, but I'd ignored it. The stand New York gays had taken in 1969 against police harassment at the Stonewall Inn was history but I knew no one actively involved in the latest phase of the gay liberation movement. I never denied that I was a lesbian but it was easier to be 'one of the lads' to survive. In truth, I'd really been sheepish about my sexuality, for when I'd seen women holding hands and embracing openly in the New York streets I'd been perturbed and had turned off, automatically, for safety. Old habits die hard, and I was still just a little frightened. Talking to Mary, we got away from the book, and I began to see the advantages in being more open about who I was. She took me to a women's bar, Bonnie and Clyde's, where women played pool and there was none of that hangdog shuffling that characterised lesbian life in London. I started to divide my evenings between listening to music, talking to people for the book, and dancing at Bonnie and Clyde's – sometimes with Stevie, sometimes alone.

Stevie never missed a chance to play music, and when she landed a gig at a neighbourhood bar asked Shaki if he'd join her on drums. Harold Mabern, whom she'd met recording with Archie, came in on piano; all she lacked was a bassist. She asked Richard Davis, one of the city's most in-demand players, for a recommendation. 'What's wrong with me, Stevie?' was his reply. As before, Rashied lent her his congas, and thus she appeared with a top-flight trio, defying the misconception that name musicians won't work with an unknown singer for Union 'scale'. Towards the end of the evening, Rashied turned up to check out the action. He had cultivated cool as part of his survival persona, and showed his approval by his presence alone, rocking back on the balls of his feet, eyebrows raised in appreciation. Dennis Charles and trumpeter Don Cherry put in an appearance as well, and the compliments flew. My woman had arrived and I was bursting with pride when I saw the response of the heavyweights.

We got back to England in time for the Victoria and Albert show. Large photographic exhibitions were still a fairly rare occurrence and press coverage, as a result, was extensive. Drummer John Stevens put together a band to play for the opening, and Margaretha Charoux was one of the many old friends who attended. She wrote me the following day: 'By now you have woken up after the night before, to the fact that you have made it. A huge success, congratulations!'

A series of concerts was held in the garden to coincide with the exhibition and the photographs were well received. Veteran critic Ainslie Ellis, writing in *The British Journal of Photography*, called it 'A really good example of photography at its eloquent and intelligent best. . . . Rich with good pictures taken with love and understanding.' However, in most other reviews the question of my race and gender continued to be debated more than what the pictures might actually be saying. *New Society* called me a 'girl', to which I responded with an irate letter, cleverly (so I thought then), paraphrasing Big Bill's 'When Do I Get to Be Called a Man? (Do I have to wait till I get 93?)'. But such failure to inspire anything other than a stereotyped appraisal of anything concerned with Black endeavour was par for the course.

Even in the most refined circles, where respect might be assumed as concomitant with my 'acceptance', it was frequently absent. Discussing plans for the poster at the Museum, the (white) designer took one look at the photographs, then rolled his eyes and fluttered his hands Al Jolson-style: 'Where all de white men, den?' Liz Bailey tutted with embarrassment and attempted to smooth my hackles. Whatever Margaretha Charoux might say, it was business as usual.

Elaine Caulker and her husband Barry turned up for the V&A opening. It was a surprise for they were on a three-year teaching tour in Dahomey, (now Benin). She invited me to go back with them when the show was over, and I thought I'd use the opportunity to return to Nigeria as well. B.B. King, the renowned Mississippi bluesman, was set for a US State Department tour of West Africa, and my drummer friend Bayo Martins had written from Lagos to say he was involved. Dahomey was but a few miles from there, and if I did a story on B.B., it would help to finance the trip.

Before leaving, though, I had to arrange a benefit gig for an old friend who was ailing. After years of ill health, Ed Blackwell's kidneys had given up on him. He had been having renal dialysis for some time; now he was considering a possible transplant. Several musicians agreed to perform and I fixed the venue, leaving John Stevens and Martin Davidson to take care of the business. A substantial sum was raised, and other similar events followed.

In Lagos, Bayo arranged for the Americans to stay at Caban Bamboo, a hotel owned by the veteran Yoruba musician Bobby Benson. When they arrived there, however, they were annoyed to find that there was no air-conditioning. The Nigerians, understandably, were upset. 'We thought you would like to stay with the people,' said Bayo. But, in the time-honoured style of Americans-on-the-road, the band threatened to mutiny and swept out, leaving Benson's humble hostelry in favour of a four-star establishment patronised by visiting dignitaries and Europeans. B.B., to his lasting credit, stayed put. 'The musicians

251

usually end up staying in a different place from me, anyway,' said he, diplomatically.

Lagos was not quite ready for the Mississippi blues and B.B. was advertised as a 'Soul' musician, sharing the bill with Nigeria's King of Afro-Beat, Fela Anikulapo-Kuti. At a reception held at the United States Ambassador's residence, Fela, ever the rebel, shocked the diplomatic corps by using bad language and attacking American imperialism. B.B. made a better impression, painstakingly answering questions from journalists who knew more about the Beatles than the blues. He went dancing at Bobby Benson's with Bayo and me and a handful of other music-lovers ('something I *never* do') and whether on television or in concert, made a point of presenting his music in a historical and sociological context. 'Maybe our forefathers couldn't keep their language together when they were taken away, but this – the blues – was a language we invented to let people know we had something to say,' he told an audience at Lagos University. 'And we've been saying it pretty strongly ever since.'

From Lagos I joined Barry in Porto Novo. Dahomey, seat of one of the great African kingdoms, is a country of vast cultural resources, but I was unable to enjoy my stay there and explore as much as I would have liked to. Elaine had decided to stay in Britain and I was disappointed. I was ill for much of the time, too, and with French the main language Europeans used in talking with Dahomeans, I found communication inhibited.

For Christmas we travelled north to Niger by lorry. It was the furthest I had ventured into the Sahel region bordering the Sahara, and encountering Fulani shepherds and Hausa-speakers, was reminded of my first visit to Northern Nigeria. We went to an ancient market at Ayeru where the temperature reached 103°F and people bought leather amulets 'off the peg', then spent New Year's Eve eating roast wild boar and sleeping out under the stars in a place called Tillaberri, where giraffe roamed wild. But it was in Niamey, the capital, that I had another unforgettable musical experience.

Out walking one evening we came across a group of drummers and a man playing an *alghaita*, a double-reed instrument like an oboe. I don't think I even had my camera with me, certainly it was not visible, but the mood towards Europeans in Niamey was belligerent, regardless of circumstance. Our presence spelt instant financial reward, and the musicians gathered around us, rapidly, demanding '*Cent francs*!' with no attention to ceremony. To my surprise, Barry exploded in an angry outburst. He had not learned to subjugate feelings of ego in a situation where one's personal history is irrelevant. He turned on his heel and walked away, leaving me pinned against a tree, the *alghaita* player blowing directly into my ear. Sixteen years on, the sound of that pipe stays in my head, startling, enthralling – and vicious. It was the first time I had come across music whose aim was a threat not a thrill.

I came home via Lomé, the capital of Togo, and spent a few days in Accra with Dot and Mike Eghan. It was a relief to speak English again and Jerry Hansen took me out for a night on the town. I had been away three months but arrived home with only a handful of photographs to show for it. I had not felt up to lugging equipment around this time, but there was another reason: I had begun to question the ethics of taking pictures just for the sake of it, especially in a situation where subject and photographer could seldom relate on anything like equal terms. By using another person for one's 'artistic' ends, it seemed to me, the photographer could only end up demeaning him or herself.

Barry had said something that dismayed and disturbed me. We had passed a group of women selling fish by the roadside, silhouetted against the setting sun, and I'd thought about taking a picture. I'd stopped, though, when he exclaimed, 'The people here make such marvellous shapes!' People, wherever they were, were always about far more than that. I'd been trying to make sense of the music through my pictures, but wherever I turned I came up against the way that images were 'consumed'. It was not a word in my vocabulary then, neither was 'representation', but I felt what was selected to be shot could have far-reaching consequences, depending on the way the subject was viewed in the consuming society. The idea of the concerned potographer was nothing new, but recognising the way people reacted to my pictures had taught me that there was a need for responsibility on the part of the photographer both in making that selection and in exercising control over the way an image was used. I felt strongly enough about this to write an article on the subject.

A white American had just had a show at one of the London galleries in which he depicted Black life in the Arkansas 'rurals', and Stevie and I had been curious to see it. She had begun to take photographs as well, and we were both very aware of the need to convey positive images of Black people, whatever their material circumstances. The show, she pointed out, showed no interaction between subject and photographer except in one case where open hostility was evident. Otherwise it was 'eyes down, shoulders bent, all hope gone'.

She said more: 'I get the impression that now he has done it, he is satisfied with his handy package of images of poverty and oppression and, because of his lack of real understanding of the people, he would not be interested in returning to show a more positive side of life – for example, the way that poverty and oppression are overcome. It's almost as if the truth would spoil his little project.'

The more I thought about it, the more I realised there was a parallel to be drawn between the way my pictures of people like Son Thomas on his broken-down doorstep were welcomed and the way the blues was seen as a music of poverty and pain. It reassured Whites of their place in society and I understood why Black people objected to images of deprivation being the only ones on display. From now on, I decided, my photography would be celebratory. Given the nature of the photographic process, I knew it would be impossible to avoid making some negative images, but, I promised myself, unless these could be viewed in a suitable context, any I did take would remain on the shelf.

I put some of these thoughts into an article, and, surprisingly, *The British Journal of Photography*, a staid professional weekly, printed it, provoking some comment in photographic circles. Some thought I was a little eccentric to take matters so much to heart, but gradually I was meeting other photographers who felt the same way. The language was naïve and the arguments still unformed, but the ideas were ones that would occupy photographers and theorists through the coming decade.

20
Ain't Gonna Let Nobody Turn Me 'Round

In a day-centre for the elderly in Meridian, Mississippi, I sat with a plate of hamhocks and greens and listened to one of the unsung heroes who helped win the right for all to vote in the South. 'I met some children one day and they were beautiful children, white and Black, and they were talking about Freedom,' said Polly Heidelberg who worked at the centre. 'I had listened to radio and TV and I had heard about Freedom. It had got all in my bones and my feet wouldn't be still.' Born in 1910, she had never been inside a school until she was well in her fifties. 'They told me they wanted me to go to school and I asked them, "For what?" They said, "To learn." I said, "I don't have time to be learning, I got to get to *Freedom*." '

I met Polly Heidelberg off to the side of the blues trail. Photographing lives outside music was not at first a conscious decision, but the warmth and hospitality we encountered as we went in search of the music made it an inevitable outcome. That Stevie was Black was an undoubted advantage, but I could never get over the amazing kindness shown me by so many Black Southerners and their generosity of spirit. And the more I plunged into the society which gave birth to the music, the less able I was to divorce the sounds of survival from everyday life.

We hadn't expected to meet anyone other than blues people on the first journey we made through the South, but someone told us about a preacher who played fire-and-brimstone guitar for the Sanctified Church in a Mississippi Delta town called Shaw. An elderly woman dressed in a floral print housedress, hair tied back neat in a bun, was pointed out as a church member, and we stopped to talk to her outside her house which stood in a field of white daisies. She was intrigued to meet people from overseas and asked us inside, a welcome respite from the relentless midsummer heat.

Sadie Saddlers told us she had a tambourine which she carried with her to the Church of God in Christ, otherwise known as the Sanctified (or Holiness) Church, where she worshipped. She had a concertina as well, and a button-accordion on which she played us a tune. Someone had left a damaged piano-accordion at the house and when Stevie admitted to being a musician, Sadie assumed she would be able to find her way around it. The instrument was unwieldy for someone with no experience and was virtually unplayable, but we shared a few laughs, trying, before Sadie suggested a drink of cool lemonade. After a while we were joined by her cousin, a strong, upright woman living across the street, who was highly amused at the idea of whitefolks being in the house with a camera. Her name was Beulah Rush, she was 81 years old, she told us, and had been involved in the fight for freedom in the neighbouring town of Cleveland.

They invited us to eat and they, too, explained later that it was unusual for a white person to want to sit at their table. We would return to stay with them on several occasions, and, although the neighbours were bemused by our relationship with the cousins, they seemed to enjoy our visits. We, in turn, were flattered to be taken into their homes in this open way. In America, Black people had built a nation, and women were one half of the team. It was inevitable that I should begin to pay more attention to what women were doing and had accomplished, for our voice was growing stronger throughout the world. The climate of the times was inescapable, and being in New York had accustomed me to women having a greater say than we did at home. Jill Krementz, a New York photographer, had documented in a book the life of 'Sweetpea', a young girl growing up in Alabama. I thought I might do something similar.

On a subsequent visit I discussed this with Sadie and Beulah, agreeing to share the proceeds should a book develop out of what, I suppose, they saw as snapshots. The Blanches were willing as well, setting up photo-opportunities in church, at Bobbie's work, and with friends and neighbours. Ruby Lee told us that whenever we were in Mississippi we should think of their place as home. But when I approached a white official for permission to take pictures in Meridian schools, his response was defensive and hostile. 'What do you want to do that for? When you say those three words – women, Black, Mississippi – you immediately stir up some sort of a picture.' Precisely, I told him, it's about time.

The V&A show had made me 'acceptable' in the eyes of the photographic establishment, and I was able to obtain Arts Council funding for a further two journeys. I distributed some of the money to the people I photographed, but in the end no book resulted. The more I came across people like Polly Heidelberg, the more I realised that no outsider could begin to picture the texture of lives such as hers. But I had to be there to reach that understanding, and in doing so, met some formidable and tenacious women.

I'd been in touch with a drummer called Alvin Fielder, who'd once worked with Sun Ra, and he invited me to Meridian where he ran the family business, a thriving pharmacy. I wanted to talk to him about his work with the AACM in Chicago for *As Serious As Your Life*, and at the same time to document women's activities away from the relentless hardship of the 'rurals'. Meridian, one of the few large towns in the state, had been a major centre in the voter registration campaign. It had achieved national prominence when two Northern Freedom Riders, Goodman and Schwerner, had been kidnapped near there along with a local young Black man named Chaney, and all murdered for their part in organising local Black voters; they were among the 'children' Polly Heidelberg befriended and who helped her attend Freedom School in her hometown. It was Alvin who insisted I meet her: 'She's for Freedom. She would stand up in the White House and say it. She's not afraid of anything.' At Freedom School said Polly, 'We learned reading, writing and arithmetic and where different places in the world were. Some of us didn't know those places was on the map. Only thing we knew on the map was Mississippi.'

Alvin introduced me to a number of prominent women, but   255 first I had to clear my activities with the Director of Neighbourhood Services. Before this, all my work had been done on an informal basis; now I had to explain myself and my reasons. I found it hard to put my intentions into words and I fumbled. The Director, who was also an NAACP official, fixed me with a disparaging look. 'I don't know how it is where you come from,' he said pointedly, 'but here in Mississippi you learn how to express yourself as a baby. If you want something, you holler. You make sure of getting someone's attention.'

I heard his words echoed when I met Jennie Ruth Crump, supervisor of the town's Early Childhood Education. With an appearance belying her age – she was in her seventies – Mrs Crump was a one-woman dynamo. She used her own car each morning to collect children from working mothers living in municipal housing, for the city provided no transportation. Her dedication brought together isolated mothers into a self-help network where neighbours would prepare children for school when mothers, who were, for example, nurses, worked nights.

Education of any kind was still not compulsory in Mississippi, and Mrs Crump travelled widely to fight against this and other injustices in the state that 'has four 'i's' and cannot see'. She told me: 'When you come from Mississippi no one's going to pay you any attention. You have to grab their attention by standing up and shouting: "Look at me!" ' I thought of the timid way children were encouraged to behave in British schools and the embarrassment I felt when I was unable to explain myself to the Director of Neighbourhood Services. The state might be 'worn-out', as one person put it, the people who ran it lacking creativity, but everywhere I went I met people fighting for whatever gains could be made.

Education was everywhere a burning priority. 'My father,' said Polly Heidelberg, 'died uneducated. Uneducated because he didn't know the value of education. He thought when you knew the horse and the cow and the chicken you were ready for society. That's all Black people knew about – or at least all they *told* that they knew. Now "smile". Isn't that funny? They helped fight a war, build America, lay out Washington. And what about Chicago, Cleveland and California? Black people built all them places.'

We sat on Sadie Saddlers' porch in the Delta one evening and witnessed some pure Mississippi politicking. Although Black people constituted the bulk of the population in the South, political office was still held, largely, by the white minority. Things had begun to change in some places, – 'hands that once picked cotton can now elect leaders,' as the saying went – and one or two Black mayors had been elected, but in Shaw the status quo was maintained. Unlike formerly, however, white candidates had now to ingratiate themselves with Black people, and this particular evening a real good ol' good boy came by with his 'Good evenin', how're y'alls'? and total disbelief when he saw Stevie and me there on the porch.

'I'm Miz Johnson's son, you know, from over in Elm Street,' he introduced himself. 'Why, sure,' said Sadie, 'I used to do housework for your mother. But I thought all the votin' was over?' 'Uh-uh,' the visitor shook his head nervously, 'You was supposed to vote for five, and people didn't do that. Now I want to do the best for the people round here, so you vote for me 'cause we all wants the best for this town.' 'That's right,' echoed Sadie, 'we all wants the best for our town.' She fingered the torn upholstery of the plastic-covered rocker on which she was sitting ('A white lady I worked for give me this. It weren't too wore out and she didn't charge me much'). Yes, she said, I'll remember: 'Make it a better place for ev-er-y-one.'

The candidate handed her his card with plenty of 'Yes, Ma'ams' and 'Now y'all remembers'. Sadie thanked him politely, and stuck the card in her apron pocket. Later that night I found it in the hearth, torn neatly in two. Over the fireplace was another, showing the local Black candidate, clearly displayed. Sadie had done as she'd said. She'd remembered.

Both cousins were impeccable housekeepers, displaying the concern for personal appearance to be found throughout the South. Their faultless dresses and linen reflected a lifetime of washing and ironing to supplement meagre wages from fieldwork, and they were amused by our rough-and-ready style, mostly T-shirts and shorts. They still washed their heavy patchwork quilts by hand and hung them out to dry in the sun, and insisted in wrapping us up each night in one of their favourites, even when the Delta night was sweltering. We brought them presents from England, cardigans for winter nights, elegant toiletries that pleased them. They were, they said, 'tickled to death' that we wanted to stay with them, and we divided our time between their two houses.

To sit down and talk with both women was more than instructive; the very texture of their language reverberated with history. There were Victorian expressions I'd heard from my grandparents, some of which dated back even earlier, words and syntax I later realised were African. Beulah's grandmother, in fact, had been taken from Africa as a child. Sadie was devout, spending several nights a week in her church where the free-for-all expressions of communality and reassurance were profoundly entrenched in African traditions. Her everyday speech resonated with phrases straight from the Bible, redemptionist, allegorical, heavy. She'd followed her mother to the Delta from Port Gibson in the hills south of Vicksburg. 'Mama,' she would say, 'was a *hero* of the church.'

They wanted to see how we cooked in England, so Stevie got busy with the pots and pans. One night after we'd eaten, Beulah told us her story. She was born in 1891.

'I come up a *hard* way,' she looked at me meaningfully. '*You* couldn't make it. I stood at the ironing-board and washed and ironed for white folks all night long. I'd leave the board, cook my breakfast and go on to the field to make the day. Talking 'bout *hard*, I've done it. I used to lay down and cry, cry, cry under the crush, but didn't see no way to get out of it. Just to ride to Memphis or Chicago was thousands of miles away in my mind. I didn't think I could take twenty or thirty dollars and go. So many people just came to the light of it. I had to stay.'

The cousins were as different as chalk and cheese, Sadie always ready to laugh and make light of everything, Beulah deeper, more profound. She made no secret of the fact that she preferred Stevie because she was a 'sister', but that did not mean being less than friendly with me. She was a woman of considerable pride and stature, that was clear, never flinching from eye-contact with whites, something which I'm sure was fairly unusual for someone of her generation locked in the 'rurals'. She looked me dead in the eye as she picked her teeth with a pin, slowly, deliberately – 'These my own teeth, Stevie,' she broke off to comment. Her gaze went through me, hard, searching, trying to fathom what made this 'li'l white gal' tick.

I drove Beulah to the doctor's on one occasion and was appalled at the way she was addressed by the slip of a girl on reception: first name only, the insult made manifest. She was far from well but that didn't deter her. 'See how these people be so *familiar*,' she said, the offender within earshot. Never, I vowed, would I make that mistake again.

A few miles north of Shaw was Mound Bayou, an 'all-colored' town founded by freed slaves in the period before Emanci[ ].tion. The hospital there was famous, said the cousins, serving the predominantly rural population of the region and preferred to nearby Clarksdale for its sympathetic treatment of Black patients. The mechanisation of agriculture had created enormous unemployment throughout the South, with the result that, for many young women, having a family provided the only secure focus for the foreseeable future. The birthrate was constantly rising and the hospital stayed busy. I wanted to photograph expectant mothers visiting the prenatal clinic at the Delta Health Centre – maybe, though I was being optimistic, even a birth. I called the Head Midwife from a payphone by the side of the highway as trucks rattled by. Being in the South had accustomed me to the slow way of speaking; I was unprepared for the sharp voice that snapped at me over the instrument. 'Sounds like someone from New York,' I said to Stevie, hanging up disconcerted. We drove to the Centre to see, none the less.

It would be hard to say who was the more surprised at our meeting. The Head Midwife was someone we knew from New York. We'd last seen her on the block below Slug's. She had been married to one of Sun Ra's musicians and had left the city to get away from the despondency and dirt of the lower East Side and raise her children nearer to nature. In Mississippi, Barbra reasoned, she could be more productive, working for herself and her family and the health of other Black people as well. Soon we were introduced to Pat White, another midwife, who came from Clarksdale, home of Ike Turner and John Lee Hooker. They took us to eat at Mrs Moore's Paradise Lounge from where home-cooked meals were carried out to the fields each day and where a group of confident women played pool in the back. I knew Barbra had not been anxious for an outsider to take pictures at the hospital, but it seemed to be all right now. I realised she must have figured that if I was down there already, I'd paid some dues.

After some discussions, permissions were arranged and Pat went off to check on the situation in the labour ward. Within minutes she was back: 'Come *on*!' and within seconds I was pulling on cap, gown and mask and readying my camera with shaking hands. The first birth I saw took place without complications. It's a cliché to say it but I felt I was in on a miracle. Thank God for fast film, I thought, for I was trembling. I didn't know whether to laugh, to cry or take pictures, so I ended up doing all three.

The road through Mississippi took us to some astonishing places. I photographed the first Black woman to get into 'Ol' Miss', a lawyer, and visited the aged fire-and-brimstone guitarist who told me that he had orders to shoot on sight anyone unauthorised who stepped on the land where he farmed as a tenant. In the Women's Camp at Parchman, the state penitentiary, we sat down in an open dormitory, unsupervised, and talked with killers, armed robbers and dope-fiends, and were invited back there to the rodeo, an annual event. There the sexes were segregated and a group of men in the Nation of Islam, heads tied with bandanas, segregated themselves, uniting only to cheer on likely riders who took on the bucking bronchos and steers.

Barbra said she wanted her children to meet Fannie Lou Hamer, who lived in nearby Ruleville and 'became like a wanted criminal' in 1962 when she attempted to register to vote there. She was fired from the plantation where she worked after being given the option of withdrawing her application or keeping her job. She refused and became one of the most vocal figures in the civil rights struggle, hounded for her political activities and forced to leave home with her husband. One of the houses where they sought refuge was riddled with gunfire. Now her front door was always open and the neighbourhood children poured in.

Ms Hamer was brutally beaten by the police, jailed and then beaten again by Black inmates paid for the job, and she had just come out of hospital following a serious operation, the legacy of years of stress and maltreatment. But when we called to see her, she told Barbra the children would be more than welcome. To me, she said: 'We always were good actors. A white man in Ruleville said to me, "Ms Hamer, we never realised you-all wasn't happy and contented." I told him, I said, "Mr So-and-so, sometimes I be grinning all up in your face but the truth of it is I'd be wanting to stick a knife through your neck!" ' And she fixed me with a look that showed she'd lost none of her fight.

I felt privileged to have had the opportunity to meet as inspirational a figure as Fannie Lou Hamer, but attempting to work in so alien an environment and one so redolent with historical implications and social expectations had me out of my depth. The sheer futility of what I was attempting came home to me when I sought to photograph a friend's mother who worked as a domestic. I wanted pictures of someone who earned a living this way – it was commonplace, characteristic – without stopping to think just how 'characteristic' it was, and why. I asked if I could come along on her job and she was evasive. Then it dawned on me that merely to ask her was being offensive. Nobody *chose* to scrub floors and make beds for a living, after all. To seek to portray this made me part of the problem, not the solution, and I was about trying to change that. I felt humbled, and gradually put the idea of the book to one side.

Staying with the cousins in the Delta, from time to time we'd run off up the road to see Eugene Powell or Son Thomas. To religious people like Sadie the blues was 'the devil's music', associated with alcohol and immorality, so we didn't say where we were going. Ruby Lee, too, though she was not judgemental, preferred not to come with us when we went to visit Jack Owens. The lifestyle and ethos of the blues musicians distanced them from others in the community, making their music very specific while in another sense what they played was at the heart of everything, whether their image fitted the expectations of conventional morality or not. There was some dislocation in dividing our days between the musicians and the wider community and, as we became more familiar with the mores of Black Southern society, there was very much the sense of entering into a forbidden world when we went out to listen to music.

Everywhere we went was religion. It was a shock after the distinctly secular nature of contemporary life in England. Ruby Lee had decided she wanted to be licensed to preach, and we went along to the quiet little Methodist church in Bentonia where she occasionally took her place in the pulpit. Her intervention was not without its critics among those hidebound by convention, but as she pointed out, 'When the three women went to the Sepulchre to anoint Christ's body there weren't any men around. The angel told them the message from Christ. If that first message was given to them, why can't we put ourselves in the right position to be used? Why can't women carry the message?'

At first we just took it in our stride, waiting for Grace to be said before meals, and genuinely pleased to go to church on a Sunday. After a while, though, the continual talk of religion and racism became overwhelming. We were worn out by what we had seen and experienced, and although most of the people we met lived better than their forebears had done, the legacy of slavery and post-Reconstruction exploitation was clearly still part of the Southern way of life. Just the sheer extent of health problems we encountered, the result of years of poor nutrition and deprivation, was depressing and shocking. It could not be ignored, however inspirational the music that came out of that environment could still be.

Blues fanciers would talk nostalgically of the apparent demise of the music and complain that its exponents were not being replaced. But, as Richard Wright had observed in his introduction to one of Paul Oliver's books, inevitably the music itself would become less important as the conditions that produced it improved. This would not, as it happens, hold totally true. A new awareness would come about, of the music's historical significance and its cultural role in sustaining the Black nation.

To us, however, there was nothing romantic about the smell of poverty we encountered in some of the places we visited. It was different when we spent time with younger people in work, but after one of our visits to Eugene, we decided to escape the pressure for a while by checking into a nearby motel. There were plenty of motels on the road outside Greenville, and we went for the cheapest one we could find. As soon as we settled in we realised our mistake. Cheap motels in that part of the world were used for one thing only, and the bed, with its threadbare grey sheets, reeked of it. It was too late to seek alternative accommodation, and anyway, we could barely afford the handful of dollars we'd paid. We had a bottle of cheap wine with us, and I suggested that if we drank it, the smell might not be so intrusive.

We fell asleep to the sound of car doors slamming, and the kind of anticipatory giggling that precedes nights of abandon. The wine seemed to work, though — until the middle of the night. I awoke to find Stevie shaking me, frantic with insomnia. 'They won't stop!' she shouted in my ear. They've been at it for hours and they just WON'T STOP!' Sure enough, through the haze, I could hear the steady thud-thud-thud of coitus from the next-door cabin. Then, wide awake all of a sudden, I sat up. On the wall by the door hung a decrepit air-conditioner, wobbling and shaking rhythmically on its moorings. I crossed the room, reached up and switched it off. 'Better now?' I enquired.

The communal nature of life in the South was reminiscent of Africa, and wherever we went we joined in. I hulled peas on the porch and went fishing, shopped for okra and greens: collards, mustards and turnips. At Ruby Lee's I dug sweet potatoes and looked on while goats were slaughtered and butchered, ate catfish and hoecakes and 'every part of the pig but its squeak'. Bobbie took us dancing at a jukejoint in the fields, showing us off to her friends, and Raife and I drank moon-shine together, conspiratorially. A trumpet player born in Mississippi viewed my pictures later with no little scorn and suggested sarcastically that I might have got a better idea of what life was like down there if I'd had to pick cotton under the sun. To him I was 'slumming', the traditional view of 'white trash', but when Sadie took me along to her church, I was back at the roots of Ray Charles. Music, as ever, took over. It was a far cry from hearing 'Sinner's Prayer' at 16, over the radio, or the majesty of that choir in Atlanta; just the rugged interaction of voices and minds set on freedom at a country prayer meeting, plain and unvarnished. 'Is you feeling tired, Brother Carruthers?' Sadie asked the elderly fire-and-brimstone guitarist. 'It's past feelin's now, just tired,' he replied, but he pounded his box with a fervour which made it sound as Beulah, not 'sanctified' suggested, 'like a freight-train loaded with rocks roaring on by!' The Rev. Genie Carruthers was a long way from being B.B. King, but when the congregation joined in, cymbals crashing together, tambourines to glory, I knew there was no further back in the music to go.

Part Six
Ringing our own Bells

Sisters are doin' it for themselves
       Standin' on their own two feet
And ringin' on their own bells.

Aretha Franklin/Annie Lennox

21
You Keep A-Knocking

By the mid-1970s, the music press had begun to sit up and notice that women were becoming more vocal in popular music, as participants and commentators alike. *Let It Rock*, which made history when it became a workers' collective, decided to devote an issue to 'Women in music', and I was asked to contribute. The struggle to inject a female voice into music criticism was just that, a struggle, and this one only made it by the skin of its teeth. I wrote a piece about women jazz musicians, a breathless attempt to shed some light on the contributions of, among others, two pianists who also composed: Mary Lou Williams and Lil Hardin, she who had written arrangements for the New Orleans greats. True to the short shrift 'jazz' got in those days — and, really, still does — the article disappeared from the issue in question, appearing as an addendum the following month.

At one of the planning meetings, though, I met Marion Fudger, who was music editor of *Spare Rib*, the women's liberation magazine. Marion had just started playing the electric bass, and was one of the few women musicians I knew in London. She was anxious to make contact with others who worked in the business, and invited me and Stevie along to a discussion. There was no formal plan, she said, it would just be a group of women getting together to talk about the ways that music had affected our lives. She was hoping that the singer Joan Armatrading would come along, too. Marion planned to tape our chat and if anything came out of it, might write it up for the magazine. Stevie was out of town working, so I suggested I bring Maggie Nicols. Marion did not know her but she agreed.

I hadn't seen Maggie for a while but I knew she was bringing up her daughter alone and running regular voice workshops which were receiving a lot of attention. I had heard vaguely that she had become politicised, too. It was only when we were on our way that I realised she had joined the Workers' Revolutionary Party and held strong views about Trotskyism and permanent revolution.

Marion had organised a cosy little get-together with two or three other women, among whom was socialist feminist historian Sheila Rowbotham, one of the important local theorists of women's liberation. I had recently taken part in a BBC Magazine programme at Bush House where the male presenter had waved a copy of her *Women, Resistance and Revolution* and said what a load of rubbish it was. I told him that if that was how he felt, then he wouldn't want to keep the book. He agreed and handed it over. I hadn't had time to read it yet, though.

There was plenty of red wine to drink and as we all got to know each other, we talked about our teenage years and how music had become important to us in different ways. Joan Armatrading turned up at one point, but she spent the entire proceedings standing by the window, staring out on to Holloway Road. I had never taken part in a conversation like this before. I was used to discussions in pubs which turned into arguments, where men talked through you, over you, and finally talked you into the ground. I would inevitably drink more and more to escape from the intellectual battering or to gather enough nerve to assert my own point of view. I was not used to doing things the feminist way, with everybody having their chance to speak, uninterrupted.

At one point, I remember, I began talking about Eden Kane. Why I should have introduced his name, a bland and uninteresting ballad singer, I am not sure. I think it had something to do with the way women were attracted to singers for conventional good looks before the Beat groups, dishevelled by comparison, came on the scene. Through an alcoholic haze, the incongruity of the situation dawned on me. Why on earth was I having this polite conversation about people whose music was so unimportant? Something I said lit a fuse in Maggie. Before anyone realised what was happening she leapt from her seat. 'Women will never be free until the people are free!' she shouted, adding other slogans about working-class struggle.

The others were amazed, even Armatrading turned around from the window. I remember thumping my fist on the table. 'Why the fuck are we talking about Eden Kane?' I bellowed. 'We ought to be talking about Albert Ayler!' That just about broke up the meeting. Unheedingly, we had managed to destroy the profitable interchange that can occur between women where everyone has their say and nobody is allowed to dominate the conversation. We drove drunkenly off into the night, yammering on about Workers' Power, Black Power and the revolution in music. We had no idea what havoc we'd left behind.

The early phase of the contemporary women's movement in Britain coincided with the resurgence of my interest in photography and the extended period I spent in the States. My involvement with feminism would affect me most strongly from now on, although my politics were by no means confined to this area. Neither were the sources of my politicisation. Through the women's movement I met people who expanded my horizons in many directions, introducing me to theories I could use to explain my experience, rather than as some politicos did, trying to live their lives according to theory. Ideologies that seemed disparate could be put together to make sense of all that had gone before. It was refreshing, rewarding and mind-blowing, and because it was all about changing, not without anxiety and terror.

From the mid-1970s, events seemed to move at a headlong pace. I became more aware, more involved, and thus felt more in control of my life. New ideas came hard on the heels of each other, catapulting me into new realities, providing food for an ever-inquisitive mind. If time itself is the process whereby the early part of this narrative has been edited, permitting an easy subjectivity about events recalled from a distance, the hectic trajectory of these new discoveries is, I feel, reflected in the pace of its latter chapters. Events are too recent, relatively speaking, for objective editing to begin.

Where feminism was concerned, there was no road-to-

Damascus conversion, no point at which I could say: 'It all began here.' Life was not a seamless continuum, and seeds sown years before would only gradually come to bear fruit. For a long time it was one-step-forward, two-steps-back, as I questioned the nature of what feminism was saying, suffered rebuffs at the hands of the damaged self-righteous and retreated into the relative safety of the status quo. With the learning process came new contradictions, the experience that all of us engaged in revolution encountered. It sure wasn't easy to reject learned patterns of behaviour, for women and men alike had been programmed from birth with rigid expectations of ourselves and each other. To go against these required an effort of will, and trauma was as much a part of the process as triumph.

Some time before I began to describe myself as a feminist, I ran into three other photographers who had been with me at the Regent Street Polytechnic. Maggie Murray was one of these, and she shared a darkroom with Sally and Richard Greenhill. Sally and I had been friendly at college, she'd come with me to see Chris Barber at the Marquee and ended up reading Ottilie's palm, but Richard, when I'd last seen him, had been a kid just out of school in sports jacket and flannels. Now they were married. The Greenhills were among the first Westerners to visit China after the Cultural Revolution and their photographs had caused quite a stir, yet although both were accomplished and established photographers, they insisted their work be jointly credited to help Sally avoid the prejudice that still attached to women who earned their living with a camera. After a gap of over ten years, the four of us started picking up threads.

All freelance photographers suffer from isolation – it's like an industrial disease – so it was a relief to talk with people who shared the concept of concerned, responsible photography. It was good to come across other women photographers, too, for after being thrown into the limelight with my V&A show, I was tired of being seen as some kind of phenomenon. There'd always been other women out there, I knew that – Julia Margaret Cameron was one of the pioneers, after all – but people were still surprised when a woman photographer turned up on a job. Even at weddings, I became used to that air of expectancy, a looking around and waiting for the 'real' practitioner to arrive.

Women in various fields of endeavour were putting out feelers to contact each other, and I became known as someone who worked in photography. I'd become an active and visible member of my union, the National Union of Journalists, and it was indirectly through this that I received a phone call from Angela Phillips. Angela would become respected for her writing on women's health and social issues, but at this time she was working as a photographer. A group of women wanted to put on a small photographic exhibition at the National Film Theatre to coincide with a season of women's films, she said, and would I come along to a meeting.

I'd attended a couple of sessions of a new group, Women in Media, but found it daunting and élitist, packed with eloquent, high-powered women who'd made it to Fleet Street and intended to stay, come what may. Now this would be the first time I'd be involved in anything to do with 'Women's Lib', as it was being disparagingly dubbed by the media, and my feelings about it were mixed. Among many people I knew in America, the movement was seen as diverting attention from the Black liberation struggle. Even among women who recognised the injustices we all experienced, there was a reluctance to acknowledge this while Black people continued to occupy an inequitable position in society. 'I'd be a contradiction to myself standing out there saying, "I want to be President of General Motors," when my man can't even get a job as a grease-monkey [mechanic],' was how Carol Blank put it.

I could not deny this, for it was clear that the American movement had been started by women, predominantly white, who had been involved in the civil rights struggle. They'd used theories developed during the Southern voter registration campaign. Tactics such as sit-ins came out of the civil rights movement, while consciousness-raising, the key process whereby women began to see their problems as common to all, rather than individual, sprang directly from the testifying of the Black church. At the same time, as a woman and a lesbian, I was tired of being trivialised, ignored and denied. Being in New York had made me aware of what women were getting into and producing together, so being involved in this photographic initiative seemed like a positive move.

We met a couple of times to plan the show and then I received a cursory call from Angela. 'We're not having you because you're too professional,' she said. I was astounded. No one had ever accused me of being *that* before. I had started to work for *The Times* as a result of my V&A show, where I had met the paper's veteran picture editor, Norman Hall. He would not have hired me had I *not* measured up to 'professional' standards. Norman was a great encouragement to me at this point, but elsewhere in the building and out on the job, I still had to run the gauntlet of Fleet Street men who felt unsettled when they saw a woman appear on their patch.

I was trying so hard to improve the way I took pictures, to develop a new vision of the world from the lessons of living in America. At the same time I wanted to assert myself as a woman. This exhibition was to be the first of its kind in England and I wanted to be part of it. I didn't realise that this anti-professionalism was a part of the movement's purism and stemmed from a reaction against male standards. It was a stance that would ultimately prove damaging. It dissuaded many well-qualified women from accepting feminist ideas, and for a while, was responsible for developing an unhelpful and unproductive Luddite attitude towards skills in some quarters. But even had it been explained to me that we were trying to devise a new set of standards against which worth might be measured, that we were attempting to create a more egalitarian climate in which all women might participate on an equal footing, I don't think I would have understood it at that point, so great had been the battle to get through this far. All I knew was that I was hurt and dismayed. I stayed that way for some time to come.

The V&A show turned me into a media event for a while. It was summertime, the 'silly season' in Fleet Street, and white-girl-snaps-Black-jazzers made good copy for some. Several hacks made their way to my door and continued to contact me in the months ahead. One of these was Beatrix Campbell, at that time a columnist on the Communist

Morning Star. Searching for feature material, she told me I 'seemed like an interesting woman'.

I knew Bea was a feminist, who had come out as a lesbian at the *Star* and caused a sensation by being the first person to talk of gay rights on a Communist Party platform. It was some time after her initial phonecall that we got together, and when she turned up, with another *Star* contributor, she asked me veiled questions about what we would then have termed 'sexual preference', as well as questions concerning my work. I squirmed in my seat, unsure of how to answer her. The idea of being that outspoken about my sexuality had frightening ramifications for me even then, and anyway, I didn't see that it had anything to do with my work. As ever, aggression took over, and I snapped back defiantly, telling her to mind her own business, or something like that. She was charm itself but I felt quite unsettled.

Another writer who wanted to meet me was Rosie Parker, who wrote about visual arts for *Spare Rib* and was an early member of the magazine's team. She opened the conversation by saying that I probably knew her aunt, Baroness Nica de Koenigswarter, a legendary figure in jazz circles, who for many years had supported a number of New York's uncompromising jazz musicians. I did know her and I also knew that the pianist and composer Thelonious Monk was living at her house in New Jersey since taking ill and retiring from public appearances. Nica kept Monk away from many well-wishers, afraid they might exacerbate his unhappy emotional state. False rumours abounded about his health and state of mind. From then on, if I wanted to know how Monk was doing, I would ask Rosie. Ten-to-one she would have seen him recently and be able to give a more accurate report.

She wrote a very generous piece about me and my work in which I was quite outspoken about the way that racial politics had influenced women's liberation. I told her about staying at Ornette's and what I had learned from the confrontations with Mary, and said that my concern for women's liberation had grown out of being exposed to the Afro-American struggle. I also made the point that many Blacks in America felt middle-class white women had lifted their theory and strategy and were angry. To the best of my knowledge, no one had made a statement like that in the magazine before. British feminists had yet to be challenged about the racism with which the movement was riddled, and indeed, internationalism of any kind would remain a hazy concept in these circles for some time to come. The movement was still in its early optimistic phase, a halcyon wave of women seeking out each other after years of thirsting, coming together to learn and grow. We thought everything could be solved by sisterhood.

However, after my decidedly unsisterly display at her cosy little gathering Marion Fudger viewed me with caution. Whatever Rosie might have written about me and my work, I was *persona non grata* in *Spare Rib's* music section. I wanted to develop my *Let It Rock* piece for a feminist readership but although Marion interviewed Stevie and other women I knew in the business, she turned down every suggestion I made. Where sisterhood was concerned it was clear she thought I was a dangerous reactionary but worse than that, I gathered she had no time for 'jazz'. That, according to her, was the only thing I knew anything about, and it was a subject that made no appearance in the magazine until responsibility for the musical contents devolved elsewhere. When it did I wrote a long piece on saxophonist Kathy Stobart, but most of my contributions after that were not about jazz. Once again I felt that I was suffering from the misunderstanding and prejudice that surrounds Black music, or anything defined by race. 'Oh, you're the person who writes about – or photographs – Black jazz,' people would say (as if there were any other kind), and I'd be placed in that compartment, stifled, unable to expand on any other interests I might have.

At this point the world of women's liberation seemed to me, as it did to many women, like a club, admission possible only through personal introduction. I'd blown mine. It was not until a year after *Jazz Seen* that I had the chance to work on a project with other women.

Having blundered into photography in such a haphazard way, I was beginning to realise I was unaware of some basic business practices. I played catch-up round at the Greenhills. Few photographers are encouraged to be aware of our rights by those buying our pictures; it is not in their interests to do so. Just as when I used to do weddings, the photographer's was always the last fee to be paid, so picture editors, by and large, had scant regard for photographer's rights, fears and feelings. They just wanted the picture. However, as Sally Greenhill pointed out, 'Even now, when people are more enlightened and realise that there's more to a picture than just releasing the shutter, I don't think it does them any harm once in a while to be reminded of what actually goes into this achievement.'

What we were talking about was respect, not only for the people we photographed but for ourselves as well. Ours was still a craft that was shunted to the sidelines unless you happened to work in one of the glamorous areas such as fashion. A spirit of confidence and solidarity grew out of our friendship which I like to think would, for us all, permeate our relationships with other photographers. As time went by, we would be involved in many initiatives to improve rates and conditions for working photographers. The most notable of these was organised by me in conjunction with another photographer, Chris Steele-Perkins. We managed to bring together a disparate band of photographers, some of whom were part of the National Union of Journalists, others who had never made this connection. It was the first time so many isolated individuals had met in this way, an ecumenical approach that was built on later in the union. Maggie Murray and I would go on to start a picture agency, all women. That agency, Format, like the Hackney Flashers, another feminist initiative, had its roots in events of ten years earlier.

Julia Meadows, who worked at the Half Moon, a community gallery attached to the East London theatre, wanted to mount an all-woman photography show. She knew my work from *Jazz Seen* but visible women photographers were still thin on the ground. I told her about Maggie and Sally; then, swallowing my injured pride, suggested Angela Phillips, whose name I now saw in *Spare Rib*.

Nobody said a word for or against professionalism this time. We were a mixture of experienced individuals and struggling beginners and the two shows we worked on together marked for all of us, with the exception of Angela, our first real contact with the consciousness-raising process of feminism. Some who came along to the first meetings said that they could see no advantage in being identified as 'women photographers' and drifted away. Those of us who made the connections began to meet regularly to look at each other's work and plan the exhibitions. The first, held in 1974, comprised our pictures of 'Women' and I showed some I had taken in Mississippi. The second was 'Men'. The meetings were eagerly anticipated, turning into social events where we not only discussed our photography and working practices, but discovered things about ourselves and each other that we had never considered or thought of before.

We began to develop new ways of looking at images, which were layered with meaning. Inevitably for the time, we were asked whether anyone could tell from looking at a photograph if it was taken by a woman or man. We could not have answered that one at the beginning, but by the end of our relationship as a group we knew what we wanted to prioritise in our work and we had developed ideas about women's particular ways of seeing. Our poster for the first show featured a 'triumphant' stereotype, a 'jolly housewife' in the kitchen, surrounded by children and chaos but making a go of things. By the time we got around to 'Men' we were more politicised and more subtle. One of the best shots showed a group of men watching a football game, backs to the camera. Behind them stood a woman, minding a baby in a pram, glancing distractedly over her shoulder. She stood in the foreground of the picture but was left out of the main event, unable and unallowed to participate. All of us could identify with that feeling. New ideas were beginning to take root and soil was fertile.

Maggie, who taught at the Polytechnic of Central London as it was now, invited the Photography School's redoubtable Head along to the opening. 'You remember Val, don't you?' she said, hiding a smile. Margaret Harker was charm itself and mentioned the V&A show favourably. The irony was not wasted on me, but I held back from reminding her what she had said when she booted me out of the Poly.

Our first show created a fair bit of attention and eventually led some of us to form a visual group at *Spare Rib* which provided an ongoing critique about how and why pictures were used. Rosie Parker asked me to write about exhibitions for the magazine and to review *The Unretouched Woman*, a booklength collection of the work of Eve Arnold, the first woman to join Magnum, the élite photographic agency run by its members. She was also the first white photographer permitted to document the activities of the Nation of Islam, at a time when the Nation was avowedly separatist and white people were seen as 'blue-eyed devils'. She had managed to establish a relationship with the Honorable Elijah Muhammad and Malcolm X, then his lieutenant, and her reputation was awesome. She was staying in London and I went to interview her at her elegantly appointed apartment in Mayfair.

Some of her pictures, of women living under Islam in Egypt and the USSR, were striking and a famous sequence on Marilyn Monroe revealed great sensitivity. But there was another series that I found upsetting. At some stage she had run into a group of lesbians involved in sado-masochistic practices. She had photographed them, whipping each other, at what was alleged to be a 'lesbian wedding' in Clapham. Such pictures of individuals who would be classed as deviants bore no

271

resemblance to the lesbian world that I knew – more likely what they were doing was a show set up for men – and I thought their inclusion was dangerous. The Half Moon discussions had developed my awareness of the damaging effect such negative images could have. These, I felt, could only feed voyeuristic fantasies, and things were difficult enough for lesbians without that. We were getting along fairly well, talking about Malcolm and swapping stories about the difficulties faced by women photographers, and I decided to broach the subject of the offending pictures.

The atmosphere changed immediately. Eve went on the defensive, pointing out that she had merely photographed something she saw, it was not a comment about *all* lesbians. I said that it was, for it was the *only* representation of a certain way of life she had included. I felt, too, that it marred an otherwise beautiful book. Our conversation deteriorated, I made an excuse and left. In the event, the story was never used, but this unfortunate experience, especially sad because I had riled a women I admired, who had herself had to struggle against all the odds, and because she had, in turn, upset me, led me to realise how fragile relationships still were between women and how easily our intentions could be misunderstood.

In 1975, the year of the second show at the Half Moon, I was back in New York. By an extraordinary stroke of luck, I had found a publisher there for my long-planned photo-documentary, *The Face of Black Music*, and was putting the finishing touches to what was intended as a visual celebration of the various musical strands that existed side by side in Afro-America. Duke Ellington was in there with Guitar Shorty; the Rev. Genie Carruthers, his guitar 'like a freight-train loaded with rocks', alongside Cecil Taylor. There was Muddy Waters in Chicago, Polo Barnes in New Orleans, Dionne Warwicke and Jimi Hendrix being international. I asked Archie Shepp to write the introduction, then realised to my dismay that few of my existing images of women were strong enough for inclusion.

Vicki Wickham took me on the road with Labelle, the group that she managed, and I saved face with some backstage shots of this outrageous trio. But saving face was not enough. However others might respond to this documentary portrait of the music, it continues to remind me of my own short-sightedness in this particular direction. I'd gone out of my way to shoot photographs with the project in mind, but failed to seek out women whose presence in music was as vital as men's. I'd been as far from acknowledging this as I'd been when I sought out those old 78s by woman singers for Louis Armstrong's trumpet accompaniments. Brainwashing went deep, but the process of unlearning was in progress.

I'd also been trying to find an American publisher for *As Serious as Your Life*. It would be the first book to deal extensively with the new music, and publication on the music's own doorstep would, I felt, be more advantageous. In the event, American publishers were reluctant to deal with some of the radical things I had to say. Much of the book was already written by now, but I continued to spend time with the musicians, learning still – frequently the hard way.

It would be pointless to pretend that the constant confrontation still the order of the day did not create psychological trauma, but as time wore on, developing an increased awareness seemed fair exchange. How I managed to remain physically unscathed, though, is a mystery to me. The city was tough and living there wasn't always a bundle of laughs.

By 1975 the New York Musicians' Festival was an important feature of the jazz lover's summer calendar. Begun as a small break-away protest from the annual Newport event which ignored the less established artists, it had now received funding and grown. It offered the chance to hear many hours of new music, bebop too, in a musician-controlled situation throughout the city's five boroughs. It attracted attention outside the small street community who knew every musician as one of 'their own', but some of the organisers remained entrenched in separatist attitudes.

Getting access to cover events was not without problems. I went to pick up a press pass at a community centre just off the Bowery, a typical SoHo building with reinforced steel doors triple-locked and no bell or other means of attracting attention. The basement, black-curtained, was covered by grilles, and I pulled one aside, without thinking. Three people sat there, gazing up at me in some surprise. And that was all I saw. A huge Alsatian dog sprang forward and latched on to my arm, burying his teeth in my cheek. Too stunned to move, I barely heard someone cry, 'Get outside!' Somehow I did, and one of the occupants came outside to fetch me. I knew her vaguely, the sister of one of the organisers, both nationalists, and the first inclination, on both sides, was to grit our teeth and 'face off' each other. Neither wanted to give in to human feelings. Rover was OK, she told me, he'd had his shots against rabies, and I followed her into the office. From the corner of my eye, though, I could see a bulge begin to appear on my cheek. While my pass was being prepared, gingerly I put my hand up to my face. It came away bloody and I began to feel sick. 'Are you OK?' asked Malkia, suddenly concerned. 'Sure,' I said, bigtime. It wasn't until I got out in the street that I started to shake.

Helen warned me to think about tetanus. At first I brushed the suggestion aside, but as the week wore on, I began to worry about the state of the streets on the Bowery and the possible chance of infection. I checked on the incubation period, ten days, and accepted Helen's invitation to bypass the system. She took me to Bellevue, the lower East Side hospital notorious among musicians for its treatment of addicts. I realised I was in Another Country when I saw the state of one of the guards. Eyes staring, he was speeding. 'What d'you expect?' said Helen, matter-of-fact. 'Hospital workers get all the best drugs.'

In the treatment room I was asked when I'd last had a tetanus shot. I couldn't recall having had one and said so. The nurse looked at me as if I was from Mars, 'I guess they don't do it over there, huh?' Two shots was the punishment, one in the right arm. I began to roll up the other sleeve for the second – 'No, drop your pants.' I did so and leaned over a trolley, bracing myself, just as all hell broke loose outside. The trolley was snatched from my grasp and in the commotion I looked around to see three Puerto Rican transvestites who had burst through the swing-doors into the treatment room, cursing and shouting. One, dressed in orange wig, high heels and scanty mauve miniskirt, carried a young boy across his sholder in a fireman's lift. The boy had OD-ed and turned blue. He was unceremoniously dumped as doctors rushed forward. The drag queens turned on their high heels and split, with staff in pursuit. I pulled up my jeans while resuscitation followed, saline injections, much slapping and cursing, from doctors in shirtsleeves.

The trolley reappeared when the fuss had died down, and the nurse came back for another attempt. Like a heavyweight punch, the needle hit the muscle above my right buttock, and I felt something unpleasant trickle down my leg. 'Oh, *shit*, honey,' she barked. 'Broke the fucking needle!' The process was repeated, this time with success, and I staggered away, wondering who else I might have the pleasure to encounter on my hospital visit.

Helen was waiting for me in Casualty, a collection of bruised, battered people ranged along benches beside her. And in one corner an injured man, his shirt ripped, lay handcuffed to a stretcher. Three cops surrounded him, hands on their guns. Outside it was scorching, midsummer weather. I walked back along Second Avenue in a daze, retracing my steps from that first New York visit when I made up my mind to leave Al Douglas. New York, New York. A helluva town.

I arrived back in London to find my relationship with Stevie was over. We had been lovers for ten years almost to the day, but had been growing apart for some time. It had begun when I'd contemplated living in New York, a move she was reluctant to make, and had been fuelled by paranoia and frustration, legacies of our hectic, dislocated lives. But the way things were set up for women in a world that puts male concerns first was not unconnected. Women's relationships were seen then, and still are, as secondary to the needs and desires of men. I'd certainly not valued what we had. I had never worked at things as much as I might, assuming that we would just stay together, like magic, however I carried on. But a rift had developed between us, and I'd been so caught up in my pursuit of other goals, other truths, that I had failed to notice it widening.

Following the demise of *Let It Rock*, I got involved with Dave Laing, the editor, on a project that had nothing to do with music. The 1973 coalminers' dispute that brought down the Conservative government had inspired many of us who were socialists with its sense of the miners in the workers' vanguard. Dave and I had collaborated on stories before; now we discussed the possibility of doing a book about coal. I needed something to take me away from home and sad memories, and it seemed like a good idea. Working together we developed a friendship that was to lead to my involvement with a new set of acquaintances and to yet another way of looking at music and other aspects of popular culture.

Bob Houston, who first published my interviews with Albert Ayler and Sun Ra in *Melody Maker*, now edited the mineworkers' national newspaper. He suggested we talk to NUM representatives in four separate coalfields, and they, in turn, arranged for us to visit four pits. Fernhill in the Rhondda was the smallest, as yet unmechanised and with a small complement of pit-ponies, Bilston Glen in MidLothian the largest, the National Coal Board's modern showplace. There was

Cadeby in Yorkshire, where management were kept out of the colliery in 1973 by mineworkers holding the bridge across a stream like medieval troops; Betteshanger in Kent was the nearest. All were among the most militant in the country. We talked to dozens of women and men in the industry and went underground in Scotland and Kent, a revealing, exciting experience.

The process took me away from the Black-centred world in which I'd been involved with Stevie and made me take a hard look at my own people's culture and history. I realised that I was as ignorant about working-class history as my friends were of gospel or blues. We met miners who had read widely, who could quote from the classics as well as from Lenin, and people who glowed with pride in their craft as they talked of seams they had opened and coal they had won. We heard tales of tragedy and celebrations of struggle; met women whose homes were glowing and spotless, who had nurtured generations of pitworkers and referred to coal as 'their' industry.

There was one elderly woman in Wales, the mother of the local Lodge secretary, who sat prim as a picture beside her raging coal fire, knitted 'teacosy' hat on her head. She smoothed down her apron as she recalled a lifetime of water-boiling and back-scrubbing and continually plied us with cakes. She was well into her eighties and going a bit deaf, but she perked up when Dave mentioned the pre-nationalisation coal-owners. 'Coalowners?' she echoed. 'Oh, those *buggers*! I'd like to blow steam up their arse!'

We were both anxious that where possible we should present women's side of the story and reveal how they had kept communities going in adversity, a debt which, incidentally, mineworkers were always swift to acknowledge. But Dave was not always too adept at putting the pointed question. We learned, for example, that in prewar Wales, all the young women left the valleys and went into 'service', leaving the way free for others to come in from cities like Cardiff to work as prostitutes. I wanted Dave to get one of the older men to discuss this.

But the subject embarrassed him and he procrastinated. Finally, he promised to try. We were to meet the leader of the longest stay-down strike in coalmining history and it was agreed this would be the day. 'Er – all the women went out of the valleys, didn't they?' he began, when the three of us were alone. 'Yes, that's right,' came the slow answer. 'So – er – there were no women here for the men to – er – spend time with?' 'That's right.' Seconds ticked by. 'The young men must have been – er – very – er – lonely, then?' Pause. 'Oh, yes, that's right.' Another pause as Dave framed the question. And just as he did so, the lady of the house put her key in the door. We never did get a quote on the subject.

On a couple of occasions I was able to meet members of the NUM executive as well as the rank-and-file. Daily the Tory press railed against these supposed anarchists and megalomaniacs who sought to bring the nation to its knees, but as elsewhere in the coalfields, I met cultured and fascinating men. Above all, most seemed to be 'gentlemen', a word which as an emergent feminist I was reluctant to use. Bob Houston, the bluff Scotsman, hired me to shoot delegate portraits in Yorkshire at a Conference on Industrial Democracy. We drove up to Harrogate with the Communist Party's Industrial Organiser and NUM

General Secretary Lawrence Daly, Miles Davis and Clifford Brown playing on the stereo. Mum was impressed to learn I was staying at the Majestic, for she knew Harrogate well. Clive and I had been born in the town during the wartime evacuation, and even then it had been a hotel of exceptional standard. Now it housed several hundred delegate mine-workers, with me the only woman among them.

Soon after our arrival I was engaged in heated debate with nationally known figures over the most unlikely of issues. Houston stayed busy lining up a row of single malts on the bar behind us, as views were aired concerning the recent controversial deselection of MP Maureen Colquhoun for coming out as a lesbian, a subject introduced by them, not me. The consensus was support for her right to self-determination and justice, even if her lifestyle clashed with the personal chapel morality of some of the delegates.

Houston advised me against shooting candid portraits of McGahey, Gormley, Scargill and others, clutching tea and biscuits and supping pints in the bar. It was something I regretted. 'Backstage' shots were a way of life to me and these would have been so revealing. So often the 'hard' unbending side of trades unionists was stressed that it was a delight to see them at ease. Not so delightful, however, was dining out with a bunch of industrial journalists.

Houston had warned me in advance that it might be a 'hairy' occasion, but years on the road with musicians had failed to prepare me for the misogyny of this particular band of brothers. I managed to get through the meal while my host muttered apologies at my elbow, but eventually I could stand them tormenting the lone waitress no longer, and said so. I rose to go back to the hotel, but a 'brother' journalist pulled me back forcibly into my seat. 'Just a minute,' he snarled. 'What about your share of the bill?' Houston leaned across, black beard bristling. 'The NUM's paying for her, laddie,' he said, restraining the man with a bearlike hand.

On the way back to the hotel I ran into one of the Scottish miners I knew and he invited me to join him for a glass of wine. As we sat in the hotel lobby I told him what had occurred and he made conciliatory noises. Then the industrial hacks poured in and the one with whom I had clashed came over to rail at me all over again. The others milled around like drunken schoolboys, harassing a group of women who were waiting for their husbands, *en route* to a dance. These were the people who formed 'public opinion' each day in the news-papers. To think I'd wanted to be one of their number.

Before we left for London, Lawrence Daly took us to lunch. At an elegant restaurant, where fine linen and glistening silver comple-mented a meal as refined as the conversation, the men made a point of including me at every turn. How instructive to compare this with the previous night's outing. I wondered what the 'general public' would have thought had they seen the two factions side by side.

I went back to Wales and Betteshanger on my own, to shoot pictures at leisure and in more intimate situations than had been possible when we had been dashing about doing interviews. We were stuck for a title so we called it *There Was Only the Pit*, after a statement that cropped up constantly. Regrettably, the book never appeared. There were problems with the publishers over the way the photographs should be used, then we were overtaken by events. Abruptly, the picture changed. The reminiscences we'd collected seemed parochial, romantic and dated. The labour movement was moving into another phase with the miners soon to fight for their lives. To bring the book into line with contemporary sentiments would have meant doing a rewrite and neither of us felt up to that.

As we travelled around the country together, Dave and I never stopped talking. From the trade union movement to sexual politics, I absorbed ideas like a sponge. Music was our common denominator, folk in particular. As a 'jazzer', I had begun to dismiss the folk-music I'd previously enjoyed because of its dated Arran-sweater, beer-swilling image. There was a desperate need in folk circles to claim that the music was still alive in Britain when it was patently dead in most places outside Ireland and Scotland, but Dave had an entirely new way of looking at it and making connections. He was interested in survivals but concentrated on the point where the traditional merged with the modern and popular. He introduced me to Celtic-rooted musicians such as Ireland's glorious Bothy Band and the Breton harp-player Alan Stivell. Another music world was unfolding.

When I split up with Stevie I was utterly lonely and for a while saw another musician who worked on the folk circuit. Music was the only thing we had in common, and it was purely coincidence that our paths should have crossed when I was discovering so many new sounds. She took me on a tour of Holland, where she shared the bill with Fairport Convention, and we hung out with the singer Sandy Denny. Then we went over to Ireland.

County Clare has a tradition of concertina players who rate as the best in the world; I photographed some for a forthcoming album. At Innis I met a musician named Sonny Murray. The coincidence was too much and I told him he had a namesake in America, a Black man who played the drums. To my surprise, this was no news to him. A cultural tour had taken him to Philadelphia, homebase for the other Murray, and a fellow musician had chanced on the drummer's name in the paper. 'Hey, Sonny,' said he to Our Man, 'I see you're playing another job on the side.'

We spent Christmas in Kilkee in the southernmost part of Ireland and saw the sea freeze over. St Stephen's Day found us at the farmhouse home in Cooraclare of Tom Carey, another concertina player. It was celebration time and he was joined in a series of duets by the virtuoso Solus Lillis. We sat up close to a generous fire, drinking whisky, perching on seats set inside the hearth. Peat spluttered and blazed, giving off a smell that can best be described as luminous. Mrs Carey sat down beside me to invite us to eat, gently taking my hand in the same way that African people will sometimes do. I was moved. There was bread, meat and tea, which we washed down with whisky, then everyone danced to the radio, breaking off only to cross themselves for the Angelus.

I was asked by some 'cool' jazzers what there was in Irish music which, to them, seemed repetitive and unexciting. It was the first time I had come across living music that performed a ritual cathartic function, just like the blues, only a few miles from my doorstep.

I began to spend more time in Yorkshire, where Dave Laing had moved while we worked on our book. Despite what was only an accidental connection by birth, I felt an affinity with the county and the solid, unchanging nature of things there. The wildness of the moors appealed to me, contrasting with the ever-present evidence of the industrial revolution in all its greatness. Yorkshire stood four-square on the face of Britain, its buildings formed out of huge blocks of stone hewn from the hills saying 'move me if you dare'. It was reassuring after the transient nature of life in London and the insecurity that had built up in me since Stevie had gone.

But being on my own once again had its positive side. Freed from what had gone before I was able to take a new look at myself, to decide what my own life had been about thus far. I developed a greater appreciation for my own history and roots, and gained from the learning. I went for a walk through Calderdale one day and stopped to admire a viaduct carrying trains from Manchester to Leeds. An elderly woman got into conversation. 'How many people died building that?' she asked. It was just as Elaine Caulker had put it; whatever the material achievements of the nation we took for granted, there was blood on each stone. I saw the spectres of the working-class that had made Britain 'great', wasted by the harshness of the industrial revolution, heard someone remind me, when I backslid on my union activities, 'People have died for the right to join a trades union.' I could never see work or workers in the same light again.

We had just returned from a trip to one of the coalfields when Dave had to rush to Birmingham to review the Geordie singer/songwriter Alan Price in concert. I'd known Alan since he played organ with the Animals and I decided to tag along with Dave and Gilly, his wife. We had a hair-raising trip across the Pennines in a hailstorm and were hardly in the mood for music. But Alan soon had us in the palm of his hand. The highlight came when he launched into his rousing 'Jarrow Song'. Just hours before we'd been talking to miners who had experienced the deprivation of the period when hunger marchers left Jarrow for London in 1936 to proclaim their plight to an uncaring south. Alan's song, previously without context for me, suddenly put it slap-bang in the pages of history. His past was there, and it was *our* past. It was folk-music still, but modern and relevant, carrying within it the story of who we all were, just as the blues did for blues people. How extraordinary that I'd been attracted to Alan in the first place because he knew how to play the blues. Now, here he was, the trenchant Geordie fellow, bringing me back home as well.

Through Dave's extended circle of friends I got to know a number of women who were feminists. For a long time, though, I had felt that women's liberation was a club that you needed a password to enter and I was not alone in this belief. Walking into the *Spare Rib* offices seemed at times like entering a minefield. Manners were seen as bourgeois and unnecessary in radical circles, but to me it was as unfriendly as *Melody Maker*, where I was one of the few women ever seen in the inner sanctum, secretaries aside.

One day I noticed in my favourite music paper a totally

gratuitous trailer to a piece I had written about the poet Gil Scott-Heron, as yet unknown outside America: 'If Women's Lib commandos are about to assault the *MM*, we would like to point out that we are honoured to present the works of the best lady photo-journalist in jazz.' I said nothing at the time, although I was a little put out. At the same time, I felt somewhat smug to be singled out for being 'as good as a man'. That, after all, was what the comment implied.

A couple of weeks later, however, there was a nasty little scene in the office. One of the editors made the comment that he could not send a woman on a particular assignment. This got up my nose. 'Don't be ridiculous,' I said, 'you could easily send me.' 'Of course I could,' he replied, 'but the point is that you're the only woman I *could* send.' When I protested, he launched into a diatribe about the hopelessness of women as reporters and how everyone on local papers knew that you couldn't send a woman along to cover a road accident because she couldn't cope with the sight of blood.

Before I could reply that if anyone was used to seeing blood on a regular basis it was us, the rest of the staff began to abuse women's liberation. Most of it was schoolboyish stuff, the highlight being when one of the newer recruits averred that his sister had read Germaine Greer's *The Female Eunuch* and thought it a load of old rubbish, so there. Such, though, was the level of debate that prevailed at *Melody Maker*. It had never been easy to make headway there, but the paper, which was yet to hire a woman on the editorial staff, seemed to become overtly hostile from then on. I missed the days when Laurie Henshaw would rap me over the knuckles for not editing 'bad language' out of my copy.

The music press is a bastion of male chauvinism, and when I got to know a woman who had worked there as a staffer, and survived it, I wanted to throw my hat in the air. Penny Valentine wrote for *Disc*, whose offices were next to *MM*'s in Fleet Street. We'd had a nodding acquaintance for years, since meeting at Georgie Fame's twenty-first birthday party when I was 22 and she a year younger. But until I started going up to Fleet Street regularly, we had never really spoken to each other at length. *Disc* was rather downmarket compared to the *MM*, and I think I tended to dismiss her as a kind of dolly-bird. As I strode down the corridor armed with the latest instalment of the Black Power saga, she'd be sitting at her typewriter looking desperately busy, with shoulder-length blonde hair and mini-skirt, invariably puffing at a cigarette. If we caught each other's eye we'd say 'hello', but as I began to feel more and more up against it next door, I would make a point of dropping in to exchange a few sentences. Eventually we'd become friends and confidantes, helping each other cross the precipices that opened up as women began increasingly to question our situation as second-class citizens.

There was music, too, and Peeve was a stone Soul fan, who'd been taught to dance by the Four Tops' Levi Stubbs and thought that Aretha was Queen. As a jazz enthusiast and lover of blues, I'd actually missed out on a lot of the more popular aspects of Black music. But I'd begun to listen to Aretha when I was staying at Benny Golson's place in New York in the 1960s and he'd given me *I Never Loved a Man* to bring home. That one record had a tremendous impact on me, not just musically but spiritually, too. No longer were my heroes all men, with

Bessie and Billie on the side. Aretha was up there with Ray Charles, opening the door to church music, and it was no coincidence that these two artists should have been the ones to change my life so dramatically at quite different stages. When I started talking to Peeve about music, we listened to records together, and I began to fill in more of the gaps.

Gradually the two of us grew closer together, as we realised how much we had in common, although our individual experiences and solutions differed considerably. But it was Peeve who was responsible, more than anyone else, for helping tie together the threads that would interconnect in my life for the foreseeable future. She was not the only catalyst to show me how to bring music, socialism and personal politics together and put them into a context, and we didn't share everything – I was a lesbian and she was not, for a start – but because we were women in what was still a man's world, we found ourselves needing each other in that way that can only be productive and lead to growth.

It was our connection with the *Let it Rock* team of writers that gave us our first opportunities for serious discussion. Away from the competitive, backbiting milieu of the straight music papers, we found ourselves into an environment, predominantly academic, where we were actually strangers. It was almost as male-dominated as the other had been, but had pretentions towards greater egalitarianism. The writers differed from the hacks of Fleet Street and brought sociological considerations to bear on their analysis of music and music practice. It was really quite alien to us, coming as we did from a tradition of thinking on our feet and making it up as we went along, but it opened up a fresh way of looking at music and gave us a new vocabulary that became useful as we made our journey to greater self-awareness through feminism.

It was not, however, until we committed ourselves to the women's movement and began reading and talking to others that our past and our present made sense. We had no roots in this new world of academia and analysis where we found ourselves, but the new world made sense of our old one. Like many other women we knew, we had suffered from our isolation. This meant seeing our problems as individual, rather than ones shared by all women. We discovered our situation had a political history and, in doing so, were empowered to move onward and upward.

Jill Nicholls, a friend of Angela Phillips, joined the *Spare Rib* collective and I persuaded her to let me write music reviews. Together we would go to hear people such as Gladys Knight when they came to London and it amused me to collect our Press tickets and end up sitting next to the man from *Melody Maker*. Jill was ten years younger than I was and we spoke a quite different language. After years of hanging out with the elders, I was beginning to find out there were things to be learned from younger people as well. Sonny Criss, the saxman from Memphis in Paris, would have been proud of me.

Jill invited me to the magazine's party and I turned up feeling defiant. It still rankled that I had been rejected for being 'too professional', my ideas on jazz called 'old-fashioned', though why I so desperately wanted to be 'one of the girls' was not readily apparent. At the party I bumped into Bea Campbell again and we started going out together, to hear music — Elvin Jones, Smokey Robinson — and exchange political views. The *Morning Star* story shelved since our first meeting finally made its appearance, updated, and we even wrote something together, a Joan Armatrading review so tortuous and clumsy it put me off collaborating with anyone again.

Bea lived at the top of an East End tower block in Cable Street, which had once been the teeming Black centre of London, with forty cafés, gambling and nightlife. Her flat gave an enchanting view of the City at night and it was there, to a background of sodium lighting, the river and stars, that I began to grasp other aspects of political history that had slipped through my fingers. Her irreverent references to 'old Charlie Marx' slightly disturbed me, but I was amazed at how little I knew about suffragism, the trade-union movement, sexual politics and class struggle, and how little she knew about music, Black history, even the place where she lived. I was daunted by the way she could leap up in the morning and plunge straight into Marxist theory, impressed by her enquiring mind. I purchased a copy of Engels's *Origin of the Family* to show willing; she wanted to know about music, so we made it a two-way thing.

By now Angela Phillips, the one time scourge of my 'professionalism', had become a good friend. We lived not far from each other and I would drop in for a meal or simply an explanation of something connected with feminism. Because I had rejected the women's movement in the early days and read none of the books apart from Greer and Shulamith Firestone's *The Dialectic of Sex* (totally daunting), I felt ignorant of some of the basics. I wanted to catch up, as I saw it, with everyone else, not realising that different experiences were equally valuable. Many women during this period joined consciousness-raising groups, and apart from the Half Moon shows I'd never done that. Much of my CR took place at Angela's kitchen table.

Radical feminism, which in its crudest analysis defines all men as the enemy, was only just emerging as an identifiable tendency in Britain and the factionalism around it was unknown to me. Nevertheless, I was aware that explanations I was getting at the top of the Cable Street tower were somewhat more oriented towards socialism's solutions to women's wants and needs than our own ways of solving the same. There was nothing wrong with this, for if I was to identify myself as 'being' anything I would have claimed Socialist, rather than Radical, feminism. But Angela, having been involved in the new stage of the movement from its earliest days in this country, offered a more woman-centred picture. My anger at the injustices I'd suffered because of my gender grew more acute, but the movement's analysis and the women I met prevented the frustration from exploding and taking me with it.

22
We Are Family

I was having dinner one night with a feminist barrister when she suddenly mentioned Peetie Wheatstraw. I nearly fell under the table. A couple of years earlier I would have been hard-pressed to find another like-minded woman who had heard of John Coltrane, let alone this obscurest of bluesmen. Peetie Wheatstraw, 'The Devil's Son-in-Law', sold plenty of 78s in the 'Race' market of the 1930s, but his was not a name to slip readily off anyone's tongue these days. I couldn't get over it for ages.

The predominantly white women's movement was not a place to find kindred spirits when it came to the music. There were feminists who wrote about music, albeit from a different perspective to mine. We tended to hang on to each other whenever we met, exchanging ideas and snippets of information, but they were just about as rare as any kind of women had been when I first started going out to the clubs. The women's movement was primarily about ideas, not the body, not the spiritual, and that for me has always been one of its failings. It certainly accounted for the lack of serious attention paid to most forms of music. Some record reviews did appear in *Spare Rib* and elsewhere, shoved in at the end as an afterthought beside careful analyses of theoretical literature and film. It was not good enough.

As time went by I got to know a number of women instrumentalists and singers who knew about Cecil Taylor, Charles Mingus and Herbie Hancock. I wrote articles about some of them and, in 1982, actually initiated a women's jazz festival, the first such held in Britain. The majority of British feminists, though, stayed antipathetic towards what took place in the world of 'jazz', not knowing how to react to the music on the rare occasions they came across it, failing to respond with applause in the right places. It was an acute reflection of the exclusive nature of the male listening coterie. There were some icons whose names were bandied about: Billie Holiday, Bessie Smith, Nina Simone, but generally speaking Charlie Parker and Thelonious Monk produced no response. No one, it seemed, had even heard of undisputed female musical giants such as Joanne Brackeen, Melba Liston or Mary Lou Williams.

Jazz got classified as 'men's music' (which, of course, it was, by and large), and many refused to listen to it for this reason. There was more than a little irony in this. Those holding this view were not artists with a worked-out separatist policy. Some musicians did distance themselves from the exclusive working practices of their male counterparts in order to play together and develop new methods of unravelling musical problems. A number of these became my good friends. Generally speaking, however, those who were the most vehement in their dismissal of what male musicians were doing continued to listen either to the concert music of long-dead European composers, Beethoven, Brahms and the like, or to run-of-the-mill chart material which was ultimately far more reactionary than the message of love and hope for which jazz music stood.

But I hadn't realised how prejudiced I was myself when it came to what women musicians had to say. The lessons of the early days went deep. I'd been living with a woman musician who was exceptional, but I related to her work on what was really a most personal level. In the back of my mind I relegated the majority of women to an essentially supportive role. Being supporting, after all, was what we had all been brought up to be. It took me quite a while to get over the notion that men were destined to be the keepers of the musical flame.

As women we write books about male endeavour in preference to women's and I was no exception. So educated are we to undervalue our own activities that we'll catch ourselves asking, 'When are the real characters coming on?' when watching a film where women take the leading roles. It was hardly surprising that for years my work dealt almost exclusively with men's activities. Indeed, in many instances I had to force myself to write about what women were doing, feeling it was something I ought to do rather than having any passionate commitment to pursuing a feminist goal. It was hard in the 1970s, and sometimes still is, to break the habits of a lifetime.

Committed as I was to jazz and the cause of Black music in general, I found myself in an ambivalent position when it came to the sounds that dominated the lives of other, younger, people who increasingly became part of mine. My relationship with pop music was complex. It would be pointless to deny that I ever listened to rock 'n' roll, indeed my first lesbian experience took place to the strains of 'Be-Bop-A-Lula' and 'Elvis' 'Good Luck Charm', records that I and my schoolfriends continued to play together into our twenties. But from the late 1960s onwards, I no longer wrote about popular music and my focus began to change. Engrossed as I became in the philosophy and politics of people such as Cecil Taylor and Archie Shepp, there seemed to me something second-rate about most popular music. Any deeper meaning that might be there was hidden by adopting this view. Even in feminist circles, my élitism hampered me. I didn't even listen to Joan Armatrading for ages, even though I had a passing acquaintance with her and was intrigued to see her become an artist of note. Joan was the idol of nearly all the women I got to know in the 1970s but it was not until I became involved with someone who played her records to wake up to that I began to appreciate her soul and originality.

As the decade wore on, the link between music and politics was becoming more widely debated. Punk, out to shock, provided an anarchic challenge to existing musical methodologies, and a group of interested parties including the band Henry Cow and some of the *Let It Rock* critics began meeting, inspired by the lively new atmosphere. They formed a talking shop, Music for Socialism, aimed at cementing the relationship between politics and various musics in ways that could be both productive and popular.

In 1977, the year that Allison and Busby published *As Serious as Your Life*, I found myself tagging along with Peeve to a series of Music for Socialism concerts, workshops and debates held over a weekend at Battersea Arts Centre. Peeve, who was now freelancing for *Street Life* after a spell with a record company, had for some time been involved with Mike Flood Page, another journalist; he, with fellow *Let It Rock*-ers Dave Laing, Gary Herman and Ian Hoare, was one of the driving forces behind the organisation. To us, though, the level of discussion was rather earnest and tedious, and we sought refuge in the bar together with others bemused by something at odds with their idea of fun. The uncomfortable alliance between disparate thinkers, élitists and folkies, Soul buffs and punks, would finally falter and be eclipsed by the rise of the campaigning Rock Against Racism, but getting to know the people behind it represented another important step for me in making sense of the music.

For the first time I heard music associated with semiotics and signifiers, heard talk about Althusser, Barthes and Lacan and the 'meaning of meaning'. It was well over my head at first, but to discover that such analysis existed was enabling, marking the beginning of my more self-conscious exploration of music's function. I'd sensed it instinctively, intuitively, before, knew that Black music meant something other to me than it did in the society whose arm it had strengthened and stayed. Now, I started to see the whole construction of something called 'jazz' as essentially European-oriented, permitting little deviation from an established view. In many ways it was a total lie. Little that had been written about it, believed, bore much resemblance to any African–American reality.

The New Left now expressed an interest in what women were saying and doing and Maggie Nicols, who was never far away from any radical happening, began to crop up at the alternative events I attended. A new group called FIG (Feminist Improvising Group) made its debut at a Music for Socialism concert at the Almost Free in Rupert Street and there was Maggie, singing alongside one of the Henry Cow members, composer and multi-instrumentalist Lindsay Cooper. Shortly afterwards, when both women appeared in another line-up during the first Women's Festival held at the Drill Hall, I wrote about it in *Melody Maker*. Some of my photographs from Mississippi were shown at the Festival, a lively event, and inspired by this new sense of 'women together', I was raring to go.

Maggie worked with a new band called Ova for a period, too, and I reviewed a gig where they appeared alongside a new trio that Stevie had formed. Despite the open hostility shown to feminist endeavour elsewhere in the *MM*, the fact that I was a respected writer on music allowed my commentary to slip through the censorial net. It was good to see women who had achieved recognition in the jazz world choosing to play for other women at these events. Maggie in particular had kept the faith in so many ways when it didn't seem as if there were many believers. It had been a struggle for both her and Stevie to keep their real identity intact in the face of overwhelming pressure to conform as though all was well in the male-dominated field of endeavour they'd chosen, and to pretend that being a lesbian 'just happened'. But this side of our lives was important. Just having them on hand, and getting to know so many other women musicians was good for me, too.

And yet although mainstream visibility of feminism was growing, the music papers would be obstructive to anyone who attempted to present the feminist view, men included, for some time to come. Earlier on, when women's liberation was still a curiosity, *Melody Maker* had found some space for women's voices, albeit as channelled by men. Michael Gray, another of the *Let It Rock* team, wrote a provocative three-part series on 'Women in Rock', in which he quoted from Sheila Rowbotham and others, relying heavily on questions that women were beginning to discuss with each other; a later panel discussion included Marion Fudger. But to the best of my knowledge, my little 'Caught In the Act' reviews marked the first incursion that anyone calling herself a feminist made into the popular music press.

The Drill Hall concert left many women at a loss. It was a freewheeling, improvised piece, played by forthright musicians who obviously knew their instruments. But the 'free music' idiom was unknown to most of the audience, and unease and uncertainty were expressed about whether, being so 'inaccessible', theirs was an élitist concept. It was bitterly frustrating for the musicians involved to be rejected this way. Most of them had a history of struggle against male refusal to allow them a place on the bandstand. Now, having shown that not only could they play their instruments but were equipped to handle the most demanding of concepts, they were under attack from the quarter where they most needed friends.

It was an ironic situation and my sympathy went out to them, even when I was sometimes out of sympathy with the music itself. FIG's attempts to incorporate 'the sounds of women's work into a work of women's sounds', Lindsay Cooper's description of a piece which used cake-whisk, hairdryer and vacuum-cleaner, did not necessarily endear it to me when I yearned for the dramatic lovecry of Albert Ayler or the double-clutching drumbeat of a New Orleans parade.

Women during this period were looking for a music they could call their own. The 'cock-rock' of the popular bands was rejected out of hand and male solo singers, whether in the Rock or Soul arena, became seen as oppressive. However much they enjoyed the Rolling Stones' funky blues rhythms, no liberated woman wanted to hear about 'Under My Thumb'. New heroines were on the agenda, but the tough, cool Chrissie Hynde, the ambiguous Annie Lennox and punk's agents of style had yet to emerge. In 1977 the choice lay between folk-music and Janis Joplin. Janis was a bit of a problem. It was an acute embarrassment to any of us with a wider knowledge of music to have to keep silent when 'our' leading cult figure was being praised. Not only was Janis a hit-and-miss 'screamer', she was an unashamed coloniser of Black women's material. To this day, most white people seem to think she wrote Big Mama's Thornton's 'Ball and Chain' and Erma Franklin's 'Piece of my Heart'. With women such as Sarah Vaughan or Bessie Smith in the pantheon, it seemed reactionary to espouse what she was doing.

We did not stop to think how inordinately lucky we might be, considering our cultural background, to have even heard people like Sarah, Aretha and Ella Fitzgerald, let alone the dozens of 'unknown' singers whom, in my case, my travels had allowed me to hear in church, night club and bar-room. Most women could only go by what was on offer, and if Janis was what was available, well, at least she was stroppy. 285

It was ironic, though, that she should have been loved for qualities condemned in others. Being aggressive on the bandstand was seen as 'masculine' in some circles and challenged an attitude that left many passionate women musicians out in the cold. After her death, too, things became really tacky, when women sold her to each other as a tragic heroine snared by society's expectations of the ordinary woman. She was taken up, shaken, and pressed to the communal breast like the bittersweet memory of Billie. Still (to my dismay) a purist, I found it unpalatable.

I was lying in bed one day with a temperature when the phone rang. It was Jill Nicholls. 'Quick, grab your camera!' she said. 'We're going down to Fleet Street to protest at the *Evening News*.' I was feeling dreadful but adrenalin fuelled me. It was the kind of moment for which I'd been waiting for years. Nobody asked me to go on news stories; now I was in on one of our own.

The *Evening News* had discovered a doctor prepared to help lesbians conceive by artificial insemination by donor (AID). A woman reporter had been dispatched to act the role of a lesbian who wanted a baby, and she had come back with a seamy piece aimed at prurient readers. Worse than this, though, the paper had uncovered the identities of some female couples raising AID children and photographed them. An attempt to take out an injunction to prevent the pictures being published was unsuccessful. A number of women were enraged by this damaging abuse of privacy and a plan of action was hastily hatched. A sympathetic reporter made an appointment to see the editor under a pretext, and the protestors followed her in.

I found the demonstrators on their way into the building. They were an assorted crowd, a few men in their number, some women were lesbians, some not. All were angry. They refused to leave when asked to do so and sat down, demanding to see the editor. The police were called but left when he agreed to a meeting. I was standing on a chair by a desk to take pictures when it was tipped up, without warning, and I saw desk and typewriter coming to meet me. I rounded on the journalist who had done this and was met with a torrent of abuse that questioned my gender. I was shaking with rage and challenged his action, and a minor scuffle ensued. Insulting comments reverberated around the newsroom before the main action adjourned to the lobby. There the demonstators confronted the editor-in-chief, presenting him with a series of hastily compiled demands. To the surprise of everyone, a right of reply was granted, and I made the back page of the *Guardian* as an unnamed statistic: 'A photographer was thrown from a chair.' A threatening crowd of Fleet Street workers gathered outside the building before the demonstration dispersed. As I stood in the lobby talking to a fellow photographer, a gobbet of spit dropped from the stairway above on to my head. I grabbed the editor in protest and he was deeply embarrassed. Although 'Lesbians Reply' sold newspapers, there had been no real need for him to grant this right of reply: it was the first ever, making history and setting a precedent for subsequent action. Nevertheless, any illusions I had about wanting to break into the mainstream media vanished in that moment of homophobia. I was surprised to see several women I knew to be straight, wearing lesbian badges, supportively. That gay people suffered discrimination was something all of *us* knew, but the specific way lesbians were reviled came as a shock to many women previously uncommitted and indifferent to what our lifestyle actually meant in practice. 'What you do in private should be your own business,' was the liberal view, but as one woman put it: 'For what I do in private I lose my job, I lose my children. Therefore I have no privacy and so I must speak as a lesbian.' From then on I became involved in several similar actions, sometimes as participant, sometimes photographer. It was time to stand up and be counted.

Prominent among those at the *Evening News* demonstration was a tough, no-nonsense Australian named Carole Spedding. I was filled with admiration at the way she had challenged the editor, standing up to him with just the right amount of diplomacy to make sure we got what we wanted. Her humour, which should have pointed the way to the form other action might take but failed to catch on, surprised other hardliners opposed to this kind of behaviour. But it won his respect. I wished I could have mustered that kind of resourcefulness as I stood snivelling with a raging temperature and anger and shouted back at my assailant. She worked at *Spare Rib*, too, and I gave her a lift back to the office, discovering, to my surprise, that she had a background in jazz. As a teenager in Adelaide Carole had started a jazz club and was befriended by Louis Armstrong and Lucille, his wife. We went to hear music together and at a memorable session at Dingwall's, joined forces with Penny Valentine to cheer on the redoubtable Etta James, whose songs had influenced a generation of British blues bands. I wrote about Etta's raunchy performance in a way that was a bit too near the knuckle for some *Spare Rib* readers, but now with Carole in charge of music reviews, I had someone in my corner who was familiar with where the music came from and had a handle on what its exponents were actually saying. I had found a new forum for self-expression which helped me look inside myself, too, and grow. Carole came with me to a story on rhythm-and-blues veteran Bo Diddley for the *Observer*, flirting lightly with him as custom demanded. In his new, spangled shirt, she said he looked 'pretty', and he was delighted. So was I, to find another woman who could speak the blues language.

Peeve had begun writing for *Melody Maker*, too, now, and with Carole we became a redoubtable team whenever we met. Dusty Springfield came back from America to sing for her new women's audience, and the newspapers beavered away, trying to discover why she had been out of the picture so long. Dusty inspired the protective instinct, and at a predominantly male press conference, Peeve and I sat in a row with other like-minded women, giving encouraging shouts of support in an attempt to avert the unfriendlier queries – much to the astonishment of 'straight' writers we worked with elsewhere. Being together with sisters in situations like this was novel for me and exciting; banded together, we thought we were something else.

Lindsay Cooper reviewed *As Serious as Your Life* for *Spare Rib*, applauding the space, limited though it was, devoted to women musicians. Her attitude contrasted with those male writers who took me to task elsewhere for being insufficiently 'feminist'. It was true that I

287

had dwelt on women's supportive rather than parpicipatory contribution, but as someone pointed out, jazz wasn't exactly a feminist area of endeavour. Many's the time I have wished since that I could rewrite that particular part of the book with a more thorough analysis of women's position. It was an intervention, though, and by and large, the response to *As Serious* was positive. Trumpeter Leo Smith called it 'A Great Black book' in a review, and other American musicians I knew wrote to thank me, some, well aware of just how much they owed their survival to women, commending me for giving credit where it was long overdue. I was warmed by their positive reception, especially as I knew there would be others who would attack me for bringing personal politics into the artistic arena and diverting attention, in their view, from the everyday struggle against racial injustice. I was quoted and interviewed, on radio and in the press, and invited to talk on Black music during a seminar organised by the Communist Party. Nervous and unsure how to handle this, I asked Ian Hoare, who had edited an insightful book about Soul, to help me out. On the same platform a drummer I knew called Josefina Cupido was talking about Women's Music. Ian played the Temptations' incantatory 'Message to a Black Man' which said more about the strength of the music in six minutes flat than all of our tentative theorising. It had the impact and power of a riff by James Brown, the passion and profoundness of a Coltrane exploration. Josefina and I sat back, stunned and startled. This was music from the heart, thrust into the commercial arena. The Marxists in search of a handle on popular culture did not know quite what had hit them.

A new world was opening up, where we thought, like fools, that the bigotry of the past would dissolve in the face of our enthusiasm for universal justice and understanding.

I sold my pictures from the *Evening News* demo to *Time Out*, which had used my music pictures since its humble beginnings as a foldover sheet listing London events. I had worked for them as a photographer in the past, but now I had proved my worth under pressure, I was given assignments where I rubbed shoulders with other 'Lefty' photographers and got myself bloodied and bruised. There was the long-running industrial dispute at Grunwick's, and the first 'Reclaim the Night' when women like Maggie Nicols marched through Soho to protest at sexual harassment on the streets, flaming torches aloft, and Angela Phillips was floored by a policeman. When the National Front staged a provocative march through Lewisham, they met with a significant show of resistance. The police lined up alongside the fascists, protecting them from the hail of missiles that rained down on them from protestors, and I was hit on the head by a flying dustbin lid. I swayed and saw stars but carried on taking pictures. I understood how photographers work in the firing line, something I'd always pondered since being enthralled by McCullin and by Capa's *Images of War*. It's an automatic reaction inspired by familiarity with one's instrument and the procedure; you carry on doing it until you have the chance to stop and consider. Then, believe me, you don't feel so good. I had a headache for days.

Time Out and *Spare Rib* began to credit me 'Val'. That was what my friends called me, after all; 'Valerie' was the name my mother used when she was angry. I thought the name-change suited my new, free-wheeling feminist persona; at least it was preferable to calling myself 'Sybilchild', replacing father's last name with mother's as some women had done. Richard Williams was now editing *Time Out* and I began to write for the magazine, too, ending up for the occasional week in the newsroom as a reporter. It struck me one day that this was what I'd always wanted. The typewriter and cigarette were there, only the green eye-shade was missing. I stopped to consider a moment: how did it feel? It was all right, I told myself, grinning, just twenty years too late.

The dispute at the Grunwick photo-processing plant in Willesden was a pivotal *cause célèbre* on a number of fronts. Not only was it the first occasion the trades union movement put its strength behind a predominantly female workforce, it was the first time that Asian women entered the public eye. There had been other industrial action involving this low-paid section of the community before, but now a handful of Gujerati women and men fighting for union recognition were regularly thrust into the news. The picket-line became almost like a pilgrimage for many photographers with a socialist conscience, and I made several early-morning trips to honour the small group of women taking on the might of the establishment as casually as if they were cooking breakfast.

The Day of Action which brought 15,000 out on to the streets in their support was breathtaking in its magnitude and defiant spirit. Peeve and Mike Flood Page came with me to join the regular crowd of demonstrators swelled by trades unionists and other supporters of every persuasion, blocking all access routes to prevent scab labour from getting into the plant. In one direction the main road curved steeply upwards towards Central London. It was solid with demonstrators who refused to budge, and at one point a group of police on horseback appeared over the hill in an attempt to disperse them. Silhouetted against the skyline, they looked, as Peeve put it, like a scene from an Eisenstein movie. There was no escaping the dramatic nature of the occasion.

Drawing breath away from the crush of the crowd, we sat on a wall outside a garage, talking with Pratibha Parmar, a Gujerati woman I knew from Bradford who would become a close friend. (Three years later when she organised the First Asian Girls Festival in Leicester, she asked me to be the official photographer.) Then, with a shout of 'Here they come!' a contingent of Kent miners, some of whom I recognised from my visits to Betteshanger, marched down the street, heads, banners and fists held high. There was a feeling that we were unstoppable.

Wherever I turned I saw familiar faces; Lindsay Cooper in there, tussling, supporting a cause that had enraged working people throughout the country. But the face of protest was changing, and when Yorkshire mineworkers' President Arthur Scargill rallied a group, 'Come on, lads!', the cry 'And lasses!' came from the crowd. 'There's no lasses down the pit!' was his immediate, patronising rejoinder, but there were many among the faithful for whom that rankled.

At times it seemed that people forgot whose struggle Grunwick's actually was; certainly, once the streets of Willesden were clear the media completely ignored the women they'd used as icons in news bulletins. But Jayaben Desai, the dispute's nominal leader, had a particular style of reasoned defiance which would have a significant effect on the way Asian women were viewed in the general community. When Peeve, now ensconced at *Time Out* herself, suggested I interview Desai one year on from the strike. I was flattered to have the opportunity. I found her as resolute as ever, despite damaged health. And, she explained, the example set by her and her striking comrades had had important ramifications among people from the sub-continent. Not only had new ideas arisen about the distribution of domestic labour as a result of women's involvement, the struggle was seen as an affirmation of Asian potential in terms of labour power.

For a while I was caught up in a headlong love affair with the alternative media. *Time Out* employed a significant proportion of women, and although not all of them would have called themselves feminists, an understanding existed between us. The movement's ideas were fresh and spoke of freedom, and certain expectations of equality and justice were formed. The men, for the moment, fell into line.

This period, from around the middle 1970s to the end of the decade, was one of great change for all women, but particularly those of us who had struggled to survive in a 'man's world'. However much we might have champed at the bit, there were none of us who had not found ourselves forced to collude with the system that held us back and trivialised our endeavour. Survival had been the main thing, but gradually a new awareness of self was emerging. But however we might think about ourselves at this point, the past would not go away just because we willed it. We might have declared ourselves eager to put women first, but the accommodationist strategies of former times could catch up with us at the most inappropriate moments.

When I first began to think of myself as a writer with something to say about music, the 'quality' men's magazines such as *Playboy* provided a market for writers who dealt with more than matrix numbers and historical fact. Hoppy and I sold our Thelonious Monk interview to one of these 'glamour' publications; it seemed like a sophisticated outlet at the time. Later, a man I knew got a job with a group that published some of these soft-porn showcases. He asked me to write a regular jazz column and I agreed. Nat Hentoff wrote for *Playboy*, after all; I could see no contradiction in what I was doing.

But situations and consciousness can change quite dramatically in a short space of time. Take *Spare Rib*, for example. Its first issues featured interviews with people like George Best, the footballer, and, to advertise an article on secretaries, had a cover shot of Marion Fudger, sitting on comedian John Cleese's knee. Nevertheless, I was deeply embarrassed around the time I began to work for the magazine to receive a call from another journalist who had found a home with the 'leisure' group, now decidedly 'hard-core' rather than 'glamour'. I had known him since my earliest days on the music scene and he had uncovered my record reviews in back issues. I remembered my brother reminding me, somewhat mischievously, that everything I'd ever written was on file at the British Library, and I groaned inwardly when he suggested I consider reviving my column. When I refused, he switched to another tack: 'What about your photography? I was thinking it might be fun to have a girl photographing girls.' No, no, I stammered abruptly, I didn't want to do that.

'Why not?' he insisted. 'We usually spend a weekend away with the models, lots of food and booze, having fun. You'd enjoy it.'

No, I said, I couldn't do that. It wouldn't be politically appropriate.

'Politically?' he echoed. 'Appropriate? What happened to that jolly, fun-loving girl I used to know?'

'She grew up!' I told him, putting the phone down with a firmness that surprised even me.

Feminism made me look at the world so differently. For a while I got involved with another journalist named Sally Bradbery; we went to Paris together and saw a major exhibition of paintings by Picasso. 'Look how he hates women,' she said. I took a fresh look and saw she was right. His figures were dissected and brutalised in the name of art, cut up into segments and ravished. No Degas or Toulouse-Lautrec he, painters who revealed their admiration for women with each appreciative brushstroke. It was not hard to believe, hearing about it later, that he could stub out a cigarette on his lover's cheek.

The women's movement introduced ideas about power and personal relationships we never dreamed about as we lurched to our destiny down the stairs at the Gateways, but it was hard to put the habits of a lifetime behind you. 'It's not easy being a revolutionary,' Jill Nicholls had said, half serious, half joking, at my 'incompetence' with new ways of being. And yet how could someone ten years my junior appreciate the times that women like me had lived through? The situation had changed so rapidly and suddenly, and yet here were all these confident, politicised women, telling elder sisters what to do. Few revolutionary movements are without their downside, and the intolerance that some women exhibited towards each other was a new kind of dues-paying it was hard to confront.

The Gateways encouraged the ghetto mentality among lesbians. But, although ghettoes are places where society forces minorities rather than places they themselves have chosen in which to be separate, they are not necessarily devoid of virtues. Women emerging from the women's liberation movement, enthused with new-found freedom, frequently sought to express their feelings of sisterhood in physical ways. There were 'political lesbians', too, women who felt that lesbianism was the 'correct' way for feminists to live, even if they did not feel attracted to women in the way that declared lesbians did, nor, in fact, become involved in physical relationships themselves. Many of these women posed problems for those of us who had developed our own 'outlaw' codes of practice in the ghetto. They wanted to be close to other women and yet we were accused of behaving 'like men' when we showed affection or made passes in what were, to us, normal, acceptable ways. Analyses of our behaviour were developed, proclaiming that some of us old-style dykes had modelled our lifestyle on the heterosexual 'norm'; but these analyses failed to take into account just how little self-respect existed before Gay Liberation. Uncertain and often self-hating, not all of us were as nice as we could afford to be later when we were free to proclaim our gayness and walk down the street hand in hand with our lover. Gradually it would be recognised that taking on male identity had been a form of resistance for some, but at this point, there was an uncomfortable feeling that once again the behaviour of some of us was being proscribed by another section of society. We were expected to call these women our sisters – wanted to, in fact – and yet they were critical of lifestyles some of us had developed for our self-expression and emotional protection. A lot of us missed the ghetto, with all its contradictions and cruelties.

It may well be that in England, at least, a lot of these attitudes stemmed from the national characteristics of sexual repression, denial and lack of demonstrativeness. Certainly, it didn't seem to be common in America. For lesbians like me, though, it was hard to escape the peculiar comparison between the lifestyle and outlook of some newly liberated women and the anything-goes libertarianism of the 1960s. The attitudes of both eras could be hurtful and more than a little stultifying for those of us who had developed our lesbian politics in the ghetto.

Sally, my journalist friend, also came from a middle-class background, but like me found the middle-class mores and purism of some feminists discomforting. She had developed her lesbian politics with a bunch of other older-style 'dykes' who'd cut their teeth down the Gateways and moved on into more radical gay liberation politics. They lived in 'squats' in the East End and had anarchistic views that made them the bane of some socialist feminists, equally angry but working for change in a more structured way. For the first time I met other lesbians with whom I could relate on a more physical, libertarian level, without the restrictions imposed by theoretical sisters, albeit often unwittingly. I was not comfortable with what I dubbed 'cultural feminism', either, but these particular women were non-conformist in every way and for a while I enjoyed their iconoclastic style. Two of them had done a book, *We're Here*, a collection of interviews with other lesbians. I read it, identifying enthusiastically and blossoming in my own lesbian identity. I no longer felt remotely ashamed.

I stopped working for *Melody Maker* when its policy changed and it became less concerned with the more serious aspects of music. I'd begun to realise that I could do more for the music by bringing it to the attention of a wider public. With the exception of the occasional piece, I gradually bowed out of the specialist press, too, preferring to concentrate on previewing events for *Time Out* and including aspects of the history that lay behind the musical notes. I wrote longer pieces for *The Observer* as well, both outlets providing an invaluable exercise in conciseness which had been neither possible nor necessary in the ego-ridden musical press with its sloppy standards.

Whenever I thought of Son Thomas on his broken-down porch, of Polly Heidelberg and Fannie Lou Hamer, resolution engraved in their faces, fighting to bring a nation to its knees, Beulah Rush denied her rightful name into her eighth decade, I felt I had a duty to make political points, not merely spread naked information devoid of any supporting historical context. By now there were few followers of popular music who did not realise where the Elvis Presleys and Janis Joplins came from, but this awareness and sense of responsibility did not extend to an earlier era. Gershwin, I told them, learned stride piano from Luckey Roberts in Harlem, Fred Astaire his dance-steps and routines from Black tutors; the list was endless. My polemical approach gained me respect in some quarters, made me distinctly unpopular elsewhere. The traditionalists among writers and listeners felt that they had an indisputable handle on Black music, formulated in part by decades of repetition of dubious legend; firsthand experience and increasing immersion in Black scholarship caused me to develop a somewhat different picture.

Over expansive, inebriated dinners at Peeve and Mike's I met other politicos who had at least heard of people such as Archie Shepp and knew their significance. The New Left was interested in popular culture, and anyone who could string a few words together about something like music and make political sense of it was welcome. I was asked to contribute to the Trotskyist *Socialist Review*, the first time I had done any such 'serious' writing. The new openness to ideas that I found all around me was encouraging, and I felt able to explore ideas that would have met with the thick blue line in the musical papers. It made such a change to be treated with respect, to have opinions and experience valued and welcomed, but as ever, disillusion was not far around the corner.

It was time, I thought, to write for one of the dailies. I interviewed Nigerian writer Flora Nwapa for the Women's Page of the *Guardian*, then approached the Arts Editor with an idea. Sebastian Clarke, a Trinidadian writer whose experience went back to the Underground press of the 1960s, had done a book about reggae. It was a break with racist convention that says music is something Black people do and whites document, and I thought it would make a good story.

However, on reading what Clarke had to say, the Arts Editor's reaction was to challenge the veracity of his remarks. He asked me to produce a 'less self-effacing re-draft' – in other words, to rewrite the piece in a way treating Black opinion with disdain. He disputed the fact that my own experience had led me to agree with Clarke's point: that Blacks are rarely allowed to comment on their own culture in the white media. 'For a Black guy to be articulate, to be intelligent, is like an affront to the white cats, editors, sub-editors, or whoever they are.' Clearly my collaboration in perpetuating the myth that Black views are irrational was being sought.

'By all means, let Clarke blow off steam about us honkies,' he wrote, adopting divisive 'us against them' racial tactics. It was an atti-tude I had encountered on numerous occasions in conversation with white editors, yet few, whatever their prejudice, would have actually committed it to paper. He felt free to write to me in this way, based on the cosy assumption that we shared the same cultural background and beliefs. No Black journalist, I felt, would have received such a letter. While I was expressing my own views, he implied, I was on relatively safe ground, yet when Clarke, supported by his own, closer to street-level experience, expressed his, he was said to be 'veer(ing) off down murky alleys'. What I was being asked to do was, essentially, to rap Clarke over his knuckles for having the gall to voice opinions that challenged the media's Eurocentric view of the world. Not only were the views of Black people disregarded, they themselves were allowed houseroom only as long as they were exotic or entertaining – or a problem. Rastafari, for example, filled all three qualifications for newspapers such as the *Guardian*, a kind of licensed buffoonery in the minstrel tradition. But, 'Who or what is Rastafari?' asked the editor facetiously. 'A brief explanation is needed for our readers.'

On New Year's Eve a group of journalists gathered for a party at Angela Phillips' flat. I took the letter along and we shared a few laughs. Once the amusement had passed, though, surprise was expressed at its belittling tone. From a collective background of many years in journalism, no one could recall receiving a letter of similar reproof. It was agreed that I should withdraw the article, stating my reasons for refusing to change it, and write in *Time Out* about what had occurred. The media at this point regarded 'anti-racist' reporting as writing about the National Front, all stereotypes about Blacks being accepted, particularly the one that maintains they had nothing to say. It was an opportunity to lobby for the inclusion of the Black voice in the media, a move that was gaining currency in some union quarters.

Overnight I turned around a challenging piece, seeking support and a quote from the Black Media Workers Association, whose spokesperson felt it a positive move. He also pointed out that I was putting my neck on the line. How true. The editorial team at *Time Out* were unsettled by what I had written, but the copy was subbed none the less. As the day wore on, however, the fact of my refusal to rewrite the original piece led to some debate over whether it had, in fact, been 'good enough' for the *Guardian*. They had seen the original letter and agreed it was shameful, but any dispute over my thoroughness could lead to conflict in professional circles. For reasons that were never fully explained, the article failed to appear.

That ranks should have closed in what I had previously considered a radical alternative magazine was an injustice. The more 'glamorous' of 'militants' could always find space in *Time Out*, even if the magazine employed no Black people on staff. But whether theirs was a minority view was unimportant. Space was allotted on the grounds of making 'good copy' rather than on that of what was actually being said. The Black 'quota' was filled and the voice of the ordinary individual excluded. It was business as usual and I could never again feel at ease with those who in cavalier fashion excluded these views.

I was becoming more involved in union matters, for I recognised that the only way to bring about change was to work together for it with others. But freelance journalists do not, as a breed, take kindly to 'organising' of any kind. Whenever the union was in dispute with a publication, it generally meant withdrawal of labour, anathema to those of us whose means of earning a living was precarious at the best of times. It was necessary to fall in with this for the communal benefit but deeply disappointing when a story might have taken weeks to research and prepare. Nevertheless, for three years I was on the NUJ's London Freelance Branch Committee.

Branch meetings held monthly could be profoundly boring but there was always someone on hand to give light relief, from Woodrow Wyatt and *The Sporting Life* reporter on up. For a while, Jo Fawkes was a branch official. She was the daughter of cartoonist Trog, who had once been a clarinettist with Humphrey Lyttelton and had an amusing tale of waking up, when she was a toddler, to find 'Mr Five By Five', singer Jimmie Rushing, asleep on the living-room couch. At a tense moment in one especially interminable meeting, I sent up an envelope to her at the top table. It was delivered with all the urgency of passing on important information, and she opened it just as events reached crisis point. Inside was an appealing snapshot of me, aged 16, hand in hand with the aforesaid Rushing. She nearly fell off the platform.

Complaints under rule were regularly brought in the union, and I sat on committees where this was done with regard to racist reporting. These initiatives seldom got very far. At first chapel representatives from the newspapers concerned would answer official summonses, later they frequently 'refused to dignify' such proceedings with an appearance. The handful of us who challenged racist reporting and the perpetuation of stereotypes were alienated from the main body of opinion. At one branch meeting I put a motion that it should become official policy to drop the derogatory term 'blacking' in descriptions of industrial and other disputes, and was laughed off the platform for trying to alter the English language. An MP member was one of those who joined the reactionaries in laughing the loudest; a few months later I saw him on television out 'on the stump', fighting, he said, for an end to racial discrimination. A *Guardian* diarist thought the idea was hilarious, writing in his column that this would eliminate four pages from the *Oxford English Dictionary*. Eventually several unions would pass motions proscribing the unacceptable term.

The *Observer Magazine* sent me to America to do a piece on the blues, but I ruined my chances of writing on women's issues elsewhere in the paper when that column's editor trivialised a complaint from a reader who objected to the white colonisation of Black women's hairstyles. I knew the complainant slightly, for she was a neighbour, and I wrote back in her defence. 'What a bigoted, narrow-minded letter you write – and miss the point as well,' was the scornful reply.

I was angry and over the top at times, but a lot of women were, and for a variety of reasons. After the early halcyon days of the movement, when everyone joined in with cheerful optimism, the inevitable backlash was beginning. No one had begun to talk about 'post-feminism' yet, but the one newspaper that offered any thoughtful coverage of women's affairs suddenly dropped the subject to a bare minimum with the installation of an unsympathetic editor. Angela Phillips, Jill Nicholls, I and a couple of other feminists who were professional journalists decided to initiate a plan of action to counteract the trivialisation of important issues. Women in Media still existed but operated on an essentially reformist level; we were a little more radical in our approach and expectations. Angela thought it would be a good idea to invite two established journalists along and sound out their views. Eileen Fairweather, one of our number, was living in an ancient tenement in what was then the red-light area of King's Cross, and it was there that we met, deriving wry amusement at the idea of our two more sophisticated sisters fighting their way past the kerb-crawlers who frequented the area.

At first the meeting went smoothly. One of the invitees had been involved in Women in Media and other campaigns and was most sympathetic. Gradually, though, it became apparent that those of us who had called the meeting had differing ideas about the speed with which events might proceed and what we considered most crucial. One concern united us, to a degree – the exclusion of the Black voice in the media. It was this that precipitated the break-up of the meeting.

The second visitor whose woman's consciousness, her regular column made clear, had only recently been slightly raised, considered Black issues of minor significance. Women, she told me, were 'more discriminated against than Black people, because there were more women than Blacks in this country'. She even quoted percentages to support her 'argument'. Both Angela and I were outraged; the others distinctly embarrassed. I felt unable to take part any further and left the room, closely followed by Susan Hemmings, who worked on *Spare Rib*. She, although calm, was equally angry. The meeting broke up and we stayed behind to finish the wine, Eileen attempting some light relief: 'You could almost hear the sound of their high heels tottering through the piles of dog shit and condoms.' Whatever had been agreed, it was obvious that women such as these were not about to relinquish their power in favour of Black issues being raised in the Media. To get anywhere was a struggle for all of us whatever our views, but there were many who failed to make the connections.

There was an interesting postscript to this story. Three or four years later I ran into Sebastian Clarke, now Amon Saba Saakana. 'Funny thing,' he said, 'the *Guardian* just did a half-page story on me, saying the same things I did in that interview with you.' Its author? The aforementioned offending columnist with whom I'd argued. It had taken uprisings and protest for Saakana's voice to scrape through. Militancy was momentarily fashionable in Fleet Street, but this journalist was in a position of power on her paper. Just half a dozen years previously, anyone who put their neck on the line could expect only ridicule, I well knew, yet still, if you looked closely, nothing had changed. It was interesting to note who was allowed to write what; those in power were still calling the tune.

March 2, 1981 saw the Black People's Day of Action, organised to protest at police attitudes and intransigence over the investigation of events that caused the deaths of 13 young people in a fire at a party in New Cross several weeks previously. The national press had been disparaging in reporting the tragedy, concluding, without any evidence, that the perpetrator was probably a guest at the party. The day was distinguished by the size of the march, estimates ranging from 3,000 (*Sun*) to 15,000 (*Westindian World*). Many had taken the day off work, being joined on the route by women out shopping and night-people seldom seen on the streets before noon. There were Whites who were angry, too, and Maggie Murray and I went along with Peeve, leaving our cameras at home as a mark of respect.

Anger was running high and reached a pitch as the procession turned into Fleet Street, shouting 'Thirteen dead, nothing said!' Journalists craned out of the windows, their expressions ranging from sneers to unease. At some point a small group of young people detached itself from the main body and took more direct action, but they were a tiny percentage. The march was a dignified occasion, a statement of assertion and intent, which was to be of immense historical and political significance.

But it was the action of the tearaways which concentrated the tabloids' attention the following day. 'Rampage of a Mob!', 'When the Black Tide Met the Thin Blue Line', 'The Spoilers!' — these were some of the headlines. The reports were full of inaccuracies, fuelled by hostility. So vicious was the tone of the reporting, in fact, that for the first time, other 'straight' white journalists were compelled to comment on the shameful coverage, notably Ivan Rowan in the *Sunday Telegraph* and Lucy Hodges in *The Times*, distancing themselves from such deliberately racist reporting. The circumstances leading up to the march aroused considerable sympathy and an unprecedented number of complaints under rule were taken out in various parts of the NUJ. For a while there was a feeling in some quarters of the press that this time Fleet Street traditions had gone too far.

Peeve, Maggie, and I were among those who brought our branch's complaints, producing witnesses to the events of the march to support our cases; the newspapers were represented by the appropriate Chapel officials. The result of these hearings was utter confusion. For a start, it was how the articles appeared as 'wholes' that had caused such outrage: headlines, layout, pictures and text taken together were what we considered encouraged discrimination on grounds of race and colour, and this was what we had challenged in the wording of the official complaint. Although we all worked professionally in the media, none of us had much Fleet Street experience. We did not realise that in some cases an article in one of the dailies went through a news process that could involve more than 30 people. To whom, therefore, could blame be apportioned? It transpired that bylines themselves gave no indication of who was responsible, for these could be arbitrarily chosen, sometimes invented. The committee disagreed about attributing responsibility for the published material and suggested that we would have done better to have brought our complaints under a different rule. On reflection, we agreed they were right, but the result of the disagreement meant the complaints had to be dropped. It was bitterly disappointing to realise that once again the system had been saved by bureaucracy.

Our complaints stirred up a lot of anger in Fleet Street and there were attempts to throw the branch and named complainants into disrepute in the union. Some journalists still thought that race was not a trades union issue. As for me, I was deeply ashamed. I'd wanted so much to be 'one of the boys' in The Street, and it still hurt to realise just what that meant. Maybe there had been a tradition of justice at one time, now being a journalist was in the eyes of many I knew to live at the level of a sewer rat.

Maggie Murray was coming to the end of an eleven-year marriage. I'd had my first experience of teaching, filling in for her at the Poly when her baby was born, and taken her a copy of Malcolm's *Autobiography* when she was in hospital. Better than fruit or flowers, she had said, it opened her eyes and started her thinking. It seemed appropriate that I should become her first woman lover and she told me I was the first woman she'd met who 'lived in the real world', moving in it and dealing with it on equal terms, the way men did without question.

I liked that but found it ironic. As a woman I was still an Outsider, and although the women's movement was exciting and inspirational, even there I often felt that I didn't fit. My ideas had been formed by a different experience. Women snarled and switched off when they heard Muddy Waters sing 'I'm a man, I'm a man, M-A-N spells *man*', not realising the enormous significance for an Afro-American man in making this statement. Indeed it annoyed me when men were called 'boys' in reaction to the disparaging 'girls', for no one had considered what those words could mean in a different environment, but when some Radical feminists organised a march through an area of London with a large Black population, protesting against sexual attack, I was one of several dismayed by the historical implications of that.

And then there was Susan Brownmiller, who attacked Emmett Till in her harrowing study of rape. My blood boiled. Sure, I could understand her analysis; as a feminist I do hold all men responsible for rape – to a degree. But crying 'rape' had historically been used as a means of controlling Black men, and to drag in the case of a 14-year-old thrown to his death in a Mississippi river in the 1950s for allegedly speaking in a familiar manner to a white woman was going too far. It was no less a lynching than the thousands of others that radicals like the author, herself a one-time civil rights stalwart, had protested for decades. How could I support the line that this boy harboured the thoughts of a rapist, even when I knew and somewhat agreed with, the interpretation lying behind it?

Maggie had always been forthright and apparently fearless. Now she was freed from convention, she was raring to go. As we spent more time together we talked about 'getting it right' with our pictures, making sure our work showed whose side we were on. Such discussion was not unusual among committed photographers now, but ours was inspired by our Half Moon collaboration in the past and what we had learnt from our journeys outside our own culture, mine in America, hers to Africa. There was a need, too, to change the way that women photographers were perceived, something about which we both felt strongly. We noted wryly that the women in other agencies were frequently there only as tokens or, as in Fleet Street, got only safe and easy assignments.

I was tired of working alone and had tried several times to persuade Angela Phillips that we ought to set up something together. Now, Maggie and I decided, the time had come for women to form a photo agency of our own. We got in touch with everyone we could think of who worked at a professional level and told them what we had in mind. As at the Half Moon, there were some who could visualise no advantage in throwing in their lot with others and, as they saw it, giving up hard-won individualism and freedom. Others saw the potential benefits and began to plan. We hoped that our example would prove an inspiration to others, and aimed to raise the consciousness of our clients where possible through the careful selection of images. We would send out a photograph of a woman when a doctor or bricklayer was requested; a Black person when the white equivalent would be routine.

It took us a year and a half, but in May 1983 Format finally emerged. 'Funny, isn't it?' said Maggie. 'This would never have happened if we hadn't been lovers.' Participation had been denied women so long; now, by giving up the security she had enjoyed as a married woman and with it society's recognition and approval, she had moved on into the real world as well.

For too long it seemed to me I'd been seen as someone who could 'only' photograph musicians; now, with the chance to accept all kinds of assignments, I gave up most of my writing. I met a man from Gambia in the street one day when I was working on a community project. We got talking when I asked if I could take his picture and I told him I'd been to his country. He said he worked as a tailor, had come here in the 1940s as a teenager, stowing away on a boat. I took his address, promising to send prints, which I did. Later, one of the photographs was used in a book and I thought he might like to have a copy. I wrote him a letter and we met. It was a winter's evening, shivery, and he invited me back to the council flat where he lived with his cousin. There the three of us sat around all evening, watching TV and drinking endless cups of tea rich with evaporated milk, African-style. He was pleased as punch to see his face in a book, impressed that I'd done as I'd said and sent the pictures along. 'People here don't do that, you know; they don't keep promises. Really – you are one of God's children.'

I felt a pleasurable glow, not just from the tea and the paraffin heater. Maggie and I had made such a point of trying to send prints back to people whenever we could, often at considerable personal inconvenience. When we'd told students at the Poly that they should never forget this responsibility, they'd sneered without understanding the give-and-take process of life, the new go-for-self already taking hold. But to be warmed by such a response on a cold winter's night was the kind of thing that made being in photography worthwhile. You couldn't buy moments like this. 'Please,' said my Gambian friend, 'you are welcome any time. You don't have to write, just come here. You are our sister.'

Format had been planned as a business, but we continued to supply our 'alternative' clients with photographs at a price they could afford. Eventually we applied for a grant which enabled us to do this and cover some of the enormous expense that photography entails, but the initial setting-up involved capital investment on the part of the members and a significant degree of financial sacrifice.

In 1984 I discovered that my mother was terminally ill. She had had cancer for some time but had kept it at bay; now her prognosis was poor. I realised that I could expect my mobility to be limited for some time to come, and would not be able to accept too many assignments. I was beginning to worry about money when I had a call from the past.

Prince Ademola Aremu (not his real name) had been a minister in the Nigerian government prior to the first military coup. I'd known him when I worked in diplomat circles but had not seen him for 16 years. Now he was in town, curious to know how I was faring, and we arranged to have dinner. This, I thought, could be the answer to some of my problems. I would ask him for money. As the eldest son of an Oba, a Yoruba king, he would be accustomed to this, flattered even to be asked for his help. I would be just one of his many supplicants, and after all he could only say no.

We met in a smart restaurant in Mayfair, and I dressed as well as I could for the occasion. I was interested to note, though, a slight breeze from the waiter showing us to a table. We chatted about this and that and I told him about some of the work I'd been doing. The atmosphere was relaxed between us, but despite this, I was beginning to think that maybe it would not be so simple to ask him for money; it was something I'd not done before. Then he said, 'You have written positive things about Black people when no one was taking us seriously. We are grateful for what you have done.' As far as I knew, Prince Aremu was unaware of my work apart from the photographs I'd taken at dances and parties back in the 1960s. I was embarrassed, but now I knew that it would be harder to go ahead with my plan. I was pleased that he no longer thought of me as the 'likely girl' he once knew, but this change in attitude placed our relationship on a different footing.

At the next table sat another white woman out with an Arab. There was champagne at their table and what looked like fresh salmon, and she was hurling both down her throat as though they were going out of style. Between swallows I heard her asking 'terribly interested' questions about 'your people's customs'. The Arab looked bored, while at our table we were getting along like a house on fire. Prince Aremu's father had recently died and that made him automatically heir to the kingdom, but, he was explaining, the government was trying to limit the power of traditional rulers. If he became Oba, he said, he would have to account for his money and ask permission to leave the country.

Out of the corner of my eye I saw a second bottle of champagne arrive and rapidly begin to go the way of the first. I made up my mind. She wasn't me, and it was definitely beneath my dignity to ask my companion for money. I relaxed, and was suddenly struck by the humour of it all. 'You know, it's terribly funny,' I said, laughing, 'here we are – you're talking about whether or not you're going to take up the throne, and here I am, a socialist! And,' I added, 'a feminist, too!' He looked puzzled. 'You know, "women's lib" and all that!'

Prince Aremu leaned forward and grabbed my arm with enthusiasm. 'Oh, but my dear, you were *then*!' I was so very pleased that I'd not put that question. Sixteen years on, I thought, I'd not let the side down.

We left the restaurant together and I thought I might give him a taste of proletarian reality by driving him back to his hotel in my battered old van. Instead, a chauffeur was waiting, and he opened the door of an elegant saloon, expecting us both to get in. To his surprise, we shook hands in the doorway. 'Any time you want an air ticket to Lagos, give me a ring,' said Prince Aremu airily and we went our separate ways.

It was early still and I had a positive feeling. I wanted to continue the evening on an upbeat note, so I made my way to the Women's Bar at the Drill Hall. I ran into a woman I knew called Linda Bellos. 'You look all smartened up,' she said. 'Where have you been?' 'Oh,' I said, with a toss of the head, 'I've been dining out with a prince in Mayfair.' She didn't believe me, but then I don't suppose I'd have believed that within a couple of years she'd be a controversial figure in London politics.

23
Keep on Pushing

When my mother died I thought of suet puddings. I wanted my childhood again and food was the key. I thought of seed-cake heavy with caraway and dripping, of capon for Christmas – never chicken – with gravy made from the giblets and coloured rich brown with sugar burnt over the gas. Whenever I came back from my travels, I'd put in my order: rhubarb crumble and steak-and-kidney pudding, please, the dough made with real suet bought from the butcher.

Food, like music, is the most important of cultural touchstones. It's small wonder that the English as a nation are so cold, given the low priority we place on both. Mum, fortunately, like her mother and grandmother, was an accomplished traditional cook who specialised in the better aspects of English cuisine. As the years went by, her repertoire expanded to take in 'foreign' dishes, encouraged by Clive and me who, like most of our generation, viewed traditional fare as 'old-hat'. My own eating habits had changed radically by the time I started to realise the importance of asking her to pass on the old recipes. But by the time I got around to thinking that way, she was too ill for us to make up for lost time.

Going through the house after Mum's death was an object lesson in never taking anyone for granted. Again and again I wondered at her neatness – she'd virtually *catalogued* all the linen – and at just how progressive she had grown with the years. In the larder I found comfrey, camomile and limeflowers, and an array of wholemeal products and grains. The old standbys had gone, thrown out by an 80-year-old woman admired by one of her friends: 'Your mother was *modern*; there aren't many people like that in Streatham.' The only echoes of childhood were a bottle of rennet used to make the junket we loved and an ancient bottle of cochineal – 'It's made from dead beetles,' I once informed her authoritatively – with which birthday-cake icing was coloured. Of the trappings of Mrs Beeton there was hardly a trace.

Cleaning out cupboards I came across objects I'd not seen for years: tiny gold-rimmed cocktail glasses, presents from Westindian friends (not quite 'her' style), hideous sundae glasses we'd won at the fair. The elegant wine glasses we'd be permitted to drink from only at Christmas were chipped, the sad legacy of my grandmother's cavalier struggles with the washing-up. In her bedroom I caught myself handling cosmetic aids with which I hadn't bothered for years. I looked into Grandma's silver-backed mirror which had lain on the dressing-table and thought of the lengths to which women went for beauty.

But food. I urgently needed to cook dishes remembered from childhood and associated with happier times. And yet I was ashamed to realise that I, who could turn out a pretty good curry goat, had paid scant attention to the way Mum routinely produced pastry to melt in the mouth. As time went by I realised that, dismissive as I'd been of her skills as a youngster, a surprising amount had been absorbed through a kind of mother-to-daughter osmosis. I sat down and read a few books, asked questions of some of her friends and was soon producing tapioca pudding and seed-cake like a veteran.

Clive turned out to have some of the cooking secrets. With children of his own he'd learnt how to do 'our' Christmas dinners, while I was rushing around the world wolfing *brinjal bhaji* and groundnut stew. It's funny how those we don't credit with a sense of tradition get the priorities right. One day he announced proudly, 'I think I've found out how to do *liver*!' I tasted the gravy and wanted to cry. Like a snatch of a song from the jukebox when you first fell in love, I was back in the kitchen at Streatham when the Stargazers were 'on-the-AIR', loved and comforted in the best way my mother knew how.

Going to register Mum's death, I had tried to make light of the situation. 'At least now we're real grown-up people,' I said. 'There's no one to tell us off now.' 'That's just the trouble,' said Clive. 'It's something you grow to depend on.'

I'd asked Mum when she was nearing 80 if she too ever felt like a child. 'Oh, yes,' she'd responded with feeling. 'Sometimes I *run* along the road and look in all the shop-windows and feel just like I did when I was eleven.' I was moved by her enthusiasm and sheer simplicity, but then, she was always that way. Small wonder, though, that it was so hard for me at times to feel like the grown-up I had become.

To travel with Mum was a joy. Her enthusiasm reminded me of the first time I got a foreign stamp in my passport. Her delight with Paris was infectious, the way she repeated information she'd gathered endearing. I took her to Berlin for the Jazz Festival with a *Melody Maker* party when she was 65. Crossing the wall to the Eastern sector she infuriated some bigots on board by declaring it far more elegant than the gaudiness of the West. She was right, of course; when grim faces were put down to repression, she saw the equally grim November weather as responsible. She'd dragged me to a party held by the Mayor of Berlin for Duke Ellington's birthday, despite a hangover I'd acquired the previous night, and said something that earned her a namecheck in the paper from Richard Williams. 'Mrs Wilmer,' he wrote, 'you are too much'. And really, she was – hanging out with Cecil Taylor and getting drunk, passing out for the first and only time in her life and leaving me to pick up the pieces.

I found it hard sometimes to remember her early unease and prejudice with 'foreigners', especially when I saw the sweet, easy way she socialised with people who embodied worlds she could have never imagined. Randy Weston stayed at our house and talked Africa and Nationalism, she cooked him bacon and eggs; the Liberian Ambassador invited her to his parties and she drank champagne. Clive took her to Italy and she knocked back *grappa* and devoured *calamari* like a veteran of foreign travel. Yoruba entrepreneurs, Malayan accountants and Sikh doctors ate at her table, all of them remembering her food, but above all, her hospitality and charm.

Several times towards the end of her life she confided in me how naïve she had been. She'd cite instances of her unworldliness and cheerfully evinced regrets at her unsophisticated behaviour. 'Remem-

302

ber that time Charlie Mingus came to dinner?' I smiled at the memory of 'that man' who'd taken over the kitchen with his barbecue chicken. I could see him seated at the scrubbed-pine table, still wearing beret and raincoat, unwrapping his greasy newspaper parcels to her general disgust. The child of her parents, she'd been raised to be hopelessly genteel; now she saw her rudeness, she said. 'But I just didn't know people carried on like that. It's different now; I've learned so much about the world and its ways from what my children have taught me.'

The idea of homosexual love was something she could never quite grasp – 'Well, not for women, dear' – yet she never made me feel uncomfortable about my lesbian friends. Unlike so many others with a similar lifestyle whose parents rejected both them and their feelings, I always knew I could bring my friends home to a warm welcome. Without such a love behind me, I doubt whether I could have even coped with the stresses of trying to be myself in an essentially homophobic society.

But racism was never far away from the surface in British life and even in death, it would not go away. As Mum lay at the undertaker's before the funeral, two of her friends expressed the desire to pay their last respects. My brother wanted to do so as well, but I was not particularly eager to participate in the experience. Clive lived outside London, though, so I accompanied the two women until his arrival. While we were waiting, the elderly mortician engaged us in conversation. Seeking a topic where he presumed he'd find a ready consensus, he launched into a diatribe on how the character of Streatham was 'changing'. He mentioned a weekend he'd spent out of London – 'Such a difference from being here, I think we only saw one Chinese all day.' I bristled, enraged at such rudeness but I couldn't ignore him. I lit a cigarette and went outside to wait. As I stood on the corner in the April drizzle, trying hard to hold back the tears, Clive came hurrying along the High Street and saw the look in my eyes. I told him what had occurred and he took my hand as we made our nervous way to the mortuary. Mum's friends went in first and as Clive waited his turn, the undertaker continued to rail at 'foreigners' for the benefit of another white, middle-class male. Tall, masculine and bearded, Clive squeezed my hand, giving me strength and willing me not to explode. 'Can't say I agree with you,' he said, summoning up his most refined put-down. 'Most of the people I teach are foreigners and I find it a worthwhile experience.' I appreciated him and loved him for making his own journey to this realisation, but could not get over the outrage being forced on us as family. My mother was lying inches away, behind a thin wall of plywood. How dare this man treat her with such disrespect? I changed my mind about going in to see her, and Clive and I held hands together in our grief.

It was a childhood friend of my mother's who produced the most unlikely of epitaphs. I'd gone to see her, anxious to touch base with someone who had known Mum for so many years. I'd hardly sat down before she baldly announced: 'Your mother wasn't a Christian, you know!' I was stunned. She'd been a lifelong believer, unquestioning, a regular churchgoer until a year or so before her illness began. Her friend enjoyed my reaction. 'Romance and ritual!' she scoffed, nearing 90. 'All the doing of *men*. Nothing to do with God or the afterlife.'

I'd gone there depressed but now I was laughing. I felt a sense of the irreverent mischief these two had shared. I'd wondered why her churchgoing had stopped, imagined she was growing tired. Hypocrisy, said her friend, that was the reason. It made sense when I remembered stories of dubious church doings she'd told me. Mum could never be called a profound thinker, but that did not mean she was anyone's fool.

I was fortunate indeed to have such an exceptional parent. Many people who have relatives with cancer say this period can often be the best time of the relationship. As she gradually became weaker, I found myself loving her more than I'd ever felt possible. We sat together and watched spring buds appear on the trees and I knew she wouldn't be there for the greening. I looked out over the Common and couldn't believe what I was seeing: a man walked by with a falcon attached to his wrist! As weak as she was, she got up to peer out of the window, her sense of amazement with her up to the end.

I rescued the old *dhurrie* that we'd played on as children and taken on picnics. I washed it carefully and watched with sadness as the fibres disintegrated and gave up after a century of use. The past, it seemed, was disintegrating, too. Now there was no one older than me and I had to be grown-up at last. For months afterwards I wanted to tell Mum of things I had done, and grew distraught at times when I realised it was no longer possible. I had no idea how much I had sought her approval. Maybe it's true that we do stay children inside while our parents are living and only change when the fact of their absence sinks in. I took plants from her garden and put them in mine, a reminder of the home where we made toast around the fire, then counted the faces that stared back out of the flames, a place where everything was possible.

My mother's death seemed to bring everything else to a head. The floodgates of misery opened and for a while I was almost knocked down by the tide. Injustices and pain I'd experienced came to the surface accompanied by the appalling sense of bereavement. Her death was followed in close succession by those of three of her friends. It was harrowing to have to cope with another round of funerals and I felt beleaguered. So many of the people I'd known were no longer there. Musicians I always took for granted would go on coming to London stopped coming, many of the people I'd met in the South had also passed on. Time stopped still for a while as I looked back over my life and considered.

The inescapable feeling that kept on surfacing was that I had always been an outsider. For a while when I hung out with Peeve and the rest of the gang, I found the sense of community I'd only known in my last year at school and going off to camp in my teens. It always seemed to elude me, no doubt the legacy of a childhood in which my mother's necessities meant that mine would be often ignored, and a schooling that failed to cater to my needs.

I'd longed for that sense of belonging, but had never found it in the lesbian ghetto nor, truth to tell, in the women's movement which had given me important direction in so many matters. Feminism had been a key factor in my personal growth, but social mores formed by a different experience meant that even there I could still feel a maverick, out on a limb. It was ironic that the knowledge which I'd used as a touchstone for living had set me apart from others who couldn't deal with my reasoning. I'd been on a journey that began when I first wrote to Baby Dodds and Jesse Fuller, asked Sister Rosetta about the whys and the wherefores of rhythm. Others put their toe in the water and stepped back after a while. I worked my way up to the deep end with all the attendant dangers and thrills.

I'd learned so much from being in contact with Black ways of seeing, but seldom found an echo at home. And yet in America, where Black autonomy was often deeply resented, I constantly met other white people who had taken on board the challenge of the times. Such people endorsed the most radical views expressed from inside the music's community, mercilessly dissecting respected critics and accepted opinion in a way that was light years ahead of most thinking in Britain.

The history of white writing on jazz has been filled with misunderstanding and misapprehension. In general, writers considered only those people they had met, mostly musicians. They saw the individual as an 'oddity', evaluating their behaviour against a string of white norms, rather than as a 'type' from within their own culture. Saxophonist Lester Young was a prime example of that, misjudged by white writers to whom he was not anxious to speak, who built up a picture of someone unrecognisable to his everyday companions. A British magazine suggested Louis Armstrong was still a 'country boy' when he turned up in Chicago in the 1920s in a straw hat. Another musician responded immediately to say such assumptions were dangerous. Straw hats, he pointed out, were the 'in' style of the day; Louis was expressing himself as a modish sophisticate.

Few Whites emerge from short contact with Black society with other than superficial burns. Whether there for the music or other sensual attractions, the pervading mood is consumerist. There's an inability to come to terms with anything that fails to fit preconceptions, even if it was that 'outsider' quality of the art that made it attractive in the first instance. An enormous gulf separates those white people who have 'participated' in the 'Black experience' by living and moving with Black people, and those who remain fixed in their own community's spirit and beliefs. Commitment to an alternative way of seeing means a move to another psychological dimension of the cultural self.

Being involved on a one-to-one basis with so many people of colour, I think I escaped sentimentalising or romanticising individual and collective needs and demands. As a result, I became out of step with many other Whites I knew. I'd meet other White people who had just had a brush with colour in some shape or form and they'd expect an echo of recognition because of the knowledge they imagined we shared. I couldn't see it that way. I'd think of Stevie and me, and other friends in interracial relationships. We cared for and loved our partners and worked hard to learn from them about their situation. Those others, white women who tell of encounters with 'studs' rather than people, white men with a stable of Black starlets to put on parade, they were collectors, the paraders of prized possessions. And there was a history to that.

Among even the most open-minded of Whites, men and women, I've found an unfailing tendency to disbelieve the extent of racism. The psychological dislocation it can create remains unknown. Feeling themselves to be blameless as individuals, they can see no need to take on board situations created by 'others'. Tell them that if they're not part of the solution, they're part of the problem and they grow uneasy. Tell them that they, too, are racist because they benefit from an unjust and unequal society, and they go off into paroxysms of protest. Such people cannot conceive that there are others who have challenged themselves and come to terms with the realisation that they are participants in the system, that there are some of us who have been torn apart by that realisation, that there are those among us who have endeavoured to do whatever we can to change the status quo.

In 1978 the last National Women's Liberation Conference held in Britain ended in uproar, disintegrating into an ideological free-for-all between feminists from different tendencies. Workshops on racism and fascism were held at the conference, the first such event I'd attended, but when a Black woman grabbed the microphone in the midst of the plenary turmoil, her comments were almost swamped by what was taking place on the 'home' front. I was shocked at the time, though, when I realised what she was saying: if white feminists didn't do something about our racism, we could kiss goodbye to the idea of Black women's continuing participation. Hers was by no means the first such call for action, but it was by far the most public. And in a movement that had always prided itself on having no leaders and in its total 'democracy', the challenge was particularly disturbing. But the challenges came fast and thick, nagging at the élitist fabric of the movement, showing up the much-lauded sisterhood as a sham. Many white women were forced to examine their individual consciences and do something about it. The movement began to take on a more international character, although there remained some who disputed the relevance and usefulness of identifying with events taking place the other side of the globe, or even as nearby as Ireland.

Gradually, as women of colour and other minority groups such as the Irish became more vocal, a greater awareness developed and affirmative action procedures became the commonplace in feminist circles. Some Black women and others began to organise autonomously, but as the inequalities that existed on our own doorstep increasingly came out into the open, anti-racist strategies began to emerge in disparate quarters. It would be fatuous to pretend that all is well in the movement where race and class are concerned, but because so many women have taken on board the idea of self-examination over racism, there is a greater understanding of the need for such progress than exists in most other political circles.

In matters of culture, though, I often think it's business as usual. It's fashionable now to read Alice Walker, just as it is to dance to Art Blakey, but the connections with the world that nurtured these artists and from where their inspiration is drawn, still seems to me, for the most part, to be missing. Even in the women's movement where the current interest in Black women writers is long overdue, this is not without its problems. Some who are interested will do as I did and go on

306

and discover a massive body of literature, music and art and try to communicate its existence to others still in the dark. But there are too many for whom Black women writers are 'flavour of the month'. They can't stop talking about the particular picture of pain Alice Walker drew in *The Color Purple* and yet they stay unaware, uninterested even, of someone like Langston Hughes, whose poetry, social comment, revolutionary writing and humour spanned half a century.

The picture has changed significantly from when I first moved in African circles. Then, those Whites who were attracted to the music, the painting and literature, were visibly enriched by the discoveries they had made. Today the approach is unashamedly consumerist. People dip into a grab-bag of international 'goodies' to come up with an Alice Walker, a Sunny Ade or a plate of jollof rice, and if they're lucky they may find out something of what it all means. There's an unwillingness to go deeper that did not exist in the old Bush House days. Colonial types some of the old radio hacks and Coasters might have been, but they really cared about Africa and the Diaspora, and knew their Soyinka from their Achebe, their *eba* from their cocoyam, their I.K. from their E.T.

By the time this appears in print, though, I expect we'll have moved on by a few notches. Black pressure to 'get it right' will make sure of that. I've always felt that those of us outsiders who were admitted to Black cultural circles had a responsibility to ensure that history was represented as accurately as possible. It's true that we cannot write with the insider's authenticity, but whenever we do have the chance to spread information, then it's incumbent on us to get it right. And as ever, those who know will be able to differentiate between those with a genuine interest in the culture and those who say, 'What's in it for us?'

When we talk about someone being 'larger than life', I wonder whose life we mean? The people who have attracted me most deeply, as comrades, as teachers and lovers, have always seemed a little larger than life to me. I have taken my inspiration from such people, gained the political wherewithal, whether or not my ultimate concerns have been the same as theirs.

I have wondered whether the musicians, the hustlers, the intellectuals and politicos I've met in the Black world were as different from their own peers as I was from mine. Yet because of their social situation, however 'progressive' the individual might be, she or he would have to be rooted. And it's that rooting, so vital to life's continuity, that is missing, being deliberately destroyed with little to replace it, in fact, in contemporary white British society and culture. Small wonder I've often felt more at home elsewhere.

The value of knowledge took on a new meaning for me because of my contact with African peoples. I don't know if I'd ever evaluated it before; learning was something you just did, generally to advance yourself in your chosen field of endeavour. The only place where knowledge is measured in terms of anything other than its earning power is in the ivory towers of academe. There scholars are involved in intellectual arguments that have little bearing on real life or the rising and setting of the sun.

It was different in Afro-America. There I discovered a respect for wisdom that was to be found in every part of society. The only place I encountered anything like it in my own society was among older people in the mining communities. As the liberation movements of the 1960s and 1970s progressed, so value was placed on everything from cultivation to cookery, from textile production to healing, on an awareness of history, philosophy and the arts. It had little to do with a redemptive cultural nationalism, a yearning for 'African' values. It was much more to do with self-liberation through learning and the reclamation of history. A process where knowledge was its own reward.

As I talked with hundreds of different people I listened to polemic, read poems, saw plays. And a new way of seeing developed, not least a new way of seeing myself. The process that had begun so many years ago when I went to hear Big Bill Broonzy and the Eureka Jubilee Singers was bringing *me* back home as well.

When Stevie's mother remarried, a small party was held after the ceremony. Everyone took a turn on the dance-floor, me included. She was not much of a one for partying, but this was a special occasion. She moved smoothly between the other dancers, joining her daughter in a skilful display of getting-down which relegated the rest of us to the sidelines. 'We'll show 'em!' she said. 'They think they can dance but however they try they can't do it like us!' The man she was marrying was white, but everyone present applauded, him included. These women could *dance*.

I knew her words were aimed at me and it hurt. At the time, I suppose, I took it personally, for I knew she was not over-keen on my friendship with her daughter, seeing me as a class intruder as much as anything. But I think what she was saying went far deeper than my personal chagrin. Racial competitiveness at this level would not exist, or would not be pursued with the same degree of cruciality were not the music and the dance and their significance of such importance to racial health and well-being. Claiming something for oneself went far beyond the parameters of the actual music.

John Graham had explained it to me years ago. When Nigerian students did their 'African thing' at a wedding, I'd seen the change that took place with my own eyes. I got to know a veteran saxophonist from Jamaica named Louis Stephenson who came to London back in the 1930s and worked with top bands. At his wife's funeral he wandered about dispensing hospitality, deliberately accentuating the 'Jamaican-ness' of his speech. 'Oh,' said a woman guest who, like him, had been in Britain for fifty years, 'that's our Jamaican language. We always do that to make us feel better.' 'Yes,' affirmed another woman. 'It just bucks you up, puts a little *spring* in you when you hear that, doesn't it?'

The resentment of what has been appropriated, stirs even the most magnanimous soul. I have yet to meet one Black musician who did not express anger about this at some point or another; the literature speaks constantly of white plunder. 'You have taken my blues and gone,' wrote Langston Hughes; Paul Laurence Dunbar's poem 'When Malindy Sings' written 90 years ago, laughs at white attempts to be 'soulful'. Small wonder when, as I write this, Fred Astaire having just died, not one tribute acknowledges the Black teachers who pointed his great talent in a specific direction.

On one of my trips to Mississippi with Stevie, Beulah Rush had given us a beautiful quilt we'd admired – or rather, tried to give it. We'd insisted on paying because neither of us believed in accepting such a valuable gift. When we stopped living together, it seemed more appropriate that Stevie should have it.

This was long before this women's art – 'the art form feminism discovered' – became chic. And indeed, although I'd seen quilts all my life, at that time I actually didn't realise that there was a serious artistic tradition of white quilting, too. True, the appreciation of women's art and of the fact that 'Anonymous was a woman' was painfully overdue, yet it is interesting to note that since the uncovering of this particular branch of endeavour, the contribution of Black quilters has been down-played in most of the literature surrounding the craft.

I missed the quilt and remembered that Barbra Jackson had told me about a noted Mississippi quilter who lived near Mound Bayou and sold her work for a living. I sometimes wished that I'd made an effort to find her. But I didn't. Then in 1980 I met Michael Thelwell at the University of Massachusetts in Amherst. Mike, who wrote the novel *The Harder They Come*, had been active in the civil rights movement and spent a period in Mississippi. His home was full of African paintings and sculptures and on his bed was a splendid checked quilt. I was headed for Mississippi again when I left Amherst, and decided that I would try to find a quilt for myself.

I'd wanted something personal from women I knew and had grown to care for, and ended up buying three, all very different, equally splendid. Two were made by a friend of Ruby Lee's; one thin, a delicate pastel, the other more robust and colourful. The third was Sadie Saddlers' own work, a 'Double T' pattern in blue, grey and orange, backed with old floursacks. They felt so precious to me as I packed them up carefully for their journey home.

But in New York I started reading *Drylongso*, a compelling collection of Afro-American oral testimony. The words of one 'dry-longso' (ordinary) speaker were chilling: 'White people, they always steal from you then go away. And after a while they come back again to see if there's anything else left to steal.'

I stopped short, thinking once again about Eugene's guitar, about what Malcolm said, and wondering whether Sadie, Ruby Lee and the others saw me this way. I felt bad, especially as ancient quilts were beginning to make their appearance in high-priced antique shops in Manhattan, and the women's movement was into a full-swing rediscovery of 'our' hidden art. I felt like a plunderer, too.

Back in England I pushed the guilty feelings into the back-ground and gave the more delicate quilt to Peeve. But still those words from *Drylongso* kept coming back, not only about the quilts but about everything. For the second time in ten years I could hear the voice of Ornette's friend Mary: 'Don't take advantage, haven't you people taken enough?' Then Carmen Lowe came to stay with me in London. Carmen is an artist who sews and lectures on African textiles and the needle-work and weaving of her own Afro-American culture. She dug the

309

quilts. With a connoisseur's eye and a reverence for tradition she told me, 'You know, you are very lucky to have these quilts.' I detected no hint of censure but felt compelled to say something of my misgivings concerning this 'luck'. She realised that, she said, but also recognised how and why I'd acquired them and what they meant to me.

Then she went on to tell me something you don't read in the books about the quilters' art. 'See those knots in the cotton? That's from when they unpicked floursacks and sugarsacks to make their thread.' This knowledge added another dimension to the whole story. Quilting had always been the art of necessity, and I realised that you couldn't ignore the circumstances in which these artifacts were produced any more than you could reject the background to the blues. It made me determine to honour the makers by protecting these covers and making sure that I acknowledged them whenever their work was admired. Now, by extension, every time I hear one of my sisters going on about how 'You *must* read Toni Cade Bambara' or whoever, I think about Mississippi and how it's something you can't buy off the shelf at the feminist bookshop.

I would never have shot pictures in Harlem or written *As Serious as Your Life* if I'd let my spirit be destroyed by the political concerns of that particular hour. It wasn't easy because I respected the views of the cultural nationalists and separatists, but I knew that what I was recording would be important one day.

Back home I was under another challenge, from those who still debated the right of Black people to be perceived on an equal footing. This came from as much inside the music world as it did from outside, indeed it was often worse nearer to home. It's not easy to live with a constant challenge, especially when it comes from both sides, but I was encouraged by those who did appreciate what I was about, and by the gradual turnaround of events.

My picture of Milford Graves playing in a Harlem street became quite a classic; few other photographers appeared to have taken pictures in similar circumstances during that period and those who had done were not always readily accessible. Some years later I had a call from a film-maker who wanted to use it in a documentary about the new music. He asked if I had any more shots from the gig and was surprised that there were only a handful. He wanted to know why. I hesitated, then decided to be open. 'Look,' I said, 'that was 1971. If I'd pushed my way nearer the stage I might have got slapped in the head.' He laughed. 'Yeah,' he said, 'I was there. And I'd probably have been one of those doing the slapping.'

In 1980 *As Serious* was published in America, and promoter Verna Gillis, who ran a studio called Soundscape, organised a launch party attended by many notable musicians. Ronald Shannon Jackson who once played drums with Ornette, Albert Ayler and Cecil, particularly asked if he could provide the music for the occasion. But indifference to my work continued at home – ironic, as there would soon be a revival of interest in jazz.

A new generation of musicians and listeners turned their attention to jazz and the music enjoyed a small surge of popularity in Britain that it hadn't known since the Trad Revival. The massive economic and cultural investment in rock had long forced it to take a back seat; now all that seemed to be changing. But this new interest developed in an increasingly conservative political climate and did not mean that ideas and feelings I had developed over more than thirty years' listening would be needed or welcome. Whereas in the two preceding decades there had been some attempt to come to terms with the factors that linked politics and popular culture, now surface glamour was what counted for most. The new breed of hipsters made it up as they went along, apparently hell-bent on ignoring the music's profoundness. It was easier for them to embrace a notion of the music that presented its heroes as icons, draped in their zoot-suits, than attempt to come to terms with what these superbad cats were actually saying. Such consumerism linked easily with the sentimental aggrandisement of the old men with the shaky vibratos that characterised the revivalists of my teens. To my sorrow, my years of immersion in the music, its culture and mores, appeared irrelevant, and I began to experience difficulty in getting published. Neither did the magazines evidence any desire to encourage the Black point of view. I persuaded Amiri Baraka to write for one local journal and with an arrogance truly stunning, the editor dismissed his contributions as dated. Baraka took it all in his stride. He'd expected such 'stupidity and racism', he said, but I couldn't get over the fact that this was the author of *Blues People* who was being rejected. His insights were not good enough for an outsider who had decided how jazz ought to be.

It was not until six years after the American publication of *As Serious as Your Life* that I felt finally vindicated. When I'd interviewed Mike Thelwell I'd been inspired by the way he included so much Jamaican cultural history in *The Harder They Come*. He'd told me of some Rasta acquaintances who had insisted he mention one of their important historical figures and how he'd had to rewrite part of the book to accommodate his constituents. It gave me another slant on the social responsibility of the artist. He'd liked what I'd written about him, too, and we'd stayed in touch.

Roberta Uno, to whom he was married, was co-ordinator of the annual Black Musicians' Conference at the University of Massachusetts in Amherst, where they both taught. She asked if I'd like to show some of my photographs at the 1986 meeting and take part in a panel discussion with musicians and other writers. As luck would have it I'd just put together an exhibition to illustrate the Black music continuum. Its title, *Sorrow Songs, Soulful Shout*, honoured toasters and testifiers, songsters and celebrants, and was a tribute to W.E.B. DuBois who had written so movingly of the 'sorrow songs', the spirituals, in *The Souls of Black Folk* at the turn of the century. The chance to take the show to the States was a godsend. For too long my rural images, of blues people and others, had stood on their own, devoid of a context. They were among my best pictures but whenever a group of them were shown here and there, they projected an impoverished and one-sided view of life in Afro-America. I'd added some shots by David Corio, another photographer in love with the music, and the show that resulted was, we felt, tightknit, informative and pacey.

Several distinguished figures were on the university faculty, including James Baldwin, and staying with Mike and Roberta, I was able to attend one of his lectures. One student asked him how he could explain to unsympathetic whites that Black people had earned the right to equal treatment through the history of their presence in America. Baldwin mused. 'Ask them how America would *sound* without us? How would the language sound? How would the music sound?' Everyone laughed. It was just so obvious, but exactly the kind of explanation that was resisted so strongly in England.

To my great pleasure, Baldwin turned up for the *Sorrow Songs* opening along with Archie Shepp and Max Roach, the drummer/composer, who were also faculty members. I'd woven a text around the photographs, using quotes from DuBois, Baraka and other writers to illustrate the celebratory and sustaining nature of Afro-American music, and the images ranged from a shot of the Blanches off to church in Bentonia to Jamaican poet Linton Kwesi Johnson on that same corner in Brixton where I saw Black people for the first time as a child. I viewed the arrival of Max Roach with some apprehension. He was not one to let any mistake or omission pass by unnoticed, and we had recently had an exchange in which he implied that I was a proselytiser for the new music to the exclusion of its historical antecedents. Now, however, he greeted me warmly: 'We haven't always seen eye-to-eye before, but what you've done here is really positive. Congratulations.'

I was surprised and gratified, but there was more. A group of students sang gospel songs, warmly, simply, for the occasion, and when all the wine and potato chips were finished, the leader offered up a speech of thanks from the keyboard: 'As I look around the room at these pictures, the main thing that strikes me is the grace that has brought us through.' A fitting way to end the proceedings, he suggested, would be joining together for 'Amazing Grace'. And so, as I stood beside him in the bend of the piano, faculty, students and visitors stopped what they were doing and joined in singing the timeless anthem. Archie and Max, Mike and Roberta, James Baldwin, so frail but clearly so loved by those around him, the voices in the room, mixing generations and nationalities, came together in a celebration of survival despite. The emotion of the moment left little room for much profound thinking. At leisure, I reasoned, grace and a determination I'd never thought I possessed had likewise brought me thus far. I wished my mother could have been there at that moment. She would have loved it, been proud.

Max came over after the singing. 'Jimmy and I are having dinner later with a few others, would you like to join us?' I said I would be delighted and asked if I could bring my writer friend Peter Guralnick, who had come along for the opening.

That night in the restaurant Peter and I sat transfixed like a couple of teenage fans in a group that included musicians, writers, mathematicians and visual artists. Max played host and the conversation ranged eloquently from his recollections of studying with master drummer Ti Roro in Haiti thirty years previously – 'He put a screen around you so you couldn't see his hands. You had to hear the sound and figure out how to re-create it' – to recording 'Money Jungle' with Mingus and Ellington: 'Duke took one look at Mingus and me and said, "Just think of me as a second-rate Bud Powell".' They talked about Papa Ibra Tall, the revered Senegalese weaver, and the need for Black visual artists to organise to get a decent price for their work. Max discussed his plans for his autobiography, saying he would like to do it as a series of books in the fashion of Maya Angelou.

Baldwin turned up later with a friend and sat quietly, that eloquent fire of his obvious just under the surface even though his pallor suggested a poor state of health. The love and protectiveness he inspired in the people around him was something to see. Nelson Stevens, the painter, sat at my elbow. 'Where's your camera?' he nudged me. 'You really should catch this.' I'd left it behind, not wanting to intrude on the learning experience, but I did regret it. It was incredible, Peter said later, 'I can't think of anywhere you could sit down for a couple of hours and hear conversation of such a high degree of knowledge, awareness and such diversity.' 'And love,' I put in. Yes, love. Very few Whites I knew could talk and write with that kind of love. I thought of the compelling works that comprised Baldwin's canon, of Richard Wright's *Twelve Million Black Voices*. Few of us could produce something of such evocative power and sustaining strength. We're too caught up in the pursuit of material ideas to have enough room for the spiritual.

Herb Snitzer, my early inspiration in music photography, came over to Amherst to see the show, and in New York I met Roy DeCarava for the first time. We did an interview together and he allowed me to photograph him out for a walk with his daughter. The midday sun beat down, casting hard shadows, my unfavourite light. I fumbled self-consciously with my equipment, joking at my apparent inexpertise, but Roy remained calm and unruffled. Later, when I gave him a copy of *The Face of Black Music*, he told me he liked my pictures.

I felt somehow my history was coming full circle. I spent time with the Blakeneys and for the first time in years met up with Herbie Lovelle. I interviewed Buck Clayton who had just written his autobiography, and met Danny Dawson who had grown up in Newark with Carol Blank and Madeleine Bell and done the photographs for Baraka's *Black Music*. He surprised me by revealing that Johnny Dodds had been one of his early heroes, too, giving the lie to popular assumptions of what Black people had listened to during that period. At New York University he introduced me to a bunch of music-lovers of varying ages and backgrounds who, I discovered, rated *As Serious as Your Life* as one of the crucial books about music; it was very encouraging.

In the space of one week I heard three powerhouse pianists. Jayne Cortez took me and her fellow poet Ted Joans to see Cecil Taylor, and a few days later the song-writer Doc Pomus invited me to go with him to catch rockabilly's crazy man, Jerry Lee Lewis. Both, in their own ways, were equally remarkable. Only in New York I kept telling myself, only in New York. Louis Stephenson, my Jamaican friend from London who used to play saxophone, came over to see his sister and together we caught McCoy Tyner. 'I've been knowing Valerie for twenty-five years,' McCoy told him. Had it really been that long, I wondered? How could time have passed by so quickly?

There's a spot that I drive past in London where I once interviewed a bass player named David Izenzon. 'The older I get the more I realise how little I know,' he told me, adding: 'Well, of course, I'm not saying anything you haven't heard before, am I?' 'Oh, no,' I affirmed, at 23 eager to show my sophistication. In reality, though, I had no idea what it was he was saying. Time has shown otherwise, of course, and his words come back to me each time I pass by that building. Now it's apparent to me, too, that there will never be time enough to learn all the answers. Memphis Slim had a song about it: 'We grow old too soon and smart too late.' I never dreamed it could catch up with me so fast as well.

I interviewed James Baldwin once in London and asked him what he missed most about America. The bars, the barbershops, the Saturday nights, he replied. 'Well, really I guess I miss my youth.' I thought of that when I saw him again, looking so small and so vulnerable, but never imagining that he didn't have long to live. Now I miss my own youth as well.

I loved all those afternoon sessions with the musicians, the hours in the bar after the interview. To see the young players rushing in and out of the hotel, enthusing about what they'd discovered on their first trip to Europe, the oldtimers taking it in their stride but never missing a trick. For years I took it for granted there'd be a hotel to go to and musicians to hang with, never ceasing to get a rush of excitement when someone said, 'Let's go for a drink.' It could be a 'living legend' of jazz or someone who had just joined the band from the back of beyond; each encounter was part of my education. I'd watch how Black professionals conducted themselves in a world that was frequently hostile, and in doing so, discover ways of dealing in circles where women's presence was still very resented. That I'd constructed a part of my life around the sound of the music, the majesty of King Louis, the eloquence of Sidney Bechet, was no accident; the music itself had been constructed as a means of telling the story, a tool for survival.

In the dark days before women's liberation, I spent many a night getting drunk with a friend from the Gateways, digging Dylan and Dusty. In more sober, businesslike moments, I was playing Charlie Parker and Coltrane, but heterosexual values predominated in the outside world and threatened to swamp me, and when I needed to remind myself who I was I'd go and see Pam. 'Like a Rolling Stone' and 'Just Like a Woman' meshed with 'Some of your Loving' in my mind as I drove across London, needful. I was sure of a welcome, confirmation as well, years before any of us became aware just how much such self-expression is necessary for spiritual survival. With *Dusty in Memphis* on the deck I felt safe. She was something of a lesbian icon, a singer we thought of as one of our own; when someone taped her old sides for me for a recent birthday, I was transported back to those nights round at Pam's. We'd gossip about our less fortunate sisters, laugh to disguise the strains of living 'the life', and I'd tell her all about my latest caper. It's so much easier now, light years away from the consuming self-oppression that characterised that period for many. It's a hard-won freedom that women fought for, whatever their differing conclusions and political philosophy, but there's something about those desperate days that I can't forget.

Really, it was all part of growing up, whatever our ages. The Flamingo and those nights with the Blue Flames, Ronnie Scott's with Vi Redd and Blossom and Rahsaan Roland Kirk blowing his heart out, and where all the pianists sounded like Wynton Kelly and Bill Evans just for a minute. In New York there was a group of gay men who would take us dancing, to exclusive loft-parties with ticket admittance, where people popped amyl nitrates and we danced as if there was no tomorrow. I wish I could dance like that now: in those Manhattan lofts, at Bonnie and Clyde's. Oh, my youth. Like the song: 'The youth of the heart and the dew of the morning . . .', where have you gone?

Music stays one of the mysteries, sometimes centrestage, sometimes in the background, always, like sex, the most powerful force in life. At the church I attended with the Guides and the Wolf Cubs, the organ stops came out and the entire building, some of its fabric dating back to the fourteenth century, shook. Even when I'd disavowed religion, I still looked sneakily forward to Church Parade for that very reason. I can still hear the dramatic key-change on 'O God Our Help in Ages Past' and feel the pews quivering around me.

Music is something that can stay with you always: Johnny Dodds blowing his heart out on 'Perdido Street' across the decades, Mahalia in *Jazz on a Summer's Day*, Kodály's Cello Sonata in the darkroom in Soho. Sitting transfixed at the feet of the Raelettes, watching Ray Charles and Margie Hendrix swap choruses on 'Don't Set Me Free' while she winked at Michael Aldred and me between numbers. The *alghaita* player in Niamey, making my heart beat fast and fearful; the woman in church in Atlanta who had me drowning in my own tears.

The pain of Mum and all that her death had brought to the surface could still come back at any moment, and music, of course, could still spark it off. More than three years had passed when I sat listening to Lester Bowie in concert play Billie Holiday's 'Good Morning Heartache' and it started me crying inside. I knew why, when someone asked me to review a set of Billie reissues, I'd refused. It wasn't just, as I'd told him, that I felt Billie was sacred, it was what her voice could do to me — to anyone open enough to receive, in fact. The irony in whitefolks being torn apart by voices like hers and still refusing to acknowledge the *why* of the music hit me as I sat there and dug into Lester.

Many of us who loved the music as if it were our own, have stayed 'fans' despite the cynicism that surrounds it and in which we are forced to share. With Peeve I read all the books and the theories, and we developed feminist ones of our own. Like me, though, she can still go wild over a soulful voice for such singing speaks volumes. Many's the time she has phoned up to play me something by one of our favourites. Even on the answering-machine she'll leave a message: 'Hey, Beast' (she calls me that), 'listen to this!' and play an astonishing Gladys Knight track she's discovered amid all the dross.

My walls are covered with photographs of the people whose music I love. I've often wondered what some of the women who come to see me make of brawny Bobby 'Blue' Bland or tattooed and bescarred Otis Spann staring out at them from under their pompadoured hair. On their walls they have feminist posters, everything from Solidarity with African Women to Marlene Dietrich and Justice Demands the Vote. Some of my images are so *macho* I've wondered about it myself on occasion, but dammit, the cats were my heroes — still are — and the music is still in my veins.

Liking music with values that can contrast with feminist perceptions is not without its ironic moments. Whenever I feel brought down by the day-to-day problems I experience as a woman or lesbian, I look to music for comfort. Some people I know would, I suppose, play something by an inspirational 'risen-above-it-all' woman artist to similarly move on up. To my surprise, I often find myself reaching for gospel music or the blues or, as I did the other day, Percy Sledge and his archetypal male lovecry, 'When a Man Loves a Woman'. How contradictory. What on earth do these patriarchal sentiments have to do with me and, for example, the woman who – so *I* think – is currently giving me a hard time?

It has something to do with establishing *sanity*. To do that I have to reach for something with which I'm familiar, that constituted part of the aural backdrop for the 'hip' people of my generation. Whether the dominance of Soul music in the lives of some of us has anything to do with the commercial interests that capitalised on music's racial crossover in the 1950s and 1960s I don't know. Probably it has more to do with the fact that church-reared singers like Percy Sledge have had four centuries of survival from which to draw inspiration. Black people have always leaned on that sound in one shape or form. It goes deeper than anything I've ever known, to the point of pain, almost. Church (gospel) singers and blues people are shamans who work *with* their listeners to establish and confirm eternal verities. And even those outside the common cultural bank can participate if they know the language.

This odd combination of influences that often makes me feel an outsider in the white feminist community is not without its amusing moments, of course. Like the night I went to a women's bar with a younger lover. I was feeling insecure because she'd just got off with an even younger woman and I was filled with a clumsy mixture of jealousy and understanding. She was being a lot warmer than usual – guilt and ego combined, I suppose – but still I felt miserable. And then from out of the sound system came Little Walter, the legendary blues harmonica player, and 'My Babe', his classic paean to loving fidelity: 'My babe don't stand no cheatin', my babe/She don't stand none of that midnight-creepin'/My baby's a true little baby, my babe.' Those women who stopped to listen to the lyrics were trying to relate the sentiments to their own particular situation. And I couldn't stop grinning to myself.

See, I'd spent some days with Little Walter when he came to London 20 years earlier. He was a battle-scarred veteran of Chicago street brawls and everyone here had been warned off him. He and I got along just famously. We got drunk together and had a little frolic; when he was shot dead at the age of 38 I was saddened.

I started to tell 'her' about it but had to give up. I felt distanced because I knew she couldn't visualise such a relationship, and close, at the same time, because she was being so affectionate. And I realised how I had to come to terms with the fact that both worlds were mine. An unholy mixture, for sure, but one you can work at if you want to.

Index

Wynter, Sylvia 50

Acknowledgment is hereby made for permission to quote song lyrics from the following publishers and copyright holders:

Mama Said (Luther Dixon) used by kind permission of Ludix Music Ltd, 14 New Burlington Street, London W1X 2LR.

Sweet Little Sixteen (Chuck Berry) used by kind permission of Jewel Music Publishing Co. Ltd, 129 Park Street, London W1Y 3FA.

'Tain't Nobody's Biz Ness If I Do (Williams/Grainger/Prince) © 1922, Leeds Music Corp., USA, used by kind permission of Redwood Music Ltd, 14 New Burlington Street, London W1X 2LR (in respect of their 33⅓% interest only) and EMI Music Publishing Ltd, London WC2H 0EA.

Feel the Need in Me (Abram Tilmon) used by kind permission of Warner Chappell Music Ltd, 129 Park Street, London W1Y 3FA.

(I'm A) Road Runner (Brian Holland/Lamont Dozier/Eddie Holland) © 1965, Stone Agate Music Co., Inc., reproduced by kind permission of Jobete Music (UK) Ltd, 35 Gresse Street, London W1P 1PN. All Rights Reserved. International Copyright secured.

Louisiana Blues (McKinley Morganfield) used by kind permission of Jewel Music Publishing Co. Ltd, 129 Park Street, London W1Y 3FA.

Furry Sings the Blues (Joni Mitchell) used by kind permission of Warner Chappell Music Ltd, 129 Park Street, London W1Y 3FA.

Sisters Are Doin' It For Themselves (Annie Lennox/David A. Stewart) © 1985, D 'N' A Limited/BMG Music Publishing Ltd. Used by kind permission of BMG Music Publishing Ltd, 3 Cavendish Square, London W1M 9HA.

My Babe (Willie Dixon) used by kind permission of Jewel Music Publishing Co. Ltd, 129 Park Street, London W1Y 3FA.